the BETTY FURNESS

Westinghouse

COOK BOOK

PREPARED UNDER THE DIRECTION OF
JULIA KIENE

SIMON AND SCHUSTER, NEW YORK

First Printing

LIBRARY OF CONGRESS CATALOG CARD NUMBER: 54-8645
DEWEY DECIMAL CLASSIFICATION NUMBER: 641.5

MANUFACTURED IN THE UNITED STATES OF AMERICA
AMERICAN BOOK—STRATFORD PRESS, INC., NEW YORK

THIS BOOK IS DEDICATED TO *YOU*

A BUSY HOMEMAKER WHO GLADLY PREPARES
THREE MEALS A DAY FOR YOUR FAMILY,
AND WHO DELIGHTS IN DOING IT

Contents

Preface

Until I began doing Westinghouse product demonstrations on television in May, 1949, I'd never realized what a delight and a marvel of convenience a really modern kitchen could be.

But through my work—and eventually in my own magnificent Westinghouse kitchen—I discovered what wonders could be performed. The whole process was so fascinating that I finally decided it would be a great idea to pass on what I had learned to you.

I'm not the worst cook on my block, but I'm afraid I'm not the best either. I realized that it might be some time—more years than any of us would care to wait—before I had enough knowledge to write a whole book by myself.

But I was lucky, because in my acquaintance there was a charming lady who knew *everything* there was to know about the subject. Her name is Julia Kiene, and she is the Director of the Westinghouse Home Economics Institute. Julia has made cooking both her profession and her hobby.

I proposed my idea to Julia; she agreed to pool her experience and knowledge with my enthusiasm—and here is our cook book. The recipes are written so they can be cooked on whatever type of range you may have in *your* kitchen.

We hope you will have fun with it. And when your Golden Rice Casserole or Leg of Lamb Orientale turns out just right, remember —you can be sure . . . if it's Westinghouse!

BETTY FURNESS

Preface

Until I began doing Westinghouse product demonstrations on television in May, 1949, I'd never realized what a delight and a marvel of convenience a really modern kitchen could be.

But through my work—and eventually in my own magnificent Westinghouse kitchen—I discovered what wonders could be performed. The whole process was so fascinating that I finally decided it would be a good idea to pass on what I had learned to you.

I'm not the worst cook on my block, but I'm afraid I'm not the best either. I realized that it might be some time—more years than any of us would care to wait—before I had enough knowledge to write a whole cookbook myself.

But I was lucky, because in my acquaintance there was a charming lady who knew everything there was to know about the subject. Her name is Julia Kiene, and she is the Director of the Westinghouse Home Economics Institute. Julia has made cooking both her profession and her hobby.

I proposed my idea to Julia; she agreed to pool her experience and knowledge with my enthusiasm—and here is our cook book. The recipes are written so they can be cooked on whatever type of range you may have in your kitchen.

We hope you will have fun with it. And when your Golden Rice Casserole or Leg of Lamb Orientale turns out just right, remember—you can be sure . . . if it's Westinghouse!

—Betty Furness

Introduction

One thing about cook books that makes them different from most books is that we seldom read the first few pages. Instead, we open them somewhere near the middle and flick backward or forward until we find what appears to be an interesting recipe.

Perhaps you have already done that very thing with this cook book, but could we ask a special favor of you? Won't you please read the first few pages, because there are some hints and suggestions right at the very beginning that may be helpful to you.

Perhaps you have never done any cooking. Don't let that disturb you, because there are hundreds of homemakers who know little or nothing about food preparation. Interestingly enough, with a willingness to learn, many of these so-called beginners develop into wonderful cooks.

There is no mystery about being a good cook. All one needs to do is:

1. Study the recipe carefully and be sure you understand it.
2. Check all recipes before actually starting to cook, to make sure you have all the necessary ingredients.
3. Be accurate in your measurements.

Helps for Being Accurate

Invest in standard measuring cups. They aren't expensive. If you decide you like the glass or aluminum measuring cups best, buy two, one for dry ingredients and one for liquid. Or, you can buy the "Mary Ann" measuring cups which usually have a ¼ cup, ⅓ cup, ½ cup, and 1 cup nested together.

Also, standard measuring spoons are a great help. They come linked together in 1 tablespoon, 1 teaspoon, ½ teaspoon, and ¼ teaspoon sizes.

All recipes call for level measurements. If you are measuring, say, baking powder, in a measuring spoon, fill the spoon quite full, then carefully level it off with the back of a silver knife or a small spatula.

Measuring Flour

Flour must be sifted before measuring. After it is sifted, pile the flour lightly into a measuring cup, but don't shake the flour down into the cup. You'll have too much flour if you shake the cup as you measure, and your food won't taste right. After the flour has been piled lightly into the measuring cup, level it off with the back of a silver knife or spatula. This may take a second longer, but it is worth the extra trouble.

Measuring Shortening

The Mary Ann cups are more convenient for measuring shortening. If you are using the glass or aluminum standard measuring cup, here's a simple way to do it. Suppose the recipe calls for ½ cup shortening. Fill the measuring cup ½ full of water, then add shortening until the level of the water is even with the 1 cup line. Be sure you pour the water off before putting the shortening in the mixing bowl.

I'll do some more arithmetic for you. To measure ¼ cup shortening, fill measuring cup ¾ full of water; ⅓ cup shortening, ⅔ full of water; ¾ cup shortening, ¼ full of water. Always stop adding shortening when the water level reaches the 1 cup line on the measuring cup.

The Following May Help, Too

A few grains	less than ⅛ teaspoon
3 teaspoons	1 tablespoon
16 tablespoons	1 cup
1 cup	½ pint
2 cups	1 pint
4 cups	1 quart

Perhaps the Recipe Calls for "Tablespoons" Instead of Cups

4 tablespoons	¼ cup
8 tablespoons	½ cup
12 tablespoons	¾ cup
14 tablespoons	⅞ cup

How to Divide Recipes by Half

Most recipes are written for 4 servings. Such recipes can easily be cut in half. However, when dividing a recipe, remember to use a smaller pan than the regular recipe calls for. If you should use a large cake pan for a small cake, you would need magnifying glasses to find the cake. For instance, if you would make half a cake recipe calling for 2 cups flour, bake it in one 8-inch round cake pan.

Most recipes are easily divided in half. For example, 1½ cups flour divided by half, would end up being ¾ cup flour. If the recipe calls for only 1 egg, that may bother you a bit. Some people say to beat the egg and divide the egg that way. What to do with the other half always seems a problem. Since eggs are used usually to make a mixture light and fluffy, it really doesn't do a bit of harm to use the whole egg. Seems much more sensible than dividing it and throwing half away. Baking times are approximately the same.

SOME COOKING TERMS

There are several different ways to mix ingredients:

Beat: To make a mixture light and fluffy by beating air into it. Should be done with a slotted spoon or a wire whisk egg beater. Care must be taken not to overbeat, particularly when using an electric mixer, since overbeating will cause tunnels and prevent the mixture from rising as it should.

Blend: To mix several ingredients (usually of different textures) very thoroughly until whole mixture is smooth.

Fold: To mix, *very gently,* ingredients which have had air beaten into them. Since that air is what will make your cakes or your omelets light and fluffy, you do not want to beat the air out when you include the final ingredient. Add ingredient very slowly, cutting down with the edge of a mixing spoon, carefully moving the spoon along the bottom of the bowl and slowly up to the surface again. Never use an electric mixer for this job.

Stir: To mix several ingredients together. Usually done with a fork or spoon, moving it in wide, slow-moving circles until ingredients are mixed.

And there are also a number of general cooking terms, some of which are:

Baste: To moisten food while it is cooking. Usually this applies to meat, and the basting material may be pan drippings, water, or some special sauce, depending on the recipe. Use a large spoon, or one of the vacuum tubes that is sold for this purpose.

Blanch: To remove skins from fruits or nuts or tomatoes by submerging in hot water. Nuts usually must stand in the boiling water for several minutes; while fruits and tomatoes need only to have the boiling water poured over them.

Braise: To brown meat or vegetables on the top of the stove in a small amount of shortening. Pan is usually tightly covered, and a small amount of liquid is added to prevent food from burning.

Caramelize: To melt granulated, or white, sugar in a heavy saucepan or skillet over very low heat until the sugar is liquid and brown in color.

Cream: To work shortening and sugar together until mixture is light and fluffy.

Cube: To cut solid food into approximately even squares.

Dice: To cut into small pieces which may be irregular in shape.

Dot: To scatter small amounts of butter, nuts, and so forth over the surface of foods.

Dredge: To coat with seasoned flour or cracker crumbs, or something of the sort, so that the entire surface of the food is covered.

Marinate: To soak foods for a period of time in French dressing, lemon juice, soya sauce, and so forth. Marination does wonders many times, particularly for meat which is to be broiled.

Mince: To chop very fine. For onions, garlic, cheese, and so on, use a medium-sized grater; but foods such as nuts and dried fruits will be more easily minced with a sharp knife.

Purée: To force foods through a very fine sieve, or to cut them up into a smooth liquid with the help of one of the new electric blenders.

Sauté: To cook in a small amount of shortening, usually on a slow heat. Frequently, recipes will ask that food be sautéed only for a short time, until it is slightly cooked or cooked to a golden brown.

SOMETHING ABOUT HERBS AND HOW TO USE THEM

If you haven't had the courage to use herbs in your cooking, don't keep wishing you knew how to use them, but start right now, today! It isn't necessary to buy a great assortment; begin by using just a few of the old standbys and find out for yourself the lift they give to just ordinary food.

It also would be wise to buy small jars of the herbs, rather than large ones, since they lose their pungency if stored for too long a period.

Another caution. Don't let your sudden enthusiasm for herbs run away with you. Forget that old trite saying, "If a little is good, more should be better." Dried herbs are used sparingly; a small pinch usually is sufficient.

If you have garden space, why not have a small herb garden? With little effort you can grow tarragon, mint, parsley, chives and thyme. You can use fresh herbs rather recklessly. An easy trick is to tie several large sprigs of parsley, a small sprig of tarragon and of thyme together. Then drop this herb bouquet into a kettle of soup, or a stew—in fact, any meat or fowl dish which is cooked by moist heat. An herb bouquet put into the cavity of a chicken you are about to roast does wonderful things to the flavor of the meat. It also eliminates the necessity of stuffing the chicken.

Following are some of the most common herbs and how best to use them:

Anise: Has a licorice-like flavor. Use very sparingly. Can be added any time during cooking process. Fresh anise is excellent in fresh vegetable salad. Anise seed or powdered anise wonderful in cookies.

Bay: Has a refreshing, rather woodsy flavor. Excellent in soups, sauces, and stews. Use a half leaf of the dried, a whole leaf of the fresh—but watch your timing.

Fennel: Another one of the herbs which tastes like licorice. Use the same as anise. In some parts of the country the stems and bulbous part are eaten like celery. The fresh herb is lacy and makes a fine garnish for salads and so forth.

Sage: Slightly bitter in flavor. Use with a light touch. Generally used in stuffings for fish or fowl. Do not cook for a long period of time. If freezing stuffing, do not use sage; it develops a bitter taste when frozen.

Savory: Not quite so bitter in taste as sage. Fine in stuffings and a touch in salads is a good idea. Do not overcook.

Marjoram: Spicy flavor which is excellent with poultry, lamb, eggs, stuffing, and bland vegetables. Good substitute for sage. Excellent to use for foods which require long cooking.

Orégano: Pronounced "o-ray'ga-no." This is really wild marjoram, and is used in the same way. Very pungent. Excellent with tomatoes, soups, pork and lamb. Very popular with Italian and Mexican cooks.

Basil: Tastes something like cloves. Excellent when cooking most vegetables, with the exception of potatoes. Wonderful in soups or any long-cooking foods. Basil vinegar adds zest to any French dressing.

Mint: Usually used fresh, although dried mint leaves are available. If added to cooked foods, put mint in shortly before food has finished cooking. Excellent in fruit cups, salads, peas and carrots, sauces for lamb.

Rosemary: Used much like mint. Spicy in flavor. Popular in fruit cups, meat sauces, stews and roasts. Do not cook too long.

Tarragon: A must for the herb shelf. May be used either fresh or dry in salads, in poultry and fish cookery, meat and fish sauces. Add a little tarragon vinegar to your French dressing. Can be cooked either a long or short time. Use with caution.

Thyme: Pronounced "time." Pungent in flavor. Excellent in soups, stuffing, chowders. May be cooked a long or short time. Use with considerable restraint.

Parsley: Has a wonderful flavor which goes with almost anything. Always use a sprig of fresh parsley or a sprinkling of dried parsley when cooking meat. Also used as a garnish. Healthful to eat, too.

Dill: Excellent with fish, fresh vegetable salads, steaks and chops. Do not cook for a long period of time. Use with a light touch.

Chives: Grow these in your garden or window sill. Best when used fresh. Wonderful in salads, egg dishes, and particularly fine with cottage cheese. Good mixed with sweet butter, too.

Soups

The history of soup goes back to the beginning of recorded time, for it has always served as a mainstay of man's diet. There is almost no limit to the variety of soups that are served all over the world, but the real honors in fine soup making must go always to the French homemaker who achieves magnificent flavored soups with the most economical of ingredients. This combination of incomparable flavor with real thrift is unusual . . . but it is one which we may all achieve.

It was from France that we learned of the "soup pot," which is always kept on the back of the stove. The French cook tosses into it every odd and end of meat, gravy, vegetable water or vegetables, and from such a seemingly random assortment she concocts soups such as we in the United States rarely have the pleasure of eating. Each country, however, has its delicious specialty. Italy has its Minestrone, Russia contributes her Borsch, and from India we get wonderful Mulligatawny Soup, with its memorable blending of spices.

In this country, soup favorites vary, depending upon the section of the country in which you live. New England favorites are Bean Soups and the sea-food Chowders. The South prides itself, and rightly, on its Gumbo Soup, its Black Bean, its Turtle, its Creole mixtures and its Bisques. A favorite vegetable of the Southern soup maker is okra, and you will be surprised and delighted if you introduce okra flavor into your own soups. And finally, the Southwest specializes in soups which they have developed with the help of their Mexican neighbors and feasts on such delicacies as Pinto Bean Soup, Mexican Stew, and Rice Soup with Shrimp.

No matter where you live you will find that soups of all kinds will add flavor, nutrition, and often excitement to the meals that you serve. Remember always, however, the cardinal rule of soup serving: If it is to be a hot soup it must come to the table *steaming* hot, and if it is to be a cold soup it must be served *icy* cold.

If the soup you select is to serve as the main part of your meal, you will want to choose a nourishing combination such as Vegetable, Bean, or Lentil Soups, or one of the Chowders. The Bouillon and Consommés are usually served simply as appetite teasers, while the Cream Soups may be used as a first course, followed by a good salad and a fairly hearty dessert.

As you and your family come to enjoy soups of all kinds you will find that a soup tureen will add a great deal to the simplest meal, for it will ensure that the soup is served piping hot, and it will add a touch of glamour and beauty to your table.

What to Serve with Soups

Here again you are limited only by your own imagination. Crackers of various shapes and flavors are always good. In New England, water crackers are usually served. The crackers can be pepped up by brushing them lightly with melted butter or margarine, then sprinkling grated cheese, poppy seeds, onion or garlic salt over the top. These should be placed on a cooky sheet and heated in a 350° oven for about 10 minutes.

Croutons are one of the better-recognized garnishes for cream soup. Make them by cutting ½-inch cubes of bread, and sauté them in hot butter, gently shaking the pan until the squares have browned and toasted. Garlic or onion salt added just before taking them from the pan will add greatly to the flavor.

Bread cut in thin strips, brushed with melted butter or margarine, and toasted in the oven is delicious. Or, after the strips of bread are toasted, sprinkle grated cheddar cheese on one side and put under broiler for about a minute—until the cheese is melted.

Split pea or lentil soup always tastes better with a topping of frankfurters cut in one-inch lengths.

Onion soup must have rounds of toast and a generous amount of Parmesan cheese. Bouillon or consommé always seem a little better when served with Melba toast, but many folks prefer a special custard, cut in cubes or fancy shapes. (Recipe on page 3.) Egg rivels are also a favorite, and matzoth balls are wonderful with chicken soup. (Recipes for these will be found on page 4.) A slice of lemon or lime is usually floated on bouillon or consommé.

Sometimes children think they don't care for soup, but a sprinkling of fluffy white popcorn over the soup gives them an urge to find out what is underneath the popcorn.

Before everyone became so conscious of calories, a touch of whipped cream was frequently floated on cream soups.

Soup should always be accompanied with something, but just what that something is to be may be left to your imagination and good judgment.

How to Clarify Soups

Remove fat from chilled soup. Then, for every quart of stock, take 1 egg white and 1 egg shell. Beat together lightly and add to it 1 tablespoon cold water. Add to stock and bring stock to boiling point over low heat. Simmer 2 minutes. Remove from heat and let stand for about 20 minutes. Strain through a fine colander.

TRICKS: To remove fat from soup stock, place a lettuce leaf in hot soup stock. Remove it when leaf has absorbed fat. Or, drag a paper napkin over surface of soup. Grease will adhere to napkin.

GARNISHES FOR SOUPS

EGG CUSTARD

Small shallow baking dish ... Preheated oven—350° F. .... Baking time—20 minutes

2 egg yolks	⅛ teaspoon salt
1 whole egg	Pinch Cayenne pepper
½ cup bouillon	

Beat egg yolks with whole egg. Do not overbeat. Add bouillon and seasonings. Pour into shallow dish, such as small glass pie plate. Place this dish in a larger pan, containing sufficient water to bring water halfway up the dish containing the custard. Bake. Cool. Cut into cubes or fancy shapes and float on clear soup, such as bouillon or consommé. Serves 4.

RIVELS NO. 1

1 whole egg or 2 egg yolks	¼ teaspoon salt
1 cup all-purpose flour, sifted before measuring	

Beat egg slightly. Sift flour with salt and add to egg. If egg yolks are used, it may be necessary to add a couple tablespoons cold water. Work these together until the mixture resembles corn meal. Drop into boiling soup. Cook about 10 minutes. Serves 4.

RIVELS NO. 2

Use ⅛ cup butter or margarine instead of the egg. Work together like pie dough. Form into small balls. Drop into boiling soup. These will separate and resemble rice. Serves 4.

MATZOTH BALLS

2 tablespoons marrow or chicken fat	¼ cup matzoth meal
1 egg	½ teaspoon salt
	Pinch of nutmeg

Cream marrow or other fat, add egg slightly beaten, add matzoth meal and seasoning. This mixture should resemble a soft dough. Place in refrigerator for 4 or 5 hours to harden. Shape into balls the size of a marble. Try one in boiling soup, and should it not hold together, add a bit more matzoth meal. Serves 4.

QUICKIE SOUPS

If your family enjoys soup, and you don't have the time or inclination to make your own, don't give up soups. There are many excellent canned soups on the market, and by using imagination, wonderful combinations may be achieved. Also, for quick soups for lunch, or a late night snack, the dehydrated packaged soups are very good. However, when using the packaged or dehydrated soups, better read the directions for making the soup carefully. Otherwise, the soup might not be to your liking.

Some Suggestions for Delicious Soups from Cans

CREAM OF TOMATO

1 can of condensed cream of tomato soup, 1 can clear bouillon, ½ soup can of water. Mix together, bring to a full boil. Serve at once. Serves 4.

BLACK BEAN SOUP

1 can condensed black bean soup, 1 can clear bouillon. Mix together and bring to a full boil. Just before serving, add ½ cup sherry. Wonderful on a cold day. Serves 4.

CELERY SOUP

1 can condensed cream of celery soup, 1 can cream of chicken soup, ½ soup can each water and milk. Mix all together. Bring to full boil. Serves 4.

CREAM OF CRAB

1 can condensed cream of mushroom soup, 1 can condensed asparagus soup, 1 soup can each milk and water, ½ cup heavy cream. Bring to full boil, remove from heat, and add ½ cup shredded crab meat and ¼ cup sherry. Serve at once. Serves 4-5.

CREOLE CLAM BISQUE

1 can condensed clam chowder, 1 can condensed chicken gumbo, 1 soup can light cream. Bring to full boil. Serves 4.

CREOLE TOMATO SOUP

1 can condensed cream of tomato soup, 1 can condensed chicken gumbo soup, 2 soup cans water. Combine soups, add water. Bring to full boil. Serve. Serves 4.

TOMATO CLAM CHOWDER

1 can condensed cream of tomato soup, 1 can condensed clam chowder, 1 soup can water. Mix soups, add water, bring to full, rolling boil. Serve. Serves 4.

MONGOLE SOUP

1 can condensed cream of tomato soup, 1 can condensed pea soup, 2 cups milk. Mix soups with milk and bring to full boil. Flavor with salt and pepper as needed. Just before serving add ¼ cup sherry. Float grated cheese on top of soup. Serves 4.

TURTLE SOUP

1 can condensed mock turtle soup, 1 can condensed pea soup, 1 can consommé. Add 2 soup cans water. Bring to full boil. Just before serving, add ¼ cup sherry. Serve. Serves 6.

HINDU SOUP

1 can condensed tomato soup, 1 can condensed green pea soup, 2 cups light cream, 1 teaspoon curry powder, 1 teaspoon dry mus-

tard, salt to taste. Mix all ingredients together. Bring to full boil. Serve. Serves 6-8.

SOUPS MADE FROM MEAT STOCK

There is no trick to making a good soup stock, except that it is something you have to plan, rather than try to make at the last minute. Good soup stock requires long, slow cooking to extract all the flavors. There are two types of soup stock, the brown stock, which is made from beef knuckle or shin, and the white stock, usually made from veal knuckle.

When you are buying a soup bone, it is best to count on about 1 part bone to 2 parts meat. If possible buy the marrow bone. The marrow adds flavor to the stock.

BROWN SOUP STOCK

5-6 pounds soup knuckle	1 turnip, cut fine
3 quarts cold water	2 or 3 sprigs parsley
Marrow from bone	1 small bay leaf
1 onion, chopped fine	2 sprigs marjoram
1 carrot, cut fine	6 whole black peppers
1 stalk celery, cut fine	1 tablespoon salt

Have soup knuckle cracked in several places. Remove half the meat and set aside. Place soup bone in large kettle, add the cold water, and start cooking on very low heat. Put the marrow from bone in skillet, and when melted, add meat which has been cut from soup bone. Brown meat. Add to soup bone and water in kettle. Cook on low heat for about 3 hours. Then add vegetables and seasonings and cook for an additional 2 hours. Strain and keep in a cool place. If you have a home freezer, freeze what you are not going to use immediately. Makes about 2 quarts of stock and is excellent as the base for onion soup and consommé. Also excellent for jellied soups.

WHITE SOUP STOCK

4-5 pounds veal knuckle	2 or 3 sprigs parsley
3 quarts cold water	2 cloves garlic, cut fine
2 stalks celery and leaves	1 small bay leaf
1 onion, cut fine	6 whole black peppers
1 carrot, cut fine	1 tablespoon salt

Have knuckle cracked in several places. Combine all ingredients. Place over low heat and cook slowly for 5-6 hours. Strain and keep in a cold place. Or, if you have a home freezer, freeze the portion not being used immediately. Makes about 2 quarts of stock. Wonderful as a base for cream soups.

TRICK: Frequently it is inconvenient to make your own stock. So, as an excellent substitute, buy canned bouillon or use either beef or chicken bouillon cubes. Use 2 bouillon cubes to each cup boiling water. Or, buy bouillon concentrate, and use 1 teaspoon of the concentrate to 1 cup boiling water.

VEGETABLE SOUP

3 pounds shank soup bone, cracked	1 cup carrots, diced
	2 cups potatoes, diced
3 quarts water	1½ cups celery, sliced
1 bay leaf	2 onions, diced
2 cups cooked tomatoes	2 tablespoons salt
1 cup cabbage, finely shredded	½ teaspoon pepper

Put soup bone, water, 1 tablespoon salt, and bay leaf in large kettle with tight-fitting lid. Cook on low heat for about 6 hours, then cool, remove bone from kettle, and skim fat from top of broth. Add the vegetables, the other tablespoon salt, and pepper. Cook on high heat until mixture steams, then reduce heat to low setting, and continue cooking for 1 hour. Serves 8-10. Any leftover soup may be frozen.

QUICK VEGETABLE SOUP

1 pound ground beef	1 onion, chopped
1 large can tomato purée	1 tablespoon salt
2 cups potatoes, diced	¼ cup uncooked rice
2 carrots, diced	⅛ teaspoon pepper
½ cup celery, diced	1¾ cups water

Brown ground beef in large kettle. No fat other than the fat in the meat is needed. Just as soon as meat is brown, add remaining ingredients. When mixture is steaming, reduce heat to low setting and cook for 45 minutes to 1 hour. Serves 4-6.

ONION SOUP AU GRATIN

12 medium-sized onions	1 teaspoon Kitchen Bouquet
4 tablespoons bacon drippings or other shortening	1 drop Tabasco sauce
	Salt and pepper to taste
14 cups homemade beef stock or	French bread, toasted
28 bouillon cubes dissolved in 14 cups boiling water	8 tablespoons Parmesan cheese
	1 teaspoon Worcestershire sauce

Slice onions thin. Sauté slowly in bacon drippings or other shortening, until a golden brown. Place beef stock in large kettle, add onions, Worcestershire sauce, Kitchen Bouquet and Tabasco sauce. Simmer, covered, on low heat, for 1 hour. Season with salt and pepper. Toast slices of French bread, top each slice with Parmesan cheese, and place under broiler until lightly browned. Place soup in heated bowls, top each bowl with a toasted slice of bread and add more cheese, if desired. Serves 6-8.

The French place the toasted French bread in the bottom of an ovenware soup bowl. Top the toast with cheese, then place under the broiler until cheese is lightly browned. Remove bowls from oven and fill bowls with hot soup. By doing this, the bowl in which the soup is served is also very hot, which keeps the soup hot much longer and is therefore more enjoyable.

OXTAIL SOUP

1 oxtail, cut in 2-inch lengths	¼ cup onions
1½ quarts water	1 cup cooked tomatoes
⅓ cup barley	2½ teaspoons salt
½ cup each of potatoes, carrots, celery, cabbage, diced fine	

Place oxtails in large kettle with tight-fitting lid. Add water and bring slowly to boiling point. Skim carefully. Add barley, reduce heat, and continue cooking for about 2½ hours. Add remaining vegetables and seasonings. Continue cooking until vegetables are tender. The vegetables may be varied according to what is available, but in any case you should have at least 3¼ cups, with tomatoes an essential. Serves 4.

SCOTCH BROTH

¾ cup barley	1 turnip, diced
2-3 pounds lamb or mutton	1 carrot, diced
6 cups cold water	4 stalks celery, chopped
1 tablespoon salt	1 grated carrot
3 tablespoons butter or margarine	¾ cup parsley, chopped
2 onions, diced	⅛ teaspoon pepper

Carefully pick over barley and soak overnight in 5 cups of water. Remove as much of the lean meat as possible from the bones. Put meat and bones in large kettle and add cold water and salt and cook over low heat for 1 hour. Add barley and continue cooking until meat is tender. This will require about 1½ hours' additional cooking. Remove bones from soup mixture, cool soup, and skim off fat. Melt butter or margarine and sauté onions, turnip, carrot, and celery to a golden brown. Add to soup mixture and cook on low heat for about 1 hour. About 15 minutes before ready to serve, add grated carrot, parsley, and pepper. Serve piping hot. Toasted French bread is excellent to serve with this soup, which is really a meal in itself. You can package and freeze what you don't use immediately. About 8 servings.

TRICK: Buy lamb neck, flank, or breast. The bones help the flavor, and the cheaper meat is just as good in soup.

BORSCH

1 cup cooked beets, finely chopped	½ teaspoon salt
	¼ teaspoon pepper
2½ cups beef stock	4 eggs, beaten
3 tablespoons lemon juice or diluted vinegar	½ cup sour cream

Add beets to beef stock. Cover and cook about 20 minutes over low heat. Add lemon or vinegar and seasonings. If vinegar is used, use half water. Heat to boiling point. Slowly pour the hot soup mixture over the beaten eggs. Stir vigorously to prevent the eggs from curdling and separating. Serve at once while still very hot, since this soup should not be reheated. Add 1 tablespoon sour cream to each serving. Serves 4-6.

Borsch may also be served cold. After the hot mixture has been blended with the egg, cool slightly, then place in refrigerator to chill. Top the cold Borsch with sour cream.

TOMATO BOUILLON

Heat together equal amounts of tomato juice and brown soup stock. For additional flavor, add 2 or 3 cloves and 1 small bay leaf, which should be removed before serving. Serve with a lemon slice. Allow 1 cup liquid per serving.

TOMATO SOUP SUPREME

4 tablespoons butter or margarine	1 small bay leaf
	2 or 3 whole cloves
¼ cup each celery, onion, and carrot, diced	¼ teaspoon crumbled tarragon
4 tablespoons all-purpose flour	2½ cups canned (No. 2 can) tomatoes
3 or 4 whole black peppers	4 cups brown stock

Melt butter or margarine in saucepan. Slowly sauté the celery, onion, and carrots until lightly brown. Blend in the flour, whole black peppers, bay leaf, cloves, and tarragon. Cook over low heat until ingredients are well blended. Add tomatoes and continue to cook over very low heat for about 1 hour. It will be necessary to stir this occasionally. Strain through a fine sieve, add the brown soup stock, and bring to boiling point. Add salt and pepper, if necessary. Serves 4-6.

JELLIED BOUILLON NO. 1

Either the brown soup stock or white soup stock when placed in the refrigerator for several hours will make wonderful jellied bouillon.

The canned bouillon will usually become firm if placed in a refrigerator overnight.

JELLIED BOUILLON NO. 2

Add a dash of onion salt and ½ teaspoon celery salt to 1 can of bouillon and heat. Soften 1¼ teaspoons unflavored gelatin in 1 tablespoon cold water. Add to heated bouillon. Add 1 cup cold water and the juice of half a lemon. Chill thoroughly. An easy way to prepare for serving is to break the jellied bouillon with a fork. A thin slice of lemon on top looks attractive and improves the flavor of the bouillon.

CHICKEN STOCK

4-5 pounds stewing chicken, cut up	1 stalk celery, cut in 1-inch lengths
3 quarts water	2 or 3 sprigs parsley
1 carrot, cut up	2 teaspoons salt

Place cut-up stewing chicken in large kettle. Add water. Cover. Cook over low heat until boiling point is reached. Skim carefully. Add carrot, celery, parsley, and salt. Cover and gently simmer for about 3 hours. Strain. Chill. If any fat accumulates over chilled liquid, remove while soup stock is cold. Makes 1½ to 2 quarts stock.

CHICKEN NOODLE SOUP

Follow directions for chicken stock, above. After straining soup, cool chicken pieces, then remove the meat, discarding the skin and bones. Place strained broth in kettle, add chicken pieces, and bring to boiling point. Add noodles. Usually an 8-ounce package of noodles is sufficient. Cook about 15 minutes after noodles are added. If you prefer to use the chicken meat in other ways, just add noodles to strained broth. Serves 4-6.

CHICKEN AND TOMATO BOUILLON

2½ cups chicken stock	Salt and pepper to taste
1 cup tomato juice	

Combine chicken stock and tomato juice. Bring to boiling point. Serve piping hot with a garnish of either sliced lemon, small toasted cheese crackers, popcorn, or a topping of whipped cream. Serves 4-5.

PHILADELPHIA PEPPER POT

½ pound honeycomb tripe	2 tablespoons parsley, minced
6 cups chicken stock	2 teaspoons salt
4 slices bacon, cut in small pieces	1 cup raw potato, diced
½ cup onion, chopped	2 tablespoons melted butter or
½ cup celery, chopped	margarine
1 green pepper, chopped	2 tablespoons all-purpose flour
1 small bay leaf	½ cup heavy cream
1 teaspoon peppercorns, pounded fine	

Cook tripe, rinse, and cut in ¼-inch cubes. Place in large kettle and add chicken stock. Fry bacon until crisp and sauté the onion, celery, and green pepper in the bacon drippings. Add to tripe and chicken stock. To this mixture add the bay leaf, peppercorns, parsley, and salt. Cover, and when mixture comes to the boiling point, add diced raw potato. Cover and simmer gently for about 1 hour. Blend melted butter or margarine with flour and stir into hot soup mixture. Season with additional salt if necessary. Just before serving, stir in the heavy cream. Serve piping hot. Serves 6 as a main dish.

TRICK: To make chicken stock use 12 chicken bouillon cubes and 6 cups water, or 6 teaspoons chicken concentrate with 6 cups water.

CHICKEN GUMBO

4 tablespoons butter or margarine	2½ cups cooked tomatoes
1 onion, chopped fine	1 small bay leaf
½ green pepper, chopped fine	1 tablespoon parsley, minced
1½ cups cooked or canned okra	1 cup cooked chicken, finely diced
4 cups chicken stock	

Melt butter or margarine in saucepan. Sauté onion, green pepper, and okra until golden brown. Stir in the chicken stock, cooked tomatoes, and bay leaf. Cook on low heat, simmering gently for about 45 minutes. Season to taste. About 15 minutes before serving, add the minced parsley and cooked chicken. Serves 4-6.

TRICK: This is an excellent way to use a small amount of left-over chicken or turkey. Boil the bones for the stock, but be sure you strain the stock before using it.

CHICKEN OR TURKEY BONE SOUP

Bones from 1 turkey or chicken
8 cups cold water
½ cup onion, chopped
½ cup celery, chopped
1 teaspoon parsley, chopped
Salt and pepper to season

Place all ingredients in large kettle. Cover and simmer gently 2 or 3 hours. Strain. Serve clear as bouillon or add rice or barley or noodles and continue cooking until whatever you add is tender. If there are any remnants of turkey meat, add them to the strained soup. Serves 6.

DRIED BEAN AND PEA SOUPS

The thrifty homemaker can pinch many a penny if she will take the time to make these delicious bean and pea soups. These are hearty soups and usually are served as the main part of the meal. A salad and a favorite dessert make this inexpensive meal take on the air of a banquet.

Use your own judgment about overnight soaking of navy and lima beans, and split peas and lentils. Some prefer to cook them without soaking, and others feel the flavor of the soup is improved by overnight soaking.

If you favor overnight soaking, wash the dried beans or peas carefully, then soak them in the amount of water called for in the recipe. No draining is necessary.

SPLIT PEA OR LENTIL SOUP

2 cups dried split peas or lentils
3 quarts cold water
1 ham bone or ¼ pound salt
   pork
1 large onion, chopped
3 stalks celery, cut fine
3 sprigs parsley
2 cups milk
Salt and pepper to season
¼ pound frankfurters

Place split peas or lentils in large kettle. Add cold water, ham bone, or salt pork. (If you are using salt pork, cut in 1-inch cubes.) To this add the chopped onion, celery, and parsley. Bring slowly to the boiling point and simmer over low heat for 3 or 4 hours. If the dried vegetable has been soaked overnight, it probably will not be necessary to simmer the mixture so long. In any event, cook until the peas or beans are very tender. For a smooth soup (and most folks prefer the smooth soup) rub mixture through a coarse sieve. Add milk and seasonings. Heat over low heat until boiling point is reached. Serve piping hot. Cut frankfurters in thin slices and serve over top of soup. Garlic bread is an excellent accompaniment to this soup. Makes 10-12 servings. Wonderful to freeze.

SPLIT PEA SOUP

2 quarts cold water	¼ teaspoon dried thyme
2 cups green split peas	¼ teaspoon dried marjoram
2 stalks celery, chopped	Dash of cayenne
2 carrots, chopped	1 bay leaf
1 onion, chopped	Salt and pepper to taste

Mix all ingredients. Be sure the thyme and marjoram are powdered. Better rub them between the fingers. Cover and cook slowly for about 1 hour, or even longer. The mixture must cook until the peas are very soft. Force through a coarse sieve. Return to range and bring to boiling point. Serve piping hot in bowls which have been heated. Serve this with dark rye bread and butter. Serves 6-8.

This is a famous recipe from the Andersons of Buellton, California. Many people travel miles to eat this fine concoction.

NAVY BEAN SOUP

1½ cups navy beans	1 carrot, diced
4 cups cold water	2½ cups milk
¼ pound salt pork	2 teaspoons salt
1 small onion	¼ teaspoon pepper
½ cup celery, diced	½ teaspoon paprika

Wash beans and place in large kettle. Cover with cold water, add salt pork, cover, and bring slowly to boiling point. Simmer for about 2 hours, then add the onion, celery, and carrot. Continue cooking slowly for an additional hour or so. When beans are soft, rub mixture through a coarse sieve. Add milk, salt, pepper, and paprika to bean mixture. Cut salt pork into fine cubes and add to soup. Return to range and heat slowly until mixture begins to boil. Serve piping hot. Serves 4-5.

ITALIAN MINESTRONE

2 cups navy beans, soaked overnight
10 cups water
2 tablespoons salt
4 peppercorns
Salt and pepper to taste
½ cup olive oil
1 clove garlic, minced
3 onions, chopped

4 tablespoons parsley, chopped
4 stalks celery, cut fine
2 cups tomato pulp, or tomato purée
2 cups cabbage, coarsely chopped
1 zucchini squash, sliced thin
2 cups cooked macaroni
Grated Parmesan cheese

Soak navy beans overnight. The following morning, drain and put in large kettle with water and salt. Cook over low heat for 1 hour or longer, until beans are tender. Add peppercorns and seasonings to taste. Heat olive oil and sauté garlic, onions, parsley, and celery to a golden brown. Add to cooked beans. Add tomato pulp, cabbage, and additional seasonings, if needed. Cook over low heat for 1 hour. About 15 minutes before soup is finished, add zucchini and macaroni. Serve hot in heated earthen bowls or large soup plates. Sprinkle Parmesan cheese over soup. If soup should become too thick, add a little boiling water. Serves 6-8.

BLACK-EYED BEAN SOUP

2 cups black-eyed beans
2 quarts cold water
Small ham bone
3 tablespoons butter or margarine
2 tablespoons onion, chopped

2 stalks celery, chopped
2 tablespoons all-purpose flour
2 teaspoons salt
¼ teaspoon pepper
¼ teaspoon dry mustard

Soak beans overnight. Drain. Place in large kettle. Add cold water and ham bone. Bring slowly to boiling point. Melt 1½ tablespoons of butter or margarine and sauté onion and celery until lightly browned. Add to bean mixture. Continue cooking on very low heat for about 3 hours, or until the beans are soft. Rub through a coarse sieve. Reheat to boiling. Blend flour, remaining butter or margarine, salt, pepper, and mustard. Mix well and stir into soup. Continue cooking for about 5 minutes. Serve piping hot. Serves 6-8.

BEAN SOUP MEXICAN STYLE

½ cup navy beans	1 cup celery, chopped
3 cups cold water	½ cup cabbage, finely shredded
2 tablespoons shortening	2½ teaspoons salt
1 clove garlic, minced	⅛ teaspoon pepper
3 tablespoons onion, chopped	1 cup cooked tomatoes
1 tablespoon parsley, chopped	1 cup cooked noodles

Wash beans, place in large kettle and add water. Bring slowly to boiling point and simmer until beans are tender. Melt shortening and sauté the garlic, onion, parsley, celery, and cabbage until lightly browned. Add to the bean mixture. Stir thoroughly. Add salt, pepper, and tomatoes and simmer about 30 minutes longer. Just before removing from heat, add noodles and continue cooking until noodles are heated through. Serves 6-8.

LOUISIANA LIMA BEAN SOUP

2 cups dried lima beans	½ cup green pepper, finely
8 cups cold water	minced
Ham bone	1 cup canned tomatoes
3 small onions, chopped	3 teaspoons salt
½ bay leaf	¼ teaspoon pepper
1 cup carrots, finely chopped	

Wash lima beans. Place in large kettle. Add water and ham bone, the onions, and the bay leaf. Cover. Simmer over low heat until beans are tender. Reserve 1½ cups of the whole beans. Force remainder through a coarse sieve. Return the whole beans to the soup mixture, add the carrots, green pepper, and tomatoes. Continue cooking over low heat until vegetables are tender. Add salt and pepper. If there is any ham on the bone, cut into bits and add to the soup. Serves 10. Excellent to freeze.

BEAN AND BARLEY SOUP

1 cup dried lima beans	1 small carrot, diced
6 cups cold water	3 tablespoons barley
2 teaspoons salt	1 cup evaporated milk
¼ teaspoon pepper	2 tablespoons butter or
¼ cup onion, finely diced	margarine

Wash beans. Place in saucepan. Add water, salt, and pepper. Cover. Cook over low heat until beans are almost tender. Add onion, carrot, barley and continue cooking over low heat until beans are tender and vegetables cooked. Add milk and butter or margarine. Bring to boiling point and serve at once. Serves 4-6.

CREAMED SOUPS

Creamed soups are wonderful for lunch or as the first course of a light dinner. Children usually love creamed soups, and they are an excellent way of making sure that children receive their essential daily quota of milk. Don't forget that milk is good for grownups, too, so all the family will benefit when you make creamed soups.

BASIC CREAM SOUP

3 tablespoons butter or margarine
1½ tablespoons all-purpose flour
1 teaspoon salt
⅛ teaspoon pepper

3 cups whole milk
1 cup puréed leftover vegetables
1 teaspoon onion, grated

Melt butter or margarine in saucepan. Add flour and seasonings and stir until well blended. Slowly add milk, stirring constantly. Bring to boiling point, then add the puréed vegetables and onion. Reduce heat and cook over low heat for about 5 minutes. Use leftover cooked vegetables such as spinach, peas, celery, carrots, asparagus, or snap beans. The only trick is either to mash them fine or force them through a sieve. If you have an electric blender, use it to purée the vegetables. Serves 4-6.

TRICK: Use cans of strained baby-food vegetables in place of the leftovers for a quick and easy soup. Use as many as you want. You'll find that they taste wonderful.

CREAM OF CELERY SOUP

Use basic recipe above, using 1½ cups milk and 1½ cups chicken broth with 1 cup of the finely puréed celery.

CREAM OF SPINACH SOUP

Use basic recipe above, but use only ¾ cup of the puréed spinach. Also add a dash of nutmeg.

CREAM OF CORN SOUP

2 cups corn, canned or leftover
2 cups boiling water
2 cups milk
1 slice onion
2 tablespoons butter or margarine

2 tablespoons all-purpose flour
½ teaspoon salt
⅛ teaspoon pepper

Place corn, boiling water, milk, and onion in saucepan. Cover. Simmer for 20 minutes. Rub through a coarse sieve. Melt butter or margarine and carefully brown flour in melted butter or margarine. Stir into corn mixture. Simmer 5 minutes. Serve piping hot. Serves 4-6.

CREAM OF TOMATO SOUP NO. 1

4 tablespoons butter or margarine	2 cups canned or cooked tomatoes
4 tablespoons all-purpose flour	⅛ teaspoon pepper
1½ teaspoons salt	½ bay leaf
2 cups milk	1 tablespoon onion, chopped
2 cloves	

Melt 2 tablespoons butter or margarine in saucepan. Blend in the flour and salt. Add milk gradually and cook over low heat until slightly thickened. In another saucepan cook the cloves, tomatoes, pepper, bay leaf, and onion over medium heat for about 10 minutes. Thicken with 2 tablespoons butter or margarine and 2 tablespoons flour which have been blended together. Slowly add milk to tomato mixture, stirring all the time. Do not allow mixture to come to a boil, as boiling may cause tomato soup to curdle. Serve at once. Serves 4-5.

CREAM OF TOMATO SOUP NO. 2

1 cup cooked or canned tomatoes	2 tablespoons butter or margarine
⅛ teaspoon soda	
2 cups whole milk	Salt and pepper to taste

Place tomatoes in saucepan and cook over low heat for about 10 minutes. Add soda and stir it carefully through tomatoes. Add the milk, stirring constantly. Do not allow to boil. Remove from heat, add seasonings and butter. Stir well. Serve at once. Serves 4.

SOUTHERN CREAM OF TOMATO SOUP

4 tablespoons butter or margarine	1¼ teaspoons salt
5 tablespoons green pepper, finely minced	⅛ teaspoon pepper
	2 tablespoons all-purpose flour
2 cups tomato juice	2 cups scalded milk

Melt 2 tablespoons of butter or margarine in saucepan, add green pepper, and sauté over low heat until green pepper is tender but not brown. Add tomato juice and seasonings. Bring to boiling point. Thicken with 2 tablespoons butter or margarine which has been blended with the flour. Add milk. Do not allow to come to boiling point. Serve piping hot. An interesting garnish for this soup is a sprinkling of browned, buttered bread crumbs. Serves 4.

POTATO SOUP

8 leeks, tops as well as white part (green onions may be used)
2 Bermuda onions, sliced thin
2 tablespoons butter or margarine
16 chicken bouillon cubes and
8 cups water, or 8 cups chicken stock

6 medium-sized potatoes, peeled and sliced
1 tablespoon salt
⅛ teaspoon pepper
1 cup top milk
1 cup light cream
1 tablespoon parsley, chopped

Sauté leeks and onion in butter or margarine until golden brown. Put bouillon cubes in large kettle, add water, and simmer over low heat until cubes are dissolved. Add leeks and onion, potatoes, salt, and pepper. Cover. Cook over low heat for about 45 minutes or until potatoes are well done. Put mixture through a coarse sieve. Return to kettle. Stir in milk. Cook over low heat until mixture comes to boiling point. Add cream, stir thoroughly. When boiling point is again reached, serve at once. Sprinkle parsley over top. Serves 8-10.

MASHED POTATO SOUP

4 cups milk
2 tablespoons onion, grated
2 cups mashed potatoes, hot or leftover
3 tablespoons melted butter or margarine

1 tablespoon all-purpose flour
1½ teaspoons salt
⅛ teaspoon pepper
¼ teaspoon celery salt
1 tablespoon parsley, chopped

Scald milk together with onion and add slowly to potatoes, blending well. Blend 1½ tablespoons melted butter with the flour, salt, pepper, and celery salt and add to the hot milk and potatoes. Stir well. Cook slowly over low heat until boiling point it reached. Add remaining butter or margarine. Serve piping hot and sprinkle parsley over the top. Serves 6.

VICHYSSOISE

(This soup is served very cold. For best blending of flavors, prepare the day before using.)

2 tablespoons butter or
   margarine
2 leeks, white part only
½ onion, chopped fine
2 cups chicken broth
2 sprigs parsley
1 small stalk celery

4 cups potatoes, finely sliced
1 teaspoon salt
¼ teaspoon nutmeg
1 cup heavy cream
1 tablespoon parsley or chives,
   finely minced

Melt butter or margarine in saucepan, add leeks, cut fine, and onion and sauté slowly until tender but not brown. Add chicken broth, parsley, celery, potatoes, and salt. Cook slowly until potatoes are tender. Put through a very fine sieve. Return mixture to saucepan. Add nutmeg and cream. Bring to boiling point. Remove from heat and chill. Serve in individual bowls. Top with chopped parsley or chives. Serves 4.

OYSTER STEW

¼ cup butter or margarine
1 pint oysters
¾ cup cold water
2 teaspoons salt

½ teaspoon celery salt
1 teaspoon paprika
4 cups milk

Melt butter or margarine over high heat. Add oysters, water, salt, celery salt, and paprika. Cook until oysters begin to curl at edges. Add milk. When mixture reaches boiling point, remove from heat. Serve at once. Serves 4.

LOBSTER STEW

2 1-pound lobsters
½ cup butter or margarine

1 quart whole milk

Boil lobsters and remove meat immediately, saving the tomalley, or liver, the coral, and the thick white substance inside the shell. Simmer the tomalley, white substance, and coral in butter or margarine very slowly for 7 or 8 minutes. Add lobster meat cut in fairly good-sized pieces. Cook for 10 minutes over very low heat. Remove from heat and cool slightly. Then add, very slowly, just a trickle at a time, the milk, stirring constantly. Allow the stew to stand 5 or 6 hours before reheating for serving. According to the very fine booklet put out by the State of Maine, such aging is an important step in fine lobster stew. You do not need salt and pepper if the stew is made properly. Serves 4.

TRICK: According to that same Maine booklet, the trick of perfect lobster stew is stirring when the milk is added. Otherwise the mixture will curdle. Experts claim the stirring must continue until the stew blossoms a rich salmon color.

CHOWDERS

Chowders, made from vegetables or fish, and accompanied by a salad, usually make a meal. Some chowders require considerable time and care in preparing, as you will see; but you will probably decide that it is worth it. Fish chowders improve with age and are always better the second day. Fish chowders also freeze wonderfully, and you would be wise, therefore, to make an extra quantity so that you can freeze what is not used immediately.

CORN CHOWDER

4 cups raw potatoes, diced	2 cups milk
2 cups boiling water	1 teaspoon salt
¼ pound salt pork, diced	⅛ teaspoon pepper
¼ cup onion, chopped	1 teaspoon paprika
2 cups corn, canned or fresh	2 tablespoons parsley, chopped

Cook potatoes in boiling water for 15 minutes. Put salt pork in skillet and fry until meat is crisp. Add onions and cook slowly for 5 minutes. Onions should be tender, but not brown. Add to potatoes. Also add corn to potatoes. Cook 15 minutes longer. Add milk, salt, pepper, and paprika. Bring to boiling point and serve piping hot. Top with parsley. Serve with crackers. Serves 4-6.

FISH CHOWDER

5 pounds potatoes, grated	3 pounds strong-flavored fish
4 large onions, grated	such as haddock
3 cups cooked tomatoes	1 quart whole milk
3 quarts water	½ pint heavy cream
5 teaspoons salt	¼ pound butter or margarine
1 teaspoon pepper	

Grate potatoes and onions. Place in large saucepan. Add tomatoes, water, and seasonings. Simmer for about 2 hours until mixture is a fine pulp. Stir occasionally. Add fish which has been finely chopped and simmer 3 hours longer.

Note: If frozen fish is used, thaw before adding. If fresh fish is used, take off as much fish from bone as possible. Cook bones in small amount of water, strain and add to chowder. Just before serving add the milk, cream, and butter or margarine. Do not boil. Bring just to boiling point and serve at once. Serves 12-15.

TRICK: Make this the day before. Add milk, cream, and butter or margarine just before ready to serve. An easy food to serve at a party, because all you need with it is a tart, tossed vegetable salad, and a simple dessert.

VEGETABLE CHOWDER

4 strips bacon, diced	1 cup corn, leftover or canned
1 onion, diced fine	3 cups milk
2 tablespoons all-purpose flour	2 cups tomatoes
2 cups cold water	Salt and pepper to season
4 potatoes, sliced fine	

Fry bacon until crisp in large saucepan. Add onion and sauté slowly until onion is tender but not brown. Add flour, stirring constantly. Add the water and potatoes. Cover. Cook until potatoes are tender. Add corn and milk. Bring to boiling point, then simmer for about 5 minutes. Add tomatoes. Just as soon as boiling point is reached remove from heat and serve at once. Season to taste. Serves 6-8.

CLAM CHOWDER

1 quart fresh clams	1 quart whole milk, scalded
¼ pound salt pork	Salt and pepper to season
1 quart uncooked potatoes, diced	Butter or margarine, if desired
1 onion, chopped	

Remove black parts from clams, saving the liquor. Cut pork in small pieces and fry until crisp and golden brown, then remove small pieces of pork from the fat. Add potatoes and onion, with just enough water barely to cover the potatoes. Cook over low heat, simmering gently, until potatoes are done. Add clams and cook 2 minutes after the mixture has reached the boiling point. Long cooking of clams toughens them. Remove chowder from heat and allow to stand a few minutes. Then add hot milk, the clam liquor, and seasoning to taste.

This recipe comes from the same fine booklet on sea-food cookery put out by the State of Maine that I have mentioned earlier. The trick to clam chowder, according to this fine book, is in adding the hot milk after the chowder has been removed from the heat, which lessens the chances of the mixture's curdling. Serves 4.

BOUILLABAISSE

(It's a little difficult to decide whether this famous southern dish is a soup, chowder, or just plain fish dish. We'll take the chance and put it under "Soups.")

2 pounds mixed fish, haddock and other strong-flavored fish	2 teaspoons salt
	1 teaspoon pepper
	¼ teaspoon saffron
1 cup lobster meat	2 cups white wine
6 onions, sliced thick	4 cups water
4 cloves	1 tablespoon parsley, chopped
2 cloves garlic	½ cup olive oil
1 bay leaf	Several slices stale bread

Tie the fish (and do be sure there are no bones in the fish), lobster meat, onion, cloves, garlic, and bay leaf loosely in a piece of cheesecloth. Do not tie tightly because the flavors will not penetrate the broth. Into a large kettle, place the salt, pepper, saffron, white wine, water, and parsley. Hang the fish mixture into the liquid. Cover. Cook over simmer heat for 1 hour. Remove the fish mixture from the liquid. Drain. Save the liquid that drains from the cheesecloth and return to kettle. When well drained, remove the onion, cloves, garlic, and bay leaf from the cheesecloth bag and place the fish back in the kettle containing the liquid. Add the stale bread. Bring to boiling point. Serve at once. Bouillabaisse is enhanced when served from a tureen. Serves 4-6.

Meats

How Much to Buy

You are the best judge as to the amount of meat to buy, for you are in the best position to estimate the appetite of your family and the portion of your food budget that you wish to spend on meat. As a rough guide, however, you may count on three to four small servings from one pound of boneless meat, such as rolled roasts, ground meat, and so on. When the meat has a bone, you may count only on two servings per pound, and for hearty eaters you may need to allow a little more.

What to Look for in Buying

There are three guides to be considered in buying meat: (1) the inspection stamp, (2) the grade stamp, (3) the appearance of the meat itself.

The object of the inspection stamp is to protect you, the customer, and assure you that the meat is from healthful animals that have been slaughtered under sanitary conditions.

The inspection stamp may be federal, state, or city. All meat-packing plants which ship outside their state must operate under federal inspection. The major portion of all meat sold in the United

States is federally inspected. A large portion of the remainder is inspected under state or city regulations. A very small portion is slaughtered on farms and in small communities where no inspection is maintained.

The various grades of meat given below refer to beef, but also apply quite closely to veal, lamb, and mutton. Pork is sold somewhat differently and is graded by the packer on a quality and weight basis. Smoked cuts usually carry the name of the packer.

Grade stamps on the meat indicate quality. Government-graded meat from a locally inspected establishment is labeled Prime, Choice, etc., while government-graded meat from a federally inspected plant is marked U.S. Prime, U.S. Choice, etc.

Prime beef is the highest quality, but don't feel too badly if you rarely see it in the butcher shop, because, first of all, there isn't too much Prime meat available. Exclusive restaurants, clubs, and hotels usually bid for this quality.

Choice beef is the highest grade available throughout the year in retail stores, and only about fifteen per cent of the total supply of beef comes within this grade.

Good beef is the most popular grade. About the only difference between Choice and Good is that the fat covering is usually slightly thinner on Good.

Commercial beef has less fat and, with the exception of rib and loin cuts, should always be cooked by moist heat.

Utility beef has still less fat, and all cuts should be cooked by moist heat.

Cutter and *Canner* beef grades are seldom found in retail markets.

Cull, comparable to Cutter and Canner, refers to veal, lamb, and mutton.

How to Care for Fresh Meat

Since a large percentage of your food budget goes for meat, the care of this expensive item is important. As soon as you get home, remove all wrappings and place the meat in the meat keeper of your refrigerator. If you have one of the older models which does not contain this useful feature, unwrap the meat, place on a platter or plate, cover lightly—*not tightly*—with waxed paper, and place meat in the coldest part of the food compartment of your refrigerator, which is directly under the freeze chest.

Remember that ground meat should be used as soon as possible after purchase, and that it must never be kept more than forty-eight hours.

How to Care for Frozen Meats

If you buy your meat already frozen, provided it is properly packaged, then place it immediately in your freeze chest or home freezer.

However, if you buy fresh meat for freezing, it must be packaged in moisture-proof, vapor-proof wrappings. The wrapping paper used by butchers MUST NEVER BE USED.

The best wrapping material to use for packaging meat to be frozen is either aluminum foil (not the household kind, for it is not heavy enough, but regular freezer foil), laminated foil, or polythene bags. It also is necessary to work all air from packages when preparing food for freezing. Proper packaging and exclusion of air are even more important than the zero temperature for storing the frozen food.

Cooking Methods

There are six different ways to cook meat, and in most cases the tenderness of the meat determines the method of cooking. In general, tender cuts are best when cooked by the dry-heat method, such as roasting, broiling, or pan-broiling. Less tender cuts of meat are made tender by cooking with moist heat, such as braising, pan-frying, and cooking in a quantity of liquid.

Thin cuts of meat, such as chops, steaks, and cutlets of pork or veal, need to be cooked well done. They are better when braised or fried, rather than broiled or pan-broiled.

During cooking, meat shrinks in size and weight regardless of the method used. Strangely enough, the higher the temperature at which meat is cooked, the greater the shrinkage.

ROASTING

Cuts Suitable for Dry Roasting

Standing ribs	Rump roast (from Choice meat)
Rolled ribs	Tenderloin roast
Tip roast	

How to Roast Meat by Dry-Heat Method

1. Season with salt and pepper, if desired. According to the home economists at the National Livestock and Meat Board, it doesn't matter when you season the meat. However, if you are on the forgetful side, better do it when you put the meat in the oven.
2. Place meat, fat side up, on a trivet in an open, shallow pan. The trivet holds the roast out of the drippings, and the fat on top of the meat melts into the roast as it cooks. So, the basting is done for you. If you are wondering what a trivet is, it is a wire rack supported by 3 or more short braces or legs.
3. Place a meat thermometer in the center of the meat. The thermometer bulb must not touch a bone or rest in the fat and must be pushed into the center of the roast.
4. DO NOT ADD ANY WATER, and DO NOT COVER. Roasting is a dry-heat method of cooking, and if the pan is covered, or water added, that luscious, expensive roast becomes just a plain pot roast.
5. Roast in a slow oven, 300° F., or according to chart, pages 26-27.

How to Roast Frozen Meat

Frozen roasts may be cooked from frozen state. Unwrap and place in shallow pan, on trivet. Place in preheated oven, 300° F. Do not add water and do not cover. However, frozen roasts require 15 minutes longer roasting time per pound than thawed or fresh meats.

If you wish to use a meat thermometer, place in meat just as soon as meat has thawed.

TIMETABLE FOR ROASTING MEATS

Roasting times are based on refrigerated (but not frozen) meats started in a preheated oven.

Roast	Weight Pounds	Oven Temperature	Temperature of Meat Removed from Oven (Use Meat Thermometer)	Approximate Minutes per Pound for Unfrozen Meats
BEEF				
Standing Ribs	6-8	300° F.	.140° F.	Rare —18-20
			160° F.	Med.—22-25
			170° F.	Well—27-30
Smaller Roast		350° F.	Same as large roast	Same as large roast

TIMETABLE FOR ROASTING MEATS (Continued)

Roast	Weight Pounds	Oven Temperature	Temperature of Meat Removed from Oven (Use Meat Thermometer)	Approximate Minutes per Pound for Unfrozen Meats
Rolled Ribs	6-8	300° F.	140° F.	Rare —32
			160° F.	Med.—38
			170° F.	Well—48
(Prime) Chuck Ribs or (Choice)	6-8	300° F.	150° F.-170° F.	Well—25-30
(Prime) Rump or (Choice)	5-7	300° F.	150° F.-170° F.	Well—25-30
PORK—FRESH				
Loin—Center	3-4		185° F.	Well—35-40
Whole	12-15	350° F.	185° F.	Well—15-20
Ends	3-4		185° F.	Well—45-50
Shoulder—Whole	12-14	350° F.	185° F.	Well—30-35
Boned and Rolled	4-6	350° F.	185° F.	Well—40-45
Cushion	4-6	350° F.	185° F.	Well—35-40
Pork Butt	4-6	350° F.	185° F.	Well—45-50
Fresh Ham	10-12	350° F.	185° F.	Well—30-35
PORK—SMOKED				
Ham—Whole	10-12	300° F.	170° F.	Well—25
Precooked	10-12	300° F.	145° F.-150° F.	Well—15
Half	6	300° F.	170° F.	Well—30
Precooked	6	300° F.	145° F.-150° F.	Well—20
Shank End	3	300° F.	170° F.	Well—40
Butt End	3	300° F.	170° F.	Well—45
Cottage Butt	2-4	300° F.	170° F.	Well—35
Picnic	3-10	300° F.	170° F.	Well—35
LAMB				
Leg	6½-7½	300° F.	175° F.-180° F.	Well—30-35
Shoulder	4½-5½	300° F.	175° F.-180° F.	Well—30-35
Rolled	3-4	300° F.	175° F.-180° F.	Well—40-45
Cushion	3-4	300° F.	175° F.-180° F.	Well—30-35
VEAL				
Leg Roast	7-8	300° F.	170° F.	Well—25
Loin	4½-5	300° F.	170° F.	Well—30-35
Rack (4-6 Ribs)	2½-3	300° F.	170° F.	Well—30-35
Shoulder	7	300° F.	170° F.	Well—25
Rolled	5	300° F.	170° F.	Well—40-45

BROILING AND PAN-BROILING

Cuts Suitable for Broiling or Pan-Broiling

Ground meat	Pinbone sirloin steak	T-bone steak
Tip steak	Boneless sirloin	Club steak
Sirloin steak	Porterhouse steak	Tenderloin steak
Rib steak	Loin chops	Calf's liver

How to Broil Meat

All tender cuts of beef, lamb, mutton chops, liver, sliced cured ham, and bacon are suitable for broiling. Fresh pork or veal, however, are seldom broiled.

Steaks and chops should be at least an inch thick for best broiling.

Ham should be at least ½ inch thick.

Liver should be from ¼ to ½ inch thick.

Here are step-by-step instructions for broiling meat:

1. Turn oven regulator to "Broil."
2. Place meat on rack of broiler pan.
3. Place pan in broiler oven so top of meat is at least 2 inches from broiler unit. Steaks and chops 1½ to 2 inches thick should be at least 3 inches from broiler unit.
4. Broil until top side is brown. The meat should be a little more than half done when the top side is brown.
5. Season top side with salt and pepper. If broiling bacon or ham, you can forget the salt. Steaks and chops brown better if browned before salting.
6. Turn and brown the other side.
7. Season the second side and serve at once on heated plates.

How to Pan-Broil Meat

1. Place meat in frying pan or griddle which has been slightly heated. Keep heat fairly low, for you will want to cook the meat slowly.
2. Do not add shortening or water. Do not cover. Pan-broiling is a *dry-heat* method of cooking. You will find that the meat cuts that are suitable for pan-broiling have enough fat to keep them from sticking to the pan.

3. Brown meat on both sides. It should not, however, be seared or browned over a high heat. Contrary to what many people believe, such searing does not "hold in the juices."

4. Turn occasionally—at least more than once, and preferably several times.

5. Cook to desired degree of doneness and serve at once on heated plates.

TIMETABLE FOR BROILING STEAKS AND CHOPS

| | Thickness | Approximate Total Broiling Time | |
		Rare	Medium
BEEF			
Club Steak	1 inch	15 minutes	20 minutes
	1½ inches	25 minutes	30 minutes
	2 inches	35 minutes	45 minutes
Rib Steak	Same as Club Steak		
Porterhouse Steak	1 inch	20 minutes	25 minutes
	1½ inches	30 minutes	35 minutes
	2 inches	40 minutes	45 minutes
Sirloin Steak	Same as Porterhouse Steak		
LAMB			
Loin Chop	1 inch	12 minutes	
	1½ inches	18 minutes	
	2 inches	22 minutes	
Rib Chop and Shoulder Chop—Same as Loin Chop			

BRAISING AND PAN-FRYING

Cuts Suitable for Braising or Frying (Cooking in Moist Heat)

Round steaks	Flank steaks	Shank knuckle
Rump	Short ribs	Oxtails
Chuck	Minute steak	Heart and beef or pork liver

How to Pan-Fry

All comparatively thin pieces of meat, made tender by pounding, scoring, cubing, or grinding, and leftover meat may be pan-fried. When a small amount of shortening is used, it is called pan-frying, and when the meat is immersed in shortening, it is called deep-fat frying. For information on deep-fat frying, turn to Chapter 8, page 221.

1. Place sufficient shortening in skillet to cover the bottom. Heat shortening. Any meat that has a coating of flour, meal, or egg and crumbs will possibly need a little more shortening than meat fried without flouring. Ham or pork chops will need no shortening.
2. Brown meat on both sides.
3. Season and serve at once.

How to Braise Meat

Braising is another method used for cooking less tender cuts of meat.

1. Dredge meat with flour which has been seasoned with salt and pepper, herbs, and spices. Go easy on the herbs and spices. A little of either goes a long way.
2. Place shortening in frying pan or suitable kettle and brown meat slowly on all sides. The browning develops flavor and color.
3. Add a small amount of liquid such as water, tomato juice, soup stock, or sour cream.
4. Cover tightly.
5. Cook at a low temperature until tender. This means simmering, not boiling.
6. Make gravy from the liquid in the pan.

COOKING MEAT IN LIQUIDS

Both large and small cuts of less tender meat are cooked in this manner.

1. Brown meat on all sides. The only exception to this rule is corned beef and cured pork, which do not need to be browned.
2. Cover the meat with water. The liquid may be either hot or cold. The main difference between braising and this method of cooking is the amount of liquid used.
3. Season well with salt, pepper, herbs, spices, such as tarragon, bay leaves, thyme, marjoram, onion, garlic, and parsley.
4. Cover kettle and simmer until tender. Too-rapid cooking shrinks the meat and makes it dry and stringy.
5. If meat is to be served cold, let it cool in the liquid in which it was cooked.

6. If vegetables are to be added, as in boiled dinners, add them whole or in large pieces, and just long enough beforehand to cook them sufficiently.

ROAST MEAT RECIPES

ROAST BEEF WITH YORKSHIRE PUDDING

This will be easier to cook if you have two ovens, since the meat is cooked at low temperature, while the Yorkshire pudding needs a much higher heat. You may, however, cook it with a single oven by removing the meat thirty minutes before serving time, covering with a clean towel, and setting it in a warm place. Remember the meat will continue to cook for a time after removal from the oven, so, particularly if you want rare beef, you must take this waiting time into consideration. You will find that meat set aside in this way will be easier to slice than that which has just come from the oven.

Roast the beef according to directions on page 26, checking cooking time with the chart on pages 26-27.

YORKSHIRE PUDDING

9- x 9-inch pan . . . Preheated oven—425° F. . . . Baking time— 30-40 minutes

½ cup hot drippings from roasting pan	1 cup all-purpose flour, sifted before measuring
2 eggs	½ teaspoon salt
1 cup milk	

Pour hot drippings from roast into pan. Beat eggs until fluffy, add milk, beat until well blended. Stir in flour and salt. Beat thoroughly. Pour batter into prepared pan. The batter should be about ½ inch deep in pan. Bake. Serve at once. Serves 8.

GLAZED LEG OF LAMB

To roast lamb, follow roasting directions on page 26. For length of roasting time, see chart on page 27.

During the last hour of roasting, baste two or three times with ½ cup grape jelly which has been dissolved in ½ cup boiling water.

Another interesting glaze is made by mixing 1 can sieved apricot baby food with ½ cup water. Use this mixture to baste the lamb during the last hour of roasting. Serve lamb with Mint Sauce, page 244.

STUFFED LAMB SHOULDER

Have the butcher remove the bone from a shoulder of lamb. Season inside of meat with salt and pepper. Fill cavity with dressing (page 94). Pile dressing in lightly, otherwise it will become soggy and heavy. Sew edges together or fasten together with skewers. Serve with brown gravy (page 246).

Roast lamb according to directions on page 26. For length of roasting time, see chart on page 27.

ROAST VEAL

Veal is very tender but contains a great deal of connective tissue and requires long, slow cooking. There is very little fat on veal. It is therefore advisable to add fat by what is called "larding." The easiest way to do this is to place several thin slices of salt pork or bacon strips, or suet which has been flattened out, on top of the meat.

Season with salt and pepper and roast according to directions on page 26. For length of roasting time, see chart on page 27.

ROAST LOIN OF PORK OR SHOULDER OF PORK

The center cuts are most desirable for roasting. For a truly delicious pork roast, cut a clove of garlic lengthwise into slender pieces. Work this garlic in between the bones on the under side. Season with salt and pepper. A trivet is not so essential with loin of pork, since the bones hold the meat away from the drippings.

Roast according to directions on page 26. For length of roasting time, see chart on page 27.

Pork shoulder, whole or boned and rolled, may be roasted the same way.

ROAST SMOKED PORK OR BAKED HAM

Tenderized hams need no soaking or precooking. Virginia or Smithfield hams should be soaked in cold water for at least 12 hours, then placed, skin side up, in a large kettle. Cover ham with water. Cover kettle and simmer meat until tender. These hams are then roasted the same as tenderized hams.

BAKED TENDERIZED HAM

Place ham on trivet in shallow pan, skin side up. For roasting time, see chart on page 27. About an hour before ham has finished roasting, remove from oven and peel off the rind. You will need a sharp knife to do this. Start at the butt end and carefully loosen the rind from that end. Pull gently, using the knife to loosen any portion which wants to cling to the fat.

Now comes the trick. You will need a sharp knife again, because you are about to "score" the fat, or top side of the ham. Starting at the left side of the hock end, cut a slit (not too deep, about ¼ inch deep) diagonally across the ham over to the right side of the butt end. Do the same an inch on the other side of the first line, until you have these slits diagonally across the entire top of the ham. Then go the other way across, making these rows an inch apart. The top of the ham now has many nice little rectangular sections on top. Do half a ham the same way. Next, stick whole cloves where diagonal lines intersect.

Here are a number of suggestions for decorating and flavoring baked ham:

1. Spread top surface of ham with 1 cup brown sugar which has been blended with ¼ cup prepared mustard.
2. Spread over surface of ham 1 cup brown sugar, 2 teaspoons dry mustard mixed with 3 tablespoons vinegar or sherry.
3. Place thin slices of unpeeled oranges over ham and sprinkle generously with 1 cup brown sugar mixed with ¼ cup all-purpose flour.
4. Cover ham with honey after scoring.
5. Place pineapple chunks in each scored section. Anchor them down with toothpicks. Baste with pineapple juice.
6. Mix 1 cup crushed pineapple with 1 cup brown sugar and ¼ cup sherry. Spread over ham. Baste occasionally with half pineapple juice and half sherry.
7. Baste with 1 can apricot nectar blended with ¼ cup sherry.

After using any of the above suggestions, return ham to oven until nicely browned. It is desirable to baste several times during this final roasting period.

ROASTED CANADIAN BACON

Shallow pan with trivet . . . Preheated oven—350° F. . . . Roasting time—about 2 hours

2 pounds Canadian bacon	1 cup pineapple juice
½ cup brown sugar	¼ cup sherry or other wine
2 tablespoons prepared mustard	

Score fat side of Canadian bacon. (See directions for scoring ham, page 33.) Combine brown sugar and mustard and spread over top. Place in shallow pan. Pour pineapple juice and sherry over and around it. Baste occasionally while roasting.

BROILED MEAT RECIPES

For broiling, follow directions on pages 28-29.

STEAK

Steaks are greatly improved by marinating for several hours before broiling. "Marinate" is a large-sounding word for something that is really very simple to do. All it means is to cover the food with a liquid and let it stand to season for two or three hours.

Any of the following marinades will make meat more flavorful:

1. Marinate in Choy Sauce. An easy way to do this is to cover the bottom of a glass utility dish with Choy Sauce. Place steaks or chops in dish. Cover with waxed paper. In about 1 hour, turn meat over and marinate other side.
2. Marinate meat in spicy French dressing.
3. Marinate in ½ cup olive oil, ¼ cup sherry, 1 teaspoon granulated sugar, mixed together.
4. Rub steak with garlic before broiling.
5. Rub prepared mustard over steak before broiling.
6. Make incisions in steak about ¾ inch deep and 2 inches apart. Pack Roquefort cheese in incisions.
7. Marinate in ½ cup olive oil in which ¼ cup Roquefort cheese has been thoroughly blended.

PENNYWISE STEAK

1½ pounds ground beef	½ cup dry bread crumbs
1½ teaspoons salt	¼ cup onion, grated
⅛ teaspoon pepper	¾ cup milk

Combine all ingredients. Do this as gently as possible so as not to press meat. Pressing meat into a compact mass ruins the finished product. Shape to resemble a porterhouse steak about 1½ inches thick. Place on broiler pan and be sure the top of the meat is about 3 inches from broiler unit. For rare steak, broil about 8 minutes, turn and broil 7 minutes. For medium, broil 12 minutes, turn and broil 10 minutes.

You can use any of the broiling tricks on pages 28-29 for pennywise steak, too.

KABOBS

Cut good quality beef, 1½ inches thick, into 1½-inch cubes. Allow at least two of the 1½-inch cubes per serving. You do the arithmetic on how much meat to buy, because the amount of meat you buy depends upon the number you plan to serve.

Marinate cubes in Soy Sauce about 2 hours.

Alternate cubes with mushroom caps and onion slices on metal skewers. Brush with melted butter or margarine and broil. Broiling time requires 25-30 minutes, brushing with melted butter or margarine every time you turn the Kabobs.

These are perfect for outdoor broiling. If you are cooking them outdoors, use slender sticks of green wood in place of metal skewers.

BROILED LIVER

Brush liver with melted butter or margarine. Season with salt and pepper. Place on broiler pan. Put under broiler unit about 2 inches from heat. Broil about 8 minutes on one side, turn, brush with melted butter or margarine and broil about 6 minutes on second side.

BROILED SWEETBREADS—See page 56.

FRYING BREADED MEATS

Veal and Pork tenderloin are the two meats most commonly breaded and fried. Both are tender meats, but the connective tissue is apt to be stringy. Therefore, for best results they should be fried slowly until browned, then steamed for 30-40 minutes.

BREADED VEAL CUTLETS

Large skillet with cover . . . Total cooking time—45-50 minutes

1 pound sliced veal, ½ inch thick, cut from leg	¼ cup milk
Salt and pepper	½ to ¾ cup bacon drippings, or other shortening
1 cup fine bread crumbs	¼ cup water or sherry
2 eggs	

Cut veal in serving-size pieces. Season with salt and pepper. Roll each piece in bread crumbs, then dip in egg and milk, which have been beaten together, and again in bread crumbs.

Fry slowly in hot bacon drippings or other shortening. Brown on one side, then turn and brown on the other side. When both sides are brown, add water or sherry. Cover skillet, reduce heat, and allow to simmer 30 minutes. Serves 4.

BREADED PORK TENDERLOINS

1 pound pork tenderloins, cut into four portions. Have butcher flatten them for you. Then proceed as for breaded veal cutlets. Serves 4.

BRAISED MEATS

POT ROAST

Large covered skillet or Dutch oven . . . Cooking time—3-4 hours

4-5 pounds chuck, rump or round beef	Salt and pepper to taste
1 clove garlic	⅓ cup shortening
¼ cup all-purpose flour	1 large onion, sliced
	1 cup water

Rub meat with garlic which has been cut in half. Mix flour with salt and pepper and carefully rub on all sides of meat. Heat shortening in skillet or Dutch oven. Brown meat evenly on all sides. Slip a trivet under the meat so it will not rest directly on bottom of cooking utensil. Add onion and water. Cover. Simmer gently for 3 to 4 hours, or until tender.

If you do not have a trivet, you may have to turn the meat occasionally. It also may be necessary to add more liquid during the cooking period. Do not allow liquid to boil. The success of a pot roast depends upon long, slow cooking. When cooking period is over, remove meat to hot platter, make brown gravy (page 246), and serve at once. Serves 8-10.

POT ROAST IN SOUR CREAM

8-inch covered skillet . . . Cooking time—1½ hours

2 pounds chuck or rump roast, cut in 1½-inch slices	5 onions, sliced
⅓ cup all-purpose flour	½ pint sour cream
Salt and pepper	2 tablespoons flour
⅓ cup shortening	4 tablespoons water or milk

Roll slices of meat in flour which has been seasoned with salt and pepper. Brown meat on both sides in hot shortening. Cover with sliced onions. Pour sour cream over all. Cover and simmer for 1½ hours, or until meat is tender. When meat is tender, remove from skillet to hot platter. Mix flour left over from dredging meat with water or milk, add to liquid in skillet, and cook until thickened. Pour over meat. Serve at once. Serves 6-8.

POT ROAST MEAL

Follow directions for pot roast (page 30). Use a large kettle with cover or, better yet, a Dutch oven. About 1 hour before cooking time is finished, place potatoes, cut in half lengthwise, and carrots, cut in half lengthwise, around the meat. Cover. Allow one potato and one carrot for each person being served. Arrange vegetables around meat, which has been placed on a hot platter.

BEEF IN WINE

Heavy covered skillet . . . Cooking time—about 2 hours

4 tablespoons butter or margarine	2 tablespoons all-purpose flour
1 carrot, diced in ¼-inch cubes	½ cup red wine
2 onions, chopped fine	½ cup beef stock
1½ pounds lean beef, chuck or round	1 teaspoon salt
	¼ teaspoon pepper
	Herbs to taste

Melt butter or margarine in skillet. Add carrots and onions and fry gently until a golden brown. Push to one side of skillet and brown meat on all sides. When meat is evenly browned, remove from skillet, add flour, and stir through mixture. Next add wine and stock, salt and pepper and herbs, if desired. Stir until sauce is smooth. Return meat to skillet. Cover. Bring to steaming point, then reduce heat to simmer and cook for 2 hours, or until tender. Remove meat to hot platter and pour sauce over it. Serves 4.

TRICK: If you do not have any beef stock, dissolve a bouillon cube in ½ cup boiling water.

SAUERBRATEN

Large covered skillet . . . Cooking time—about 4 hours

1½ cups vinegar	2 large onions, sliced thin
1½ cups water	1 cup cooking or olive oil
2 bay leaves	3 to 4 pounds beef, chuck or heel of round
12 whole cloves	
¼ teaspoon pepper	½ cup all-purpose flour
½ teaspoon mace	Salt and pepper
1½ teaspoons salt	4 tablespoons shortening
1 tablespoon sugar	

Heat vinegar, water, spices, salt, and sugar to boiling point. Pour over sliced onions and allow to stand until cool. Stir in oil. Place meat in crock or large casserole, pour marinade (the mixture you just finished cooking) over meat. Place in refrigerator for two or three days, turning meat once a day so it will pickle evenly. Remove meat from marinade. Strain, but save the liquid. Wipe meat dry. Dredge with flour, seasoned with salt and pepper. Brown meat on all sides in hot shortening. When brown, add 1 cup strained marinade. Cover. Bring to steaming point, then reduce heat to simmer. Cook until tender. Remove meat to hot platter. Make brown gravy (page 246). Some cooks add raisins and gingersnaps to gravy. You can suit yourself about that detail. Serves 10-12.

TRICK: Heat 3 cups of dry red wine with spices given in Sauerbraten recipe. Cool. Pour over meat and marinate for about 18 hours, turning frequently. Then continue as for Sauerbraten.

HUNGARIAN GOULASH

Covered skillet or Dutch oven . . . Cooking time—1½ to 2 hours

2 pounds lean beef, cut in 1-inch cubes	1 bay leaf
	2 tablespoons paprika
¼ cup all-purpose flour	1½ teaspoons salt
Salt and pepper	Dash of cayenne pepper
4 tablespoons shortening	4 medium-sized potatoes, diced
2 cloves garlic, cut in strips	4 tablespoons all-purpose flour
2 cups water	4 tablespoons cold water
1 cup canned tomatoes	

Dredge cubed meat in flour seasoned with salt and pepper. Heat shortening in skillet and brown meat and garlic. When meat is brown on all sides, add water, tomatoes, bay leaf, paprika, salt, and cayenne. Cover. Cook over high heat until steaming, then reduce heat to a low setting. Cook 1 hour, or until meat is tender. Add diced potatoes and cook 30 minutes longer. Blend the flour with water. Stir until the mixture forms a smooth paste, then add to goulash and cook until thickened. Serves 6-8.

TRICK: Use only ½ cup tomatoes and, just before serving, and after thickening has been added, stir in ½ cup sherry or red wine.

STUFFED FLANK STEAK

8-inch skillet with cover . . . Cooking time—2 hours

2 pounds flank steak (have butcher score the steak)	4 tablespoons all-purpose flour
	4 tablespoons shortening
1 clove garlic, cut in half	2 cups tomato juice
2 teaspoons salt	2 tablespoons all-purpose flour
¼ teaspoon pepper	

Rub steak on both sides with clove of garlic which has been cut in half. Season with salt and pepper. Spread stuffing (see page 39) evenly over steak and roll with fiber of meat. Fasten ends together with skewers, toothpicks, or tie with string. Roll in flour, brown meat on all sides in hot shortening in skillet. Add ½ cup of the tomato juice. Cover. Bring to steaming point over high heat, then reduce heat to simmer setting. Cook for 2 hours, or until meat is tender. It may be necessary to turn the meat occasionally. When tender, remove from skillet to hot platter. Remove fastenings. Mix flour with remaining tomato juice, add to liquid in skillet, and cook until thickened. Pour over meat. To serve, cut in slices across fiber of meat. Serves 4-6.

Stuffing for Flank Steak

3 cups bread cubes
1 tablespoon chopped parsley
2 teaspoons salt
⅛ teaspoon pepper

2 tablespoons shortening
¼ cup onion, finely chopped
¼ cup celery, finely chopped

Combine bread cubes, parsley, salt, and pepper. Heat shortening, add onions and celery and simmer gently until onions are cooked and lightly browned. Mix with bread cubes.

TRICK: Better use bread that is at least 2 days old. If very dry bread is used, you may have to add ¼ cup water.

BEEF STROGANOFF

8-inch skillet with cover . . . Cooking time—45 minutes

1 pound round steak, sliced thin
¼ cup all-purpose flour
½ teaspoon salt
⅛ teaspoon pepper
4 tablespoons shortening
½ cup onions, chopped
1 can (6 ounces) mushrooms (or 1 pint fresh)
1 clove garlic, minced

1 cup thick sour cream
1 can condensed cream of tomato soup
1 tablespoon Worcestershire sauce
¼ teaspoon Tobasco sauce
½ cup green pepper, diced
1 package (8 ounces) spaghetti
Parmesan cheese

Cut meat in ¾-inch cubes and dredge with flour seasoned with salt and pepper. Brown meat in hot shortening. Add onions, mushrooms, and garlic. Combine cream, tomato soup, sauces, and green pepper. Pour over meat. Cover. Cook on high heat until steaming, then reduce heat to simmer. Cook spaghetti (pages 253-54). Serve meat over spaghetti. Sprinkle Parmesan cheese over top. If you

prefer, steamed rice (page 265) may be used instead of spaghetti.
Serves 4-5.

SUKIYAKI

8-inch skillet with cover . . . Cooking time—35-40 minutes

2 tablespoons cooking oil	1 cup celery, cut diagonally in
1½ pounds sirloin steak, cut in	1½-inch strips
thin diagonal slices 2 inches	1 can (10-12 ounces) bamboo
by ½ inch	shoots, thinly sliced
¼ cup sugar	1 can (8 ounces) mushrooms,
¾ cup Soy Sauce	stems and pieces
¼ cup water or mushroom stock	1 bunch green onions, cut in 1-
2 onions, sliced thin	inch lengths with tops
1 green pepper, cut in thin	
strips	

Heat oil in skillet, add meat and brown lightly. Combine sugar,
Soy Sauce, and water or mushroom stock. Add this to meat. Cover.
Bring to steaming point. Cook about 40 minutes, or until tender.
Add remaining ingredients except green onions. Cover and cook
on high heat only a short time, about 2 or 3 minutes. Add green
onions and cook 1 minute more. Serve with hot steamed rice (page
265).

Sukiyaki must be served as soon as the vegetables are done so
they will retain their crispness. Serves 4-6.

SAVORY SKILLET MEAL

8-inch skillet with cover . . . Cooking time—1 hour

1 pound round steak, cut in serv-	4 medium-sized carrots, cut in
ing pieces	half, lengthwise
¼ cup all-purpose flour	1 large onion, peeled and sliced
1 teaspoon salt	quite thin
½ teaspoon pepper	1 teaspoon chopped parsley
4 tablespoons shortening	1 tablespoon meat sauce
4 medium-sized potatoes, quar-	1 can condensed cream of mush-
tered	room soup

Dredge meat in flour seasoned with salt and pepper. Brown meat
in hot shortening. When beef has been browned on both sides,
place vegetables in skillet with meat. Mix meat sauce and mushroom soup and pour over top. Cover. Just as soon as steaming point
is reached, reduce heat to simmer setting. Cook until meat and
vegetables are tender. Serve at once. Serves 4.

SWISS STEAK

Skillet with cover . . . Cooking time 1¼ hours . . . OR . . . Casserole
with cover . . . Baking time 1½ hours 375° F.

2 pounds round, rump, or chuck, cut 2 inches thick	¼ cup shortening 1 onion, sliced
¼ cup all-purpose flour Salt and pepper	2 carrots, sliced 1 No. 2 can tomatoes

Pound meat with the edge of a heavy-plated or wooden mallet.
Dredge with flour seasoned with salt and pepper. Brown meat on
all sides in hot shortening. Add onion, carrots, and tomatoes. Cover.
Bring to steaming point over high heat, then reduce heat to simmer. Or place meat, after it has browned, in casserole. Add vegetables and tomatoes. Cover. Bake in oven. This may be served
from casserole, or, if cooked in skillet, should be served from hot
platter. Serves 6.

POT ROAST OF VEAL

Large covered skillet or Dutch oven . . . Cooking time—2 hours

3½ to 4 pounds rump of veal	2 or 3 peppercorns
2 tablespoons all-purpose flour	1 bay leaf
Salt and pepper	1 cup water
½ teaspoon paprika	8 or 10 small onions, peeled
2 tablespoons shortening	

Dredge meat with flour which has been seasoned with salt, pepper,
and paprika. Brown meat on all sides in hot shortening. Add peppercorns, bay leaf, and water. Cover. Bring to steaming point, then
reduce heat to simmer. Cook 1½ hours. Place onions around meat.
Simmer for ½ hour longer, or until meat and onions are tender. Remove meat to hot platter, surround with onions. Make brown
gravy (page 246). Serves 6-8.

VEAL SCALLOPINI

Large skillet with cover . . . Cooking time—about 45 minutes . . .
OR . . . 2-quart casserole with cover . . . Baking time—about 1
hour at 375°

2 pounds veal steak, sliced very thin	4 tablespoons salad oil 1 can (8 ounces) mushrooms,
½ cup all-purpose flour Salt and pepper	sliced 2 cups sauterne wine

Cut meat in 2-inch pieces. Dredge with flour which has been seasoned with salt and pepper. Brown on both sides in hot salad oil in large skillet. When veal is well browned, remove from skillet to casserole. Put well-drained mushrooms in skillet in which veal was cooked and sauté in remaining oil. Add wine to mushrooms, and when hot, pour over veal. Cover casserole. Place in oven. May be served with hot steamed rice (page 265).

Or, if it is not convenient to use the oven, after the veal has browned, remove from skillet. Sauté the mushrooms, add wine, and bring to boiling point, then return veal to skillet, making sure all meat is covered with the sauce. Cover. Just as soon as mixture comes to steaming point, reduce heat to simmer. Serves 6-8.

VEAL PAPRIKA

8-inch covered skillet . . . Cooking time—1¼ hours

1 egg	4 tablespoons shortening
1 tablespoon water	1 clove garlic, cut in half
1½ teaspoons salt	½ cup water
1½ pounds veal, cut in 2-inch cubes	1 cup sour cream
	1 tablespoon paprika
⅔ cup fine bread crumbs	

Beat egg together with 1 tablespoon water and salt. Dip veal cubes into egg mixture, then into dry bread crumbs. Heat shortening and fry garlic. Remove garlic, add the veal and brown cubes on all sides. Add ½ cup water. Cover. When mixture reaches steaming point, reduce heat to simmer and cook 1 hour. Add cream. Do not stir. Sprinkle with paprika. Cover. Cook 15 minutes longer. Serve over hot rice (page 265) or noodles (pages 253-54). Serves 4-6.

MOCK CHICKEN

8-inch covered skillet . . . Cooking time—35 minutes

1½ pounds veal steak	2 tablespoons shortening
¼ cup all-purpose flour	1 can chicken rice soup
½ teaspoon salt	⅓ cup pimiento stuffed olives, sliced
¼ teaspoon paprika	

Cut veal in one-inch strips. Roll in flour seasoned with salt and paprika. Brown on all sides in hot shortening. Add soup. Cover. When mixture comes to steaming point, reduce heat to simmer. Cook for about 20 minutes. Add olives and cook for 15 minutes longer. Serve at once. Serves 4-6.

VEAL AND VEGETABLE ONE-DISH MEAL

Dutch oven or large covered skillet . . . Cooking time—40 minutes

1½ pounds veal shoulder, ground	2 tablespoons all-purpose flour
2 tablespoons melted butter or margarine	3 tablespoons shortening
½ cup bread crumbs	6 small potatoes, quartered
½ teaspoon Worcestershire sauce	6 small carrots, sliced and halved
½ teaspoon parsley, minced	6 small onions
1 teaspoon salt	1 cup green pepper, chopped
1 teaspoon sugar	1 cup hot water
1 egg, beaten	3 tablespoons tomato catchup
	½ teaspoon pepper

Mix ground veal, melted butter or margarine, bread crumbs, Worcestershire sauce, minced parsley, salt, sugar, and beaten egg. Form into balls, roll in flour, and brown in hot shortening in skillet. When veal balls are brown, pour off any surplus drippings and add potatoes, carrots, onions, green pepper, and the hot water which has been mixed with the tomato catchup. Add pepper. Cover tightly and allow mixture to cook on low heat for 35 minutes. Serve while hot. Serves 6.

PORK CHOPS

Almost anyone can fry pork chops, but here's one of grandmother's tricks. Since pork chops are fatty, there really is no need to put shortening in the skillet. So, grandmother used to sprinkle salt over the bottom of the skillet, then put in the pork chops and fry them slowly, 12 to 15 minutes on each side. They brown beautifully, without sticking, and when they are ready to turn, there is sufficient grease in the skillet to brown the second side nicely.

PORK CHOP CASSEROLE

2-quart covered casserole . . . Preheated oven—375° F. . . . Baking time—45 minutes

4 or 5 pork chops, cut ½ inch thick	1 can condensed cream of mushroom soup
Salt and pepper to season	

Brown pork chops (using salt in the pan, as above, if desired). Season with additional salt, if necessary, and pepper. When brown on both sides, place in casserole. Pour mushroom soup over chops. Cover. Place in oven and cook. You can serve these from the casserole. Serves 4-5.

SPARERIBS WITH SAUERKRAUT

3-quart covered casserole . . . Cold or preheated oven—350° F. . . .
Cooking time—2 hours

2-3 pounds spareribs (have butcher crack spareribs)	Salt and pepper to taste 4 cups sauerkraut

Season spareribs with salt and pepper and brown in hot skillet.
If there is considerable fat on them, do not add grease to skillet.
Place half the sauerkraut in casserole; next, half the browned
spareribs. Repeat. Cover. Place in oven. Cook. Serves 4.

This dish may also be done on the top of the stove. Simply cook
spareribs in large skillet. After they have browned, pour off grease
which has accumulated. Pour sauerkraut over spareribs, cover,
and cook on simmer heat for 1½ to 2 hours.

CANADIAN BACON AND SCALLOPED POTATOES

2-quart covered casserole . . . Preheated oven—375° F. . . . Baking
time—1 to 1¼ hours

4 cups potatoes, sliced	½ cup milk
2 tablespoons all-purpose flour	1 can condensed cream of mush-
1 teaspoon salt	room soup
⅛ teaspoon pepper	½ cup buttered crumbs
8 slices Canadian bacon, ½ inch thick	2 tablespoons butter or marga- rine

Wash, peel, and thinly slice potatoes. Combine flour, salt, and pepper. Put 4 slices Canadian bacon in bottom of greased casserole.
Top with half of the sliced potatoes. Sprinkle with half the flour
mixed with seasonings. Put remaining 4 slices bacon on top of potatoes. Next, the remaining potatoes, and sprinkle remaining seasoned flour on top. Mix milk with mushroom soup. Pour over bacon
and potato mixture. Top with crumbs and dots of butter or margarine. Bake. Keep covered for first ½ hour of cooking, then remove
cover. Serve from casserole. This makes a fine one-dish meal. Thin
slices of ham may be substituted for Canadian bacon. Serves 4.

CURRIED HAM ROLLS

9-inch square baking dish . . . Preheated oven—375° F. . . . Baking
time—30 minutes

2 cups cooked rice (page 265)	½ teaspoon salt
1 medium onion, minced	½ teaspoon curry powder
¼ cup parsley, finely chopped	8 slices boiled ham (not too thin)
1 tablespoon melted butter or margarine	4 hard-cooked eggs (page 273)

Mix cooked rice, onion, parsley, melted butter or margarine, salt, and curry powder together. Place about ⅛ cup of rice mixture on each slice of ham. Roll up and place, seam side down, in baking dish. Cut hard-cooked eggs in half lengthwise and place ½ egg, cut side down, on ham roll. Pour curry sauce over rolls. Bake. May be served on thin wedges of toast, if desired. Serves 4.

Curry Sauce

¼ cup butter or margarine	2 tablespoons cornstarch
½ teaspoon curry powder	½ teaspoon salt
½ teaspoon monosodium gluta-mate	2 cups milk

Melt butter or margarine in saucepan. Add curry powder, mono-sodium glutamate, cornstarch, and salt. Blend well. Add milk. Cook over medium heat until thick.

STEWING MEAT RECIPES

BEEF STEW

Large covered skillet or kettle . . . Cooking time—1½ to 2 hours

2 pounds beef, chuck or shank, cut in 1-inch cubes	Pinch marjoram, thyme, tarragon
¼ cup all-purpose flour	6 small onions
2 teaspoons salt	6 small carrots
¼ teaspoon pepper	6 medium-sized potatoes, cut in quarters
3 tablespoons shortening	
3 cups hot water	

Roll cubed meat in seasoned flour. Melt shortening in large skillet or kettle and brown meat in hot shortening. When meat is brown on all sides, add water and herbs. Cover utensil, and when steaming point is reached, turn heat to simmer setting and cook until meat is almost tender, about 1 hour. Add vegetables. Turn heat to high until steaming, then reduce heat to a lower setting, and cook until vegetables are tender, about 30 minutes. Serve at once. Serves 6.

JELLIED VEAL LOAF

2 pounds knuckle of veal, sawed in half	1 onion, cut in half
	Salt and pepper
1 pound lean veal	2 sprigs parsley
4 cups boiling water	3 hard-cooked eggs (page 273)

Place knuckle of veal and lean meat in deep saucepan. Add boiling water, onion, salt, pepper, and parsley. Cook slowly until meat is tender, about 2 hours, or maybe more. Drain mixture through a fine sieve which has been placed inside a crock or bowl. Remove meat from veal knuckle and cut in medium-sized pieces. Cut other meat in same size pieces. Return meat broth to kettle and continue cooking until 2 cups liquid remain. Cut hard-cooked eggs crosswise in medium pieces. Garnish bottom of bread pan, or any mold, with eggs. Next put in a layer of meat, a second layer of egg slices, and cover with meat. Pour meat broth over the meat mixture. Chill thoroughly. Cut in ½-inch slices for serving. A wonderful food for hot weather. The knuckle of veal, if cooked slowly enough, makes its own gelatin. Serves 8-10.

VEAL OR LAMB STEW WITH PARSLEY DUMPLINGS

Large kettle with cover . . . Cooking time—2 to 2½ hours

3 pounds stewing veal or lamb	2 tablespoons celery tops,
¼ cup all-purpose flour	chopped
3 tablespoons shortening	½ teaspoon marjoram
4 cups boiling water	12 small onions, whole
1 clove garlic, sliced	6 medium carrots, quartered
2½ teaspoons salt	and cut in 2-inch pieces
¼ teaspoon pepper	Parsley dumplings (page 312)

Cut veal or lamb in 2-inch cubes. Dredge with flour and brown in hot shortening in large kettle. When meat is browned on all sides, add the boiling water, garlic, salt, pepper, celery tops, and marjoram. Cover. Just as soon as mixture reaches steaming point, reduce heat to simmer. Cook over simmer heat for 1 hour, or until meat is almost tender. Add peeled onions and carrots. Cover and bring mixture to steaming point. Then reduce heat to a low setting and cook 30 minutes longer, or until vegetables are tender. Make dumplings and place over the stew and cook 15 minutes longer. Carefully place stew in large serving bowl, with dumplings on top, and serve at once. Serves 8.

NEW ENGLAND BOILED DINNER

Large kettle with cover . . . Cooking time—3 to 3½ hours

3 pounds corned beef	6 carrots, cut in half lengthwise
3 cups water	6 potatoes, cut in half lengthwise
1 medium-sized head of cabbage	6 turnips, cut in quarters

Place corned beef and water in large kettle. Cover. Cook over high heat until steaming, then reduce to a medium heat. Cook for 2½ hours. Remove meat from kettle and put vegetables in, returning meat to kettle, but on top of the vegetables. Cover. When mixture is steaming briskly, reduce to a medium heat and continue cooking for about 30 minutes, or until vegetables are tender. Ham may be substituted for corned beef. Serve at once on large platter. Serves 6.

OXTAIL STEW

Large kettle with cover . . . Cooking time—about 2½ hours

2 oxtails, cut in 2-inch pieces
¼ cup all-purpose flour
¼ cup shortening
4 cups boiling water
3 tablespoons barley
5 or 6 peppercorns
4 whole cloves
1 bay leaf

1 tablespoon Kitchen Bouquet
2 tablespoons salt
6 medium potatoes
6 small carrots
1 large or 2 small onions
Mushroom dumplings (page 312)

Dredge oxtails in flour. Heat shortening in kettle and brown oxtails on all sides. Add boiling water, barley, peppercorns, cloves, bay leaf, and the Kitchen Bouquet. Cover. When mixture comes to steaming point, turn heat to simmer. Cook about 1½ hours. Add salt and vegetables. Cover. Continue the slow cooking for 45 minutes, or until vegetables are tender. Make dumplings and place over stew, cover, and cook 15 minutes longer. Serve at once in large dish, placing dumplings on top of stew. Serves 5-6.

CURRIED BEEF OR LAMB

(A wonderful recipe for those who really like curry)

Large covered skillet or stew kettle . . . Cooking time—2 hours

2 pounds lean beef or lamb cut in 1-inch cubes
1 cup water
2 bouillon cubes
1 can tomato paste
½ teaspoon ginger
1 clove garlic, diced
1 teaspoon salt
½ teaspoon pepper
1 teaspoon Worcestershire sauce

1½ to 2 tablespoons curry powder
½ cup grated coconut
¼ cup seedless raisins
2 tart apples
1 large onion, diced
1 teaspoon dried parsley
½ teaspoon coriander (optional)

Place meat in large skillet or stew kettle. Add all ingredients. Cover. When mixture comes to steaming point, reduce heat to simmer. Stir occasionally. Should more liquid be needed, add either water or tomato juice. This mixture should end up more like a thick sauce than a thin mixture. Serve over hot rice (page 265). Serve with chutney, ground peanuts, or coconut sprinkled over the top. Serves 4-6.

CHOP SUEY

Large skillet with cover . . . Cooking time—45 minutes

1¼ pounds veal steak	1 can (8 ounces) mushrooms
2 tablespoons shortening	(caps or pieces)
3 cups celery, diced	1 teaspoon salt
2 cups onions, diced	4 tablespoons all-purpose flour
¾ cup water from bean sprouts	2 tablespoons water
1 cup water from mushrooms	3 tablespoons Soy Sauce
1 can (2¼ cups) bean sprouts	

Cut veal in small cubes. Brown in hot shortening in skillet. Do not flour meat. Add celery, onions, water from sprouts and mushrooms. Place lid on skillet. When steaming point is reached, reduce heat to a simmer setting. Cook for 35 minutes, then add sprouts, mushrooms, and salt. Make a thickening of the flour, water, and Soy Sauce and add to mixture. Cook over high heat until thickened, about 5 minutes. Serve on hot rice (page 265) or canned Soy noodles. Serves 6-8.

GROUND MEAT RECIPES

CHILI STACK

8-inch covered skillet . . . Cooking time—about 40 minutes

2 tablespoons shortening	1 tablespoon chili powder
1 onion, chopped fine	1 teaspoon salt
1 clove garlic, chopped fine	Dash of pepper
1 green pepper, chopped	1 can (No. 2½) tomatoes
1 pound ground beef	½ cup sharp cheese, grated
2 tablespoons all-purpose flour	

Put shortening in skillet. When hot, add onion, garlic, and green pepper and cook until onions are slightly browned. Add meat and cook until crumbly. Next, blend flour through mixture, then add remaining ingredients, except cheese. Turn heat to a low setting and cook for 30 minutes. Just before serving stir in the cheese. Delicious served on toast or toasted hamburg buns. Serves 4-5.

MEAT LOAF

Bread pan or flat utility pan . . . Cold or preheated oven—375° F. . . . Baking time—1½ hours

1 pound ground beef	½ cup tomato soup
½ pound ground pork	1 egg
½ pound ground veal	1 cup soft bread crumbs
½ cup onion, finely chopped	½ teaspoon pepper
½ cup celery, finely chopped	2 teaspoons salt
¼ cup butter, margarine or drippings	

Have meat ground twice. Brown onions and celery in butter or margarine, or drippings. Add tomato soup to onion mixture, then beat egg into mixture. Add bread crumbs and seasonings to meat, then add onion mixture. Work well with hands until ingredients are thoroughly blended. Pack in greased bread pan or form into a loaf. This meat loaf is excellent when served cold, and wonderful for sandwiches. Serves 5-6.

COMPANY CASSEROLE

2-quart casserole . . . Preheated oven—350° F. . . . Baking time—30 minutes

8-ounce package noodles	8 ounces cream cheese
1 pound ground meat	¼ cup thick sour cream
3 tablespoons butter or margarine	½ cup green onions, chopped
2 cans (8 ounces each) tomato sauce	1 tablespoon green pepper, chopped
1 cup cottage cheese	2 tablespoons butter or margarine, melted

Cook noodles according to directions on pages 253-54. Brown the ground meat in butter or margarine. Stir in tomato sauce. Remove from heat. Combine cottage cheese, cream cheese, sour cream, onions, and green pepper. Spread half the cooked noodles in greased casserole. Cover with cheese mixture, then with remaining noodles. Pour melted butter or margarine over the noodles. Pat the ground-meat sauce mixture on top. Bake. Serve from casserole. Serves 6-8.

PARTY MEAT LOAF

2-quart loaf pan . . . Cold or preheated oven—375° F. . . . Baking
time—1½ hours

½ cup onion, chopped	3 cups soft bread crumbs
¾ cup celery, diced	½ cup water
¼ cup shortening	2 pounds ground beef
½ cup green pepper, diced	½ cup tomato juice
1 tablespoon salt	2 tablespoons butter or
2 eggs	margarine, melted

Brown onions and celery in hot shortening. Combine with green
pepper, salt, eggs, bread crumbs, and water to make a stuffing.
Add half the stuffing (1½ cups) to the meat, mixing well. Pat out
half the meat mixture in loaf pan. Cover with remaining stuffing,
then top with remaining meat mixture. Bake. Baste twice during
baking period with tomato juice and melted butter or margarine
to keep loaf moist. Serves 10-12.

PORCUPINE BEEF BALLS

3-quart covered casserole . . . Cold or preheated oven—375° F. . . .
Baking time—1½ hours

½ cup uncooked rice	2 tablespoons green pepper,
1 pound ground beef	chopped
1¼ teaspoons salt	3 tablespoons onion, chopped
¼ teaspoon pepper	2 tablespoons all-purpose flour
2 cups canned tomatoes	
3 tablespoons butter or	
margarine	

Combine uncooked rice, ground meat, salt, pepper, and ¼ cup of
the tomatoes. Mix and form into 12 meat balls. Place in a greased
casserole. Heat butter or margarine in skillet and lightly brown
green pepper and onion. Blend in the flour and add remaining tomatoes slowly. Cook until thickened. Pour over meat balls. Cover
and bake. Serve from casserole or on heated platter. Serves 6.

BEEF BALLS IN CABBAGE LEAVES

8-inch skillet with cover . . . Cooking time—about 1 hour

6 large outer cabbage leaves	½ cup cooked rice
1 pound ground beef	1 cup tomato juice
3 teaspoons salt	1 medium-sized onion, sliced
½ teaspoon pepper	2 tablespoons sugar
2 tablespoons onion, chopped	2 tablespoons vinegar

Scald cabbage leaves in boiling water, leaving them in water only long enough to soften them. Combine ground beef, 1 teaspoon salt, pepper, chopped onion, and rice. Form into 6 meat balls. Wrap each ball in cabbage leaf and fasten edges with toothpicks. Place in skillet. Add tomato juice, sliced onion, remainder of salt, sugar, and vinegar. Cover. Cook over high heat until steaming, then reduce heat to simmer. Serve at once on hot platter. Serves 6.

GROUND BEEF AND VEGETABLE CASSEROLE

2-quart uncovered casserole . . . Cold or preheated oven, 375° F.
. . . Baking time—1½ hours

2 pounds ground round steak	4 tablespoons shortening
½ teaspoon sage	3 tablespoons all-purpose flour
2 teaspoons salt	2 cups canned tomatoes
¼ teaspoon pepper	Buttered crumbs
10 onions, sliced and fried (page 161)	2 tablespoons butter or margarine

Season ground meat with sage, salt, and pepper. Mold into 6 balls and place in bottom of casserole. Over this, place the fried onions. Heat shortening in skillet, add flour, and blend. To this add the tomatoes. Cook until thickened. Pour over onions. Cover with buttered crumbs. Bake uncovered. Serve from casserole. Serves 6-8.

KIDNEY BEAN AND BEEF BALL CASSEROLE

3-quart casserole . . . Preheated oven—375° F. . . . Baking time—1 hour

1 egg, beaten	2 teaspoons salt
¼ cup milk	2 teaspoons dry mustard
½ cup quick-cooking oatmeal	2 tablespoons vinegar
1½ teaspoons salt	1 can (6 ounces) tomato paste
1 pound ground beef	½ cup sorghum molasses
⅓ cup chopped onions	½ cup green pepper, chopped
¼ cup shortening	½ cup onions, chopped
2 cans (No. 2) kidney beans or about 5 cups cooked beans	

Mix egg, milk, oatmeal, and salt; soak 5 minutes. Add meat, onions; mix well. Shape into 1-inch balls. Brown on all sides in hot shortening. Place in casserole. Mix remaining ingredients and pour over meat balls. Bake. Serve from casserole. A good meal when the budget has been overspent. Serves 6-8.

CHILI CON CARNE

Covered skillet . . . Cooking time—1½ hours

1 pound coarsely ground beef	1 tablespoon paprika
½ cup onion, chopped	1 can (No. 2) tomatoes
2 tablespoons shortening or drippings	1 teaspoon salt
1 tablespoon garlic, chopped	3 cups cooked red beans (or 1 No. 2½ can red beans)
2 tablespoons chili powder	

Cook meat and onions in shortening or drippings until meat is brown but not crusty. Add garlic, chili powder, paprika, tomatoes, and salt. Cover. Cook over high heat until steaming, then reduce heat to simmer and cook for 1 hour. Add cooked beans and cook long enough for them to heat thoroughly. Serve in heated bowls with crackers. Serves 4-6.

TRICK: For really delicious chili, make it the day before, then reheat for 1 hour on simmer.

RANCHBURGERS

1 pound ground beef	¼ cup onion, grated
1 teaspoon salt	¼ cup milk
½ teaspoon pepper	4 hamburger buns

Combine meat, seasonings, grated onion, and milk thoroughly. Split buns and spread each half with meat mixture, spreading well over the edge. Arrange buns on broiler rack and broil about 8 minutes. These should be about 4 inches away from broiler unit. Serves 4.

HAMBURGERS DE LUXE

1 pound ground meat	1 teaspoon salt
2 tablespoons onion, finely chopped	2 tablespoons shortening

Combine ground meat, salt, and onion, tossing the ingredients together with a fork. Lightly shape into 4 medium-thick patties. Pan-brown in shortening in skillet. Serve hot. Serves 4.

TRICK: For a truly luscious hamburger, don't press the meat. In fact, the very best hamburgers are made by separating the meat with a fork, tossing into hot shortening in a skillet, or broiling, and seasoning after they are cooked. Pressing the meat into patties makes them heavy, and not nearly so good.

BROILED HAMBURGERS

Hamburgers de luxe can be broiled as well as pan-fried. In fact, they are even better when broiled. Broil at least 3 inches from broiler unit. Turn once during cooking time. Requires from 6-10 minutes, depending upon how you like them.

Before serving, you might spread the hot hamburger with one of the following:

2 tablespoons butter mixed with 1 tablespoon prepared mustard.

2 tablespoons butter mixed with 2 tablespoons blue cheese.

2 tablespoons butter mixed with 2 tablespoons chopped chives.

These may be served with or without the buns, depending upon how the family likes them.

CREAMED HAMBURGERS

8-inch skillet . . . Cooking time—about 20 minutes

½ cup onion, minced	¼ teaspoon pepper
¼ cup butter or margarine	¼ teaspoon paprika
1 pound ground beef	1 pound mushrooms, sliced
1 clove garlic, minced	1 can condensed cream of
2 tablespoons all-purpose flour	chicken soup
2 teaspoons salt	1 cup sour cream
¼ teaspoon monosodium	2 tablespoons parsley or chives,
glutamate	chopped

Sauté onion in butter or margarine until golden brown. Stir in beef and cook until crumbly. Add garlic, flour, salt, monosodium glutamate, pepper, paprika, and mushrooms. Stir and fry slowly for about 5 minutes. Add soup and simmer, uncovered, for 10 minutes. Stir in sour cream, sprinkle with parsley or chives. Serve on baked or mashed potatoes, hot steamed rice (page 265), noodles (pages 253-54), or toast. Serves 4-6.

INDIVIDUAL HAM RINGS

6 individual ring molds . . . Preheated oven—350° F. . . . Baking time—40 minutes

⅓ pound ground ham	⅛ teaspoon pepper
⅔ pound ground pork	1 egg, beaten
½ cup dry bread crumbs	½ cup milk

Combine all ingredients and mix thoroughly. Put into well-greased, individual ring molds. Bake. Remove from oven. Allow to stand about 5 minutes before taking out of mold. They will come out a little easier. Turn out on hot rusks and fill with a creamed vegetable. Wonderful for party luncheon. Serves 6.

HAM LOAF

Large loaf pan . . . Preheated oven—375° F. . . . Baking time—1½ to 2 hours

1 pound ground ham	½ teaspoon salt
1½ pounds ground veal	⅛ teaspoon pepper
2 eggs	6 slices pineapple
1 cup cracker crumbs	10 maraschino cherries
1 cup milk	

Sauce

¾ cup brown sugar	¼ cup vinegar
1 teaspoon dry mustard	

Mix together the meat, slightly beaten eggs, cracker crumbs, milk, salt, and pepper. Place the slices of pineapple with a maraschino cherry in center of each slice in bottom of loaf pan. Combine the ingredients for the sauce and spread ½ the sauce over pineapple, next spread the meat, packing it in firmly. Spread remaining sauce over the top of loaf. Bake. To serve, turn out on platter. Garnish with parsley, and you really have an attractive dish. Good cold, too, for sandwiches. Serves 10.

DRIED AND CORNED BEEF

CREAMED CHIPPED BEEF

4 tablespoons butter or marga-rine	½ pound chipped beef
6 tablespoons all-purpose flour (or more, if very thick gravy is desired)	1 quart whole milk

Place butter or margarine in skillet and allow it to become quite brown. Use a medium heat, or the shortening will burn. Add flour and stir into butter or margarine until all particles of flour are browned. Next add chipped beef which has been torn into small pieces. Allow mixture to become brown and well coated with the flour mixture. Add milk, stirring as needed to prevent lumping. The creamed chipped beef will be golden brown in color and much more appetizing than if made without browning the butter or margarine, flour, and chipped beef. Serve over hot baked potatoes, rice (page 265), or toast. Delicious food. Serves 4.

CORNED BEEF

10 pounds brisket of beef	½ cup water
1 cup brown sugar	1 medium-sized onion, chopped
1 cup smoked salt	2 bay leaves
4 cloves garlic, cut in pieces	¼ cup vinegar
1 teaspoon paprika	1 large carrot, sliced
½ teaspoon ground mustard	⅓ cup brown sugar
½ teaspoon saltpeter	1 tablespoon salt

Have the butcher remove the bones and surplus fat from the brisket. Wash the beef well, dry with a cloth, and place in a stone jar with brown sugar, smoked salt, garlic, paprika, ground mustard, and saltpeter dissolved in ½ cup water. Cover the jar with a plate weighed down. Let stand 12 hours and then add enough cold water to cover the beef. Leave the jar in a cool place for 10 days. Then take the beef from the brine, but do not wash it. Place the beef in a kettle with onion, bay leaves, vinegar, carrots, brown sugar, and salt. Cover with cold water and boil until tender. Let the beef cool in the liquid. This meat is delicious almost any way you want to use it.

CORNED BEEF HASH

2 cups corned beef, ground	1 onion, ground
3 cups cold boiled potatoes, ground	Salt and pepper to taste
	4 tablespoons shortening

Mix corned beef, potatoes, onion, and seasonings together. If the mixture seems dry, moisten with a little milk or cream. Heat shortening in skillet. Spread ground mixture evenly over skillet. Cook on medium low heat and cook until hash is slightly brown on bottom. Serves 4.

TRICK: Just before serving put a poached egg (page 274) in center of each mound of hash. Makes a handsome dish and a wonderful meal.

VARIETY MEATS

Sweetbreads

Sweetbreads are a delicacy and should be handled with great care. They do not keep well, so should be cooked and used soon after purchasing. However, they may be precooked, then stored in the refrigerator for near-future use.

Sweetbreads are the thymus glands of beef, calves, and lamb. There are two kinds, the heart sweetbread and the throat sweetbread. As the animal matures, these glands disappear. 1 pair serves 2.

HOW TO PRECOOK

Simmer sweetbreads 15 minutes in salted water, to which I tablespoon lemon juice or vinegar has been added for each quart of water. Drain. Then plunge in cold water and remove the membranes.

HOW TO COOK

Fried. Sweetbreads are delicious pan-fried, but take care not to use too high a heat. Brush the precooked sweetbreads with melted butter or margarine. Pan-fry until delicately browned, about 10 minutes. For something really special, pan-fry a few mushrooms along with the sweetbreads and serve on toast wedges.

Broiled. Brush sweetbreads with melted butter or margarine. Place on broiler pan which has been brushed with butter or margarine, so that the sweetbreads will not stick. Place broiler pan at least 3 inches from broiler unit and broil 10 to 15 minutes. They do not need to be turned.

SWEETBREAD CASSEROLE

1-quart casserole . . . Preheated oven—350° F. . . . Baking time—45 minutes

2 pairs sweetbreads, precooked	2 cups mushrooms, sliced
¼ cup all-purpose flour	Rich white sauce
Salt and pepper to season	4 slices Canadian bacon, ½ inch
4 tablespoons butter or marga-	thick
rine	Buttered toast

Divide the precooked sweetbreads into serving sizes. Roll in seasoned flour and pan-fry in butter or margarine until lightly browned. Do this at a medium-low heat. Remove sweetbreads from skillet and sauté the mushrooms, also on low heat. Place sweetbreads and mushrooms in casserole. Cover with white sauce (page 57).

While the sweetbread casserole is cooking, slowly pan-fry the Canadian bacon. Place bacon on buttered toast, then serve the sweetbread casserole over this combination. For decoration and added flavor put a thick slice of peeled, ripe tomato on the plate. Serves 4.

Rich White Sauce

4 tablespoons butter or margarine	1 teaspoon salt
	1½ cups light cream
2 tablespoons all-purpose flour	

Heat butter or margarine in skillet, add flour and blend thoroughly. Add salt and top milk, stirring frequently to prevent sticking and lumping.

TREAT: Substitute ½ cup dry white wine for ½ cup of the milk.

LIVER

Some people think they do not like liver, yet it is very healthful and should be eaten by every member of the family at least once a week.

Neither beef nor calf's liver needs to be parboiled before cooking, but both pork and lamb liver should be scalded before cooking.

To parboil liver, place liver in shallow dish. Pour boiling water over it. Allow to stand about 5 minutes. Then drain.

BROILED LIVER

See page 28.

FRIED LIVER AND ONIONS

8-inch skillet with cover . . . Cooking time—25-30 minutes

1 pound liver	¼ cup bacon drippings
¼ cup all-purpose flour	2 pounds onion, sliced thin
1 teaspoon salt	1 tablespoon water
⅛ teaspoon pepper	

Parboil liver, if either pork or lamb. Drain. Otherwise do not parboil. Dredge liver with seasoned flour. Heat bacon drippings in skillet. Brown liver on both sides. Place onions over liver, add water, cover, and cook over low heat for 25 to 30 minutes. Serves 4.

FRENCH-FRIED LIVER—See page 232.

LEFTOVER LIVER PATTIES

1 cup leftover ground liver	½ cup fine bread crumbs
1 cup leftover potatoes, mashed	4 tablespoons bacon drippings or
1 egg	shortening

Mix liver, potatoes, and egg. Add seasoning, if necessary. Shape into patties. Dip into crumbs and brown in hot shortening. Serves 4.

LIVER WITH SOUR CREAM

8-inch skillet . . . Cooking time—45 minutes

1½ pounds calf's liver, sliced ½ inch thick
¼ cup all-purpose flour
1 teaspoon salt
¼ teaspoon pepper
4 tablespoons shortening
2 tablespoons onion, minced
2 bay leaves (optional)
1 cup thick sour cream
2 hard-cooked eggs (page 273)
Dash cayenne pepper

Dredge liver with flour seasoned with salt and pepper. Brown quickly in hot shortening. Add onion, bay leaves, and sour cream. Cover and cook on simmer heat until liver is tender. Add chopped eggs and cook 1 minute longer. Add cayenne pepper. Stir. Serve on toast or hot biscuits. Serves 6.

LIVER AND BACON PATTIES

½ cup cooked, minced, or ground liver
2 tablespoons cooked, diced bacon
½ cup fine dry bread crumbs
1 egg, slightly beaten
1 teaspoon onion, finely chopped
1 tablespoon parsley, finely chopped
1 tablespoon chili sauce
¼ cup milk
1 teaspoon salt
⅛ teaspoon pepper
4 tablespoons bacon drippings or shortening

Combine all ingredients except bacon drippings. Shape into patties. Fry in hot shortening until brown on both sides. Serve with tomato sauce (page 245) or catchup. Serves 2-4.

PORK LIVER-BEEF LOAF

Large loaf pan . . . Cold or preheated oven—375° F. . . . Baking time—1½ hours

1 egg
½ cup tomato soup
½ cup celery, finely chopped
½ cup onion, finely chopped
1 cup soft bread crumbs
1 tablespoon salt
½ teaspoon pepper
½ pound ground beef
1 pound ground pork
¾ pound ground pork liver
4 strips bacon

Beat egg slightly, add tomato soup, celery, onion, and bread crumbs. Stir until bread is well soaked. Add salt and pepper, then ground meats, and mix well. Pack into greased loaf pan. Lay strips of bacon crosswise over loaf. A little tomato soup poured between the bacon strips gives a colorful effect. Bake. Serve piping hot. Excellent cold for sandwiches. Serves 8-10.

TRICK: If the butcher won't grind the liver for you, parboil it, remove the outside membrane, and grind it yourself in a food chopper.

COLUMBUS CASSEROLE

2 quart casserole . . . Preheated oven—350° F. . . . Baking time—45 minutes

4 ounces elbow macaroni	½ cup sweet onions, sliced
4 slices bacon	1 can condensed cream of
½ pound beef liver, cubed	mushroom soup
2 tablespoons all-purpose flour	1½ tablespoons steak sauce
1 teaspoon salt	1 cup whole kernel corn

Cook macaroni according to directions on pages 253-54. While macaroni is cooking, fry bacon in skillet until lightly brown. Pour off all but 2 tablespoons bacon drippings. Dredge liver in flour, seasoned with salt, and brown in remaining bacon drippings. When liver is brown on both sides, add onions, cover skillet, and cook until onions are slightly tender. Pour soup into bowl, stir until smooth. Add steak sauce. Fold in macaroni, liver, onions, and corn. Pour into greased casserole. Top with bacon strips. Bake. Serve piping hot from casserole. Serves 4-6.

SOUTH AMERICAN GOULASH

8-inch covered skillet . . . Cooking time—30-40 minutes

¾ pound beef liver	1 small clove garlic, chopped
¼ cup onion, chopped	2 teaspoons salt
½ cup green pepper, chopped	⅛ teaspoon pepper
3 tablespoons shortening	2 tablespoons all-purpose flour
2 cups canned tomatoes	4 ounces uncooked noodles
⅓ cup celery, chopped	

Cut liver in one-inch cubes and brown with the onion and green pepper in hot shortening. Add tomatoes, celery, garlic, and seasonings. Cook slowly for 30 minutes. Mix flour with 4 tablespoons cold water and add to mixture. Cook until thickened. Cook noodles according to directions on pages 253-54. Serve goulash over noodles. Serves 5.

TONGUE

FRESH TONGUE

3 fresh calves' tongues   1 teaspoon whole pepper
3 bay leaves   1 tablespoon salt
1 onion, sliced

Place tongues, bay leaves, onion, pepper, and salt in kettle. Cover with water. Cook slowly, allowing 20 minutes to the pound, or until tongues are tender. When tongues are cooked, plunge into cold water, remove skin, and cut away roots at base of tongue. Serve cold with horse-radish, or hot with tomato sauce (page 245). Serves 6-8.

CASSEROLE OF TONGUE

3-quart casserole . . . Preheated oven—375° F. . . . Baking time—1¼ hours

1 beef tongue   1 cup turnips, diced
2 tablespoons shortening   1 cup carrots, diced
2 tablespoons all-purpose flour 1 cup celery, diced
1 teaspoon salt   1 cup onions, diced
¼ teaspoon pepper   ½ cup green pepper, sliced
2 cups broth from cooking tongue

Cook tongue according to directions (page 60). Place in casserole. Heat shortening, add flour, salt, pepper, and 2 cups broth from tongue. Arrange vegetables around tongue. Add sauce made from broth. Cover. Bake. Serve piping hot on platter, with vegetables surrounding the tongue, and the thickened sauce poured over both tongue and vegetables. Serves 4-6.

CORNED TONGUE

1 large beef tongue   ¼ cup water
2 tablespoons smoked salt   1 medium onion, chopped fine
2 cloves garlic   2 bay leaves
½ cup brown sugar   ¼ cup vinegar
5 tablespoons smoked salt   1 large carrot, sliced
½ teaspoon paprika   ⅓ cup brown sugar
⅛ teaspoon saltpeter   1 tablespoon salt

Wash tongue and remove all ragged edges. On bottom of stone jar sprinkle 2 tablespoons smoked salt and 1 clove garlic cut in 4 sections. Place tongue in jar and cover it with the brown sugar, remaining smoked salt, paprika, remaining clove of garlic, cut in 4 sections. Dissolve saltpeter in water and pour over tongue. Cover with a plate, weighted down. Let stand 12 hours, then add sufficient water to cover the tongue. Set the jar in a cool place and leave for 10 days. At the end of that time remove the tongue from the brine, but do not wash. Put in kettle, add onion, bay leaf, vinegar, carrot, cut in slices, brown sugar and salt. Cover with cold water, bring to quick boil over high heat, then reduce to simmer and continue cooking until tongue is tender. Let stand in liquid until cool.

KIDNEYS

Kidneys from beef, veal, lamb, sheep are all available in markets today and make very fine eating.

How to Buy

Allow, for each serving, ½ beef kidney, 1 veal kidney, 2 or 3 lamb kidneys, and 2 sheep kidneys.

How to Prepare

Split and remove central fat and white tubes. Soak in salted water for about 30 minutes. Cook quickly in small amount of water, because overcooking toughens kidneys.

How to Broil Kidneys

Marinate prepared kidneys in French dressing. Broil about 10 minutes total time and turn two or three times to cook evenly. Serve on rusks or toast. Broiled kidneys don't need much dressing up, so melt ¼ cup butter or margarine, and to it add ⅛ teaspoon cayenne pepper and 1 tablespoon lemon juice, and dash over broiled kidneys.

How to Pan-Fry

Kidneys must be pan-fried at a low temperature. Cut kidneys in ¼- to ½-inch slices. Sprinkle with salt and pepper. Melt butter or margarine in skillet and brown kidneys slowly. Pour a little lemon juice over kidneys before serving.

KIDNEY STEW

8-inch skillet with cover . . . Cooking time—about 1 hour

2 beef kidneys or 4 veal kidneys
2 tablespoons all-purpose flour
1 teaspoon salt
⅛ teaspoon pepper
2 tablespoons butter or margarine
2 onions, sliced

2 cups water
2 cups carrots, sliced
2 cups potatoes, diced
1 cup canned tomatoes
1 teaspoon salt
½ teaspoon paprika
1 teaspoon Worcestershire sauce

Prepare kidneys as directed on page 61. Drain and cut in ½-inch slices. Roll in flour seasoned with salt and pepper. Heat butter or margarine in skillet, add onion and cook until a golden brown. Push onions aside, add kidneys and sauté until brown. Add water and carrots. Cover. Simmer for 30 minutes. Add potatoes, tomatoes, and seasonings. Cover. Cook 30 minutes longer. Serve piping hot on heated platter. Serves 4.

KIDNEY AND MUSHROOM STEW

8-inch skillet with cover . . . Cooking time—about 1½ hours

1½ pounds mushrooms or 1 can (8 ounces) mushrooms
12 lamb kidneys
2 large onions
¼ pound butter or margarine
½ cup white wine
1 tablespoon sherry
1 bay leaf

1 teaspoon salt
½ teaspoon pepper
3 drops Worcestershire sauce
⅛ teaspoon nutmeg
1 tablespoon butter or margarine
1 tablespoon all-purpose flour
1½ cups light cream

If you are using fresh mushrooms, slice them medium thin. Chop stems and put both stems and sliced mushrooms in a saucepan. Cover with salted water, allowing ½ teaspoon of salt to a cup of water. Simmer gently while preparing the kidneys. To prepare kidneys, see page 61. Slice thin. Mince onions and sauté the mushrooms (either those you cooked, or the canned ones, being sure to drain whichever you are using). Now add kidneys and onions to skillet. Add wine, sherry, bay leaf and seasonings, and the strained juice from the mushrooms. There should be about a cup of mushroom liquid. Cover and allow to simmer gently for about 1½ hours. When kidneys are tender, blend the butter or margarine and flour together and add to mixture. Continue cooking after adding the thickening. Stir in the cream. Remove bay leaf. Do not continue cooking after adding the cream. Serves 4-6.

BREADED KIDNEYS

8-inch skillet, covered . . . Cooking time—about 20 minutes

4 veal kidneys	¼ cup shortening
1 egg, beaten	Salt and pepper
1 tablespoon water	2 tablespoons water
1½ cups fine bread crumbs	

Soak and cook kidneys as directed on page 61. Slice each kidney in two pieces. Dip slices in bread crumbs, then in egg mixed with water, then again in bread crumbs. Brown in hot shortening. Season to taste. Add the water. Cover. Reduce heat to simmer and cook 20 minutes. Serves 4.

WAYS TO USE LEFTOVER MEAT

HEARTY MEAL-IN-ONE

8-inch square pan or casserole . . . Preheated oven—325° F. . . .
   Baking time—1 hour

8 slices day-old bread	3 eggs, slightly beaten
¼ cup butter or margarine	1½ cups milk
2 cups ground cooked ham	1 cup tomato sauce (page 245)
2 tablespoons prepared mustard	1 teaspoon salt
2 cups grated cheddar cheese	Dash of pepper

Remove crusts from bread and spread with softened butter or margarine. Arrange 4 slices in a greased pan or casserole. Mix ham with mustard and spread over bread. Sprinkle about 1¼ cups of the cheese over ham. Cover with remaining slices of bread. Combine eggs, milk, tomato sauce, salt, and pepper. Pour over bread and sprinkle with remaining cheese. Chill 1 hour to allow bread to absorb flavors. Bake and serve at once. Serves 4-6.

LEFTOVER MEAT AND RICE CASSEROLE

Covered casserole . . . Preheated oven—400° F. . . . Baking time—
   45 minutes

1 medium-sized onion, sliced fine	2 cups canned tomatoes
3 tablespoons shortening	1 cup water
1 cup diced, cooked meat	1½ teaspoons salt
½ cup uncooked rice	⅛ teaspoon pepper

Brown onion in hot shortening. Add the meat and rice and cook slowly until rice is golden brown. Add tomatoes, water, and seasonings. Stir well and pour into greased casserole. Cover and bake 30 minutes, then remove cover and bake 15 minutes longer. Serve at once from casserole. Serves 4-5.

RAGOUT OF VEAL

2 cups leftover veal, cut in cubes   1 teaspoon Worcestershire sauce
2 cups leftover gravy   Salt and pepper to season

Heat veal in gravy. Season to taste. Serve with hot rice (page 265) or baked potatoes. Serves 4.

SCALLOPED LEFTOVER MEAT (Veal, Lamb, or Beef)

Uncovered casserole . . . Preheated oven—375° F. . . . Baking time—
    25 minutes

2 tablespoons butter or   ½ teaspoon pepper
    margarine   2 cups diced cooked meat
2 tablespoons all-purpose flour   ½ cup fine buttered bread
2 cups tomato juice   crumbs
2 teaspoons salt

Melt butter or margarine. Add flour and blend well. Add tomato juice slowly, then salt and pepper, stirring frequently until mixture has thickened. Place a layer of meat in greased casserole, then pour half the sauce over the meat, repeat with a layer of meat, ending with the sauce on top. Sprinkle with buttered crumbs. Bake. Serve from casserole. Serves 4-5.

QUICK STEW FROM LEFTOVER BEEF, LAMB, VEAL, OR PORK

Large skillet or heavy saucepan . . . Cooking time—about 20
    minutes

2 cups leftover brown gravy   1 onion, cut fine
2 cups cooked meat, cut into   1 to 1½ cups raw carrots, diced
    bite-size pieces   1 to 1½ cups raw potatoes, diced

Put gravy and meat into skillet. (If gravy supply is short, make a little extra by browning 2 tablespoons flour in 2 tablespoons drippings. Add as much milk to this as needed to make 2 cups.) Cook on medium heat until gravy reaches boiling point. Add onions, carrots, and potatoes. Cover and cook over medium heat for about

20 minutes, or until vegetables are tender. If marjoram, tarragon, or thyme are available, put a pinch of each in mixture. Serves 4.

OVEN HAM CROQUETTES

Utility baking dish . . . Preheated oven—375° F. . . . Baking time—40-45 minutes

2 cups ground cooked ham	1 teaspoon salt
1 cup carrots or celery, grated	¼ teaspoon pepper
1 cup soft bread crumbs	¼ cup melted shortening
¼ cup onion, grated	1 cup dry bread crumbs
1 egg, well beaten	

Combine all ingredients except the melted shortening and dry bread crumbs. Mix well. Shape into six croquettes. Roll in melted shortening, then in crumbs. Place in utility dish and bake in preheated oven until browned. It may be necessary to turn the croquettes once for even browning. Serve with tomato sauce (page 245). Serves 6.

HOT, OPEN-FACED MEAT SANDWICHES

Put two slices of buttered bread on plate. Warm leftover gravy in skillet or make gravy from meat juices left from roast. Cut meat from leftover roast in medium-sized pieces. Place in gravy and simmer for about 10 minutes. Season to taste. Place mixture over bread. Any leftover meat, such as beef, pork, lamb, or veal is delicious served this way.

SHEPHERD'S PIE

3-quart casserole . . . Preheated oven—400° F. . . . Baking time—30 minutes

2 cups meat stock or gravy	½ cup cooked carrots, sliced
3 tablespoons all-purpose flour	1 tablespoon parsley, chopped
2 cups diced cooked meat	2 teaspoons Worcestershire
½ cup canned tomatoes	sauce
½ cup cooked onion, sliced	¾ teaspoon salt

Topping

2 cups seasoned mashed potatoes	2 tablespoons melted butter or margarine

If you do not have meat stock or gravy on hand, dissolve a bouillon cube in water or brown flour in shortening and make a gravy with water. Bring stock to full steaming point. Add meat, tomatoes, onion, carrots, parsley, Worcestershire sauce, and salt. Turn into greased casserole. Cover with mashed potatoes. First spread potatoes around sides, sealing the juices in. Then spread remainder toward center, leaving opening for steam to escape. Brush mashed potato with melted butter or margarine. Bake. Serves 5-6.

SOUTHERN HASH

8-inch skillet . . . Cooking time—about 35 minutes

5 medium-sized potatoes, uncooked	½ cup cooked tomatoes
2 medium-sized onions	2 cups cooked, leftover meat, diced
4 tablespoons shortening	1 teaspoon salt
1 cup leftover dark brown gravy	¼ teaspoon pepper

Put vegetables through a food grinder, or in lieu of that, chop them fine, or even grate them. Melt shortening in skillet, add vegetables, gravy, and cooked tomatoes. Cover. Cook over medium heat until vegetables are tender. Add diced meat and seasonings. Cook slowly for another 10 or 15 minutes, or until the mixture is brown on the bottom. Serves 4.

MEAT CURRY

8-inch skillet . . . Cooking time—about 30 minutes

3 tablespoons butter or margarine	4 tablespoons all-purpose flour
1 cup onion, finely sliced	1 teaspoon salt
3 cups diced or ground leftover lamb, veal, or beef	⅛ teaspoon pepper
1 cup celery, finely diced	2 cups tomato juice
1 tablespoon curry powder	1 tablespoon lemon juice (optional)

Melt butter or margarine in skillet and add onions. Cook slowly until onions are golden brown. Add ground meat and brown lightly. Add celery, stir through cooked mixture. Mix curry powder, flour, salt, and pepper together and stir through the above mixture. Slowly stir in the tomato juice. Cook over low heat until thickened, stirring occasionally. Stir in lemon juice just before serving. Serve on hot, steamed rice (page 265). Serves 5-6.

BARBECUED MEATS

BARBECUED SPARERIBS

Large roasting pan . . . Preheated oven—350° F. . . . Roasting time—
1½ to 2 hours

5 pounds spareribs	3 tablespoons Worcestershire
2 tablespoons drippings	sauce
1 large onion, cut fine	2 teaspoons dry mustard
2 tablespoons vinegar	1 cup water
4 tablespoons lemon juice	½ cup celery or 1 tablespoon
2 tablespoons brown sugar	celery salt
⅛ teaspoon cayenne pepper	1 teaspoon paprika
1 teaspoon horse-radish	½ cup wine
1 cup catchup	

Brown spareribs in oven. When spareribs are nicely browned,
pour off all drippings. It is essential that the drippings be poured
off, otherwise it will make the barbecued spareribs too greasy.

Brown onion in the drippings, then add remaining ingredients
and bring to boil. Pour sauce over spareribs in roasting pan. Cover.
Continue cooking for about an hour, basting occasionally with the
sauce. Serves 5-6.

TRICK: If you are short on time, brown the spareribs in a skillet,
or under the broiler, then transfer ribs to large roasting pan. However, by roasting in oven first, you can collect more of the drippings from the spareribs.

STEAMED BARBECUED SPARERIBS

Large saucepan with cover . . . Cooking time—1 to 1½ hours

3 pounds spareribs, cut in 2- or	3 tablespoons Worcestershire
3-inch lengths	sauce
1 medium onion, chopped fine	½ tablespoon ground mustard
2 tablespoons vinegar	1 cup water
4 tablespoons lemon juice	1 tablespoon celery salt
2 tablespoons brown sugar	1 teaspoon salt
⅛ teaspoon cayenne pepper	½ teaspoon black pepper
1 cup catchup	

Brown spareribs on both sides in skillet. Place browned spareribs
in saucepan. (If you have a deep-well cooker on your range, this
is wonderful to use.) Mix remaining ingredients together and
pour over spareribs. Cook on high heat until steaming, then reduce

heat to simmer. Cook until spareribs are tender. May be served between buns or plain. Serves 4-6.

BARBECUED HAMBURGERS
Large covered skillet ... Cooking time—about 45 minutes

2 pounds ground beef	¼ cup shortening
2 cloves garlic, finely chopped	

Barbecue Sauce

½ cup salad oil	1 teaspoon liquid smoke
½ cup catchup	2 teaspoons salt
1 tablespoon Worcestershire sauce	4 tablespoons brown sugar
	¼ cup vinegar
1 teaspoon dry mustard	1 teaspoon paprika

Lightly form the ground beef into 6 patties. Don't press down on meat. Use a fork to separate the meat and lightly mold with your fingertips.

Melt shortening. Brown the garlic and then brown the hamburger patties. When patties have browned, remove from skillet. Pour off any excess grease. Mix remaining ingredients together and cook in covered skillet. When mixture reaches boiling point, add hamburg patties, reduce heat, and cook slowly for about 20 minutes, basting frequently. Serve on toasted buns. Serves 6-8.

BARBECUED FRANKFURTERS
3-quart covered casserole ... Preheated oven—350° F. ... Baking time—1 hour

1½ pounds large skinless frankfurters	1 tablespoon brown sugar
	2 teaspoons salt
1 medium-sized onion, chopped fine	1 teaspoon paprika
	¼ teaspoon pepper
1 tablespoon all-purpose flour	1 teaspoon chili powder
2 tablespoons vinegar	2 tablespoons water
1½ tablespoons Worcestershire sauce	½ cup tomato catchup

Pierce each frankfurter several times with a fork and place in casserole. Combine remaining ingredients. Pour over frankfurters. Cover. Bake. Serve between buns or plain. Serves 4-6.

Poultry and Game

CHICKEN

How to Buy

Chicken is sold in many ways: whole, cut up, or by the piece, and all these may be purchased either fresh or quick-frozen.

You may find that it is actually less expensive to buy chicken by the piece, even though the price per pound may be higher, since in that way you are sure of getting only what you want, rather than buying a whole chicken and then having to decide what to do with the parts that no member of the family will eat.

In general, the age of the chicken will determine its tenderness, and this, in turn, determines the type of cooking method you will use.

The common classes of chicken are: broiler, fryer, roaster, pullet and hen, which is also sometimes called a stewing chicken. Capon is another class which may be found in some markets.

The following chart will help you to identify each class:

HOW-TO-BUY CHART

Market Term	*Characteristics*	*Quantity to buy per person*	*Method of Cooking*
Broiler			
1 to 2½ pounds 8-12 weeks old	Smooth, thin skin Flexible tipped breastbone	¼-½ bird	Broiling Roasting Frying
Fryer			
2½ to 3½ pounds 14-20 weeks old	Same as above except size	¾ to 1 pound	Frying Roasting
Roaster (male)			
Over 3½ pounds 5-9 months old	Flexible tipped breastbone Excellent layer of fat underneath skin	½ to ¾ pound	Roasting Frying
Capon			
4 pounds or over 7-10 months old	Popular size: 6 to 7 pounds Full breasted	½ to ¾ pound	Roasting
Pullet (young hen)			
2½ to 5½ pounds 4-9 months old	Similar to roaster Body shorter and plumper	½ to ¾ pound	Frying Roasting
Hen			
Over 1 year	Thick, coarse skin Breastbone not flexible Large amount of fat	¼ to ¾ pound	Braising Stewing Soup Making

How to Broil

Broiling is cooking by dry heat. The heat may come from above or below the chicken. All sizes of tender, small chickens may be broiled, but the preference is usually for a 1½- to 2½-pound bird.

Step-by-step instructions for broiling chicken follow:

1. Split the chicken in half, lengthwise, remove the backbone, neck, and keel bone. Larger sizes may be cut crosswise. Flatten the pieces.

2. Place chicken halves skin side down either in bottom of broiler pan or on broiler rack. Bring wing tip onto back under the shoulder joint.

3. Season with ¼ to ½ teaspoon salt and ⅛ teaspoon pepper for each half.

4. Brush well with melted butter, margarine, olive oil, or any desired shortening.

5. Place pan in broiler so that surface of chicken is 7 to 9 inches from the heat. Broil slowly; browning should not begin until after 10 to 15 minutes of cooking.

6. Turn every 15 minutes, brushing with additional butter or margarine each time.

7. Broil until tender, nicely browned, and crisp on the outside. Chicken is done when the drumstick and wing joints yield easily to fork pressure. The broiling time for a 2- to 2½-pound chicken is 50 to 60 minutes.

8. The liver (uncooked) and the precooked gizzard and heart may be brushed with melted butter or margarine and placed on broiler pan the last 15 minutes of broiling.

   To precook gizzard and heart, cook in covered container in small amount of water until tender. Cook slowly; do not boil rapidly.

9. Serve on warm platter, skin side up. Pour pan drippings over the chicken.

TREATS: Herbs may be rubbed into the chicken before broiling, or the chicken may be marinated in French dressing 2 or 3 hours before broiling. Lemon juice may be poured over the chicken during broiling, or you may baste with barbecue sauce.

How to Broil Frozen Broiler

It is not necessary to defrost a frozen broiler first. Follow directions given above, but allow about 20 minutes' additional time.

How to Pan-Fry Chicken

There are about as many ways to pan-fry chicken as there are homemakers to fry it. However, there is one step all agree upon, and that is that it must be fried in some type of shortening. The *kind* of shortening and how much to use depend simply upon regional likes and dislikes.

Some folks prefer to pan-fry chicken by the following method: a chicken that weighs about 3 pounds is selected. The chicken is disjointed, rolled in seasoned flour (see page 72), and fried in about ½ cup shortening. After the chicken is brown, and remaining grease is poured from the skillet, a little water is added, the skillet is tightly covered, the heat reduced, and the chicken cooked for an hour or so longer. Cooked in this way, the chicken is beautifully tender, but the skin is not crisp.

Those who like a crisp outer skin, select a smaller chicken, disjoint it, and use about 1 cup of shortening. The chicken is rolled in seasoned flour (see below), browned slowly, covered for the first half of the cooking period, and uncovered for the last half of the cooking period. Chicken fried this way has a crisp outer skin and requires about 30 minutes total cooking time.

As to shortening, those who claim to be the best chicken fryers say that half butter or margarine and half leaf lard is the only shortening which can be used.

You'll have to settle such weighty problems to suit yourself and your family.

Coatings

Another point in agreement on chicken frying is that the chicken must be coated before frying. This prevents drying out of the meat and aids in the browning crispness of the chicken, but again there are a great many popular coatings. You will have to pick one.

1. Four and seasoning. For each pound of chicken, blend ¼ cup flour, 1 teaspoon paprika, ¾ teaspoon salt, and ⅛ teaspoon pepper. Place this in a clean sturdy paper bag. Place 2 or 3 pieces of chicken at a time in the bag, shake three or four times, or until the chicken pieces are well coated with the flour. Save any leftover flour for gravy. If time permits, place coated chicken on a rack for about ½ hour to dry.

   In some sections of the country the chicken pieces are dried thoroughly before coating with flour; in other sections the chicken pieces are lifted from water into the seasoned flour. Do as you like. Either way makes excellent chicken.

2. Egg, flour, and seasoning. For each pound of chicken, blend ½ egg, 1 teaspoon water, and ¾ teaspoon salt. Dip chicken into mixture. Then coat with flour. (See above.) You will need about ⅓ cup flour per pound. Sprinkle paprika and pepper over chicken during the frying.

3. Some folks prefer to use half flour and half cornmeal, or all cornmeal, for coating chicken. Others declare there is no coating equal to a quick-mix buckwheat pancake mix.

4. Dip cut pieces of chicken in buttermilk. Then dip into flour seasoned with paprika, salt, and pepper.

How to Fry Frozen Chicken

It is not necessary to defrost frozen chicken before frying, although it may be necessary to allow the chicken to remain at room temperature until the pieces can be separated. However, as soon as that is possible, prepare for frying as suggested above. Allow 10-15 minutes' extra frying time.

Oven-Fried Chicken

Disjoint the chicken and roll each piece in melted butter or margarine. Lay on a shallow pan, skin side up. Preheat the oven to 425° F. and place chicken in preheated oven. Cook at this temperature for about 20 minutes. Reduce heat to 325-350° F., sprinkle with salt, pepper, and a generous amount of paprika. Brush with melted butter or margarine several times during the cooking process, which will require 50-60 minutes, depending upon the size and age of the chicken.

Deep-Fat-Fried Chicken

This method is adapted only to chickens which are young and very tender. Heat 3 pounds shortening to 350° F. Place coated chicken in frying basket and slowly lower into the hot shortening. Cook until tender, about 20-25 minutes.

Larger chickens may be cut up, cooked for about 30 minutes in water, drained, then coated, and fried in deep shortening.

And so, to sum up, you may fry your chicken in a minimum of shortening or in quite deep shortening. Use your own judgment about the type of shortening you wish to use. You may fry the chicken covered or uncovered and with several different coatings. Just remember, however, not to crowd the chicken pieces into a skillet, to fry the meaty pieces first, to fry at medium-low heat, and never, never to burn the chicken.

ROASTING

Roasting is slow cooking by dry heat in an oven in a shallow pan. There must always be a trivet under the chicken. All sizes of tender chicken may be roasted, but plumpness is definitely a desirable quality.

STUFFING AND TRUSSING

1. Rub cavity of prepared bird with ½ to 1 teaspoon salt. DO NOT STUFF BIRD AHEAD OF TIME, BUT JUST BEFORE ROASTING. Stuffing prepared in advance must be refrigerated. See pages 95-97 for stuffing recipes. Stuff body and wishbone cavity lightly.

2. Trussing or shaping assures compactness to permit even cooking and browning. Also, the chicken is more attractive and easier to carve. To truss: Fasten neck skin to the back with skewers. Shape wings "akimbo" style and bring wing tips onto the back. Close abdominal opening with skewers and cord. Tie drumsticks to tail. A skewer above the tail on the back helps to hold this cord in place.

HOW TO ROAST

1. Brush skin thoroughly with melted butter, margarine, or chicken fat.

2. Place trussed bird, breast side up, on a trivet at least ½ inch high in a shallow open pan.

3. Cover top of chicken with a thin cloth which has been brushed with melted butter, margarine, or chicken fat. Do not wrap bird in cloth, merely place over top of bird, and be sure none of the cloth is hanging out over the sides of the roasting pan. The cloth helps in uniform browning and makes basting unnecessary.

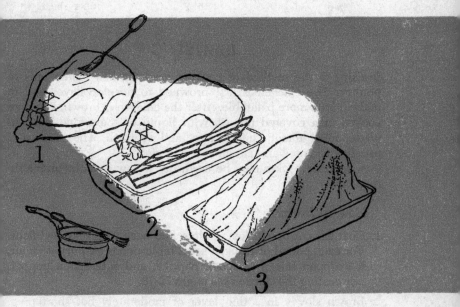

4. Roast at a constant low temperature. See Timetable on page 76.
5. DO NOT SEAR. DO NOT ADD WATER. DO NOT COVER.
6. If cloth dries during cooking, moisten cloth with drippings from pan.
7. To test for doneness, press the thickest part of the drumstick between the fingers. The meat should feel very soft to the touch. Or, move drumstick up and down. Leg joints should move readily or might even break. Better protect your fingers with a piece of paper toweling or clean cloth.
8. Remove skewers and any cord. Place chicken on warm platter while preparing gravy with drippings from roasting pan. Make brown gravy (page 246).

TIMETABLE FOR ROASTING

Ready-to-Cook Weight	Oven Temperature	Approximate Roasting Time (All times are based on preheated oven)
1½-2½ pounds	325° F.	1¾-2 hours
2½-3½ pounds	325° F.	2-3 hours
3½-4¾ pounds	325° F.	3-3½ hours
4¾-6 pounds	325° F.	3½-4 hours

BRAISING

Braising is the method of cooking used for less tender cuts of poultry. The chicken is first browned to develop flavor and to make it look more palatable. After the chicken is brown, it is then cooked in a covered utensil, with liquid of some kind, such as water, milk, tomato juice, wine, and so forth. The chicken is usually disjointed and cut into serving pieces.

A pressure cooker may be used, but follow manufacturer's directions.

How to Braise

1. Coat the cut-up chicken, giblets, and neck with seasoned flour. For each pound of chicken use 2 tablespoons all-purpose flour, ½ teaspoon salt, ¼ teaspoon paprika, and ⅛ teaspoon pepper. For coating the chicken see pages 72-73.

2. Brown slowly in a thin layer of moderately hot shortening, turning once during the browning. About ½ hour is required to brown a 4-pound chicken.

3. Remove pan from heat. Pour off any excess grease. Add ⅛ to ½ cup liquid. Cover tightly.

4. Replace over very low heat or place in slow oven, 300° F., and cook slowly until the thickest pieces are fork tender, 2½ to 3 hours.

5. Lift chicken to hot platter.

6. Prepare gravy with the pan drippings. See the recipe for brown gravy, page 246.

TRICK: A fine way to serve this type of chicken is to barbecue it. See barbecue sauce for chicken (page 240).

STEWING OR SIMMERING

Stewing is the method most commonly used for chicken that is a year or older. This age chicken requires long, slow cooking in a quantity of water, because the toughened connective tissue takes a long time to soften. Rapid boiling will only make the tissue tougher.

However, any size chicken may be stewed, either whole, disjointed, or cut up.

Steps in Stewing

1. Place the chicken, whole or cut up, in kettle. Choose a kettle with a tight-fitting lid.
2. Add ½ cup water and ½ teaspoon salt for each pound of chicken to be cooked, including the neck and giblets. If chicken is to be served with gravy and dumplings, noodles, biscuits, or mashed potatoes, increase water to 1 cup and the salt to a scant ¾ teaspoon per pound of chicken.
3. For additional flavor, 1 small carrot, 1 small onion, 2 or 3 large celery tops, a whole clove, and 2 or 3 peppercorns may be added.
4. Bring water to steaming point. Skim and reduce heat to simmer. Cook over very low heat until thickest pieces are fork tender, from 2½ to 4 hours.
5. At this point noodles may be added, or dumplings made (see page 312), or the chicken served as is over hot mashed potatoes or rice (page 265).

CARE OF COOKED CHICKEN

Knowing how to care for cooked chicken is as important as knowing how to cook it. Always refrigerate cooked leftover chicken immediately after the meal. If you are cooking chicken in advance of need, such as stewed chicken, refrigerate it just as soon as chicken has cooled. Never, never leave chicken at room temperature. IT MUST ALWAYS BE REFRIGERATED. Many a person has been made sick because the homemaker failed to take proper care of the cooked chicken.

If roast chicken has been stuffed, remove any stuffing from the cavity and store it separately.

CHICKEN PAPRIKA

Large skillet with cover . . . Cooking time—1 to 1½ hours

2 to 2½ pounds chicken for
    frying
½ cup all-purpose flour
1 teaspoon salt
⅛ teaspoon pepper

½ cup shortening
½ cup onion, chopped
1 cup thick sour cream
1 tablespoon paprika

Cut chicken in serving pieces. Mix flour, salt, and pepper together. Roll chicken in seasoned flour. Heat shortening and brown chicken. Remove chicken from skillet. Pour off all but 2 tablespoons of the shortening remaining in skillet. Add onion and cook over low heat until golden brown. Return chicken to skillet. Add sour cream and sprinkle paprika over top. Cover. Cook over very low heat for 30 minutes, or until chicken is tender. Serve on hot platter, covering chicken with the mixture in which it was cooked. Serves 4.

CHICKEN CONTINENTAL

7x11x1½-inch baking dish . . . Preheated oven—400° F. . . . Baking
    time—20-25 minutes

4 large chicken breasts
½ to ¾ cup water
2 teaspoons salt
2 packages frozen broccoli
1 recipe hollandaise sauce
    (page 242)
    Rich cream sauce (see page 79)

¾ cup almonds, blanched and
    cut in thin slivers
¼ cup butter or margarine
1 cup heavy cream, whipped
    (optional)
½ cup Parmesan cheese, grated

Cook the chicken breasts and 1 teaspoon salt in water. When chicken is tender, remove from liquid. Cool. Slice each breast in several pieces. Cook broccoli with 1 teaspoon salt (page 140). Drain. Place broccoli stalks in bottom of greased baking dish. Arrange chicken slices over the broccoli and cover with the hollandaise sauce. Spread the cream sauce over the hollandaise sauce. Brown the slivered almonds in the butter or margarine and sprinkle over top of white sauce. Place in oven until thoroughly heated through. Remove from oven, top with whipped cream, and sprinkle with Parmesan cheese. Place under broiler until top is brown, about 5 minutes. Serves 8.

Rich Cream Sauce

2 tablespoons butter or margarine	½ teaspoon salt
2 tablespoons all-purpose flour	1 cup light cream
	½ cup sherry wine

Melt butter or margarine in a saucepan over low heat. Add flour, blend well, add salt and cream, stirring constantly while adding. Cook until thick, stirring occasionally. Remove from heat. Add sherry.

CHICKEN WITH WINE

Large skillet with cover . . . Cooking time—1½ to 2 hours

¾ cup cooking oil or olive oil	½ cup chicken stock or water
4 pounds tender chicken, cut in pieces for serving	½ cup dry white wine
¾ cup all-purpose flour	1 can (6 ounces) tomato paste
2 teaspoons salt	1 herb bouquet (see below)
⅛ teaspoon pepper	1 clove garlic, chopped fine
2 tablespoons all-purpose flour	½ pound mushrooms

Heat oil in skillet. Roll chicken in flour which has been mixed with salt and pepper. Brown chicken in hot oil, turning the pieces as necessary, so they will be a rich, golden brown. When chicken has browned, remove from skillet. Pour off all but 4 tablespoons fat. Stir in 2 tablespoons all-purpose flour and moisten with chicken stock or water, and wine. When well blended, add tomato paste, herb bouquet (see below), garlic, and mushrooms which have been washed and cut in pieces. Replace the chicken. Cover. Cook very, very slowly on simmer heat for an hour, or until chicken is tender. Remove herb bouquet, place chicken on hot platter, and pour sauce over chicken. Serves 5-6.

Herb Bouquet

Don't decide this is too much trouble, because you need this touch for a truly delicious mixture. Take 3 or 4 sprigs of parsley, a sprig of thyme, and a small bay leaf. Tie the herbs together with string so they may be removed before serving the food. Or, if you do not have the fresh parsley or thyme, take ¼ teaspoon powdered thyme, 1 teaspoon parsley flakes, and the bay leaf. Tie them in a piece of cheesecloth, but be sure to remove before serving.

QUICK CHICKEN CONTINENTAL

7x11x1½-inch baking dish . . . Preheated oven—400° F. . . . Baking
time—20-25 minutes

4 large chicken breasts	2 cups medium white sauce
½ to ¾ cup water	(pages 245-46)
2 teaspoons salt	½ cup Parmesan cheese, grated
2 packages frozen broccoli	
1 can condensed cream of	
mushroom soup	

Cook chicken breasts in water to which 2 teaspoons salt has been
added. When chicken is tender, remove from liquid. Cool. Slice
each breast in several pieces. Cook broccoli until tender (page
140). Drain. Place broccoli stalks in bottom of greased baking
dish. Mix soup and white sauce together. Pour half mixture over
broccoli. Place chicken slices over broccoli and sauce. Cover
with remaining sauce. Place in oven until thoroughly heated
through. Remove from oven, sprinkle with Parmesan cheese. Place
under broiler for 5 minutes. Serves 8.

CHICKEN CASSEROLE

2-quart casserole with cover . . . Cold or preheated oven—350° F.
. . . Baking time—2 to 2½ hours

3 to 3½ pounds chicken	¾ cup shortening
¾ cup all-purpose flour	2 cups milk
1½ teaspoons salt	1 can (8 ounces) broken
½ teaspoon pepper	mushrooms
1 teaspoon paprika	

Cut chicken into serving pieces. Season flour with salt, pepper,
and paprika. Place in clean paper bag. Drop 2 or 3 pieces of
chicken in bag, shake several times, or until chicken is well coated
with flour. Repeat until pieces of chicken are all floured. Heat
shortening in skillet. Brown chicken pieces, putting meaty pieces
in first. As chicken browns, place in casserole. When all the chicken
has browned, pour off all but about 3 tablespoons of the hot drippings. Scrape the bottom of the skillet to loosen the browned portions. (This helps to make good gravy.) Add flour left over from
flouring the chicken. Stir flour through the melted drippings. Add
milk. You can also use the liquid drained from mushrooms in place
of part of the milk. When thickened, add mushrooms. Pour over
chicken. Cover casserole. Bake. This makes a wonderful Sunday

dinner, because the chicken can cook while you are at church. Serves 5-6.

TRICK: Substitute 1 can cream of mushroom soup for the milk and mushrooms. Better thin the soup down with about ½ cup milk or water.

STEWED CHICKEN AND NOODLES

Large kettle with cover . . . Cooking time—2½ to 3 hours

4 to 4½ pounds plump hen	1 onion, sliced
4 cups boiling water	⅛ teaspoon pepper
2 teaspoons salt	1 package (8 ounces) noodles
1 herb bouquet	

Cut chicken into serving pieces. Place in kettle. Add water, salt, onion, pepper, and herb bouquet (An herb bouquet consists of some celery tops, a small bay leaf, 1 carrot cut in fine cubes, 1 sprig parsley, all tied into a cheesecloth bag, so you can remove it easily.) Cover. As soon as steaming point is reached, reduce heat to slow simmer. About 15 minutes before ready to serve, remove herb bouquet, add noodles, and simmer until tender, about 15 minutes. Place chicken on hot platter and surround with noodles. Pour a small amount of any remaining liquid over all. Serve at once. Serves 5-6.

STEWED CHICKEN WITH DUMPLINGS

Large covered kettle . . . Cooking time—2½ to 3 hours

4-5 pounds plump hen, cut in serving pieces	2 teaspoons salt
3 cups boiling water	Dumplings

Be sure you select a plump young hen. Cut into serving pieces. Place in kettle, add boiling water and salt. Cover. When steaming, reduce heat to a gentle simmer. Cook until tender. Just before ready to serve meal, bring mixture to boiling point. Drop dumplings (page 312) by teaspoonfuls into the boiling broth, leaving chicken in to help hold the dumplings in place. Cover tightly. Cook dumplings. When ready to serve, place chicken on hot platter, place dumplings over chicken, and pour gravy left in kettle over all. Serves 5-6.

TRICK: There must be plenty of liquid in order to have enough left for gravy. Remember the dumplings will absorb a little of the liquid. Be sure to check liquid before adding dumplings, and if more water is needed, add it before dropping in dumplings.

CHICKEN CURRY

Large saucepan with cover . . . Cooking time—1 to 2 hours

3½ to 4 pounds young chicken
½ cup celery, diced
1 cup carrots, diced
1 tablespoon salt
3 cups boiling water
3 tablespoons butter, margarine, or chicken fat
¼ cup onion, chopped

1 to 2 teaspoons curry powder, depending on your fondness for curry
3 tablespoons all-purpose flour
2 cups chicken stock
2 egg yolks
½ cup cream or top milk
3 cups cooked rice (page 265)

Place chicken, cut in serving pieces, celery, carrots, and salt in saucepan. Add boiling water. Cover. When steaming, reduce heat to simmer and cook until chicken is tender. (*Note:* The cooking time will depend upon the age of the chicken.) When the chicken seems almost tender, melt butter, margarine, or chicken fat in skillet. Add chopped onion and fry until onion is tender and golden brown. Add curry powder and flour and stir until thoroughly blended. Take 2 cups broth from saucepan in which chicken is cooking and slowly stir into the flour mixture. Stir until smooth. Beat egg yolks, add to cream, and blend into the sauce. The rice should be cooking while you are making the sauce. When chicken is tender, remove to platter, arranging on outer edge of platter. Pile rice in the center. Pour sauce over all and serve at once. Serves 6-8.

CHICKEN PIE

8-inch-square baking dish or shallow oblong dish . . . Preheated oven—425° F. . . . Baking time—25-30 minutes

½ pastry recipe (page 365)
2 cups cooked chicken, cut in medium-sized pieces
2 tablespoons onion, finely minced
3 tablespoons butter or margarine

4 tablespoons all-purpose flour
2 cups chicken stock (chicken bouillon cubes may be used)
1 teaspoon salt
⅛ teaspoon pepper
1 cup potatoes, diced (optional)

Mix the pastry recipe. Roll out as for pastry. Place casserole over pastry and cut around dish. Cut pastry about ½ inch larger than dish, to allow for tucking into the casserole and crimping. Prick pastry with fork, or cut in any desired design. This is done to allow steam to escape while baking, otherwise the pastry will be lifted off the chicken during the cooking period.

Place chicken and minced onion is casserole. Make a sauce by melting the butter or margarine. To this add the flour and blend thoroughly. Slowly add the stock, salt, and pepper and stir until mixture thickens. Pour over chicken in casserole. Carefully lift the pastry over the hot mixture, pressing it firmly to the edges. Bake. Serve at once. Serves 4.

TRICK: If you should happen to have ½ cup or so of either peas or carrots, you might add these to the chicken mixture for added flavor.

SCALLOPED CHICKEN (Wonderful for church suppers)

10x14x2½-inch pan or 2 8x8x2½-inch pans . . . Preheated oven—
350° F. . . . Baking time—1 hour

4 to 5 pounds stewing chicken	1 onion, sliced
2 quarts hot water	2 celery stalks, cut
2 carrots, cut in slices	4 teaspoons salt

Cover chicken with hot water. Simmer, covered, until partially tender, then add the carrots, onion, celery stalks, and salt. Continue cooking slowly until chicken is very tender. Cool in broth. When cold, remove meat from the bones. Cut meat into cubes. Grind chicken skin and add to meat.

Dressing

14 cups stale bread, cubed	½ teaspoon pepper
2 teaspoons salt	2 eggs, well beaten
1 teaspoon sage	1½ cups chicken broth

Combine all ingredients. Mix thoroughly.

Special Sauce

1 cup fat skimmed from chicken broth, or 1 cup butter or margarine	¼ teaspoon pepper
	6 eggs, well beaten
	5 cups milk, part of which may be chicken broth
1 cup all-purpose flour	
1 tablespoon salt	

Melt fat in large saucepan or skillet. Blend in flour, salt, and pepper. Beat eggs and add to milk. Pour liquid mixture slowly into flour mixture and cook over low heat until thickened. Stir occasionally.

Topping

2 cups bread crumbs   4 tablespoons butter or
                                       margarine, melted

Soften bread crumbs in melted butter or margarine and sprinkle over top of casserole.

Now, place dressing in bottom of pan, spoon half the sauce over the dressing. Spread chicken evenly over sauce, then pour remaining half of sauce over chicken. Next, sprinkle topping over casserole. Bake. To serve, cut in squares. Will serve 18-20.

LEFTOVER CHICKEN

OVEN CHICKEN CROQUETTES

Shallow pan . . . Preheated oven—375° F. . . . Baking time—40-45
   minutes

2 cups cooked chicken, ground   1 teaspoon salt
1 cup celery, finely chopped   ¼ teaspoon pepper
1 cup soft bread crumbs   ¼ cup melted butter or margarine
1 egg, well beaten   ½ cup dry bread crumbs

Combine all ingredients except melted butter or margarine and dry bread crumbs. Shape into 6 croquettes. Roll each in melted butter or margarine, then in crumbs. Place in shallow pan. Bake until a golden brown. It may be necessary to turn the croquettes once during the baking period. Serves 4-6.

TRICK: You might bake corn bread (pages 307-308) at the same time and have a really delicious oven meal.

CREAMED CHICKEN AND HARD-COOKED EGGS

2 cups cooked chicken, cut in   ½ teaspoon salt
   strips or diced   ⅛ teaspoon celery salt
2 cups white sauce (page 245)   4 hard-cooked eggs (page 273)

Heat chicken in white sauce over very low heat. Add seasonings. Leftover vegetables, such as peas or carrots, may also be used. Shortly before removing creamed chicken from range, add the eggs which have been cut in halves lengthwise, then in quarters, crosswise. Serve over Chinese omelet (pages 276-77), hot biscuits (page 309), or toast. Serves 4.

CHICKEN STEAKS

Large skillet . . . Frying time—15-20 minutes

2 cups cooked chicken, minced	1 teaspoon onion, minced
¼ cup canned pimientos, chopped	1½ cups bread crumbs
1 can (4 ounces) mushrooms chopped, or ½ cup fresh mushrooms	1 egg, slightly beaten
	½ cup milk
	1 teaspoon salt
	⅛ teaspoon pepper
2 tablespoons butter, chicken fat, or margarine	¼ cup all-purpose flour
	4 tablespoons shortening

Combine all ingredients except shortening for frying and flour for dipping. Form into individual steaks or patties. Chill. Dust with flour and pan-fry in hot shortening until a golden brown. Arrange chicken steaks on platter and garnish with parsley or sliced tomatoes. Serves 4.

CHICKEN CHOPS

See Deep-Fat Fried Foods, pages 221-22.

CHICKEN AND ASPARAGUS AU GRATIN

7x11x1½-inch baking dish . . . Preheated oven—350° F. . . . baking time—30 minutes

4 cups soft bread crumbs	¼ teaspoon pepper
1 cup grated cheddar cheese	3 cups milk
½ cup melted butter or margarine	2 cups cooked chicken, diced
2 cups cooked asparagus	(may substitute veal, turkey,
½ cup all-purpose flour	or shrimp)
2 teaspoons salt	

Mix bread crumbs with cheese and ¼ cup of the melted butter or margarine. Line a glass utility dish with half the crumbs. Arrange asparagus on crumbs. Melt remaining butter or margarine, blend in flour, salt, and pepper, then add milk, stirring until all ingredients are well mixed. Cook until thick, stirring occasionally. Add chicken to sauce and pour over asparagus. Sprinkle top with remaining crumbs and cheese mixed together. Bake until crumbs have browned on top. Serves 8.

CHICKEN A LA KING

2-quart saucepan or skillet . . . Cooking time—about 20 minutes

3 tablespoons chicken fat, butter, or margarine	1 cup thin cream or top milk
1 cup fresh sliced mushrooms, or 1 can (14 ounces)	1½ cups cooked chicken, cubed
	1 whole canned pimiento, cut in strips
4 tablespoons all-purpose flour	½ teaspoon salt
1 cup chicken stock or milk	⅛ teaspoon pepper

Melt chicken fat, butter, or margarine and slowly cook the mushrooms. (If canned mushrooms are used, add to cream with chicken and pimiento.) Add flour to mushrooms which are cooking and blend well. Add stock and cream or top milk. Cook slowly until thick, stirring constantly. Add chicken (mushrooms if canned), pimiento, and seasonings. Serve in pastry shells (page 365), toasted bread cups, or over hot biscuits. Serves 4-6.

CHICKEN SOUP FROM ROASTED CHICKEN CARCASS—See page 12.

BARBECUED CHICKEN

Covered roasting pan or casserole . . . Cold or preheated oven—350° F. . . . Cooking time—1 to 1½ hours

1½ to 2½ pounds young chicken   Barbecue sauce

Cut chicken in half or quarters. Arrange in casserole or baking pan. Brush with barbecue sauce. Cover. Bake until about half done. Uncover, continue cooking, basting frequently with the hot barbecue sauce until tender and nicely browned. Cooking time depends upon size and weight of chicken. Serves 2-4.

Barbecue Sauce

¼ cup cooking oil or melted butter or margarine	1 teaspoon celery salt
	⅛ teaspoon cayenne pepper
¾ cup white table wine	¼ teaspoon black pepper
1 clove garlic, minced fine	⅛ teaspoon dried tarragon
1 large onion, minced fine	¼ teaspoon dried thyme
1 teaspoon salt	1 tablespoon parsley, chopped

Mix all ingredients thoroughly. Let stand overnight, if possible.

TRICK: Chicken for broiling may be marinated in this barbecue sauce several hours before broiling. Baste with sauce while broiling.

TURKEY

Not too many years ago most people thought of turkey as either a Thanksgiving or Christmas delicacy. Not so today. Turkey is available the year around due to the great development in turkey breeding and raising. The turkeys we find on the market today are uniform in quality: tender, plump, and juicy, with a wonderful flavor.

Better yet, these delicious, modern turkeys come in ways to suit any need. You may buy large or small turkeys, halves, quarters, disjointed and cut up, and, in many markets, by the piece. Formerly, the only way turkey could be cooked was by roasting. The excellent turkeys we now have may be barbecued, broiled, fried, fricasseed, or roasted.

Frozen turkeys are also available the year around.

How to Buy Turkey

Very few turkeys are graded, and since the size does not necessarily indicate age or tenderness, it is wise to know what you are looking for when buying turkey.

The marks of high quality are:

1. Clean, waxy skin with few pinfeathers and no bruises or discolorations.

2. Well-fleshed breast and legs and a generally plump appearance.

3. Streaks of fat under the skin on breast, legs, thighs, and back. The quantity of fat increases with the bird's age.

4. Short body and broad breast indicate a meaty bird.

5. Frozen turkeys should be frozen hard and should show no discoloration.

Buy a hen turkey if you want an 8- to 15-pound bird. Hen turkeys mature quickly and are usually better finished than toms of the same weight. ("Finish" means they are better filled out.)

Tom turkeys are best when you wish a 16- to 25-pound bird. They are at their best at this weight.

It has been my experience, however, that when a 25-pound turkey is needed, it is a good idea to buy two of the 12-pound turkeys. You get more drumsticks, thighs, and white meat that way, and at little, or no, extra expense.

How Much to Buy

Actually, the amount to buy depends somewhat on the age of the people who will eat the turkey. Small children usually don't eat as much as older children and grownups. However, allow from ¾ to 1 pound of turkey per person to be served. In this way, you'll have enough for a small second helping and some left over for eating cold.

Types of Turkey Available

New York or market-dressed turkeys are found in some localities. This type of turkey comes with head and feet on, picked but not drawn. Ask your butcher to draw the turkey, clean the giblets, and cut the neck off close to the body (first slitting the neck skin down center of back to shoulder) leaving skin over the breast intact. Ask him to remove the tendons from the leg before he cuts off the feet. Tendons become hard and dry during roasting and make the drumstick meat less desirable and more difficult to slice.

Full-drawn or eviscerated turkeys, which are ready to cook, come fresh or frozen. Most full-drawn turkeys are government inspected and usually quick-frozen.

Cut-up turkeys—half-turkeys (split lengthwise) or individual pieces—are not available in all markets.

How to Defrost Frozen Turkeys

The easiest and simplest way to defrost a frozen turkey is to unwrap the bird, place on trivet in shallow roasting pan, cover lightly with a piece of household aluminum foil, turn the oven control to 275° F., and when the bird is defrosted, usually in about 2 hours, remove from oven and prepare for roasting.

Another method is to keep at room temperature about 18 hours. Do no unwrap. Or, unwrap and place in refrigerator for about 36 hours.

How to Prepare Turkey for Roasting

1. Remove any pinfeathers. Use eyebrow tweezers, a strawberry huller, or a paring knife and the thumb.

   If the pinfeathers are stubborn, place turkey in sink and turn on the cold-water faucet. Then scrape stubborn spots with back of knife.

2. Singe bird, if necessary; although today's turkeys will seldom need singeing.
3. Remove any bits of lung, kidney, etc., which may be left in cavity.
4. Wash the outside carefully, rubbing with cloth or soft brush.
5. Rinse cavity with cold water. Drain bird thoroughly by standing upright in sink for a few minutes.
6. Refrigerate, unless bird is to be roasted at once.

The gizzard, heart, and particularly the liver spoil rather quickly and should be cooked immediately after removing from bird. Also, they must be cooked tender before adding to gravy or dressing.

How to Cook Giblets

Place gizzard, heart, and neck in saucepan. Cover with water. Add salt, a little minced onion, 1 bay leaf, and celery tops, if desired. Cover. Cook slowly about 2 hours. Add the liver the last 30 minutes of cooking.

Refrigerate promptly if giblets are not to be used immediately.

When to Stuff Turkey

Recent research by the American Institute of Baking proves that turkey should not be stuffed until just ready to put in oven to roast. Furthermore, it is no longer wise to stuff a bird and then freeze it. If I am not going to serve the turkey at the table, I roast it without stuffing, and prepare the stuffing in a separate casserole or pan. In some ways, I like this method better, for when prepared this way, the stuffing is never soggy, as it sometimes is when the stuffing is packed inside the turkey. This method is particularly suited to frozen turkeys.

Allow 1 cup of dressing per pound of bird, New York dressed weight, or 1½ cups per pound for full-drawn weight.

For stuffing recipes, see pages 94-97.

How to Roast a Turkey

First stuff the wishbone cavity. You will have to put the stuffing in with a spoon through the neck opening. Don't pack the stuffing in, do it lightly. Then skewer neck skin to back. This gives a nice smooth finish to the top of the turkey.

Lift wing up and out, forcing the tip back, until it rests flat against neck skin.

Place the turkey, breast down, in a deep bowl. Rub cavity with salt. Spoon stuffing into body cavity. Shake bird to settle stuffing, but do not pack it in. Place skewers across the opening and lace shut with clean string. Tie drumsticks securely to tail bone with string. Grease skin thoroughly with melted shortening, butter or margarine, or turkey fat.

Place turkey on rack or trivet in a large shallow pan. Brush a piece of clean white cheesecloth, or any soft cotton material, with melted fat. Lay over the turkey. Make certain the edges of the cloth are inside the shallow pan, otherwise you may get a smoky kitchen.

Place in preheated oven at proper temperature indicated in chart given below.

DO NOT SEAR. DO NOT ADD WATER. DO NOT COVER EXCEPT
WITH CHEESECLOTH BRUSHED WITH MELTED BUTTER
OR OTHER SHORTENING.

If cloth becomes dry during roasting period, moisten with fat from bottom of pan.

You may roast breast down until ¾ done, or breast up during entire roasting period,

ROASTING CHART FOR WHOLE TURKEY

Ready-to-Cook Weight	Oven Temperature	Total Cooking Time Approximate Hours Preheated Oven
4-8 pounds	325° F.	3-4 hours
8-12 pounds	325° F.	4-4½ hours
12-16 pounds	325° F.	4½-5 hours
16-20 pounds	325° F.	5½-7 hours
20-25 pounds	325° F.	7-8½ hours

Because there is variation among turkeys, the time indicated in the chart is approximate cooking time.

It might be wise, when dinner is set for a definite hour, to start the bird 20 or 30 minutes ahead of schedule to avoid delay in case the turkey should take longer to cook. The additional time also helps you make gravy, remove trussing, and so forth.

To judge when the turkey is done, test about 30 minutes before cooking time is over by moving drumstick up and down. The leg joint should give readily, or even break. Or, press the fleshy part of the drumstick, protecting the fingers with a clean cloth or paper toweling. The meat should feel very soft.

How to Roast Half Turkey

Wash bird thoroughly, both inside and out. Remove any pin-feathers. Rub cavity with salt. It is a good idea to skewer skin to meat along the cut edges to hold skin to meat during roasting. Tie leg to tailpiece and tie cord around breast end to hold wing flat. Place turkey skin side up on a rack in a shallow pan. Grease with melted butter, margarine, or turkey fat and cover with piece of cheesecloth which has been brushed with melted fat. If cheesecloth becomes dry during roasting period, moisten with fat drippings from pan.

Quarter turkeys may be roasted the same way.

ROASTING CHART FOR HALF OR QUARTER TURKEY

Ready-to-Cook Weight	Oven Temperature	Approximate Roasting Time
3½-5 pounds	325° F.	3-3½ hours
5-8 pounds	325° F.	3½-4 hours
8-12 pounds	325° F.	4-4½ hours

How to Prepare Stuffing for Half or Quarter Turkey

Prepare stuffing (page 95), allowing about ⅔ cup per serving. Press lightly into greased pan or casserole. Cover. Or, place lightly in aluminum foil and fold foil loosely. In either case, bake during last 1 to 1½ hours of turkey roasting time. The stuffing may be basted with pan drippings or giblet broth.

How to Broil Turkey

1. Choose a young turkey about 4 pounds in weight. Have turkey split in half lengthwise. Snap drumstick, hip, and joints to keep bird flat during broiling. Skewer leg to body. Fold wing tip back under wing. Skewer wing flat against cut edge of backbone.

2. Season each half turkey with 1 teaspoon salt and a sprinkling of pepper. Place turkey in broiler pan, not rack, brush with melted butter or margarine, and place skin down.

3. The trick in broiling turkey is to do it slowly, at least 7 inches from broiler unit, and preferably 10 inches. The turkey should not begin to brown during the first 15 minutes of broiling.

4. After about 30 minutes, turn turkey, brush with melted butter or margarine, and broil second side. It is advisable to baste several times during the broiling process.

5. The turkey is done when the meat on the thickest part of the drumstick cuts easily and no pink color shows.

6. Serve on warm platter and pour the pan drippings over turkey.

FRIED TURKEY

Large skillet with cover . . . Cooking time—about 1½ hours

Young turkey, about 4 to 5 pounds ready-to-cook weight, disjointed and cut into serving pieces.

½ cup flour	¼ teaspoon poultry seasonings
2 teaspoons paprika	(optional)
2 teaspoons salt	About 1 cup shortening for
¼ teaspoon pepper	frying

Combine flour and seasonings in paper bag. Shake 2 or 3 pieces of turkey at a time in bag until well coated. Save any leftover flour for gravy. Cook to a uniform golden brown in about 1 inch of hot shortening. Do not crowd pieces in skillet and cook the meaty pieces first. Browning requires about 15 or 20 minutes for each piece.

Pour off any excess grease, add 1 or 2 tablespoons of water, if desired, cover skillet, reduce heat, and cook until tender, about 50-60 minutes. The turkey is done when the thickest pieces are tender. Uncover last 10 minutes of cooking to recrisp skin. Serves 4-6.

TRICK: You can precook the gizzard and heart and fry with turkey. The liver does not need to be precooked before frying.

OVEN-FRIED TURKEY

Shallow baking pan . . . Baking time—50-60 minutes

Buy turkey as indicated in recipe for fried turkey, above. Coat with seasoned flour as for fried turkey. The pieces may be pan-fried, as for fried turkey, or fried in deep fat, 350° F., until golden brown. Requires about 10 minutes when deep-fat fried. Place browned turkey, one layer deep, in a shallow baking pan. Melt ¼ pound butter or margarine and to it add ¼ cup milk. Pour this over the turkey. Place in oven and cook until turkey is fork tender. Turn once to crisp evenly. The butter or margarine mixture may be basted over the turkey once or twice as it cooks. Serves 4-6.

FRICASSEE OF TURKEY WINGS

Large skillet with cover . . . Cooking time—1½ to 2 hours

4 flat turkey wings	¾ cup shortening
⅓ cup all-purpose flour	½ cup broth, tomato juice, or
1 teaspoon salt	sherry
⅛ teaspoon pepper	

Coat turkey wings with flour seasoned with salt and pepper. Fry in hot shortening until golden brown. Pour off excess grease. Add liquid. Reduce heat. Cover tightly and simmer until fork tender. Serves 4.

BARBECUED TURKEY WINGS—See Barbecued Chicken, page 86.

FOR LEFTOVER TURKEY RECIPES—See Leftover Chicken Recipes, pages 84-86.

DUCK

How to Buy

Allow 1 pound of duck per person being served.

How to Cook

Duck may be stuffed with apple stuffing (page 96) or chicken stuffing (page 94). Many people prefer 2 cored and quartered apples inside cavity, or 1 apple and 1 sliced orange is delicious, while a handful of celery leaves tossed into cavity gives a wonderful flavor to the meat as it cooks.

Place duck on trivet in shallow baking pan. Roast at 325° F., allowing about 30 minutes per pound. DO NOT ADD ANY WATER. You do not need to baste duck, since ducks are very fatty. However, it is advisable to prick the skin several times during the roasting and also occasionally to turn the duck so it will brown evenly. Pour off fat as it accumulates in pan.

GOOSE

How to Buy

Allow about 1¼ pounds per person. Goose has more bone and fat than duck.

How to Cook

Goose may be stuffed with apple stuffing (page 96), or the cavity may be filled with cored and quartered apples with a few celery leaves tossed in for good measure.

Roast like duck. A 10- to 12-pound goose will require about 4 hours to cook.

GUINEA HEN

Roast like roast chicken (pages 74-76). Broil young guineas like broiled chicken (pages 70-71). It is difficult to tell the age of a guinea hen, so it is well to get your butcher's assurance that your guinea hen is young. Guineas are so active that an old bird will require long, slow roasting, and even then it is difficult to have a tender roast.

SQUAB

Stuffed and cooked like roast chicken (pages 74-76), or broiled like broiled chicken (pages 70-71).

STUFFINGS

Amount to Make

For a 4-pound hen, allow approximately 4 cups stuffing.
For a 10-pound turkey, allow approximately 1¾ pounds of bread.
For a 15-18-pound turkey, allow approximately 2 pounds of bread.

STUFFING FOR CHICKEN OR FISH

½ cup melted butter or margarine,   1 teaspoon powdered sage or
    or chicken fat   poultry seasoning
2 small onions, chopped fine   1 teaspoon salt
3 tablespoons celery, cut fine   ½ teaspoon pepper
4 cups day-old bread, cubed   4 tablespoons parsley, chopped
                                           fine

Melt butter or margarine and slowly cook onions and celery until light golden brown. Add bread cubes and remaining ingredients. Toss lightly with a fork so all ingredients are thoroughly blended.

STUFFING FOR 15-18-POUND TURKEY

Cooked giblets, finely chopped
½ cup melted butter or margarine
1 cup celery, finely chopped
2 medium-sized onions, finely chopped
2 pounds bread (21 cups), measured after cutting in cubes

1 tablespoon salt
1 tablespoon poultry seasoning
½ teaspoon pepper
1 teaspoon sage
3 eggs, beaten
1 cup liquid from cooking giblets
½ cup parsley, chopped

Cook giblets and chop fine. Melt butter or margarine and slowly simmer the celery and onions. Cube the bread and to it add the salt, poultry seasoning, pepper, and sage. Combine celery and onion mixture with bread. Add beaten eggs, liquid, and parsley. Toss lightly with a fork until all ingredients are well blended.

OYSTER STUFFING

1 quart oysters
4 cups dry bread, cut in ½-inch cubes

2 teaspoons salt
¼ teaspoon pepper
½ cup melted butter or margarine

Combine all ingredients and use as a stuffing for a 10-pound fowl.

CORN BREAD STUFFING

8-inch-square pan . . . Preheated oven—450° F. . . . Baking time—30 minutes

Corn Bread

1 cup corn meal
2 teaspoons baking powder
1 teaspoon salt

1 egg
1 cup sweet milk

Sift corn meal, baking powder, and salt. Add egg and milk. Pour into greased pan and bake. Makes 4 cups crumbled.

Dressing

½ cup onion, chopped
1 cup celery, chopped
¼ cup butter or margarine
4 cups crumbled corn bread
4 cups stale bread, cubed

1 teaspoon salt
¼ teaspoon pepper
½ teaspoon poultry seasoning
1 egg
1 cup stock

Slowly cook onion and celery in butter or margarine until golden brown. Add corn bread and bread cubes. Continue cooking until golden brown. Add salt, pepper, poultry seasoning. Beat eggs slightly, add to stock, pour over dressing, stir well. Excellent for stuffing turkey, veal, or flank steak. Half a recipe is ample for a chicken or a 1½-pound flank steak.

APPLE STUFFING FOR GOOSE

¼ cup butter or margarine or bacon drippings
½ cup celery, chopped
½ cup onion, chopped
4 tablespoons parsley, chopped

2 quarts tart apples, diced
¼ cup brown sugar
1 teaspoon salt
¼ teaspoon pepper
2 cups dry bread, cubed

Melt butter or margarine or bacon drippings and slowly cook the celery, onions, and parsley. Add apples, brown sugar, cover, and cook slowly until apples are tender but not mushy. Add salt, pepper, and dry bread cubes. Toss lightly with a fork until all ingredients are well blended.

APPLE AND PRUNE STUFFING

To the above stuffing recipe add 1 pound prunes which have been cooked, pitted, and chopped. Add to apple mixture after apples have cooked.

CHESTNUT STUFFING

½ cup melted butter or margarine
2 small onions, chopped fine
3 tablespoons celery, cut fine
1 pound chestnuts, cooked and cut coarsely

4 cups day-old bread, cubed
1 teaspoon salt
½ teaspoon pepper
4 tablespoons parsley, finely chopped

Melt butter or margarine and slowly cook the onions and celery until tender and golden brown. Add chestnuts, which have been chopped coarse, and cook for about 5 minutes. Add to bread cubes. Add remainder of ingredients. Toss lightly with a fork until all ingredients are well blended. Sufficient to stuff a small turkey.

Cooked Chestnuts: To cook chestnuts, slash each chestnut twice and toss into boiling water. Boil 20 minutes and peel while hot. Chop or cut into medium-coarse pieces.

WILD-RICE STUFFING

2 cups wild rice
1 teaspoon salt
½ teaspoon pepper
1 tablespoon onion, grated

4 tablespoons celery, finely chopped
¼ cup melted butter or margarine

Cook rice as directed on page 265. Dry and fluff the rice by shaking pan over very low heat for about 10 minutes. Add remaining ingredients. Sufficient to stuff a 4-pound fowl.

GAME

RABBIT—HUNTER'S STYLE

Large covered skillet . . . Cooking time—1 to 1½ hours

1 rabbit	1 teaspoon curry powder
1 cup olive or salad oil	1 teaspoon powdered thyme
1 clove garlic	2 teaspoons salt
1 cup all-purpose flour	½ teaspoon pepper
2 tablespoons dry mustard	1 cup light cream

Cut the rabbit into pieces, rub all over with olive oil, and leave in a cool place overnight. Next day rub the pieces with a cut clove of garlic. Put flour in clean paper bag and to it add the mustard, curry powder, thyme, salt, and pepper. Shake the pieces of rabbit in the bag until well coated, then fry them to a golden brown with olive or salad oil. Watch the rabbit carefully, because it burns easily. Turn it over and over until golden brown and crisp. Reduce heat to simmer and pour cream over rabbit. Cover and allow to simmer for an hour, or until rabbit is tender. Serve on hot platter and pour cream sauce over rabbit. Serves 4-5.

WILD GOOSE

Shallow baking pan . . . Cold or preheated oven—350° F. . . . Baking time—depends on weight and age of goose

1 loaf stale bread	1 cup onion, finely chopped
1 tablespoon salt	1 cup celery, finely chopped
2 teaspoons pepper	1 wild goose
1 tablespoon powdered sage	½ cup salad or olive oil
½ pound salt pork	2 teaspoons salt

Crumble a loaf of stale bread into fluffy bits. Do not use the crusts. Add salt, pepper, and sage. Cut salt pork into ½-inch cubes and slowly fry until cubes are crisp and brown. Add, together with drippings in skillet, to seasoned bread. Toss lightly with a fork. Stir in the onion and celery. Fill the goose with stuffing and sew opening, or use skewers and string. Rub the goose outside with olive or salad oil, sprinkle with salt. If desired, place one or two strips salt pork or bacon over top of goose. Bake in shallow, uncovered pan, allowing 20-25 minutes per pound. Baste every 15 minutes with a mixture of olive or salad oil and water, about half and half. When goose is done, place on hot platter, and make gravy from drippings in pan. Serves 4.

VENISON ROAST

Shallow baking pan ... Cold or preheated oven—350° F. ... Baking time—2 to 2½ hours

4-5 pounds venison roast	1 clove garlic, cut in half
1 cup wine vinegar	1 tablespoon salt
1 cup cold water	1 teaspoon pepper
1 onion, cut in thin slices	¾ cup all-purpose flour
1 bay leaf	½ cup bacon drippings
2 whole cloves	3 strips salt pork, ¼-inch thick

Gravy

3 tablespoons bacon drippings	½ cup currant jelly
3 tablespoons all-purpose flour	3 gingersnaps
1½ cups liquid venison was soaked in	

Soak the haunch of venison in a mixture of the wine vinegar and water, with the onion, bay leaf, cloves, garlic, salt, and pepper added to the liquid. Allow to soak three days, turning meat over each day. Remove venison from liquid, dry with paper towels, pat flour all over it, and brown the haunch on all sides in sizzling hot bacon drippings. Lard the top side of the venison with strips of salt pork. Roast in shallow pan, basting with liquid it was soaked in. Allow 20-30 minutes per pound for roasting, depending somewhat upon the tenderness of the venison. To make the gravy, melt bacon drippings in skillet, blend in flour. Add liquid venison was soaked in, crumbled gingersnaps, and currant jelly. Stir until mixture is thickened. Serves 5-6.

WILD DUCK

Shallow baking pan ... Cold or preheated oven—350° F. ... Baking time—20-30 minutes per pound

Wild duck	1 cup water
1 tablespoon salt	2 tablespoons orange rind, grated
1 stalk of celery, or 1 onion and 1 apple	2 oranges, cut in ½-inch slices
1 cup orange juice	½ cup French dressing

Scrub the duck well in cold water and salt it generously on the outside. Stuff with celery stalk or apple and onion. This stuffing is not eaten. Put duck in shallow pan and roast. Baste with mixture of orange juice, water, and grated orange rind. Allow 20-30 minutes per pound for roasting. Garnish duck with slices of orange that have been marinated in French dressing and broiled to a golden brown. Serves 2-4.

BELGIAN HARE FRICASSEE

Large skillet with cover . . . Cooking time—about 2 hours

4 pounds tame rabbit or 2 game rabbits, cut into serving pieces	½ cup shortening
	1 bay leaf
	1 small onion, sliced
¾ cup all-purpose flour	1 cup top milk
2 teaspoons salt	Additional seasoning, if
1 teaspoon pepper	necessary

Dredge rabbit with seasoned flour. Heat shortening in skillet, brown rabbit. When rabbit is brown and crisp, pour off all but 3 tablespoons of grease, add bay leaf, onion, and milk. Turn heat to a lower setting and simmer gently until meat is tender. Serves 4-6.

TRICK: If rabbit is bloody, or if it is a game rabbit, soak bloody pieces in salted water for about 30 minutes before cooking.

Fish

How to Buy

When you are buying fresh fish, your best guide will be a reliable fish merchant, who will tell you which is the best fish to buy at any particular season and will provide you with only good, fresh, fish.

Frozen fish is an excellent buy, provided your merchant has proper freezer storage facilities. When you buy frozen fish, get it home as quickly as possible and place it at once in the freeze chest of your refrigerator, or in your home freezer, for the fish should not be allowed to defrost.

How Much to Buy

When buying fish whole, or buying slices from fish with bone, allow 1 pound of fish for two servings.

When buying fillets of fish (fillets have the bone removed), allow 1 pound of fish for 3 servings.

Types of Fish

Fish (shellfish not included) fall into two classes:

Lean Fish (this is the type of fish for those on a reducing diet): Flounder, Cod, Halibut (in steaks), Red Snapper, Whiting, Pickerel, Swordfish, Pike, and Haddock.

Fatty Fish: Bass, Halibut (bought whole), Mackerel, Pompano, Salmon, Shad, Trout, Tuna, Smelts, and Herring.

How to Care For

Be sure you wash the fish after you get it home. Wrap in household aluminum foil so odors will not be transferred. Store in coldest part of your refrigerator, which is right under the freeze chest. Do not keep more than 2 days at the most.

How to Prepare for Freezing

Clean fish thoroughly. Wrap tightly in freezer aluminum foil. Do not keep frozen fish more than 3 months.

How to Cook

Fish may be baked, broiled, pan-fried, deep-fat fried, or steamed.

Baked Fish

The easiest way to bake fish is to bake it on aluminum foil. Shape foil so it resembles a shallow baking pan, making sure it is large enough to hold the fish. Place foil on a cooky sheet.

A fish for baking should weigh between 3 and 5 pounds.

Have the fish merchant clean and prepare the fish for you. Rub seasonings on flesh side of fish. Stuff with bread stuffing (page 94). Be careful not to pack the stuffing in too tightly, or it will cause the fish to burst, and the stuffing to become soggy.

One of my favorite ways of baking fish is: first, prepare the fish as suggested above. After the fish is stuffed, cut two or three gashes across the top of the fish to help hold it in shape while baking, and then dot the top with butter or margarine. The amount of butter or margarine to use depends upon the type of fish, but on a 5-pound lean fish, I usually use about ¼ pound. Wrap loosely in household aluminum foil, place on a cooky sheet, and bake about 50 minutes at 425° F. When ready to serve, pour drippings in foil over fish. Serve with lemon wedges.

Broiled Fish

When broiling fish, you may leave a small fish whole, but, generally speaking, it is better to broil fillets, rather than a whole fish.

Brush the fish with melted butter or margarine and lay skin side down on broiler rack. Fillets are just laid on the broiler pan, either side up. Broil about 4 inches from broiler unit for about

15 minutes, or until fish flakes break apart easily. Season with salt and pepper.

Unless the fish is very thick, which it rarely is, you will not need to turn the fish during broiling.

To remove from broiler, use a pancake turner. Serve with lemon wedges.

Never salt the outside of a fish before baking or broiling. Always rub seasoning on flesh side of fish.

Fried Fish

When pan-frying fish you should have about ½ inch melted shortening in the skillet. Do not attempt to pan-fry a fish which will not fit in a skillet, but small whole fish, fillets, and sliced fish are wonderful pan-fried.

Roll fish in corn meal, which has been seasoned with salt and pepper. Of course, cracker crumbs, bread crumbs, and flour may also be used.

Do not fry fish too quickly. Let it brown nicely on one side, and with a pancake turner, or broad spatula, turn and brown on other side. Serve with lemon wedges and garnish the plate with parsley or watercress.

Deep-Fat Fried Fish—See pages 233-37.

Steamed or Poached Fish

Steaming fish in a small amount of liquid, such as bouillon, water, or milk, preserves the flavor of the fish more than any other method. The liquid must be kept below the boiling point. If you have a steamer with a rack in it, put liquid in the steamer to a depth that will not touch the fish. Grease the rack upon which you place the fish, season with salt and pepper, and steam fillets, slices, or small whole fish which have been cut in half. Allow from 10 to 20 minutes per pound according to thickness.

The liquid in which the fish was steamed or poached may be used as a base for a cream sauce to serve with the fish.

Very oily fish are not adapted to steaming or poaching.

If poaching fish in milk, follow the same method as for poaching eggs (page 274), keeping the milk below the boiling point. The remaining milk may be thickened and used as a cream sauce to pour over the fish.

This method of preparing fish is particularly fine for those who cannot eat fried food and for those whose diet restricts them from butter or margarine.

FISH LOAF

Loaf pan ... Preheated oven—350° F. ... Baking time—1 hour

2 cups cooked, flaked fish	1 cup fine, soft bread crumbs
2 tablespoons green pepper, chopped	1 teaspoon salt
	1/8 teaspoon pepper
1 tablespoon onion, finely minced	2 egg yolks
	1/2 cup milk
2 tablespoons butter or margarine	1 tablespoon lemon juice
	2 egg whites

Shred the fish. Sauté green pepper and onion in butter or margarine. Add to the fish along with bread crumbs and seasonings. Beat egg yolks, add to milk, then add to fish mixture. Stir in the lemon juice. Fold in stiffly beaten egg whites. Pour into greased loaf pan. Set pan in another pan of hot water. Bake. Serve with cheese sauce (pages 245-46). Serves 4-5.

BAKED HALIBUT WITH SPANISH SAUCE

Shallow baking dish ... Cold or preheated oven—375° F. ... Baking time—1 hour

2 pounds frozen or fresh halibut fillets	Spanish sauce (page 277)

Place fish in greased baking dish. Pour Spanish sauce over fish. Bake. Serve with sauce over fish. Serves 4-6.

SALMON LOAF

Loaf pan ... Preheated oven—350° F. ... Baking time—1 hour

1-pound can salmon	1/2 teaspoon salt
3 tablespoons butter or margarine	1/4 teaspoon pepper
	2 tablespoons onion, minced
3 tablespoons all-purpose flour	2 cups bread cubes
Salmon liquid plus sufficient milk to make 1 cup	1 egg, beaten

Drain canned salmon, saving liquid. Remove skin and bones. Make white sauce by blending butter or margarine with flour over medium heat. Add salmon and liquids and cook, stirring frequently. Add seasonings. Mix sauce with salmon and remaining ingredients. Shape into a loaf and place in greased loaf pan. Bake uncovered. Serves 4-6.

TRICK: Use pink salmon, which is less expensive and almost as good in flavor when served this way.

SALMON WITH BISCUIT TOPPING

1½- to 2-quart casserole . . . Preheated oven—425° F. . . . Baking time—20-25 minutes

4 tablespoons butter or margarine	1-pound can salmon
4 tablespoons all-purpose flour	¾ cup grated cheese
1 teaspoon salt	½ recipe baking powder biscuits (page 309)
¼ teaspoon pepper	
Liquid from salmon plus enough milk to make 2 cups	

Melt butter or margarine in saucepan over medium heat. Blend in flour, salt, and pepper. Add salmon liquid and milk and cook until thickened, stirring frequently. When mixture has thickened, remove from heat and add to it the salmon, from which the skin and bones have been removed, and cheese. Pour into greased casserole. Place small biscuits on top. Bake. Serves 4-6.

TRICK: Spread 2 or 3 slices bread generously with butter or margarine. Cut each slice into thirds, lengthwise. Lay on top of salmon mixture. Almost as good as biscuits, and much quicker.

SALMON NOODLE BAKE

3-quart casserole . . . Preheated oven—350° F. . . . Baking time— 40-50 minutes

1 package (8 ounces) medium noodles	3 hard-cooked eggs, sliced (page 273)
2 cans condensed cream of mushroom soup	1-pound can salmon
1¼ cups water	½ cup fine cracker crumbs
⅔ cup cheddar cheese, grated	1 tablespoon butter or margarine
½ teaspoon Worcestershire sauce	

Cook noodles according to directions on page 253. Heat soup and water over medium heat. Stir until smooth. Remove from heat. To soup, add cheese and Worcestershire sauce, all but one of the sliced, hard-cooked eggs, salmon, and noodles. Pour into greased casserole. Sprinkle cracker crumbs over top and dot with butter or margarine. Garnish with remaining egg slices. Bake. Serves 10-12.

TRICK: 2 cans (7 ounces each) tuna fish may be used instead of the salmon.

CREAMED SALMON AND PEAS

Large skillet with cover . . . Cooking time—about 20 minutes

6 tablespoons butter or margarine	1-pound can salmon
5 tablespoons all-purpose flour	1 can (No. 2) peas
1 teaspoon salt	2 tablespoons green pepper, chopped
¼ teaspoon pepper	1 tablespoon onion, finely minced
1 cup milk	
1 cup liquid from salmon and peas	2 tablespoons pimiento

Melt butter or margarine over medium heat. Blend in flour, salt, and pepper. Add milk and liquid from salmon and peas. Stir until thick. Break salmon into large pieces. Add salmon and peas to white sauce. Sprinkle green pepper, onion, and pimiento over top. Cover. Reduce heat to simmer setting and cook for 20 minutes. Serves 4-6.

SALMON CREOLE

Large skillet with cover . . . Cooking time—50-55 minutes

3 strips bacon	2 tablespoons green pepper, chopped
¾ cup rice	
2 tablespoons onion, chopped	1 teaspoon Worcestershire sauce
2 tablespoons celery, finely cut	1 teaspoon salt
1 can (No. 2) tomatoes	1-pound can salmon
2 cups water	2 slices onion, cut ¼ inch thick

Cut bacon into pieces and fry until brown and crisp. Remove bacon to a piece of paper to drain. Add rice and chopped onion to bacon drippings. Cook until light brown. Add celery, tomatoes, water, green pepper, Worcestershire sauce, and salt. Remove skin and bone from salmon and arrange salmon in whole pieces in center of sauce. Put slices of onion on top of salmon. Cover. When mixture comes to full steaming point, reduce heat to simmer setting and cook for 45 minutes. Serves 4-6.

SALMON PATTIES

8-inch skillet . . . Cooking time—about 15 minutes

1-pound can pink salmon
2 eggs, beaten
¼ cup milk
½ teaspoon salt

⅛ teaspoon pepper
½ cup fine cracker crumbs
6 tablespoons shortening

Drain and remove bones and skin from salmon. Flake. Beat eggs and add to milk, then add to salmon. Add seasonings and cracker crumbs. Form into six large patties. Melt shortening in skillet, place patties in hot shortening, and brown on both sides. Serves 4-6.

TUNA FISH CASSEROLE

1½-quart casserole . . . Preheated oven—375° F. . . . Baking time—25 minutes

1 can (7 ounces) tuna fish
1 can condensed cream of mush-
    room soup

½ cup milk
½ teaspoon salt
¾ cup crushed potato chips

Place tuna fish in greased casserole. Blend mushroom soup and milk together. Add salt. Pour over tuna fish. Sprinkle crushed potato chips over top. Bake uncovered. Serves 4.

TUNA BAKE WITH CHEESE SWIRLS

8x12-inch baking dish . . . Preheated oven—425° F. . . . Baking time—25-30 minutes

3 tablespoons onion, chopped
3 tablespoons green pepper,
    chopped
⅓ cup butter or margarine
1 teaspoon salt
⅓ cup all-purpose flour

1 can condensed cream of
    chicken soup
3 cups milk
1 can (7 ounces) tuna fish
1 tablespoon lemon juice

Brown onion and green pepper in the butter or margarine. Add salt and flour. Blend thoroughly. Add chicken soup and milk, stirring until a smooth thin sauce has formed. Add tuna fish and lemon juice. Pour into baking dish. Top with cheese swirls. Bake. Serves 6.

Cheese Swirls

Baking powder biscuit recipe
    (page 309)

½ cup shredded Cheddar cheese
½ cup pimiento, chopped

Roll biscuit dough to about ¼-inch thickness. Sprinkle shredded cheese and pimiento over top of rolled dough. Then roll as for jelly roll. Slice in ½-inch slices. Place cut slices on top of tuna mixture.

TUNA CURRY

Large skillet with cover . . . Cooking time—about 20 minutes

1 can (7 ounces) tuna fish
1½ cups medium white sauce (pages 245-46)
2 tablespoons onion, minced
2 tablespoons green pepper, chopped
2 tablespoons celery, chopped

½ cup ripe olives, cut from pits
2 hard-cooked eggs (page 273)
½ teaspoon curry powder, or more to taste
Hot steamed rice (page 265)
¼ cup pimiento, cut in strips (optional)

Heat tuna fish in white sauce. Add onion, green pepper, celery, ripe olives, and hard-cooked eggs, cut into cubes. Carefully blend in the curry powder and bring to steaming point over low heat. Serve over hot steamed rice. Garnish with pimiento. Serves 4.

SEA FOOD WITH RICE

Covered skillet . . . Cooking time—20 minutes

1 can (7 ounces) tuna fish
1 can (6 ounces) lobster, or any sea food
3 cups cooked rice (page 265)
2 cups coffee cream
½ teaspoon curry powder

½ teaspoon monosodium glutamate
¼ teaspoon basil
¼ teaspoon orégano
1 teaspoon salt

Place tuna fish and lobster in skillet. Add cooked rice. Pour cream over mixture. Add seasonings. Cover. Bring mixture to steaming point. Then reduce heat to simmer and cook. Serve on toast or Holland rusks. Serves 6-8.

BAKED SCALLOPS

Shallow baking dish . . . Preheated oven—350° F. . . . Baking time 45-50 minutes

1 pound fresh scallops
⅓ cup all-purpose flour
1 teaspoon salt
⅛ teaspoon pepper

¾ cup milk (cream would be better)
3 tablespoons butter or margarine

Wash scallops in cold water. Drain and dry well. Remove hard piece, which is found on the side, from each scallop. Roll in flour which has been seasoned with salt and pepper. Put in greased shallow pan. Fill to about ½ the depth of scallops with rich milk. Dot with butter or margarine. When baked about ½ hour, turn each and brown on other side. Serves 4.

FRIED SCALLOPS—See Deep-Fat-Fried Foods, pages 221-22.

BROILED MACKEREL WITH MUSTARD PASTE

3 pounds mackerel	1 teaspoon salt
1 tablespoon butter, margarine, or salad oil	⅛ teaspoon pepper

If fish is large, split in middle of back. Otherwise, broil whole. Mix butter, margarine, or salad oil with salt and pepper and rub over flesh part of fish. Broil. Turn fish when first side has browned and broil on second side. Before removing from broiler, spread with mustard paste and broil until bubbly, about 1 minute. Serves 6.

Mustard Paste

1 teaspoon prepared mustard	2 tablespoons parsley, finely minced
2 tablespoons butter or margarine	2 tablespoons lemon juice

Cream mustard and butter or margarine together. Add parsley and lemon juice.

MACKEREL MAINE STYLE

Oblong baking dish . . . Preheated oven—400° F. . . . Baking time —30-40 minutes

2 mackerel, about 2 pounds each	¾ cup vinegar
1 large onion, chopped fine	½ teaspoon salt
1 large carrot, diced fine	1 tablespoon parsley, chopped
½ green pepper, chopped	¼ teaspoon thyme, minced
	1 bay leaf

Place cleaned mackerel in baking dish and cover with sauce made by cooking onion, carrot, green pepper, vinegar, salt, parsley, thyme, and bay leaf for about 20 minutes over low heat. Before pouring sauce over fish, remove bay leaf. Bake. Serves 4-6.

FRIED FILLETS OF MACKEREL

8-inch skillet . . . Cooking time—about 25 minutes

1¼ pounds mackerel fillets	1 teaspoon paprika
2 tablespoons salad oil	¼ cup all-purpose flour
1 teaspoon vinegar	1 egg
1 teaspoon grated onion	1 cup fine cracker crumbs
½ teaspoon salt	¼ cup butter or margarine

Marinate the mackerel fillets in dressing made by mixing salad oil, vinegar, onion, salt, and paprika. Allow fillets to marinate about an hour, turning frequently. When ready to cook, lift from marinating mixture, drain, roll in flour, and dip in beaten egg. Roll again in fine cracker crumbs. Fry to a golden brown in hot butter or margarine. Serves 4.

FRIED SALT FISH BALLS—See Deep-Fat-Fried Foods, page 237.

CURRIED FISH

Covered saucepan . . . Cooking time—about 30 minutes

2 pounds fresh cod, halibut, or other fish	3 tablespoons all-purpose flour
4 tablespoons butter or margarine	2 cups liquor from the simmered fish
1 tablespoon green pepper, chopped	1 teaspoon curry powder
	¼ teaspoon tabasco sauce
1 small onion, chopped	1 teaspoon salt
¼ cup chopped celery	2 tablespoons parsley, chopped
	2 cups cooked rice (page 265)

Simmer the fish about 10 minutes in a small quantity of water. Be sure to cover the saucepan. When tender, drain, keeping the liquid in which fish was cooked. Melt butter or margarine and lightly brown the green pepper, onion, and celery. Do this over low heat. Then add the flour, stirring until well blended. Add the fish liquor. Stir, and cook until thickened. Add remainder of seasonings. This sauce will taste much more pungent if cooked over simmer heat about 10 minutes after it is blended, and before pouring over fish. Remove the skin and bones from the fish. Arrange on a heated platter with a border of flaky steamed rice. Pour hot sauce over fish. Garnish with parsley. Serves 6.

FISH HASH

8-inch skillet . . . Cooking time—about 25 minutes

Cold flaked fish	½ teaspoon salt
Cold boiled potatoes	⅛ teaspoon pepper
¼ cup onion, finely chopped	¼ pound salt pork

Take equal parts cold fish and cold boiled potatoes and chop together until quite fine. Add finely chopped onion and seasonings and blend thoroughly through fish and potato mixture. Cut salt pork into small cubes, place in hot skillet, and cook slowly until there is sufficient grease in skillet to moisten fish and potato mixture. Remove any bits of salt pork. Put mixture in hot grease, smooth firmly in skillet, and fry over medium heat until bottom side is nicely browned. Turn. When second side is brown, fold like an omelet. Number of servings depends upon amount of fish and potatoes used.

FRIED SMELTS

8-inch skillet . . . Cooking time—about 5 minutes

24 smelts	4 tablespoons butter or marga-
1 teaspoon salt	rine
6 tablespoons flour or corn meal	

Clean smelts, remove heads and tails, and wipe with a damp cloth. Roll smelts in salted flour or corn meal. Fry for about 5 minutes in hot butter or margarine, turning them frequently until a golden brown. Serve with tartar sauce (page 245). Serves 4-6.

MAINE THREE-WAY FISH PIE

3-quart casserole . . . Preheated oven—375° F. . . . Baking time—45-50 minutes

1 small onion, whole	2 tablespoons all-purpose flour
1 carrot, cut in quarters	2¼ cups strained stock
1 stalk celery	1 teaspoon parsley, finely
Salt and pepper to taste	chopped
1 quart water	¼ teaspoon tarragon, finely
1½ pounds halibut	chopped
1 chicken bouillon cube	½ pound cooked shrimp
2 tablespoons butter or marga-	½ pound steamed scallops
rine	½ recipe pie crust (page 365)
1 tablespoon onion, chopped	

Boil whole onion, carrot, celery, salt, and pepper in one quart of water. After boiling for 10 minutes, add fish, cover, and simmer until fish is tender. Remove skin and bones from fish and place fish aside. Return bones and skin to the onion and carrot mixture. Add bouillon cube. Cover. Cook about 20 minutes longer at simmer heat. Strain and reserve the stock.

Melt butter or margarine in small skillet. Add chopped onion and sauté several minutes over low heat. Stir in flour slowly. When well blended, add strained stock, parsley, tarragon, and additional seasoning, if necessary. Break fish in large pieces, place in a deep greased casserole, alternating with the cooked shrimp and scallops. Pour the sauce over all and cover with pastry. Make several slits in crust. Bake. Serves 6-8.

TRICK: Any lean white fish may be substituted for halibut.

SHAD ROE

Usually the roe from 1 shad yields 2 servings. It may be either broiled or pan sautéed. It is best to parboil shad roe before either broiling or frying.

To Parboil

To 1 quart water, add 1 tablespoon salt and 1 tablespoon vinegar or lemon juice. Bring to a boil. When mixture is boiling, add shad roe, reduce the heat, and simmer for about 15 minutes, although 5 minutes is sufficient for very young roe. Drain, cover with cold water, and let stand about 10 minutes. Drain.

To Sauté

6 to 8 bacon strips   Salt and pepper to taste
2 shad roe (parboiled)

Fry bacon until crisp. Remove from pan and drain on absorbent paper. Cut roe in pieces and fry in hot bacon drippings, using a slow frying temperature. Season with salt and pepper. Serve with fried bacon strips.

HALIBUT AU GRATIN

Oblong baking dish . . . Preheated oven—350° F. . . . Baking time—about 30 minutes

1 quart boiling water   1 cup Cheddar cheese, finely
½ teaspoon salt   shredded
1 tablespoon lemon juice   ½ cup fine bread or cracker
2 pounds halibut   crumbs
½ recipe for medium white sauce
   (pages 245-46)

To the water, add the salt and lemon juice. Bring to a brisk boil. Either wrap halibut in cheesecloth or place in wire basket. Lower fish in boiling water, making certain the fish is completely covered by liquid. Cover. Bring slowly to boiling point, then reduce heat. Simmer fish for about 20 minutes, or allow 10 minutes per pound. When tender, drain, and break into pieces about the size of an egg. Place in greased baking dish. Cover with white sauce to which the grated cheese has been added. Sprinkle bread or cracker crumbs over top. Bake. Serves 6.

TRICK: Fish loses both flavor and food value if boiled actively. It should always be simmered, in a covered pan.

FROGS' LEGS—See pages 232-33.

SMOKED AND SALT FISH

The fish most commonly salted are cod, haddock, herring, and mackerel. The fish most commonly smoked are herring and haddock (finnan haddie). Salmon and sturgeon are frequently smoked, but these are used mostly for snacks.

How to Freshen Salt Fish

Salt fish may be purchased in bulk, or packaged. If purchased by the piece, it usually requires several hours to freshen. Either shred the fish or cut in chunks and pour boiling water over it. It may be necessary to repeat this several times before the fish has been freshened to your taste.

When buying the packaged salt fish, follow directions on the package for freshening.

CREAMED CODFISH

8-inch skillet . . . Cooking time—about 15 minutes

6 tablespoons butter or margarine	3 cups milk
1 pound freshened codfish	Pepper to taste, usually about
6 tablespoons all-purpose flour	¼ teaspoon

Melt butter or margarine over medium heat and add freshened codfish. Allow to cook slowly until butter or margarine is bubbly and the codfish a light, golden yellow. Blend in the flour and stir carefully. Add milk and cook until thickened, stirring occasionally. Add pepper just before removing from heat. Delicious served on baked or mashed potatoes or toast. Serves 4.

TREAT: Just before removing creamed codfish from range, add 2 eggs which have been slightly beaten. If you have extra egg yolks, use them instead of the whole egg.

CODFISH PATTIES

8-inch skillet . . . Cooking time—about 10 minutes

3 cups potatoes, sliced medium thick	2 eggs, slightly beaten
	¼ cup milk
1 pound freshened codfish	¼ teaspoon pepper
2 tablespoons butter or margarine	6 tablespoons shortening

Put potatoes and freshened codfish in saucepan. Cover with boiling water and cook until both potatoes and codfish are tender, about 25 minutes. Drain and mash thoroughly. Add butter or margarine, eggs, milk, and pepper and beat until light and fluffy. Drop by spoonfuls into hot shortening and brown on both sides. Or, the mixture may be cooled, then shaped into balls, and fried in deep fat at 375° F. Serves 4.

BROILED FINNAN HADDIE

Allow 1½ pounds finnan haddie for 4 servings.

Finnan haddie to be broiled should first be steamed. To do this, place finnan haddie in a wire basket and lower over boiling water. Do not immerse the fish in water and do not pile pieces of fish on top of each other. Steam about 15 minutes.

Place steamed finnan haddie on greased broiler rack, brush with butter or margarine, pepper, and paprika. Place under broiler and allow to broil for about 5 minutes. The fish should be at least 5 inches from broiler unit.

FINNAN HADDIE CASSEROLE

2-quart casserole . . . Preheated oven—400° F. . . . Baking time— 20 minutes

1 finnan haddie	1 onion, finely minced
Milk to cover fish	4 tablespoons all-purpose flour
2 tablespoons butter or margarine	¼ teaspoon pepper
	2½ cups milk
¾ cup green pepper, chopped	1 teaspoon paprika

Cut fish into 3 or 4 pieces. Place in saucepan and cover with milk. Place over simmer heat and cook slowly for about 30 minutes. When fish has cooked, remove bones and skin. Melt butter or margarine in saucepan, add green pepper and onion, and cook slowly for about 10 minutes. Add flour and pepper. Blend thoroughly. Then add milk and cook until thickened, stirring occasionally. Place prepared fish in a greased casserole, pour thickened sauce over fish, sprinkle top with paprika, and bake. Serves 4-5.

POACHED FINNAN HADDIE

Place finnan haddie in skillet. Cover with milk. Bring slowly to steaming point and allow to simmer about 15 minutes. Serve with butter or margarine and lemon wedges.

TRICK: To remove the bones from finnan haddie easily, soak in warm water for about 5 minutes, or until bones have loosened.

SHELLFISH

CLAMS

Clams are available fresh, frozen, or canned. When you buy fresh clams, be sure the shell is tightly closed, because this proves the clam is still alive. It is difficult to tell how many clams to allow per serving, because tastes vary, and also the type meal with which clams are being served. It is best to allow from 12 to 20 clams per serving.

If you buy fresh clams at the market, the best idea is to have them opened for you. If not, let them soak in cold water a while, then scrub the shell thoroughly, rinse again, to make sure that all sand is removed. To open the shells, either steam for a short period or pry open with a knife.

To Steam Clams

Place clams in wire basket and lower into boiling water. Cover and keep water at steaming temperature. The shells will open in 10-15 minutes. If you have washed the shells carefully, be sure to save the clam liquor.

To Open Clams with a Knife

Take a strong, sharp knife and insert between the shells, cutting through the muscle which holds the two halves together. Open flat and remove the clam.

CLAM CHOWDER

See Soups, page 21.

CLAMBURGERS

8-inch skillet . . . Cooking time—about 10 minutes

1 pint clams, chopped fine	1 teaspoon salt
1 egg, well beaten	¼ teaspoon pepper
1 cup cracker crumbs	

Combine ingredients in order given and mix well. Form in round cakes and fry in hot shortening which is about 1 inch deep. Drain and serve piping hot. Wonderful served on hot, toasted, buttered buns. Serves 4.

CRABS

We always refer to crabs as hard-shell or soft-shell crabs. All crabs are really hard shell, but during the moulting season the shell is soft, and so, seasonally, we have soft-shell crabs.

How to Cook Hard-Shell Crabs

Fill a large kettle with water to which about a handful of salt has been added. Bring water to a boil. Drop in the large crab, head first. Cover and boil briskly for about 5 minutes, then allow to simmer 20-25 minutes.

If the crab is to be eaten cold, plunge immediately into very cold water and refrigerate as quickly as possible. To serve hard-shell crab, break the shell and the claws. A wooden mallet, or a rolling pin may be used. Break off the tail and loosen the upper and lower shell of the crab so the digestive track may be removed. Wash thoroughly, then heap on a platter or in a large bowl, and let everyone fall to. Serve with mayonnaise, hollandaise sauce (page 242), or plain. The meat is so delicious it really needs little or no seasoning.

If the meat is to be used in a salad, or in any of the numerous ways it may be served, pick out the meat, but take care to watch for bony pieces, and particularly the hard cartilage which separates the meaty portions of the crab.

How to Cook Soft-Shell Crabs

Soft-shell crabs are usually purchased alive and are killed by sticking a knife between the eyes. Then lift the pointed end of the top shell and remove the spongy substance which is found between the shell and the body. Place the crab on its back and remove the tail. Wash thoroughly to remove all sand. Drain.

Soft-shell crabs are either fried or broiled and are eaten shell and all.

To Broil Soft-Shell Crabs

After preparing the crab, sprinkle with salt, pepper, and lemon juice and brush generously with melted butter or margarine. Place on broiler rack, at least 3 inches from broiler unit, and broil for about 10 minutes. Turn after the first 5 minutes of broiling and brown the other side.

To Fry Soft-Shell Crabs

After preparing the crab, season with salt, pepper, and lemon juice. Dip in flour, corn meal, or egg and crumbs. Fry in hot shortening, but do not fry too rapidly, for quick frying has a tendency to toughen the meat. Serve with tartar sauce (page 245) or lemon wedges.

CREAMED CRAB IN AVOCADO

Avocado halves . . . Preheated oven—350° F. . . . Baking time— 20-25 minutes

1 can (7 ounces) crab meat	Salt, pepper, and cayenne to
1¼ cups milk	taste
3 tablespoons all-purpose flour	3 medium-sized avocados
4 tablespoons soft butter or	3 tablespoons Cheddar cheese
margarine	or Parmesan cheese, grated

Heat crab meat and milk over low heat. Blend flour and butter or margarine together. Add to heated milk mixture. Add seasonings. Stir until mixture has thickened. It is a good idea to stir with a fork so that the crab meat will not break.

Cut avocados in half, remove pit. It may be necessary to remove a little of the flesh around the pit, so there will be plenty of room for the crab mixture. Pile the creamed crab mixture into the avocado. Sprinkle cheese over top. Place avocados in shallow pan and bake. Serves 6.

CRAB SUPREME

Crab Shells or ramekins . . . Preheated oven—400° F. . . . Baking time—20-30 minutes

4 tablespoons butter or margarine	½ teaspoon celery salt
1 teaspoon onion, chopped	1 teaspoon Worcestershire sauce
4 tablespoons all-purpose flour	1 egg yolk, beaten
2 cups milk	2 tablespoons sherry
Dash of cayenne or tabasco	1 cup soft bread crumbs
Salt and pepper to taste	2 cups crab meat
	1 tablespoon parsley, minced

Melt butter or margarine, add onion, and cook over low heat until onion is lightly browned. Add flour, blend together thoroughly. Add milk and seasonings and cook until mixture has thickened, stirring occasionally. Add egg yolk, stir, and remove saucepan from heat. Add sherry and most of the bread crumbs, reserving a small portion to sprinkle over top of mixture. Then add crab meat and parsley. Mix well and fill crab shells or ramekins. Top with remaining bread crumbs. Bake. Serves 6-8.

ABALONE

Abalone is not strictly a shellfish, but since it comes equipped with a shell, we will place it in this section.

Abalone is a delicious fish, native to California waters. When you buy it, better buy it sliced and count on 1 pound serving 2. (Have the steaks pounded at the store, if possible.)

To Fry Abalone

Prepare abalone steaks exactly as you would Swiss steak, by pounding vigorously with a wooden mallet or the flat side of a cleaver. Otherwise it will be exceedingly tough. Sprinkle with salt and pepper, dip into well-beaten egg, then roll in fine cracker crumbs. Brown quickly in hot shortening. Don't let it fry more than 2 minutes to each side and take care not to let it burn.

TRICK: Use salad oil or shortening for frying abalone and have it about 1-inch deep in the skillet. Cooked in this manner, the fish will fry quickly without burning.

SHRIMP

How to Cook Green Shrimp

Large kettle with cover . . . Cooking time—about 15 minutes

2 quarts water	1 teaspoon thyme
½ cup coarse salt	1 teaspoon rosemary
¼ cup vinegar	2 bay leaves
All the leaves from a bunch of celery	5-6 whole cloves
	Green shrimp

Put water in large kettle. Add remaining ingredients except shrimp. When water reaches boiling point, add green shrimp. Bring to boiling point rapidly and cook 15 minutes. Allow shrimp to cool in water in which they were cooked. Remove shells and de-vein, if necessary.

If you are cooking frozen green shrimp, do not thaw before cooking. Plunge frozen shrimp into boiling water. Do not cook more than 2 pounds at one time.

How to De-Vein Shrimp

Remove the black vein running down the back of the shrimp by using the point of a sharp knife.

SHRIMP CURRY

Skillet with cover . . . Cooking time—25-30 minutes

¼ cup butter or margarine	1 cup light cream
4 tablespoons all-purpose flour	2 cups cooked and de-veined shrimp
2 teaspoons curry powder	1 can (8 ounces) mushrooms (stems and pieces may be used)
1 teaspoon salt	
⅛ teaspoon pepper	
1 cup milk	

Melt butter or margarine. Blend in flour, curry powder, salt, and pepper. Add milk and cream and continue cooking, stirring frequently until mixture thickens. Add shrimp and sliced mushrooms. Cover and cook 5 minutes longer. Serve at once on steamed rice (page 265). Serves 4-6.

TRICK: Use the liquid from the mushrooms in place of part of the milk.

JIFFY SHRIMP

2-quart sauce pan . . . Cooking time—about 15 minutes

4 hard-cooked eggs (page 273)	1 tablespoon parsley, chopped
1 can (7 ounces) shrimp	1 tablespoon green onion,
2 cans condensed cream of	chopped
mushroom soup	1 teaspoon paprika
½ cup milk	¼ cup sherry

Chop eggs and combine with remaining ingredients. Heat slowly to boiling point. Serve on toast or Chinese omelet (page 276). Serves 4-6.

SHRIMP JAMBALAYA

Large skillet with cover . . . Cooking time—about 35 minutes

3 tablespoons butter or marga-	1 cup rice, uncooked
rine	1 can (4 ounces) mushrooms,
1 medium onion, chopped	with liquid
½ green pepper, chopped	1½ cups shrimp, cut in halves
1 clove garlic, finely minced	(canned or fresh)
3 cups tomato juice	¼ cup pimiento, cut into strips
1 teaspoon salt	

Melt butter or margarine in large skillet. Add onion, green pepper, and garlic. Cook until lightly browned. Add tomato juice, salt, rice, and mushrooms with liquid. Cover. When mixture reaches full steam, turn heat to simmer setting. Continue cooking for 25 minutes, or until rice is tender. Add shrimp and pimiento. Cook until shrimp is thoroughly heated, about 10 minutes. Serves 6.

CREOLE SHRIMP

Skillet with cover . . . Cooking time—30-40 minutes

3 tablespoons all-purpose flour	1 clove of garlic, chopped
3 tablespoons bacon drippings	1½ tablespoons parsley, chopped
2 cups cooked tomatoes	1½ cups hot water
⅓ cup tomato paste	2 teaspoons salt
6 tablespoons onion, chopped	¼ teaspoon pepper
6 tablespoons green pepper,	1 can (7 ounces) shrimp
chopped	Rice (page 265)

Brown the flour in the bacon drippings as for gravy. Add the rest of the ingredients except the shrimp and bring to a rolling boil.

Reduce heat to simmer and cook for 20 minutes. Add shrimp and continue cooking for another 10 minutes. Serve on rice. If fresh shrimp is used, simmer for 15 minutes instead of 10 minutes. Serves 6.

FRENCH-FRIED SHRIMP—See Deep-Fat-Fried Foods, page 234.

SHRIMP NEWBURG

8-inch skillet . . . Cooking time——15 minutes

1 cup butter or margarine	2 tablespoons Worcestershire
3 pounds fresh cooked shrimp	sauce
12 tablespoons cornstarch	3 cups top milk
2 teaspoons salt	2 cups heavy cream
¼ teaspoon cayenne pepper	1 cup sherry
2 teaspoons paprika	
1 teaspoon monosodium gluta-	
mate	

Melt butter or margarine in skillet and to it add the shrimp, which have been cut in halves. Stir until shrimp are well coated with butter, then add cornstarch. Continue stirring until cornstarch is well blended. Add other seasonings; then add milk and cream slowly, stirring constantly while adding. When mixture has thickened, add sherry very slowly. Blend into mixture. Serve over Holland rusk, toast, or crackers. Serves 12.

HOT SEA FOOD SALAD

Individual shells or ramekins . . . Preheated oven—350° F. . . . Baking time—25-30 minutes

6 tablespoons green pepper,	1 cup shrimp
chopped	½ teaspoon salt
3 tablespoons onion, chopped	½ teaspoon pepper
1 cup celery, chopped	½ teaspoon Worcestershire sauce
1 cup mayonnaise	¾ cup crushed potato chips
1 cup crab meat	

Mix all ingredients together except potato chips. Fill individual shells or ramekins, or if neither is available, spread in well-greased 8-inch square pan. Sprinkle potato chips over top. Bake. Serve at once. Serves 6-8.

LOBSTER

To Cook Lobster

Lobster is cooked as directed for hard-shell crabs, page 116.

MAINE LOBSTER DE LUXE

Large kettle . . . Preheated oven—450° F. . . . Baking time—10-15 minutes

4 medium-sized lobsters	½ cup cream
3 small lobsters	2 egg yolks
1 cup diced celery and celery tops	1 cup lobster stock
¼ cup parsley	1 cup toasted bread cubes
2 teaspoons salt	2 tablespoons sherry
2 tablespoons butter or margarine	1 cup fine bread or cracker crumbs

Drop live lobsters into kettle of boiling salted water. Boil 10 minutes. Set 4 medium-sized lobsters to one side, belly side up, so juice does not run out of shell. Remove meat from 3 small lobsters. Cook lobster shells with celery, parsley, and salt for about 15 minutes. Longer if you wish. Strain. This becomes the lobster stock. To make the dressing, melt butter or margarine over low heat, add cream and egg yolks. Stir as this thickens. Add lobster stock. Cook until slightly thickened. Remove from range, add lobster meat, toasted bread cubes, and sherry.

Split the four lobsters which have been set aside. Remove intestinal vein, stomach, and liver. Cut under shell from tail so meat will show, crack large claws, fill body cavity with the dressing. Be generous. Sprinkle with fine bread crumbs. Bake. Set under broiler to brown bread crumbs. Serves 4.

TRICK: Make this in advance of need. Store in refrigerator until ready to broil for serving.

MAINE LOBSTER NO. 2

Large kettle . . . Preheated oven—450° F. . . . Baking time—19
minutes (no more)

4 medium-sized lobsters	¼ cup whole milk
16 round crackers, rolled fine	¼ cup sherry
1 teaspoon salt	1 pound fresh crab meat
¼ teaspoon pepper	1 cup Parmesan cheese
¼ cup melted butter or marga-rine	1 teaspoon paprika

Prepare fresh lobster as on page 122, or buy them already prepared. Roll crackers very fine. Season with salt and pepper. Mix
crumbs with melted butter or margarine, ¼ cup milk, and add
sherry until mixture is a soft consistency, but not runny. Stir in
crab meat and stuff lobster as full as possible. Sprinkle cheese
and paprika over top. Bake. Serve with melted butter or margarine. Serves 4.

LOBSTER NEWBURG

3-quart saucepan . . . Cooking time—about 15 minutes

2 cups fresh or canned lobster meat, or 2 medium-small fresh lobster tails	½ teaspoon sodium monogluta-mate
½ cup butter	1½ cups milk
3 tablespoons cornstarch	1 cup heavy cream
1 teaspoon paprika	2 eggs, beaten
½ teaspoon salt	½ cup sherry

If you use lobster tails, cook as follows: Bring water to a boil in
large utensil. Add 2 tablespoons of tarragon vinegar and 1 teaspoon salt (or 2 tablespoons cider vinegar and ¼ teaspoon powdered tarragon may be used). When water is boiling vigorously,
add lobster tails and continue cooking for 20 minutes. Lobster
shells will be pink. Allow lobster to cool in liquid in which they
were cooked. When cool, shell and cut lobster meat into pieces.

Sauté lobster meat in butter which has been melted in large
skillet. Use medium heat and do not brown. Cook gently so lobster meat is not broken into fine pieces. Blend cornstarch and seasonings. Blend into butter and lobster. Add milk and cream, stirring constantly until mixture thickens. Just before serving, add
eggs, then slowly add sherry. *Be Sure* lobster mixture is not at the
boiling point when eggs and sherry are added, or mixture will
curdle. Serves 6.

OYSTERS

ESCALLOPED OYSTERS

1½-quart casserole . . . Preheated oven—400° F. . . . Baking time—
30 minutes

1 cup coarsely crumbed crack-
    ers
1 pint oysters
8 tablespoons butter or marga-
    rine

1 teaspoon salt
½ teaspoon pepper
1½ cups milk

Place one half the crackers in bottom of greased casserole. Add
half the oysters. Dot generously with butter or margarine. Sprinkle with salt and pepper. Add ¾ cup of the milk. Repeat. Bake.
Serves 4.

Vegetables

Vegetables are one of our most essential foods. In fact, they should form a good part of our daily diet, for they contain a generous supply of the vitamins and minerals we all need for health. However, too often, far too often, they lose much of their nutritional value before they reach the table because of faulty or careless cooking. Vegetables can offer us a priceless gift of health-protecting food elements. We owe it to ourselves to take the trouble to cook them properly.

But careful cooking of vegetables does more than protect your health. It also rewards your palate! Many people who say that they don't like vegetables have simply never had a chance to find out how good tasting a well-cooked vegetable can be.

Here are a few simple rules for cooking vegetables. Try them—if only for an experiment. You'll be surprised at how quickly your family will notice the difference in flavor of the vegetables you cook this way, and you may think it worth while to cook your vegetables this way all the time.

Four Simple Rules for Protective Cooking of Vegetables

1. Use Little or No Water

To minimize mineral and vitamin loss, most vegetables should be cooked in only ¼ to ½ cup water. When you are cooking with 2 tablespoons water or less, first place 2 tablespoons butter or margarine in utensil, then water, then vegetables. Spinach and other greens require only the water which clings to leaves after washing. Tomatoes require no water. (These amounts of water are for cooking on electric ranges. If you are using a gas range, it may be necessary to increase amount of water used.)

2. Start Fast—Cook Quickly

Bring vegetables to steaming point on high heat, then turn control to low.

3. Avoid Violent Boiling

4. Cook in Covered Utensils

Do not stir, for this fills food with extra air which destroys certain vitamins.

The following tables for cooking vegetables are based on 4 servings, or 1½ pounds of fresh edible vegetable. For most vegetables, use 6-inch unit and a 2-quart covered saucepan. Salt to taste.

Vegetables That Cook in 10-15 Minutes

Practically all frozen vegetables cook in 10 minutes. Use 2 to 4 tablespoons of water. The following fresh vegetables also cook in 10-15 minutes after steaming point is reached.

Asparagus
Brussels Sprouts, whole
Cabbage, shredded
Carrots, sliced thin
Celery, cut in ½-inch pieces
Eggplant, cut in cubes

Lima Beans
Garden Peas
Spinach
Summer Squash
Tomatoes

Vegetables That Cook in 20-25 Minutes

Beets
Broccoli
Cabbage, quartered
Snap Beans, young and whole
Snap Beans, old, and cut in 1-inch lengths or shoestringed

Carrots, cut in half lengthwise
Cauliflower
Kale
Onions
Parsnips, halves with center core out
Potatoes (Sweet or Irish), cut in half if small, quartered if large
Rutabagas, cut in ¼- to ½-inch slices or diced
Hubbard Squash, removed from shell, diced in ½-inch cubes
Turnips, cut in ¼- to ½-inch slices

Artichokes cook in 30-45 minutes. Cook whole in enough water to cover, to which has been added 1 tablespoon vinegar, 2 teaspoons salt. (Add 1 clove garlic if you prefer.) Add artichokes after water comes to boil. Cook in 5- or 6-quart covered saucepan.

Cooking in Pressure Cooker

If you use a pressure cooker, stand by and watch it, and the clock like a hawk. Many vegetables, if pressure cooked even a minute too long, lose flavor as well as vitamins. A pressure cooker is fine, if the timing is done accurately.

How to Cook Most Canned Vegetables

To cook any vegetable canned with liquid, such as peas, snap beans, carrots, etc., first drain liquid into saucepan. Boil down to about ½ the amount. Add vegetables and heat. Season to taste. Serve immediately after vegetable has heated through.

Tomatoes, corn, etc., are placed in saucepan and heated.

Frozen Vegetables

Frozen vegetables should be cooked from the frozen state, in as little water as possible. For really delicious frozen peas, beans, and so forth, use 2 tablespoons water, 2 tablespoons butter or margarine, add frozen vegetable, cover, and cook 8-10 minutes. Break the frozen block into several sections by hitting package several times against edge of kitchen table. Vegetables cook much better if frozen block is broken.

Exception: Corn on the cob must be completely thawed before cooking; otherwise, the cob will remain cold and spoil the flavor of the kernel.

COOKING INDIVIDUAL VEGETABLES

ARTICHOKES

Cook according to directions on page 127.

May be served hot, as part of main course, or chilled, as a salad.

To Serve Hot

Have a small side dish of melted butter or margarine or hollandaise sauce. Pluck off leaf, dip the tip of it into the sauce. Place the soft or inner edge between the teeth and pull gently, scraping off the pulpy portion. Discard the rest of the leaf. Continue until you reach the center, or "choke." This is an inverted cone-shaped segment you will want to cut around, remove, and discard. The "heart" of the artichoke—that is, the base from which you have removed the choke—will remain. You will find it delicious, particularly when dipped, with the aid of your fork, into the remaining sauce.

To Serve as a Salad

Served and eaten the same way, cold artichoke will taste best with a dip of French dressing or mayonnaise. Be sure to chill them in the refrigerator, since a lukewarm artichoke pleases no one.

ASPARAGUS

How to Buy

One pound of fresh asparagus will serve two or three people.

How to Cook

Steamed Asparagus—Method No. 1

Use deep well cooker on your electric range, or any other pot deep enough for the asparagus to stand upright, yet still be covered.

Wash asparagus carefully, snapping off tough lower portions. It's a good idea to remove the scales, too, for there is apt to be sand under them. Stand, tip ends up, in mesh wire basket.

Put 1 cup of water and 1 teaspoon salt in deep utensil. Bring to a boiling point. Lower basket of asparagus into utensil, making sure that the water doesn't come into actual contact with the asparagus. Cover and steam for 15 minutes.

If you have no cooking pan deep enough, try a coffeepot. Since you will not be able to use a wire basket, the lower portion of the asparagus will have to stand in the water. Still, the tips of the asparagus will be out of the water and will not overcook.

Method No. 2

If you have neither a deep pot nor a coffeepot you can use, you will have to make do with a saucepan. In that case, use only enough water to cover the bottom of the utensil. Bring water to boiling point, placing a trivet in the pan if you have one, and then carefully lay the asparagus flat in the pan. Use this method only if absolutely necessary, for it will always mean that the tips of your asparagus will cook more quickly than the stalks, so that one end will be improperly cooked when you serve the vegetable.

How to Cook Frozen Asparagus

Cook from frozen state. Steam if possible. If not, melt butter or margarine, add seasonings, and cook the frozen asparagus in the melted shortening. Start on high heat until steaming, then reduce to low setting. Cook about 10 minutes.

How to Open Canned Asparagus

Open the bottom of the can, rather than the top. It's easier to remove the asparagus without bruising the tip ends.

How to Serve

1. Piping hot with melted butter or margarine.
2. Piping hot with browned butter or margarine. Brown a few slivered almonds in the butter or margarine. Delicious.
3. On toast with melted butter or margarine. Butter the toast, too.
4. Add some chopped, hard-cooked eggs to medium white sauce (page 245) and serve over asparagus, either plain or on toast.
5. Serve with hollandaise sauce (page 242).

ASPARAGUS WITH CHEESE SAUCE

2-quart saucepan . . . Cooking time—about 15 minutes

2 tablespoons butter or margarine	1 can (No. 2) asparagus, or 1 pound fresh, cooked
2 tablespoons all-purpose flour	1 teaspoon salt
1 cup milk	1/8 teaspoon pepper
1 cup American cheese, grated	4 slices bacon, chopped
	4 slices toast

Make a white sauce by melting butter or margarine and blending in the flour. Add the milk and stir until sauce thickens. Let cook over low heat for 5 minutes. Add cheese, and when cheese has melted, remove from heat and add asparagus, cut into 1-inch lengths, and the salt and pepper. Fry bacon until crisp and drain on absorbent paper. Serve creamed asparagus on toast slices with bacon sprinkled over the top. Serves 4.

ASPARAGUS RAMEKINS

4 ramekin or custard cups . . . Preheated oven—350° F. . . . Baking time—45-50 minutes, or until a knife inserted in center comes out clean

3 tablespoons butter or margarine	1½ cups chopped, drained, cooked asparagus
3 tablespoons all-purpose flour	2 cans (2¼ ounces each) deviled ham
1½ teaspoons salt	Dash of pepper
1½ cups milk	Paprika
3 eggs, slightly beaten	

Melt butter or margarine in a saucepan over medium heat. Blend in flour and salt. Add milk, stirring until thickened. Beat eggs and stir white sauce into eggs a small amount at a time. Add asparagus, ham, and pepper and mix well. Pour into cups. Sprinkle with paprika. Set in a pan of hot water. Bake. Makes 4 servings.

ASPARAGUS AU GRATIN

2-quart casserole . . . Preheated oven—350° F. . . . Baking time— 30 minutes

1 pound cooked asparagus, or 1 box frozen asparagus, cooked, or 1 can (No. 2) asparagus	Liquid from asparagus and enough milk to make 1½ cups
2 tablespoons butter or margarine	1 cup Cheddar cheese, grated
2 tablespoons all-purpose flour	4 hard-cooked eggs, sliced
½ teaspoon salt	½ cup soft bread crumbs
	Paprika

Save liquid from asparagus. Melt butter or margarine, and blend in flour and salt. Add liquid and cook until thickened, stirring frequently. Remove from heat. Add cheese; stir until cheese is melted. Alternate layers of hard-cooked eggs (page 273), asparagus, and cheese sauce. Cover with bread crumbs in greased casserole. Sprinkle paprika over crumbs. Bake. Serves 4.

SNAP BEANS

How to Buy

1½ pounds good quality snap beans will serve 4.

How to Cook

Wash carefully, break off stem end, but leave blossom end on. Many healthful vitamins are hidden in blossom end. If beans are young and tender, cook whole. If not, snap in 1-inch pieces, or shoestring by cutting lengthwise. Place ¼ cup water and 1 teaspoon salt in saucepan. Add beans. Cover. When steaming, reduce heat to low setting. Cook 20-25 minutes. Drain liquid. Add 2 tablespoons butter, margarine, or bacon drippings. Reheat quickly. Serve very hot. Serves 4.

SNAP BEANS WITH CRUMB TOPPING

2-quart covered saucepan . . . Cooking time—20-25 minutes

3 tablespoons butter, margarine, or drippings	1 tablespoon parsley, chopped
½ cup dry bread crumbs	½ teaspoon onion, grated
2 tablespoons raw carrot, grated	¼ teaspoon salt
	1 pound snap beans, cooked

Melt shortening and add bread crumbs. Remove from heat. Add carrots, parsley, onion, and salt. Place hot beans in serving dish and sprinkle with topping. Serves 6.

Buttered Crumbs

3 tablespoons butter or margarine	1 cup fine bread crumbs

Melt butter or margarine in small skillet or saucepan over low heat. Add crumbs and stir until crumbs are coated. If not used at once, these should be stored in covered container in refrigerator to prevent butter from becoming rancid.

SCALLOPED SNAP BEANS

Shallow baking dish . . . Preheated oven—350° F. . . . Baking time— 35 minutes

1½ pounds snap beans, cooked	⅓ cup cheese, grated
1½ teaspoons salt	½ cup soft bread crumbs
1 can condensed cream of tomato soup	4 tablespoons butter or other shortening

Cook beans in salted water until tender. Place beans in a shallow greased baking dish. Cover with the tomato soup; sprinkle with grated cheese, then the bread crumbs, which have been buttered. (See page 131.) Bake. Serves 6.

CREAMED FRESH SNAP BEANS

8-inch skillet . . . Cooking time—20-25 minutes

1½ pounds fresh snap beans	3 tablespoons water
2 tablespoons butter, marga- rine, or bacon drippings	1 teaspoon salt
	½ cup light cream

Wash beans carefully. Snap off stem end. If beans are tough, snap into 1-inch pieces. Place shortening in skillet. When melted, add water, salt, and beans. Cover. Cook over high heat until steaming, then turn to low. Cook for 20-25 minutes. Just before ready to serve, add cream. Turn control to high and bring cream to a quick steam. Serve at once. Serves 4.

SNAP BEANS AU GRATIN

2-quart casserole . . . Preheated oven—350° F. . . . Baking time—45 minutes

2½ cups cut snap beans, cooked	½ teaspoon pepper
4 tablespoons butter or marga- rine	1 cup milk
4 tablespoons all-purpose flour	½ cup liquid from beans
½ teaspoon salt	1 cup Cheddar cheese, grated Paprika

Place beans in a greased casserole. Melt butter or margarine and add flour and seasonings. Add milk slowly, stirring constantly until thickened. Add bean liquid and grated cheese. Pour over beans, sprinkle with a little paprika, and bake. Serves 4-5.

DUTCH SNAP BEANS

2-quart covered saucepan . . . Cooking time—25 minutes

2 slices bacon, diced	⅛ teaspoon pepper
4 tablespoons onion, diced	1 cup hot water
2 tablespoons all-purpose flour	1 tablespoon vinegar
1 teaspoon salt	4 cups snap beans, cooked

Brown the bacon, add onion, and brown lightly. Add flour and seasonings and brown. Add hot water and cook, stirring constantly until smooth and thickened. Add vinegar and beans. Heat thoroughly. Serves 6.

FROZEN OR FRESH SNAP BEAN CASSEROLE

2-quart uncovered casserole . . . Cold or preheated oven—350° F.
. . . Baking time—45 minutes to 1 hour

2 cups cooked snap beans, or	1 can (4 ounces) broken pieces of
1 package frozen beans	mushrooms (optional)
1 can condensed cream of mush-	1 teaspoon salt
room soup	

Place cooked beans or frozen beans (do not thaw) in greased casserole. Pour contents of can of mushroom soup over beans. If additional mushrooms are used, place these over beans; add salt. Cooked, whole, medium-size onions may be used instead of beans, if desired. Serves 4.

CELERY AND SNAP BEANS

2-quart covered saucepan . . . Cooking time—10 minutes

2 cups cooked or canned snap	½ teaspoon salt
beans	⅛ teaspoon pepper
½ cup cooked celery	1 tablespoon butter or
½ cup vegetable liquid or water	margarine

Place all ingredients in saucepan. Cook for 10 minutes. Serves 4.

BUTTERED SNAP BEANS

2-quart covered saucepan . . . Cooking time—10 minutes

2 cups drained canned snap	½ teaspoon salt
beans, or 1 pound fresh,	⅛ teaspoon pepper
cooked	1 tablespoon butter or
⅓ cup vegetable liquid	margarine

Mix ingredients. Bring to a boil and heat 10 minutes. Serves 4.

Variations

With thyme—Add ⅛ teaspoon thyme to above mixture.

With onions—Brown 2 tablespoons grated onions in 1 tablespoon butter or margarine. Add to first mixture and cook for 10 minutes.

With other vegetables—Combine with equal quantities of hot, cooked carrots, celery, peas, lima beans, or onions. Butter or cream to taste.

With salt pork or bacon—Fry ¼ cup diced salt pork or diced bacon until brown. Add snap beans and cook as buttered snap beans. Omit other shortening.

GREEN SNAP BEANS WITH SOUR CREAM—NO. 1

2-quart uncovered casserole . . . Preheated oven—350° F. . . . Baking time—40-45 minutes

2 packages French-style frozen snap beans, or 2 pounds fresh snap beans	1 cup thick sour cream
	½ teaspoon salt
	⅛ teaspoon pepper
¼ pound sharp Cheddar cheese	

Cook frozen snap beans until thoroughly heated through. If you use fresh snap beans, cook about 15 minutes. Drain thoroughly. Cut cheese in small cubes. When beans are cool, mix cheese, sour cream, and seasonings lightly through the beans. Place in greased uncovered casserole. Bake. Serves 6-8.

TRICK: Serve these at a party. Save yourself precious time by putting ingredients in the casserole ahead of time. Then pop them in the oven 45 minutes before ready to serve.

GREEN BEANS WITH SOUR CREAM—NO. 2

2 tablespoons butter or margarine	½ cup sour cream
	¼ cup shredded, blanched almonds
1 medium-sized onion, grated	
1 can (4 ounces) mushrooms, sliced	1 package frozen French-style snap beans
1 tablespoon all-purpose flour	½ teaspoon salt

Melt butter or margarine in skillet. Sauté onion and mushrooms. Blend in flour. Add sour cream and almonds. Turn heat to simmer. Cook green beans according to directions on page 127 and add salt to beans. Do not overcook. Add cooked beans to sauce and continue to simmer 10 minutes. Serves 4.

TRICK: Sauce may be prepared in advance. Then all you need do is cook beans, place in sauce, and reheat. Or, if you are doing an oven meal, make sauce, cook beans, place in greased casserole, and cook for 30-40 minutes.

LIMA BEANS AND DRIED BEANS

How to Buy Lima Beans

1½ pounds in the shell will serve 2.

How to Cook Lima Beans

Wash pod carefully before shelling. Then you won't have to wash the shelled bean and thereby wash away valuable vitamins and minerals.

Lima beans have a tendency to scorch easily. Watch them carefully while cooking.

Place ½ cup water and 1 teaspoon salt in saucepan. Add shelled beans. Cover. Cook over high heat until steaming. Then reduce heat to low setting. Cook 15 minutes. Serve with butter or margarine. May be served with cream instead of butter or margarine.

To Cook Frozen Lima Beans

2-quart covered saucepan . . . Cooking time—10 minutes

⅓ cup cream
2 tablespoons butter or
    margarine

1 teaspoon salt
1 package frozen lima beans

Place cream, butter or margarine, and salt in saucepan. Break block of frozen lima beans in several pieces. An easy way to do this is to hit the package hard against the end of the kitchen table.

Add frozen lima beans. Cover. Cook over high heat until steaming. Then turn heat to low setting. Cook about 10 minutes. You may need to lift cover and stir once to make sure frozen blocks of beans are breaking up. Serves 4.

LIMA BEAN SCALLOP

2-quart casserole . . . Preheated oven—375° F. . . . Baking time—
    30 minutes

1½ cups dried lima beans
3 cups water
2 teaspoons onion, finely
    chopped
5 tablespoons shortening
4 tablespoons all-purpose flour
1½ teaspoons salt

⅛ teaspoon pepper
1 cup evaporated milk
¾ cup liquid drained from
    beans
1 cup grated cheese
¼ cup bread crumbs

Wash beans and soak overnight in the 3 cups water. In the morning, cook on simmer heat until beans are tender (about 2 hours). Drain beans and save liquid. Cook onion in shortening until tender, but not brown (5 minutes). Blend in the flour and add the salt and pepper. Add the milk and ¾ cup liquid from the beans, stirring constantly until thickened. Add cheese, stirring only until cheese is melted. Put alternate layers of beans and cheese sauce into greased casserole. Sprinkle with the bread crumbs. Bake. Serves 6-8.

LIMA BEAN CAKES WITH CREOLE SAUCE

8-inch skillet . . . Cooking time—about 15 minutes

1½ cups cooked, mashed lima beans	½ teaspoon sage
1 cup soft bread crumbs	½ teaspoon salt
⅓ cup onion, minced	⅛ teaspoon pepper
	3 tablespoons drippings

Combine mashed beans, bread crumbs, onion, and seasonings. Shape into flat cakes. Brown on both sides in the hot drippings. Serve with Creole sauce (see page 242). Makes 6 cakes.

CREAMED DRIED LIMA BEANS

2-quart covered saucepan . . . Cooking time—about 1½ hours

1½ cups dry lima beans	¼ teaspoon pepper
3 cups cold water	1 tablespoon butter or
½ cup cream or top milk	margarine
1 teaspoon salt	

Wash beans, then soak in cold water several hours. Cook beans slowly until tender in water in which they were soaked. Drain. Add remaining ingredients, heat, and serve. Serves 6.

BAKED LIMA BEANS WITH SOUR CREAM

3-quart casserole . . . Preheated oven—375° F. . . . Baking time— 1 hour

2 cups dried lima beans	⅛ teaspoon pepper
2 teaspoons salt	1 cup sour cream
½ teaspoon dried mustard	3 strips bacon
¼ cup brown sugar	

Wash beans, then soak overnight in enough water to cover. Cook beans slowly until tender in water in which they were soaked. Add 1 teaspoon of the salt and ¼ teaspoon of the dried mustard when beans are partly cooked.

Drain, reserving bean liquid, and place beans in buttered casserole. Add sugar, remainder of salt, dried mustard, and pepper and mix well. Add the cream and 1 cup of bean liquid. Lay strips of bacon over beans. Cover and bake. Serves 6-8.

BAKED LIMA BEANS

Covered casserole . . . Preheated oven—350° F. . . . Baking time—
1½ hours

1½ cups dried lima beans	1 tablespoon brown sugar
3 cups water	1 teaspoon salt
½ pound salt pork, diced	¼ teaspoon dry mustard
1 tablespoon Sorghum molasses	

Pick over and wash lima beans carefully. Soak in water overnight. In the morning, add the salt pork to the beans and cook on simmer heat until tender in the same water in which the beans were soaked. Drain and reserve liquid. Place lima beans in greased casserole. Combine molasses, brown sugar, salt, and mustard. Add bean liquid to make 1 cup. If there is not enough liquid, add water. Pour over lima beans and cover. Bake. Serves 6.

BAKED NAVY BEANS

Bean pot or covered casserole . . . Preheated oven—300° F. . . .
   Baking time—6-8 hours

1 quart dried navy beans	1 teaspoon dry mustard
6 cups water	1 pound salt pork, scored down
1 tablespoon salt	to rind, but not through rind
½ cup Sorghum molasses	1 large onion, peeled and scored
½ cup brown sugar	on top

Wash beans and discard imperfect ones. Cover with cold water and soak overnight. The next morning drain off water, place beans in large kettle. Cover with 6 cups water, or more if necessary. Cook slowly until skins burst when you take out a few and blow on them. Drain. Save the liquid. Now mix the salt, molasses, brown sugar, and mustard with the liquid.

Place beans in bean pot or covered casserole. Lay salt pork and onion on top of beans. Add the liquid. Cover. Bake. You may need to add more liquid. The last half hour of cooking, remove the cover. Serves 10-12.

If you have any beans left over, freeze them.

BAKED KIDNEY BEANS—Follow same procedure as described above for Navy Beans.

QUICK BAKED BEANS

2-quart casserole . . . Cold or preheated oven, 350° F. . . . Baking
time—1 hour

3 slices bacon, chopped	½ cup Sorghum molasses
1 onion, chopped	1 tablespoon prepared mustard
1 green pepper, chopped	2 cans (No. 2) baked beans

Fry bacon until crisp. Add onion and green pepper and cook until
onions are clear. Add remaining ingredients and place in baking
dish. If there is too much liquid on canned beans, drain before
adding. Bake. Serves 5-6.

SAVORY DRIED BEANS

2-quart covered saucepan . . . Cooking time—1½-2 hours

1 cup dried beans (any kind)	1 teaspoon salt
2 cups water	⅛ teaspoon pepper
2 tablespoons bacon drippings	⅛ teaspoon thyme
or butter or margarine	1 small bay leaf
2 teaspoons onion, grated	

Wash and soak beans overnight in the 2 cups water. In the morning, bring the beans to a boil in the same water and then cook
slowly until tender. Twenty minutes before serving, add the shortening, onion, salt, pepper, thyme, and bay leaf and let simmer
until serving time. Serves 4.

HOT PINTO BEANS

2-quart covered saucepan . . . Cooking time—1½-2 hours

2 cups washed pinto beans	1 teaspoon salt
1 quart water	⅛ teaspoon pepper
⅓ pound salt pork	

Wash beans and soak in water overnight. Dice salt pork, add to
the beans, and cook slowly until tender in the same water in which
they were soaked. Add salt and pepper and serve hot. Serves 8.

DRIED BEANS WITH MUSTARD SAUCE

2-quart covered saucepan . . . Cooking time—1½-2 hours

1 cup dried beans (any kind)	1 teaspoon sugar
2 cups water	2 tablespoons butter or margarine
1 teaspoon salt	or drippings
1 teaspoon dry mustard	1 teaspoon lemon juice

Wash and soak beans overnight. Cook until tender in the same water in which they were soaked. Drain, reserving ½ cup of the liquid. Combine the ½ cup liquid with the salt, mustard, sugar, shortening, and lemon juice. Pour over the beans, bring to a boil, and cook 2 minutes. Fresh lima beans may also be prepared in this way. Serves 4.

PANNED RED KIDNEY BEANS

2-quart covered saucepan . . . Cooking time—1½-2 hours

1½ cups dried beans	1 cup onion, finely chopped
3 cups water	1½ teaspoons salt
2 slices bacon	⅛ teaspoon pepper

Wash beans and soak overnight in the water. Next day cook beans until tender in the same water in which they were soaked. Fry bacon until crisp, add onions, and sauté until lightly browned. Pour over beans and add salt and pepper. Serves 5.

KIDNEY BEAN LOAF

Loaf pan . . . Preheated oven—325° F. . . . Baking time—1½ hours

2 cups dried kidney beans	½ cup shortening
2 cups water	1 egg
4 cups stale bread crumbs	1½ teaspoons salt
2 cups cheese, grated	½ teaspoon pepper
½ cup onion, chopped	

Wash beans, then soak overnight in the 2 cups water. In the morning, bring to a boil in the same liquid and then simmer until beans are tender. Drain. Mash beans fine and add all the other ingredients, mixing well. Pack into loaf pan and bake. Baste occasionally with 1 tablespoon melted butter or margarine and ¼ cup water. Serves 6-8.

BEETS

How to Buy

1½ pounds will serve 4. Try to buy fresh beets with nice green tops. Use the tops for beet greens.

How to Cook

If the beets are young and tender, peel them and either slice, dice, or shred.

Put ¼ cup water, 1 teaspoon salt, 2 tablespoons butter or margarine in saucepan. Add prepared beets. Cover. Bring to quick steam on high heat. Then reduce heat to low. Total cooking time is about 10 minutes.

If beats are old and tough, do not peel them. Wash carefully. Cover with water and cook 30-40 minutes. Peel as soon as beets can be handled after cooking. Slice. The best way to use such beets is to pickle them.

To do this: Mix ½ cup water, ½ cup vinegar, ¼ cup brown sugar, 1 teaspoon salt, ½ teaspoon cinnamon, 6 or 8 whole cloves, and bring to boiling point. Pour over sliced, cooked beets. Some people like to add a couple of hard-cooked eggs to their pickled beets.

HARVARD BEETS

1-quart saucepan . . . Cooking time—15 minutes

⅓ cup sugar	½ teaspoon salt
2 tablespoons all-purpose flour	2 tablespoons butter or
¼ cup water	margarine
½ cup mild vinegar	2 cups cooked beets, diced

Mix sugar and flour together in saucepan. Add water and vinegar. Cook on medium heat until thick, stirring occasionally. Add salt, butter or margarine, and diced beets. Cook until beets are heated through. Serves 4-5.

BROCCOLI

How to Buy

1½ pounds will serve 4.

How to Cook

Soak broccoli in cold water, using ¼ cup salt to each quart water. Broccoli is a favorite hiding place for little worms, and soaking makes them come out of hiding. Soak for about 15 minutes. Then, remove tough lower portion, any coarse leaves, and peel off the coarse outer portion of the stalk. If stalks are large, slit them in half, lengthwise.

Place ¼ to ½ cup water and 1 teaspoon salt in saucepan. Add prepared broccoli. Cover. Bring to steam on high heat, then reduce heat to lower setting. Cook 15-20 minutes. Serve with melted butter or margarine, mock hollandaise sauce (page 243), or hollandaise sauce (page 242). Almonds, cut lengthwise and browned in butter or margarine, also make a pleasant topping for broccoli.

Frozen Broccoli

Break the block of frozen broccoli. Follow directions for cooking on page 127. Add 3 tablespoons butter or margarine and 1 teaspoon salt.

BRUSSELS SPROUTS

How to Buy

1½ pounds will serve 4. Buy nice green ones. The yellow ones are old.

How to Cook

Soak in cold salted water, as directed above for broccoli and for the same reason. Cut off stem end and any wilted leaves before soaking. Cook as for broccoli, using only ¼ cup water. Don't overcook; they become limp and tasteless.

CABBAGE

How to Buy

Heads should be firm. Medium-sized head will serve 4. There are many interesting varieties on the market: young green cabbage, the beautiful savoy cabbage with its crinkly leaves, Chinese cabbage, and the delicious red cabbage. One cannot overlook, however, the good, sturdy, solid heads of white cabbage which are usually available in early winter and are always good.

How to Cook

Remove any wilted leaves from a young green cabbage. Cut cabbage in quarters and shred medium fine. Place 2 tablespoons water, 2 tablespoons butter or margarine, 1 teaspoon salt in saucepan. Add shredded cabbage. Cover. Cook over high heat until steaming. Then turn to low. Total cooking time is 7-10 minutes.

SCALLOPED CABBAGE

2-quart casserole . . . Cold or preheated oven—350° F. Baking
time—1 hour

4 cups cooked cabbage	Salt and pepper to taste
2 cups white sauce	¼ cup buttered bread crumbs

Place layer of cooked cabbage in greased casserole, cover with
white sauce (page 245), season with salt and pepper. Add second
layer of cabbage and white sauce. Top with bread crumbs. Bake.
Do not cover. Serves 4-6.

HOT CABBAGE SLAW

2-quart covered saucepan . . . Cooking time—10 minutes

3 tablespoons butter or margarine	1 tablespoon water
¼ cup onion, finely grated	1 teaspoon salt
1 medium-sized head of cabbage, shredded fine	

Place butter or margarine and onion in saucepan. Cook on high
heat until shortening is melted. Add cabbage, water, and salt.
Cover. Let come to full steam. Remove cover, blend dressing (see
below) through cabbage, using a fork. Cover. Cook 1 minute
longer. Serve at once. Serves 4.

Dressing

1 egg	4 tablespoons vinegar
½ cup sour cream	

Beat egg slightly. Add sour cream, vinegar, beating thoroughly.
Use fork to toss dressing through cabbage.

TENNESSEE CABBAGE

8-inch covered skillet . . . Cooking time—15 minutes

3 tablespoons butter or margarine	⅛ teaspoon pepper
5 cups cabbage, shredded	1 teaspoon salt
	½ cup cream or evaporated milk

Put butter or margarine into a skillet and let brown slightly. Add
cabbage and stir well. Cover skillet tightly and simmer for 5 minutes. Stir and cook another 5 minutes. Add pepper, salt, and cream

or evaporated milk. Cover and simmer 4 more minutes. It is very important not to overcook the cabbage. Serves 5.

SAUERKRAUT

8-inch covered skillet . . . Cooking time—25-30 minutes

2 tablespoons drippings	1 can (No. 2½) or 1 quart sauerkraut

Heat drippings in utensil until beginning to brown. Add sauerkraut, juice and all. Bring to boil, reduce heat. Cook in covered utensil. Serves 4.

SWEET-SOUR RED CABBAGE

3-quart covered saucepan . . . Cooking time—25-30 minutes

3 tablespoons butter, margarine or bacon drippings	3 tart apples, sliced thin
1 small onion, finely minced	¼ cup mild vinegar
4 tablespoons brown sugar	Salt and pepper to taste
1 medium head red cabbage, shredded (about 4-5 cups)	

Melt shortening and add onion and brown sugar. Cook until a golden yellow. Add remaining ingredients. Cover. Cook on high heat until steaming, then reduce to low heat. Serves 4.

CARROTS

How to Buy

Young carrots should have bright green tops. Old carrots should be firm. 1½ pounds will serve 4.

How to Cook

Wash carrots and scrape. Some people leave outer skin on when preparing young carrots. Suit yourself about that point.

If carrots are young and tender, leave whole or cut in half lengthwise. Otherwise better slice them in about ½-inch slices.

Put 2 tablespoons butter or margarine, 2 tablespoons water, and carrots in saucepan. Cover. Cook on high heat until steaming, then reduce heat to low. Cook 10-15 minutes, depending upon size of carrots.

DUTCH CARROTS

2-quart covered saucepan . . . Cooking time—10 minutes

3 slices bacon	4 cups cooked carrots, diced
½ cup onion, sliced	Salt and pepper to taste

Cut the bacon into small pieces and cook until crisp. Remove the bacon from the drippings. Cook the onion in the drippings until slightly brown. Add the carrots, heat, and season to taste with salt and pepper. Turn carrots into a hot vegetable dish and garnish with bacon. Serves 6.

GLAZED CARROTS

1-quart casserole . . . Preheated oven—375° F. . . . Baking time—1 hour

5 medium-size carrots, cut in strips	½ cup sugar
¼ cup butter or margarine	¼ cup water
	½ teaspoon salt

Place peeled and cut carrots into casserole. Add remaining ingredients, cover, and bake. This is excellent with oven meals. Serves 4.

OVEN-STEAMED CARROTS

Place peeled, quartered carrots in casserole with ½ cup water, 1 teaspoon salt, and 2 tablespoons butter or margarine. Cover carrots. Place in oven and cook for 45 minutes to 1 hour at 375° F.

SCALLOPED CARROTS AND CELERY

Uncovered casserole . . . Preheated oven—350° F. . . . Baking time—25 minutes

1½ cups raw celery, diced	1 teaspoon salt
1½ cups carrots, diced	⅛ teaspoon pepper
½ cup water	1 tablespoon onion, finely minced
2 tablespoons butter or margarine	3 tablespoons cheese, grated
2 tablespoons all-purpose flour	¼ cup buttered crumbs
1 cup milk	

Cook celery and carrots together in water only until tender. Melt butter or margarine, add flour, and blend well. Add milk slowly, stirring constantly until thick and smooth. Add salt, pepper, onion, cheese, and cooked vegetables. Pour into greased casserole and cover with buttered crumbs (see page 131). Bake. Serves 5-6.

SHREDDED CARROTS AND CABBAGE

2-quart covered saucepan . . . Cooking time—about 15 minutes

- 2 tablespoons butter or margarine
- 2 cups carrots, shredded
- 2 cups cabbage, shredded
- 2 tablespoons water
- 1 teaspoon salt
- ⅛ teaspoon pepper

Melt butter or margarine in saucepan over high heat. Add carrots, cabbage, water, salt, and pepper. Mix well. Cover. When steam appears, reduce heat. Cook 12 minutes longer. Serves 4-6.

CARROT MOLD

Ring mold . . . Preheated oven—375° F. . . . Baking time—45 minutes

- 8 medium-sized carrots
- 2 small onions
- 1 teaspoon salt
- ⅛ teaspoon pepper
- 3 eggs
- ½ cup all-purpose flour
- 2 cups milk
- Buttered peas

Cook carrots and onions in small amount of water until tender and rub through coarse sieve. Add salt and pepper. Beat eggs and flour until well blended. Add milk slowly and beat until smooth. Mix with sieved carrots and onions and pour into well-greased ring mold. Place in refrigerator until ready to use. Bake. Turn from mold and fill with hot buttered peas. Serves 6 to 8.

BUTTERED CARROTS AND PEAS

Combine an equal quantity of diced, cooked carrots and cooked or canned peas. Season with butter or margarine, salt, and pepper. Heat thoroughly.

CAULIFLOWER

How to Buy

Select head of cauliflower with bright green lower leaves. The head should be white, with no dark, bruised spots. Medium-sized head will serve 4.

How to Cook

Remove any tough outer leaves. Little tender ones may be cooked. Remove stalk end. Wash carefully in cold water.

Method No. 1

Place whole cauliflower upright in saucepan. Add ½ cup water and 1 teaspoon salt. Cover. Bring to steaming point over high heat, then reduce to low. Steam 20-25 minutes.

When cauliflower is cooked in this way, it is delicious with hollandaise sauce (page 242) or cheese sauce (page 245).

Or, place steamed head of cauliflower in casserole. Cover with cheese sauce (page 245), sprinkle buttered crumbs over this (see page 131), and bake 15 minutes in preheated 400° F. oven.

Method No. 2

If you wish to separate the cauliflower into flowerets, place ¼ to ½ cup water, 1 teaspoon salt, and flowerets in saucepan. Cover. Bring to steaming point on high heat. Then reduce heat to low. Cook for 10-12 minutes.

Whichever method you use, be sure that you do not overcook this vegetable, for when it is overcooked, the cauliflower becomes dark in color, limp in texture, and strong in flavor.

Uncooked flowerets are delicious raw. Wonderful in vegetable salad. Also excellent on canapé tray. A quick plunge in a flavorsome dip, and they become an instant favorite.

FRENCH-FRIED FLOWERETS

Dip uncooked flowerets in batter (page 226). Drop each floweret in deep hot fat, 375° F. Cook until brown, 3 or 4 minutes. Delicious served plain or with cheese sauce (page 245).

BAKED CAULIFLOWER WITH CANNED MUSHROOM SOUP

Heat contents of can of condensed cream of mushroom soup. It is not necessary to thin soup. Place whole cooked cauliflower in casserole. Pour hot mushroom soup over vegetable. Sprinkle generously with Parmesan cheese. If desired, sprinkle buttered crumbs over top. Place in preheated 400° F. oven for 15 minutes. Quick, easy, and delicious.

CELERY

How to Buy

Whether you buy celery hearts, bleached stalks, or the green pascal depends upon your own taste and the way in which you are going to use the celery. For eating raw, celery hearts and pascal are best. For both eating and cooking, the bleached stalks are probably best.

How to Serve

Wash thoroughly. Celery frequently hides dust and soil. After washing, place in Humidrawer of your refrigerator to keep crisp.

Celery is delicious served raw. It is also excellent when cut in 2- or 3-inch lengths and filled with your favorite cheese.

How to Cook

Cut celery in ½- to 1-inch lengths. 2 cups will serve 4. Place ¼ cup water, 2 tablespoons butter or margarine, 1 teaspoon salt in saucepan. Add celery. Cover. Cook over high heat until steaming. Then reduce heat to low. Cook 12-15 minutes. Use such liquid as is left to serve with celery. Or, cook as above, substituting milk for water.

THRIFTY TRICK: Save the fresh, green celery leaves. Wonderful to add to soups, or dry them to use later as seasonings.

CELERY ROOT

How to Buy

1 pound will serve 4. Try to buy firm roots that have not wilted or become soft. Celery root is not found in all markets but it makes very good eating.

How to Cook

Scrub carefully. Peel. Cut in ¼-inch slices and cook as directed for celery. Can also be mashed.

CORN

How to Buy

Be sure corn has been freshly picked. You'll have better-tasting corn if you buy it with the husks on.

How to Cook Corn on the Cob

First cut off about 1 inch at base of ear. Remove husks, silks, and any wormy spots.

Method No. 1

Cook in tall kettle, or, if you have a deep well cooker on your range, in that. Place corn upright in wire basket. Place 1 cup water in kettle. Cover. When water boils, lower basket of corn into kettle. Cover. Steam 5 minutes.

Method No. 2

Bring a quantity of water to boiling point. Add corn—just as many as you will need for first serving—to boiling water. Cook for 2-5 minutes, depending upon freshness of corn and your own taste.

TRICK: It's a neat trick to roll each ear of hot, cooked corn in melted butter or margarine before bringing to the table.

Method No. 3

Carefully lay back husks, remove silks and any wormy portions. Season with salt and brush melted butter or margarine over corn. Return green husks around ear; tie down if necessary. Place on shallow baking sheet, or lay on oven racks. Cook for 45 minutes in oven at 350° F. Remove husks before serving.

Method No. 4

Remove husks, etc., season with salt, brush with melted butter or margarine, and broil until golden brown, turning corn as it browns. This method is excellent for outdoor broiling, over glowing coals in an open fireplace.

Frozen Corn on the Cob

Frozen corn on the cob must be completely thawed before cooking. Otherwise the cob will be cold when served. Frozen corn takes about 4 hours at room temperature to thaw. Either steam, as suggested for fresh corn, or plunge in boiling water for 3-4 minutes.

Corn off the Cob

Corn may be cut from the ear before cooking. To get full goodness from corn, after cutting off cob, take the back of a silver knife and scrape down the cob. You get all the good juices from the corn by doing this. Be sure to use back of knife. Otherwise, you will get many unwanted husks.

To 2 cups scraped fresh corn, add ¼ cup light cream, salt, and pepper to taste. Place in saucepan. Cover. Cook over high heat until steaming, then reduce to low heat and continue cooking for about 5 minutes. Or, after corn has been scraped from cob, place 3 tablespoons butter or margarine in skillet or saucepan. Slowly sauté the corn until tender.

Note: Any of the following recipes may be made either with canned, freshly cooked corn, or leftover cooked corn.

SCRAMBLED CORN

8-inch skillet . . . Cooking time—about 10 minutes

¼ pound bacon, cubed	¾ teaspoon salt
2 cups whole kernel corn	⅛ teaspoon pepper
3 eggs	

Brown the bacon in skillet. Drain the corn and add to the bacon. Beat eggs with salt and pepper and add to the hot bacon and corn. Stir well until eggs are done. Serves 4.

SQUAW CORN

8-inch skillet . . . Cooking time—about 10 minutes

4 slices bacon, cut into 1-inch lengths	2 cups whole kernel corn
1 medium-sized onion, sliced	2 eggs
½ green pepper, diced	½ teaspoon salt

Fry bacon until lightly browned, add onion, and brown. Add green pepper and corn. Cook slowly until well blended, about 5 minutes. Beat eggs slightly, add to corn mixture. Stir constantly until eggs have thickened. Season with salt. Serves 4.

TRICK: Add a dash of Worcestershire sauce to this recipe, and you really have a delicious concoction. An excellent way to use leftover corn.

SCALLOPED CORN

2-quart casserole . . . Preheated oven—350° F. . . . Baking time— 30-40 minutes

2 cups fresh or cooked corn	2 tablespoons butter or margarine
2 eggs, beaten	¾ cup milk
1 teaspoon salt	Strips green pepper or pimiento
Dash of pepper	
½ cup cracker crumbs	

Grease casserole. Combine corn with beaten eggs, salt, and pepper. Place in casserole. Sprinkle top with cracker crumbs. Dot with butter or margarine. Pour milk over mixture. Lay strips of green pepper or pimiento over top. Bake uncovered. Serves 6.

CORN AND CHEESE SOUFFLÉ

Baking dish . . . Preheated oven—350° F. . . . Baking time—60
  minutes •

¼ cup butter or margarine	1 cup sharp cheese, grated
¼ cup all-purpose flour	2 cups, whole kernel corn
2 cups milk	4 eggs, separated
½ teaspoon salt	
Pepper to taste	

Melt shortening and stir in flour. Gradually add milk and season-ings. Cook until thickened, stirring occasionally. Add cheese and stir until melted. Add corn. Remove from heat and gradually stir in well-beaten egg yolks and fold in stiffly beaten egg whites. Turn into greased baking dish. Place dish in pan of hot water to bake. Serves 6.

CORN CAKES

8-inch skillet or griddle . . . Cooking time—about 10 minutes

2 eggs	½ cup cracker crumbs
1 cup corn	1 teaspoon baking powder
½ teaspoon salt	
1 tablespoon butter or margarine, melted	

Beat eggs slightly. Add corn, salt, and butter or margarine. Mix crumbs and baking powder. Add to first mixture. Drop by spoon-fuls on preheated griddle and fry to a golden brown on each side. Serves 4.

CORN FRITTERS—See page 227.

CUCUMBERS

How to Buy

Select medium-sized, firm green cucumbers without any yellow blemishes.

How to Serve

Cucumbers are almost always eaten raw. Wash cucumber thor-oughly and slice, skin and all. Serve in salads or cut them in strips as a side dish for a summer meal.

Years ago it was thought necessary to soak cucumbers in salted water before serving. However, that is not necessary.

Many people enjoy eating cucumbers sliced very thin and served with a dressing of vinegar, salt, and pepper.

CUCUMBERS AND SOUR CREAM

2 cucumbers, sliced thin	1 tablespoon water
1 large onion, sliced thin	½ teaspoon salt
4 tablespoons sour cream	Dash of black pepper
1 tablespoon vinegar	Pinch powdered tarragon

Peel cucumber and slice very thin. Peel and slice onion very thin. Make a dressing of the sour cream, vinegar, water, salt, pepper, and tarragon. Pour over cucumbers. Serves 4.

EGGPLANT

How to Buy

Look for good purple color and eggplants that are firm to the touch. Usually one medium-sized eggplant will serve 4.

How to Cook

Wash eggplant. Peel and slice the desired thickness. If you will be cubing, it is desirable to make the slices about ½ inch thick. If you plan to fry slices, they may be sliced ¼ to ½ inch thick. Do not soak eggplant after slicing.

PAN-FRIED

Cut eggplant in ¼-inch slices. Dip in all-purpose flour or corn meal, seasoned with salt and pepper. Brown slowly in bacon drippings or butter or margarine, turning to brown evenly on both sides.

EGGPLANT BROILER MEAL

8-inch skillet . . . Cooking time—about 20 minutes

1 large eggplant	8 slices tomato
2 eggs, beaten	8 slices Cheddar cheese
¾ cup cracker or bread crumbs	8 slices bacon
8 tablespoons shortening, half butter	

Peel eggplant and cut in ½-inch slices. Dip in beaten eggs, then in the cracker or bread crumbs. When shortening is hot, fry the eggplant on both sides until a golden brown and until tender, about

12 minutes. Place the eggplant on broiler rack, and on each piece of eggplant, place a slice of tomato, then a slice of cheese. Cut the bacon strips in half and place them crisscross over the cheese and broil until the bacon is brown and crisp. Serve with cheese sauce. Serves 8.

Cheese Sauce

3 tablespoons butter or margarine	¼ teaspoon salt
	Dash of pepper
2 tablespoons all-purpose flour	½ cup cheese, grated
1 cup milk	

Melt the butter or margarine, blend in the flour, add the milk, and cook over low heat until medium thick. Add seasonings and cheese and stir until cheese is blended.

EURASIAN EGGPLANT

8-inch covered skillet . . . Cooking time—25 minutes

1 clove of garlic, sliced	1 can (No. 2) bean sprouts
3 tablespoons shortening	3 stalks green onions, cut in
¾ pound lean pork, sliced thin	½-inch pieces
1 large onion, sliced	1 teaspoon salt
4 stalks celery, diced	1 tablespoon Soy Sauce
1 green pepper, diced	½ cup hot water
1 large eggplant, peeled and diced	1 tablespoon cornstarch
	⅓ cup cold water

Brown garlic in hot shortening. Remove garlic and brown the pork. Add onion, celery, green pepper, eggplant, and stir until blended. Add bean sprouts, green onion, and salt. Combine Soy Sauce and hot water and pour over vegetables. Cover and cook 15 minutes, or until vegetables are just tender. Combine cornstarch and cold water and add to the vegetables. Bring to a boil. Serve immediately. Serve with fried noodles or rice. Serves 8.

SCALLOPED EGGPLANT

Uncovered casserole . . . Preheated oven, 350° F. . . . Baking time 25-30 minutes

1 eggplant	½ teaspoon salt
½ cup water	⅛ teaspoon pepper
¼ cup melted shortening	½ teaspoon onion, minced
½ cup soft bread crumbs	Buttered bread or cracker
2 eggs, well beaten	crumbs

Peel and slice eggplant, then cut into cubes. Cook in water until tender. Drain. Add melted shortening, soft bread crumbs, eggs, seasonings, and onion. Pour into greased casserole. Sprinkle with buttered crumbs. Bake. Serves 6-8.

BAKED STUFFED EGGPLANT
Shallow utility dish . . . Preheated oven, 375° F. . . . Cooking time—about 30 minutes

1 eggplant	Salt and pepper to taste
1 small onion, chopped fine	1 cup soft bread crumbs
3 tablespoons butter or marga-	¼ cup catchup
rine, melted (Bacon drip-	Buttered bread crumbs
pings would also be excellent	1 cup leftover meat, ground, or
to use.)	cheese (optional)
1 egg, beaten	

First steam the whole eggplant for 25-30 minutes. When tender, cut in half lengthwise. Scoop out pulp, but do it carefully so you won't break the outer shell. Chop scooped-out portions.

Cook onion with shortening until golden brown. Add eggplant pulp. Cook until heated through. It may be necessary to add a tablespoon or so of liquid. Sherry would be excellent to use. Add beaten egg and leftover ground meat or cheese, if desired, salt and pepper, soft crumbs, and catchup. Refill shell of eggplant. Sprinkle crumbs over top. Bake. Serves 4-6.

GREENS

How to Buy

1 pound serves 2 generously. However, some greens do not cook down, so you will probably have to regulate your amounts by the type of greens being purchased and family likes and dislikes.

There are many kinds of greens on the market: mustard, kale, dandelion, beet tops, turnip tops, Swiss chard, collards, chicory, escarole, spinach. All are good. Be sure to buy fresh, bright-colored greens.

How to Clean and Cook

Before washing, look the greens over, discarding all discolored or bruised leaves. Cut off roots. If you are using turnip tops or collards, tear leafy part from stem. The stem is tough and does not cook tender.

Wash in several waters, the first two waters being slightly warm, to remove sand or grit more effectively. The last water should be cold. Lift greens from water into a large kettle. Greens are bulky and should never be pushed down into the kettle. Add no water. The water that clings to leaves is sufficient. Cover. Cook over high heat until steaming. Then turn heat to a lower setting. Cook about 10 minutes. Drain and serve.

TRICK: When washing greens, always lift leaves from water, never drain water off. In this way, any sand or grit will settle to bottom of pan, rather than through the leaves.

How to Serve

Greens may be chopped or served as cooked, with butter or margarine and seasonings. Hard-cooked eggs make a fine garnish. Lemon juice adds a pleasing flavor.

A sour-cream dressing is also good. Combine ½ cup sour cream, 1 tablespoon horse-radish, 1 teaspoon salt, and a dash of pepper. Add to drained, cooked spinach or kale. Reheat quickly. Serve at once.

To Cook with Salt Meat

Many prefer turnip tops, collards, or mustard greens cooked in boiling liquid in which fat meat has cooked.

Cook fat meat in quantity of water until meat is tender. Then add greens. Reduce heat. Cook until greens are tender. It may be necessary to turn the greens occasionally during early stages of cooking. Usually cook from 45 minutes to 1 hour. Lift greens from liquid in which they cooked. "Pot liquor," as it is called, is excellent to serve as a hot soup. Above all, don't waste it, for it will add flavor to almost any food you cook.

CREAMED SPINACH WITH GARLIC

8-inch skillet . . . Cooking time—15 minutes

2 pounds fresh spinach, or 1 box frozen	2 tablespoons all-purpose flour
	1 cup milk
¼ cup butter or margarine	Salt and pepper to taste
1 small clove garlic, grated	

Clean and cook fresh or frozen spinach as directed. Melt butter or margarine in skillet. Add grated garlic, blend in flour, and brown slightly. Add milk and cook until thickened. Add cooked spinach and seasonings. Reheat. Serves 4.

PENNSYLVANIA DUTCH SPINACH

2-quart saucepan . . . Cooking time—10 minutes

2 slices bacon, diced	1 tablespoon vinegar
3 cups raw spinach, chopped	1 teaspoon salt
2 tablespoons all-purpose flour	⅛ teaspoon pepper
1 cup hot water	2 hard-cooked eggs
1 tablespoon sugar	

Fry bacon until crisp. Add bacon to spinach. Add flour to drippings and blend. Add hot water and cook until thickened. Add sugar, vinegar, salt, and pepper. Pour over spinach. Stir until well mixed. Garnish with sliced hard-cooked eggs. Serves 4.

SCALLOPED SPINACH WITH CHEESE

2-quart baking dish . . . Preheated oven—375° F. . . . Baking time—20 minutes

2 pounds fresh spinach	⅛ teaspoon pepper
4 tablespoons butter or margarine	½ cup cheese, grated
	½ cup soft bread crumbs
2 tablespoons all-purpose flour	2 tablespoons butter or margarine
1 cup milk	
1½ teaspoons salt	

Wash spinach and cook as directed on page 153. Drain. Make a white sauce of butter or margarine, flour, milk, ½ teaspoon salt, and the pepper. Add cheese and stir until melted. Place alternate layers of spinach and sauce in greased baking dish. Cover with the bread crumbs that have been browned in butter or margarine. Bake. Serves 4.

SPINACH MOLDS

Custard cups or 6x10-inch baking dish . . . Preheated oven—375° F. . . . Baking time—35-45 minutes

2 cups cooked spinach	1½ teaspoons salt
1½ cups soft bread crumbs	¼ teaspoon pepper
2 eggs, beaten	1½ cups milk
1 teaspoon onion, finely chopped	

Drain spinach, reserving liquid for soups, and chop medium fine. Mix all ingredients together and place in greased custard cups or baking dish. Set baking dish or custard cups in pan containing 1 inch of water and bake. To serve, unmold from custard cups or cut into squares and serve with creamed hard-cooked eggs or mushroom cheese sauce (page 244). Serves 4.

SPINACH DELIGHT

2-quart covered saucepan . . . Cooking time—15 minutes

1 package frozen spinach, or	½ teaspoon onion, minced
1 pound fresh spinach	¼ teaspoon accent
1 tablespoon butter or margarine	½ teaspoon salt
1 tablespoon all-purpose flour	¼ teaspoon pepper
½ cup sour cream	

Cook spinach and drain. Melt butter or margarine in saucepan. Blend in flour, add cream, and cook, stirring constantly, until thickened. Stir in spinach. Add onion and seasonings. Heat over low heat. Serves 4.

OVEN-COOKED FROZEN SPINACH

Covered casserole . . . Preheated oven—350° F. . . . Baking time— 45 minutes

1 package frozen spinach	¼ cup water
½ teaspoon salt	

Remove spinach from package while frozen. Cut block into four pieces. Place with salt and water in a tightly covered casserole. Bake. Serves 4.

HOMINY

How to Buy

Hominy is usually purchased in cans, although some markets sell it in bulk.

BROWNED BUTTER HOMINY

2-quart saucepan . . . Cooking time—15 minutes

1 can (No. 2½) hominy	1 teaspoon salt
3 tablespoons bacon drippings	⅛ teaspoon pepper

Drain hominy. Brown in bacon drippings with seasonings. Cover. Cook over low heat until well heated. Serves 4-6.

HOMINY AND MUSHROOM SOUP

Uncovered casserole . . . Preheated oven—375° F. . . . Baking time
—25-30 minutes

1 can (No. 2½) hominy
3 tablespoons butter or
     margarine
3 tablespoons onion, minced
2 tablespoons green pepper,
     minced

1 can condensed cream of
     mushroom soup
⅓ cup milk
1 teaspoon salt
⅛ teaspoon pepper

Wash hominy and drain. Heat butter or margarine in a skillet and
sauté onions and green pepper until they begin to brown. Add
hominy and soup which has been diluted with milk, add seasonings, and mix well. Pour into well-greased casserole. Bake uncovered. Serves 4-6.

HOMINY AU GRATIN

Uncovered casserole . . . Preheated oven—375° F. . . . Baking time
—25-30 minutes

1 can (No. 2½) hominy
2 tablespoons butter or
     margarine
2 tablespoons all-purpose flour
2 cups milk

1 teaspoon salt
¼ teaspoon pepper
¾ cup cheese, grated
½ cup buttered bread crumbs

Drain hominy. Make a sauce by melting butter or margarine, blend
in the flour, add the milk slowly, stirring constantly until sauce
thickens slightly. Remove from heat. Add salt, pepper, and cheese,
stirring until cheese has melted. Place hominy and sauce in alternate layers in greased casserole. Top with the buttered crumbs
(see page 131). Bake until crumbs are lightly browned. Serves 6.

HOMINY CROQUETTES

Greased utility pan . . . Preheated oven—425° F. . . . Baking time—
30 minutes

1 can (No 2½) hominy
3 tablespoons butter or margarine
3 tablespoons all-purpose flour
1 cup milk

2 teaspoons salt
1 egg
1 cup fine bread or cracker
     crumbs

Drain hominy and put through a food chopper, or mash. Make a
white sauce by melting the butter or margarine, adding flour, milk,

and salt. Cook until thickened. Mix this with hominy and add part of bread crumbs, or a sufficient amount so that mixture will form easily. Place in refrigerator and allow to chill thoroughly. When ready to cook, shape into croquettes. Beat egg and add 1 tablespoon water. Dip croquettes first in a few of the bread crumbs, then egg, then bread crumbs. Brush the croquettes with milk. Place in a greased pan and bake in hot oven, 425° F., until nicely browned. They may be cooked in deep fat, but from the standpoint of economy the oven is preferable. Serves 4-6.

HOMINY GRITS

2-quart covered saucepan . . . Cooking time—1 hour

1 cup hominy or soya grits	4 cups boiling water
2 teaspoons salt	2 tablespoons butter or margarine

Pour hominy into salted, boiling water. Stir until it boils. Cook on simmer heat for one hour, stirring frequently. When ready to serve, add 2 tablespoons of butter or margarine. Beat well. Makes 6 servings.

TO FRY HOMINY GRITS

Place cooked grits in mold or pan which has been rinsed in cold water. When cold, cut in ½-inch slices. Dip each slice into beaten egg, diluted with 1 tablespoon cold water. Brown on both sides in bacon fat. Serve with bacon slices.

MUSHROOMS

How to Buy

1 pound serves 4, unless mushrooms are main part of meal. Then buy 2 pounds for 4. Select firm ones, free from dark spots.

How to Cook

Clean carefully. A stiff brush is excellent. Some people say mushrooms should not be washed, but usually there is soil clinging to them, and light washing is therefore essential.

Do not peel mushrooms and do not cut off or discard the stem. Do, however, cut off any broken or jagged portion of the stem and trim the rough end, if mushrooms are old.

SAUTÉED MUSHROOMS

To each pound mushrooms, use 4 tablespoons butter or margarine. Heat over medium setting. When butter has melted, add mushrooms, either whole or sliced, depending upon size of mushrooms. Season with salt. Cook over medium setting for about 10 minutes, stirring occasionally.

TREAT: Cook as directed above. Just before removing from range, sprinkle 1 tablespoon all-purpose flour through mushrooms. Use a fork to stir with and be sure flour is thoroughly blended. To this, add ½ cup sherry. Cook until thickened. Wonderful with steak.

BROILED MUSHROOMS

Select large mushrooms. Remove stems, but don't throw them away. (Save them for soup, or to flavor other vegetables. Stems are good with steamed carrots or peas. Or you can chop the stems quite fine and use them to fill hollows.) Place mushroom caps on broiler pan, hollow side up. Brush generously with melted butter. Season with salt. Broil 10 minutes.

MUSHROOMS ON TOAST

Prepare mushrooms and place in shallow casserole with smooth side down. Dot generously with butter. Season with salt and pepper. Pour ¾ cup light cream over mushrooms. Place in preheated oven, 450° F., for 10-15 minutes. Remove mushrooms to slices of buttered toast. Pour cream remaining in casserole over the mushrooms and toast.

ONIONS

How to Buy

1½ pounds medium-sized onions will serve 4.

How to Peel without Weeping

Several ways of peeling onions are recommended. Some swear by one, some by another; you may try them all.

1. Peel onions under water. Keep cold-water faucet running and the onion in the flow of water.
2. Start peeling from root end.
3. Pour boiling water over them, then cold. Skins are supposed to slip off.

PLAIN STEAMED ONIONS

Peel onions; slice. Or use whole, preferably medium-small ones. To saucepan add ¼ to ½ cup water, 1 teaspoon salt, and onions. Cover. Cook until tender, 20-25 minutes. Drain. Serve with butter or margarine, or add ¼ cup light cream to drained onions. Reheat. Serve at once.

AMBER ONIONS

Casserole dish . . . Preheated oven—350° F. . . . Baking time—1 hour

6 medium-sized onions	2 tablespoons tomato soup (or
2 tablespoons butter or	tomato juice)
margarine	¼ teaspoon paprika
2 tablespoons honey	½ teaspoon salt

Peel onions and cross cut each end. Parboil 10 minutes until slightly tender. Place onions in greased casserole. Combine remaining ingredients and pour over onions. Bake. Serves 4.

ONIONS IN MUSHROOM SAUCE

Covered casserole dish . . . Preheated oven—375° F. . . . Baking time—45 minutes

8 to 10 small (whole) onions	¼ cup grated cheese (Parmesan
1 can condensed cream of	may be used)
mushroom soup	

Place onions in greased casserole. Pour soup over onions. Sprinkle cheese over top. Cover. Bake. Serves 4.

CREAMY FRIED ONIONS

8-inch covered skillet . . . Cooking time—20 minutes

4 medium-sized onions (about	¾ cup water
1¼ pounds)	1 teaspoon salt
3 tablespoons drippings	Few grains pepper
2 tablespoons all-purpose flour	¾ cup evaporated milk

Peel and cut onions into ⅛-inch slices. Heat drippings in skillet, add onions, and cook over medium heat for 15 minutes, or until golden brown. Sprinkle flour over onions. Add water, salt, and pepper. Lastly, add the evaporated milk. Let cook slowly for two minutes. Serves 4.

ONIONS AU GRATIN

2-quart casserole . . . Preheated oven—375° F. . . . Baking time—
20 minutes

4 cups onions, sliced ⅛ inch thick	⅛ teaspoon pepper
	1 cup milk
2 tablespoons butter or margarine	¼ cup liquid from onions
	½ cup Cheddar cheese, grated
2 tablespoons all-purpose flour	½ cup buttered bread or cracker crumbs
½ teaspoon salt	

Cook onions in boiling salted water until tender, about 15 minutes.
Drain and save liquid. Place onions in greased casserole. Melt
butter or margarine, add flour, salt, and pepper and stir until
smooth. Gradually add milk and cook until thick and smooth,
stirring occasionally. Add the liquid from onions and cheese, stirring until cheese has melted. Pour sauce over onions and top with
buttered crumbs. Serves 6-8.

FRENCH FRIED ONIONS—See page 228.

SMOTHERED ONIONS

8-inch covered skillet . . . Cooking time—20-25 minutes

4 large onions	2 tablespoons bacon drippings
1 teaspoon salt	

Peel onions and cut crosswise in thin slices. Place bacon drippings
in skillet. When hot, add sliced onions and salt. Cover. Cook over
medium heat until onions are tender and slightly golden in color.
Turn occasionally. Serves 4.

PARSNIPS

How to Buy

1½ pounds serve 4. Best to buy in spring when they have been
freshly dug.

How to Cook

Wash carefully. Peel. Cut in half lengthwise and remove the core.
Many people think they do not like parsnips but discover they
like them when core is removed. You may prefer to cook them first
and then remove the core. To cook, slice parsnips and cook in small

amount of water from 10-15 minutes. Serve with melted butter or margarine, or add ¼ cup cream.

How to Pan-Fry

Heat drippings in a skillet. Brown cooked parsnips in drippings and serve.

PEAS

How to Buy

2 pounds, unshelled, will serve 4. Select bright green pods. To test, open a pea, eat one and see if it's sweet.

How to Cook

Peas will keep their bright green color if properly cooked. Better not use a pressure cooker on fresh, green peas. You are apt to end up with a purée!

Place ¼ cup water, 1 teaspoon salt, and peas in saucepan. Cover. Cook over high heat until steaming, then reduce to low. Cook 10 minutes. Serve with butter or cream.

TREATS: Some like to add 1 teaspoon sugar to peas. Add 1 tablespoon chopped fresh mint to peas. Peas and carrots make a fine combination. Use about half and half. Put 2 tablespoons butter or margarine in saucepan, salt to season, add the peas and place 2 or 3 large-leaf lettuce leaves which are slightly damp over peas. Cover. Cook on high heat until steaming, then low. Cook about 10 minutes. Throw lettuce leaves away. Peas will have a distinctive taste. Almond slivers cooked in brown butter and added to peas also are delicious.

GREEN PEPPERS

How to Buy

Allow one medium-sized green pepper per serving, Select firm, well-shaped, thick-fleshed, bright-colored green peppers.

How to Cook

Wash, remove stem and seeds. Cut in thin slices or rings. Leave whole to stuff or bake. Large green peppers may be cut in half lengthwise for stuffing.

FRIED GREEN PEPPERS

Prepare 2 or 3 medium-sized green peppers. Slice in ¼-inch slices. Sauté in 3 tablespoons butter or margarine until crispy, tender, and lightly browned. Season with salt. Very fine served with steak.

SCALLOPED GREEN PEPPERS

1½-quart covered casserole . . . Preheated oven—350° F. . . . Baking time—45 minutes

2 hard-cooked eggs, sliced thin	⅛ teaspoon pepper
2 cups green pepper, diced	¾ cup milk
½ pound processed cheese, sliced thin	1 cup bread crumbs
½ teaspoon salt	2 tablespoons butter or margarine

Place a layer of sliced egg in the bottom of greased casserole. Cover with a layer of green pepper, then cheese, repeating until all is used. Add salt and pepper. Pour the milk over the mixture. Cover with bread crumbs that have been mixed with the butter or margarine. Cover and bake. Serves 4.

FRENCH-FRIED GREEN PEPPERS—See page 229.

EASY STUFFED PEPPERS

Shallow baking dish . . . Preheated oven—375° F. . . . Baking time—45 minutes

4 medium-sized green peppers	1 egg, slightly beaten
2 cups cooked leftover meat, ground	2 tablespoons onion, finely minced
¾ cup soft bread cubes	1 can condensed cream of tomato soup
½ teaspoon salt	

Remove tops and seeds from peppers. Steam shells about 5 minutes. Combine remaining ingredients, using only ½ can of soup. Mix well. Fill peppers with stuffing. Place in shallow baking pan. Bake 30 minutes in preheated 375° F. oven. Remove from oven and pour remaining half of soup over peppers. Return to oven and continue baking 15 minutes. Serves 4.

TRICK: Stuffed peppers offer a thrifty way to use almost any leftovers. Leftover rice may be substituted for bread. Leftover dried cheese may be ground and used for part of meat. Any meat is excellent, but leftover ham scraps are particularly good.

POTATOES

How to Buy

The amount of potatoes to buy depends upon how you are going to use them. For a small family, buy only enough for immediate needs. 1½ pounds usually will serve 4. For baking, buy only matured, firm potatoes. For mashing, buy medium-sized, matured potatoes. New potatoes are best steamed whole.

BOILED—WHOLE POTATOES

Potatoes may be peeled, or not, depending upon your family's preference.

Place ½ cup water, 1 teaspoon salt, and whole potatoes in saucepan. Cover. Cook over high heat until steaming. Then reduce to low heat. Cook 25-30 minutes, depending upon size of potato. When cooked, drain, return to heat, and cook another minute or so. This seems to fluff the potatoes. Serve with butter or margarine.

NEW POTATOES

Cook as above. Combine 3 tablespoons butter or margarine, 4 tablespoons finely minced parsley, 1 tablespoon lemon juice. Toss this mixture over drained potatoes. Be sure you cook plenty. Members of the family not on diets will call for seconds.

BAKED POTATOES—SWEET OR WHITE

Select smooth and unblemished potatoes of uniform, medium size, so they will bake in the same length of time. Scrub potatoes thoroughly. Dry. Rub lightly with unsalted fat or cooking oil. Bake for 1 hour in 400° F. oven. Before serving, roll gently back and forth in palm of hand to make mealy. Slit lengthwise, push down on slit, fill opening with butter or margarine, and serve at once.

Creamed chipped beef (page 54) is delicious on baked potatoes.

MASHED POTATOES

Cook peeled potatoes as described in recipe for whole boiled potatoes. If potatoes are large, cut in half lengthwise, then half crosswise. When cooked, drain off any remaining liquid, and return potatoes to heat a minute or so to dry and fluff up. If you have an electric mixer, use it for whipping the potatoes. Otherwise use a potato masher or a ricer.

Mash potatoes vigorously. To sufficient potatoes to serve 4, add ½ to ¾ cup whole or top milk which has been heated, 4 tablespoons butter or margarine. Keep on beating until the potatoes resemble a fluffy cloud.

BAKED STUFFED POTATOES

Buy large potatoes for stuffing. Bake according to directions on page 164. Then cut in half lengthwise. Carefully scoop out insides. Mash. Use plenty of salt, butter or margarine, and cream and mash until fluffy. Refill shells, piling mashed potatoes in lightly. Sprinkle grated cheese over top. Return to oven to brown, about 10 minutes at 400° F.

TRICK: Stuffed potatoes may be fixed in advance and reheated just before ready to serve. If potatoes are cold, better allow 15 minutes at 400° F. for heating and browning filling.

FRANCONIA POTATOES

Peel medium-sized potatoes and steam for 10 minutes. Drain. Place in pan in which you are roasting meat. Place around meat the last hour meat is to cook. Baste occasionally, and for really golden brown potatoes, turn them once or twice.

TRICK: You may fix potatoes this way without meat. Place steamed potatoes in casserole, with about 4 tablespoons heated shortening, such as bacon drippings. Place in oven, 375° F., and bake about 1 hour, turning occasionally. Or, roll the steamed potatoes in buttered crumbs, then proceed as above.

O'BRION POTATOES

Covered 8-inch skillet . . . Cooking time—25 minutes

2 slices onion	4½ cups raw potatoes, diced
3 tablespoons green pepper, diced	1½ teaspoons salt
	1 tablespoon parsley, chopped
3 tablespoons butter or margarine	

Sauté onion and green pepper in butter or margarine. Add potatoes and salt. Cover and cook slowly until done. Stir occasionally. When served, sprinkle with the parsley. Serves 4-6.

DUTCHESS POTATOES

10x14-inch cooky sheet . . . Preheated oven—450° F. . . . Baking
time—20 minutes

2 tablespoons butter or margarine	2 cups hot riced or mashed potatoes
½ teaspoon salt	Dash of paprika
1 egg, slightly beaten	

Add butter or margarine, salt, and egg to mashed potatoes. Beat.
Shape into mounds on cooky sheet. Sprinkle top with paprika.
Brown in hot oven. Serve piping hot. Serves 4.

TREAT: Add 2 tablespoons parsley or ¼ cup finely minced
chives to potatoes.

FRIED UNCOOKED POTATOES

Wash, pare, and slice potatoes very thin. Heat shortening in skillet.
Bacon drippings are excellent to use when frying potatoes. When
shortening is bubbling hot, lay in potatoes, sprinkle with salt, and
turn heat to medium setting. When potatoes are brown on bottom,
turn and fry slowly on other side. Do not cover. If desired, finely
chopped onion may be fried with potatoes.

FRIED COOKED POTATOES

Slice cooked potatoes in ¼-inch slices. Fry in bacon drippings until
brown and crisp. It will be necessary to turn the potatoes occasionally. Season to taste.

TREAT: Instead of slicing the cooked potatoes, dice them in
about ½-inch cubes. Melt butter or margarine in skillet, add diced
potatoes, and for a family of 4, stir in about ⅔ cup light cream. Cook
slowly until cream is absorbed, and potatoes are light brown in
color.

HASHED BROWN POTATOES

8-inch skillet . . . Cooking time—25-30 minutes

3 cups cooked potatoes, cut in ¼-inch cubes	½ cup light cream or evaporated milk
1½ teaspoons salt	2 tablespoons bacon drippings or butter or margarine
1½ tablespoons all-purpose flour	

Put diced potatoes in bowl. Sprinkle with salt and flour. Carefully
work the salt and flour through the potatoes, using a fork to stir.
Add cream or milk and stir through potatoes. Place shortening in
skillet. When hot, add potatoes. Let brown on one side. Take a

pancake turner and flip potatoes over. Brown on other side. Serve piping hot. Serves 4.

SCALLOPED POTATOES

Uncovered casserole ... Preheated oven—375° F. ... Baking time —1-1½ hours

6 medium-sized potatoes	2 teaspoons salt
4 tablespoons butter or margarine	2½ cups milk
4 tablespoons all-purpose flour	1½ cups Cheddar cheese, grated

Peel potatoes and slice thin. Make a white sauce of butter or margarine, flour, salt, and milk. When thickened, remove from range and add grated cheese. Place sliced potatoes in casserole, cover with hot cheese sauce. Bake uncovered. Serves 6-8.

TRICK: Instead of making a white sauce, dilute 1 can of condensed cream of mushroom soup with ½ cup milk. Pour this over the potatoes. Cook as indicated above.

ROUMANIAN POTATO CAKES

6x10-inch utility pan ... Preheated oven—350° F. ... Baking time —1 hour

4 or 5 large raw potatoes (1 quart shredded)	¼ teaspoon pepper
4 eggs, slightly beaten	½ cup fine, uncooked cereal
¼ cup all-purpose flour	¼ cup dry bread or cracker crumbs
2 teaspoons baking powder	⅓ cup chicken fat or other shortening
2 teaspoons salt	

Grate potatoes. Add eggs, mixing well. Mix dry ingredients, cereal, and bread crumbs and add to the potato mixture. Melt fat and add. Pour into greased utility dish and bake. Cut into squares and serve with creamed meat, chicken, or eggs. Serves 8.

FRENCH-FRIED POTATOES—See page 229.

AU GRATIN POTATOES

Shallow baking dish ... Preheated oven—400° F. ... Baking time —30-40 minutes

2 tablespoons butter or margarine	1 cup cheese, grated
2 tablespoons all-purpose flour	2 cups cold boiled or baked potatoes, cubed
1 teaspoon salt	
1 cup milk	

Melt butter or margarine. Add flour and salt. Stir until well blended. Add milk gradually, stirring constantly. When thickened, add grated cheese. Remove from heat. Place potatoes in greased baking dish. Cover with sauce. Bake. Serves 4.

SWEET POTATOES

BAKED SWEET POTATOES

Bake as for white potatoes (page 164), allowing about 45 minutes' baking time.

BOILED OR MASHED SWEET POTATOES

Cook potatoes with skins on in boiling, salted water until tender, about 25 minutes. Be sure to keep kettle covered during cooking period. When tender, peel and drain. Serve whole with salt, pepper, and butter or margarine, or mash, add enough hot milk to make them fluffy, and season with salt, pepper, and butter or margarine.

SWEET-POTATO CASSEROLE DE LUXE

2-quart casserole . . . Preheated oven—350° F. . . . Baking time—30-40 minutes

Cook about 6 medium-sized sweet potatoes. Remove skins. Mash. To the mashed sweet potato, add ½ cup drained, crushed pineapple (baby-food size would be excellent) and ½ cup chopped nut meats. Place in greased casserole. Cover with marshmallows. Bake until marshmallows are melted and slightly brown. Serves 4-6.

FRIED SWEET POTATOES

Fry leftover cooked sweet potatoes like leftover white potatoes (page 166).

FRENCH FRIED SWEET POTATOES—See page 229. (Same as White Potatoes.)

CANDIED SWEET POTATOES

Shallow oblong baking dish . . . Preheated or cold oven—375° F. . . . Baking time—1 hour

4 medium-sized sweet potatoes   ½ cup brown sugar
½ cup butter or margarine   ¼ cup hot water

Wash and steam or bake sweet potatoes. Peel and cut in length-wise slices about ½ inch thick. Place in greased baking dish. Pour over potatoes a sirup made of butter or margarine, brown sugar, and hot water. Bake. Serves 4-5.

SQUASH

ACORN SQUASH

How to Buy

Usually ½ squash per person is sufficient.

How to Cook

Cut squash in half, remove seeds and fibers. Sprinkle with salt and pepper. Brush with melted butter or margarine, ham or bacon drippings. Place on cooky sheet, cut side down. Bake in hot oven, 400° F., for 30 minutes. Then turn cut side up, brush with butter or margarine, and bake until brown, about 25-30 minutes.

TREAT: For something especially good, put little link sausages in squash when turned cut side up. Serve right from shell.

HUBBARD OR BANANA SQUASH

How to Buy

3 pounds will serve 4.

How to Cook

If you possibly can manage to use a whole squash, do so, because they are much better baked whole. Don't do a thing but wash the squash. Then put in 350° F. oven and bake 3 or 4 hours, de-pending upon size of squash.

When baked, cut in half. Remove seeds, scoop out pulp, season with salt, pepper, butter or margarine, mash, and serve.

If you can't manage a whole squash, then buy what you need. Cut in 2- or 3-inch squares, removing seeds, stringy portions, etc. Brush with butter or margarine or bacon drippings. Sprinkle a tea-spoon of brown sugar on each square. Bake 45-50 minutes at 350° F., keeping squash covered the first half hour.

TRICK: Use up leftover squash by following pumpkin pie recipe (page 377), substituting squash for the pumpkin.

SUMMER SQUASH

How to Buy

There are several kinds available most of the year. The white cymling, straight-necked or crook-necked yellow; chayote, a light green; or zucchini, a dark green. Buy 2 pounds for 4 servings. Summer squash must be extremely immature, fresh, and heavy for its size. The skin may be smooth or worty, depending upon variety. It must be tender and easily pricked.

How to Cook

Wash, but do not peel. Remove stem and blossom ends. Cut into ½-inch slices or cubes.

Place 2 tablespoons water, 2 tablespoons butter or margarine, and salt in saucepan. Add prepared squash. Cover. Cook over high heat until steaming, then reduce heat to low setting. Cook 10-15 minutes. May be mashed, or served as cooked. ½ cup cream added just before serving is a pleasant variation.

SAUTÉED SQUASH

Slice or dice squash. Sprinkle with salt and pepper. Sauté slowly in butter or margarine over medium heat until a golden brown. Several good shakes of garlic salt, especially on zucchini, greatly improve the flavor. Or, grate a clove of garlic very fine and add to squash as it is cooking.

ZUCCHINI PIE

9-inch pie pan . . . Preheated oven—375° F. . . . Baking time—25 minutes

4 cups zucchini squash, chopped	⅛ teaspoon pepper Dash of nutmeg
½ cup onion, finely chopped	2 eggs, well beaten
1 teaspoon salt	½ cup dry bread crumbs

Chop squash rather fine, about the size of a small pea. Blend all the ingredients thoroughly and press into greased pie pan. Bake. Cut into wedges and serve while hot. Serves 6.

TOMATOES

Tomatoes are probably best served without cooking, especially during their normal growing season.

To peel tomatoes easily, give them a quick dip in boiling water, then cold water. Remove stem, blossom end, and skin. Cut in halves or quarters, according to size of tomato.

For stewed tomatoes, etc., it is far cheaper to buy canned tomatoes, unless you happen to raise tomatoes yourself.

FRIED GREEN TOMATOES

Cut good-sized green tomatoes in ¾-inch slices. Do not peel. Dip in all-purpose flour or bread crumbs, seasoned with salt and pepper. Fry in hot shortening (bacon drippings add flavor). Turn once with pancake turner.

SAVORY TOMATOES

8-inch skillet . . . Cooking time—20 minutes

½ cup bacon or salt pork, diced	1 teaspoon salt
1 cup onion, sliced	⅛ teaspoon pepper
4 cups tomatoes, stewed or canned	4 tablespoons all-purpose flour

Fry bacon or salt pork until nearly crisp. Add onion and cook until onion is light brown. Add tomatoes, salt, and pepper and simmer for 10 minutes. Mix the flour with a small amount of cold water and stir into the tomatoes. Cook until thickened. May be served in sauce dishes or over cooked rice or spaghetti. Serves 5-6.

SCALLOPED TOMATOES

Uncovered casserole dish . . . Preheated oven—350° F. . . . Baking time—1 hour

2 cups onion, thinly sliced	½ teaspoon celery salt
1½ cups bread cubes	¼ teaspoon pepper
2 tablespoons shortening	2 tablespoons brown sugar
2 teaspoons salt	2 cups canned tomatoes

Precook onions 5 minutes. Drain. Sauté bread cubes in shortening until brown. Add seasonings and sugar to onions. Mix with tomatoes. Pour into greased casserole dish. Top with bread cubes. Bake uncovered. Serves 6.

BROILED TOMATOES

Do not peel tomatoes for broiling. Cut in half. Season with salt, pepper, dot with butter or margarine. A little Parmesan cheese sprinkled over top adds flavor. Broil, cut side up, for 5-6 minutes. Attractive to serve as a garnish with broiled meat.

TOMATOES SUPREME

2-quart casserole . . . Preheated oven—350° F. . . . Baking time—
   1-1½ hours

3 cups tomatoes, canned or stewed	1 teaspoon salt
½ cup celery, diced	⅛ teaspoon pepper
1 average onion, cut fine	1 cup buttered toasted bread, cubed
2 tablespoons butter or margarine	

Mix all ingredients together. Pour into buttered casserole. Bake. Serves 4-6.

   TREAT: A No. 2 can of corn may be added to this recipe for variation.

STEWED TOMATOES

1 can (No. 2) tomatoes	1 teaspoon sugar
2 tablespoons butter or margarine	
Salt and pepper to taste	

Place tomatoes in 2-quart covered saucepan. Turn heat to high to bring tomatoes to steaming point. Then simmer for 5 minutes. Add butter or margarine, salt, pepper, and sugar. Bread cubes may be added for thickening, or 2 tablespoons thick cream added just before serving. Serves 4.

TURNIPS AND RUTABAGAS

How to Buy

White turnips are available the year around. Rutabagas during fall, winter, and early spring. White turnips are sold in bunches with tops attached, or by the pound. If turnips still have tops, select turnips with fresh, green foliage. The vegetable should be firm to the touch and heavy for its size.

   Rutabagas are sold without tops. They, too, should be firm to the touch and heavy for their size. Count on 2 pounds serving 4.

How to Cook

Scrub thoroughly and peel. May be sliced thin, or cut in cubes, or they may be cooked whole, if small in size and very tender. Place ¼ cup water, 2 tablespoons butter or margarine and ½ teaspoon salt in saucepan. Add turnips. Cover. Cook over high heat until steaming, then reduce heat to low setting—young turnips will cook in 15-20 minutes when sliced or diced. Older turnips or whole turnips will take about 30 minutes.

Method No. 1

Mash, season with salt, pepper, butter or margarine, and add a little milk, just as when mashing potatoes.

Method No. 2

If turnips are sliced or diced, season with salt, pepper, butter or margarine. Or the diced turnips may be served with light cream.

TURNIP PUFF

Casserole dish . . . Preheated oven—375° F. . . . Baking time—40 minutes

2 tablespoons butter or margarine	3 cups mashed turnip
	1 teaspoon salt
1 tablespoon onion, finely minced	1 tablespoon sugar
	⅛ teaspoon pepper
2 tablespoons all-purpose flour	2 eggs, separated

Melt butter or margarine, add onions, and cook until onions are tender but not brown. Add flour and blend well. Add mashed turnip, salt, sugar, pepper, and beaten egg yolks and stir well. Beat egg whites until stiff but not dry and fold into above mixture. Pour into buttered casserole and bake. Serves 6.

MIXED VEGETABLES

VEGETABLE PLATE

4 large carrots, cut in strips	2½ cups cleaned Brussels sprouts
1 head cauliflower	2½ cups string beans, cut through lengthwise
2 bunches beets, peeled and sliced	Cheese sauce (page 245)

Cook carrots and cauliflower in one pan and all the other vegetables in separate pans, adding ¼ cup water, ½ teaspoon salt, and 1 tablespoon butter or margarine to each separate vegetable. Put cauliflower in the center of a large plate and arrange other vegetables around the cauliflower. Pour hot cheese sauce over the cauliflower. Serves 4-6.

VEGETABLE CASSEROLE

Uncovered casserole dish . . . Preheated oven—350° F. . . . Baking time—20 minutes

1½ cups cooked carrots, diced	⅛ teaspoon pepper
1½ cups cooked celery, diced	½ cup shredded cheese
¾ cup cooked onions, sliced	2 cups medium white sauce
1½ cups cooked peas or snap	(page 245)
beans	½ cup buttered bread crumbs
1 teaspoon salt	

Mix vegetables and salt and pepper. Stir cheese into white sauce (page 245) and place alternate layers of vegetables and sauce in buttered casserole. Sprinkle with buttered bread crumbs and bake. Serves 10-12.

TRICK: This dish may be made in advance and placed in refrigerator, in which case, allow an extra 10 minutes' baking time.

VEGETABLE SCRAPPLE

1 onion, chopped fine	1 teaspoon salt
1 carrot, chopped fine	¼ cup peanut butter
2 cups hot corn-meal mush	

Cook onion and carrot in salted water until tender. Drain. Cook the corn-meal mush (see below), and to it add the cooked onions, carrots, salt, and peanut butter. Mix well. Turn into a loaf pan rinsed in cold water. Chill until firm. Slice ½ inch thick. Sprinkle with flour and fry brown on both sides in bacon drippings. Serve with crisp bacon. Serves 6.

CORN-MEAL MUSH

¾ cup corn meal	½ teaspoon salt
2½ cups boiling water	

Add corn meal and salt to boiling water and cook 5 minutes, stirring constantly. Reduce heat and continue cooking 15 minutes longer.

SUCCOTASH

Method No. 1

1 cup cooked corn, cut from cob   1 cup cooked, shelled lima beans

Combine corn and lima beans, add ½ cup light cream. Cook over medium heat until vegetables are heated through. Season to taste. Serves 4.

Method No. 2

1 cup uncooked corn   1 teaspoon salt
1 cup uncooked, shelled lima   ½ cup water
      beans   ½ cup light cream

Cook vegetables in salted water until tender. Drain. Add cream. Reheat. Serve at once. Serves 4.

Method No. 3

1 box frozen corn kernels   1 teaspoon salt
1 box frozen lima beans   ½ cup light cream

Break packages of frozen vegetables into 3 or 4 portions each. Place in saucepan, add salt and cream. Cover. Cook on high heat until steaming, then reduce heat and continue cooking for 10 minutes. Serves 8.

Salads

Salads are no longer considered an extra-fancy touch to be reserved only for company dinners. It was not too many years ago, however, that most men claimed that all they wanted was meat and potatoes, with perhaps a pie for dessert. Things are not so today. Men—and even boys—are not only eating salads, but insisting upon them as a part of the meal!

There probably is a good reason for this change in attitude. In the first place, women have learned to use a little more imagination in making salads, and we have also learned that a salad, to be good, must be cold. Modern refrigeration has been one of the big contributing factors in the wholehearted acceptance of salads.

The finest salads in the country are served in California. Of course, in that climate, wonderful fruits and vegetables are available all year round from which to concoct salads. But even the best fruits and vegetables can't make a good salad unless they are carefully blended and served very cold. It is not unusual, in California, to see salads mixed over a large bowl of ice, so deeply do Californians believe that the colder a salad is, the better tasting it will be. And I believe that they are right!

When to Serve Salads

There is no hard and fast rule as to when to serve a salad. A tossed salad may serve as a first course, or it may be served as a part of the meal. There are those who like their salad after the meat course has been served, and it is not unusual to see a salad served alone as the main dish, particularly for luncheon. The time you pick should be determined by family preference, and the rest of the menu. Suit yourself as to when you serve it—making certain that you do not overlook the salad as an important part, no matter when it is served, of any meal.

Salad Greens

Don't limit your energies to one or two salad greens. There is a great variety: head lettuce, leaf lettuce, chicory, escarole, endive, Chinese cabbage, spinach, water cress, parsley, and romaine are all wonderful served separately or when several different kinds are blended together.

How to Prepare

When you are buying salad greens, be sure to buy fresh, crisp greens. As soon as you get them home, wash carefully, discarding all wilted and discolored leaves. Drain and put immediately in the Humidrawer of your refrigerator. The temperature and humidity in the Humidrawer is exactly right to crisp and cool the vegetable.

If you are going to use the head lettuce within a day or so, take a sharp knife and cut out the core at the bottom. Turn on the cold water and let it trickle slowly through the lettuce. The leaves will separate and cup at the same time, and the lettuce will stay crisp until time for use.

When preparing any of the leafy vegetables with a thick or coarse stem, carefully pull the leaf from the stem and discard the stem. This should be done particularly with spinach, romaine, escarole, water cress and parsley.

TRICK: When you are planning a tossed salad for dinner, wash and prepare the salad greens in the morning. Dampen a clean tea towel. Place the salad greens in the tea towel, taking care not to bruise the leaves. Place in Humidrawer of your refrigerator. When ready to serve, place in salad bowl, toss on the dressing, and the salad is ready in a second.

Salad Vegetables

Most vegetables are wonderful in salads. They may be used either raw or slightly cooked. An overcooked vegetable is not crisp and therefore not particularly good in a salad.

The vegetables most commonly used are: carrots, cauliflower, celery, radishes, tomatoes, cucumbers, young onions, tops and all, dried onions, asparagus tips, beets, potatoes, broccoli, and artichoke hearts.

If members of the family don't like, or cannot eat, raw vegetables, parboil them. It is an easy thing to do. First, prepare the vegetable in desired sizes. Carrots are usually cut in medium-small cubes, cauliflower is broken into flowerets, celery is sliced, and broccoli broken into medium-sized buds. If you are planning to use a combination of these vegetables, place in a saucepan, add about ¼ cup water, season with salt, heat until boiling point is reached, then reduce the heat and cook about 8 minutes. Drain off any remaining water. Place vegetables in a bowl and spoon a small amount of French dressing over them. Place in refrigerator to chill. This process is called "marinating," and it can add flavor and pungency to your vegetable salad.

Tricks in Salad Making

Tomatoes should always be peeled before they are put into a salad. Dip the tomato in boiling water, then place it in refrigerator to chill. When ready to use, the skin slips off easily. Or, you can rub the back of a silver knife over the tomato. This loosens the skin and makes it come off easily.

Carrot curls are an attractive garnish and are made by cutting the carrot through the center. Then take your handy vegetable peeler and, starting at the top of the carrot, push the vegetable peeler down the entire length of the carrot. Place shavings in a bowl of ice water, and they curl beautifully.

Cucumbers will add distinction as well as taste to salads if you score them. To score a cucumber, run the tines of a silver fork along the sides of the cucumber. Press firmly so that the tines will break through the skin. When sliced, the green perforated skins will add beauty to your salads.

Celery circles are wonderful in a salad and are easy to make. They also make an excellent accompaniment to a salad. Here's how to make them.

Mix ½ cup grated sharp cheese with a dash of garlic salt, 1 teaspoon onion juice, dash of red pepper, ¼ teaspoon Worcestershire sauce, and 1 teaspoon mayonnaise. Take 6 crisp stalks of celery and stuff with cheese mixture. Then carefully put together just as they were originally on the stalk. Tie with a string. Wrap in waxed paper and place in refrigerator to chill. When ready to serve, cut in ¼-inch slices.

Never wash your wooden salad bowl. After using, wipe it out with a clean dish towel or a paper towel that has been slightly dampened; then cover the bowl and put it away. Your bowl will have a beautiful luster as well as providing excellent flavor to the salad.

What You Will Need When Making Salads

It's a wise homemaker who keeps a supply of salad needs in one corner of her kitchen cabinet. You won't use all the following for one salad, but as you grow more daring and expert in this culinary art, you'll find yourself using more and more of the out-of-the-ordinary things.

For a good start you will need salad oils, either vegetable or olive, good cider vinegar, plus a small bottle of tarragon vinegar, and garlic vinegar. For a truly wonderful vinegar, you might splurge and buy a bottle of pear vinegar. Then you should have various condiments, such as dry mustard, curry powder, Worcestershire sauce, paprika, garlic, onion, poppy seed, celery seed, and a small assortment of herbs, such as tarragon, rosemary, dill, sweet basil. Of course, there really is no limit to what you can use, but those listed above are fundamental and will carry you along in fine shape in your salad making.

How to Make a Tossed Salad

Use a large bowl, preferably a wooden one. Rub the inside of the bowl with a clove of garlic which has been cut in two, so that you will be able to rub the cut edge along the bowl.

Tear the greens to the desired size—never, *never* cut them. Try to keep them just good bite size, for if you tear them into very small pieces, your salad will not look or taste as well. Then spoon chilled salad dressing over the mixture, adding only enough to coat the leaves, but not enough to collect in a little pool at the bottom of the bowl. Too much dressing will make the salad soggy and will rob it of a great deal of its flavor.

Before using the dressing, shake it very thoroughly to be sure that all ingredients are well blended. You may use a fork to toss the dressing through the greens, or you may follow the expert salad makers and simply use your hands. Remember to be gentle, yet thorough, as you toss the greens, for you must guard against crushing the leaves.

It is that simple to make a plain tossed salad. You may want to try some of the variations and special combinations you will find later on in this chapter, but all will be made after the same procedure. A good tossed salad, you will find, adds a great deal to any meal and is worth the small amount of extra care that makes the difference between the crisp inviting salad and the defeated-looking, soggy bowl of greens that no one enjoys.

Fruit Salad

There is practically no limit to the fruit which may be used in salads. The fruit may be raw, cooked, dried, or spiced. Apples, peaches, pears, avocados, pineapple, melon, grapes, oranges, grapefruit, bananas, cherries—all make excellent salads individually or blended together.

However, it is important to remember that the fruit must be thoroughly chilled, and if canned fruit is to be used, it must be carefully drained.

How to Make Grapefruit and Orange Sections

Grapefruit and oranges find their way into most fruit salads. They are best when served in sections, and while sectioning may seem like quite a task, it really is simple, and worth doing.

With a sharp paring knife, peel the grapefruit or orange, just as you would an apple. Be sure you cut clear through and remove the white portion from the fruit. When the fruit has been peeled, take the point of your knife and remove the little pithy white center at both ends. Now hold the fruit in your hand and insert the point of the knife under the thin skin which separates each section. This will be easier if you first run the knife across the outer edge and loosen the skin. Then, with the sharp edge of the knife, push down to the center of the orange or grapefruit, gently loosen the section, and lift it out. From this point on the job is easy, as you loosen the skin on the next section and lift out, and so on all the way around.

Better practice first on grapefruit. They are a little easier to do than oranges.

VEGETABLE SALADS—NOT MOLDED

This is probably the simplest of all salads to make. However, the future of the salad depends upon the crispness of the greens, which means they must be thoroughly chilled. Never start a mixed green salad unless all vegetables used have been washed, drained, and placed in the Humidrawer of your refrigerator to chill.

You may use head lettuce, romaine, endive, escarole, water cress, young dandelion leaves, and spinach.

To serve 4, use about ½ head lettuce and ¼ pound each of 2 or 3 of the other leafy vegetables listed above.

You may also add finely sliced young green onions, tops and all, radishes, green pepper, cucumber, tomato, cauliflower, or bits of leftover vegetables such as snap beans, beets, carrots, peas, and so forth.

Here's How to Do It

Rub the salad bowl with a clove of garlic which has been cut in half. Break the salad greens into the salad bowl in fair-sized chunks. Be sure to break and not cut the salad greens. Then toss the salad greens, onion slices, chopped green pepper, and so forth. If you find a small amount of leftover cooked vegetables in the refrigerator, add those for good measure.

Pour over the mixture about ¼ of the French dressing recipe (page 204). Toss carefully with two forks, but however you toss it, don't bruise the vegetables. Then add about ¼ additional cup of French dressing.

You should only use enough dressing to coat the leaves thoroughly. Any additional amount will make the salad too runny.

There you have an outline of how mixed salads are made. Remember the three basic rules . . . keep it crisp . . . keep it cool . . . and keep experimenting with new combinations. Your salads will repay the effort you put into them.

How to Garnish Vegetable Salads

Again your imagination will help you. To start with, however, try some of the easiest of the garnishes: radish roses, carrot curls, red or green pepper rings, slices of unpeeled cucumber which have been scored before slicing, hard-cooked egg slices, lemon wedges, stuffed olives, sliced, sprigs of parsley or water cress. A generous dash of paprika also helps to pep up the appearance of a salad.

COUNTRY-CLUB SALAD

1 clove garlic	1 head lettuce
4 strips bacon, cut fine	3 egg whites, hard cooked
¼ cup chives, cut fine	Egg French dressing (page 204)

Peel and cut garlic in half. Rub bowl with garlic. Fry bacon which has been cut fine and drain off drippings. Chop chives fine. Place lettuce in garlic-rubbed bowl. Then add bacon and chives. Cut egg whites left from salad dressing and add to mixture in bowl. Pour thoroughly chilled dressing over salad. Serves 4-6.

SPRING SALAD BOWL

1 clove garlic	3 tomatoes, peeled and cut in
½ lemon French dressing (page	quarters
205)	4 green onions, sliced fine
1 head lettuce	6 radishes, sliced fine
1 bunch water cress	Salt and pepper to taste
1 heart of endive	3 hard-cooked eggs, chopped
1 cup celery, sliced	½ cup parsley, chopped

Rub a salad bowl with garlic which has been cut in half. Pour in lemon French dressing. Tear lettuce, water cress, and endive in bite-sized pieces, and toss with a fork until leaves are well coated. Add celery, tomatoes, onions, radishes, salt, and pepper, if needed, and toss again until well mixed. Sprinkle chopped eggs and parsley over the top. Will serve about 8.

HEARTY SALAD

1 clove garlic	1 cup Thousand Island dressing
1 head lettuce	(page 208)
4 green onions, sliced fine	¼ pound cooked ham, tongue, or
1 cup sharp Cheddar cheese, cut	chicken, cut in long, slender
in small cubes	lengths

This salad is best made in individual servings. Use either individual wooden salad bowls, or bowls used for cereal or soup. Rub each bowl with the garlic which has been cut in half. Shred lettuce quite fine. Add onion and cheese to lettuce and mix carefully with Thousand Island dressing, reserving about ¼ cup of the dressing to place on top of salad. Place lettuce mixture in bowls. Lay the cooked meat strips over top. Place a small amount of dressing over this. Serve as the main part of a meal. Serves 4.

TRICK: This is an excellent salad to make if you have a small amount of leftover boiled ham, chicken, or tongue. All three meats may be used if you wish. In fact, it makes the salad even better to use mixed meats.

CAESAR SALAD

2 cloves garlic	1 head curly endive
½ cup olive oil	1 bunch water cress
¼ teaspoon salt	¼ cup Parmesan cheese
⅛ teaspoon pepper	¼ cup bleu cheese, crumbled
1 tablespoon Worcestershire sauce	1 raw egg
1 head lettuce	½ cup lemon juice
	2 cups crisp croutons

Peel garlic. Place in olive oil and allow to stand for several hours. Remove garlic before using. To ⅛ cup of the oil, add the salt, pepper, and Worcestershire sauce. Break crisp greens into a salad bowl. Add cheese. Pour flavored olive oil over greens, break egg over mixture, add lemon juice, and carefully toss all together. Toss croutons in remaining garlic-flavored oil. Let stand about 1 minute. Add to salad and mix lightly. Serve at once before croutons become softened. Serves 8.

To Make Croutons

Cut crusts from bread. Cut bread in about ¼-inch cubes. Either brown in oven slowly or brown in small amount of butter or margarine in a skillet.

COLESLAW

1 small head cabbage	Evaporated milk dressing (page 206) or sour cream dressing (page 209)

Place cabbage in Humidrawer of your refrigerator several hours before using. The cabbage must be very crisp. Cut cabbage in half, then in quarters. Remove the core. Use a very sharp knife and shred cabbage very fine. Toss with whichever dressing you prefer. Serves 4-6.

HOT SLAW

2 egg yolks, slightly beaten	1 tablespoon sugar
¼ cup cold water	½ teaspoon salt
¼ cup vinegar	3 cups cabbage, shredded fine
1 tablespoon butter or margarine	

Combine egg yolks, water, vinegar, butter or margarine, sugar, and salt. Cook over low heat, stirring constantly until mixture thickens. Add cabbage and reheat, stirring gently with a fork. It will take about 1 minute for the cabbage to heat. Serves 4-6.

CUCUMBERS, EUROPEAN STYLE

Wash half-grown cucumbers and serve on a plate as you would apples. Shake a little salt on the cucumber when eating.

DANDELION SALAD

1 pound tender young dandelions	1 teaspoon salt
4 slices bacon, diced	½ teaspoon pepper
2 tablespoons butter or margarine, melted	½ teaspoon paprika
	1 tablespoon sugar
½ cup thick cream, sweet or sour	4 tablespoons vinegar
2 eggs, beaten	

Wash and dry dandelions (preferably some which have been picked from flowerless stalks). Place in salad bowl. Dice and fry bacon until crisp. Pour bacon pieces and hot drippings over dandelions. Place butter or margarine in skillet in which bacon was fried. Add cream, beaten eggs, salt, pepper, paprika, sugar, and vinegar. Cook over low heat, stirring constantly until mixture has thickened. Pour this piping hot over dandelions and blend thoroughly by tossing up and down with a fork. Serves 4-5.

GRATED CARROT SALAD

Wash young, tender carrots very carefully. They do not need to be peeled, if they are very tender and carefully washed. Grate on fine grater and gently toss French dressing (page 204) through them, using a fork. Place on lettuce leaf and serve at once. A bit of cheese may be grated with the carrots. Allow about 1 medium-sized carrot per person.

SNAP BEAN SALAD

2½ cups snap beans, cooked	¼ cup French dressing (page 204)
2 hard-cooked eggs, chopped	
Salt and pepper to taste	

Place beans, eggs, and seasoning in bowl. Pour on French dressing and toss lightly with a fork. Serve on a lettuce leaf. Serves 4.

   TREAT: Try using a little grated onion or finely sliced green onion in this salad.

LIMA BEAN SALAD

2½ cups cooked lima beans,
    dried or fresh
2 hard-cooked eggs, chopped
1 tablespoon onion, finely
    chopped

1 cup Cheddar cheese, diced
Salt and pepper to taste
½ cup mayonnaise (page 207)

Place beans in bowl. Add hard-cooked eggs. Blend thoroughly. Add onion, cheese, salt, and pepper. Pour on mayonnaise and toss together gently, using a fork. Serve on lettuce leaf. Serves 4-5.

KIDNEY BEAN SALAD

2 cups cooked kidney beans,
    thoroughly chilled
4 sweet pickles, cut fine
½ cup celery, cut fine

1 small onion, grated fine
½ cup peanuts, chopped
½ cup boiled salad dressing
    (page 211)

If you are using canned kidney beans, be sure to drain them. Add remaining ingredients to kidney beans and toss carefully. Serve on a lettuce leaf. Serves 4-5.

LEAF LETTUCE AND SPINACH SALAD

¼ pound leaf lettuce
¼ pound fresh spinach
5 spring onions

4 to 5 radishes
½ cup evaporated milk dressing
    (page 206)

Wash lettuce and spinach carefully. Remove stem portion of spinach. If lettuce leaves are large, break into smaller sections. Slice spring onions, tops and all, and add to spinach and lettuce. Slice radishes very thin and add to mixture. Pour dressing over all, toss carefully, and serve at once. Serves 4.

TURNIP AND CARROT SLAW

3 cups turnips, grated
1½ cups carrots, grated
¼ cup mayonnaise (page 207)
¼ cup thick sour cream

½ teaspoon salt
⅛ teaspoon pepper
¼ teaspoon dry mustard
¼ cup sweet pickle, chopped

Mix turnips and carrots. Combine mayonnaise, sour cream, salt, pepper, mustard, and pickles. Toss vegetables and dressing together lightly. Serve on lettuce. Serves 4-5.

WILTED LEAF LETTUCE

½ pound leaf lettuce
1 medium onion, sliced very thin
2 slices bacon, diced
⅔ cup vinegar
½ cup water

1 tablespoon sugar
1 teaspoon salt
1 egg, slightly beaten
2 tablespoons sour cream or
    evaporated milk

Mix lettuce and onion together. Fry bacon until crisp. Remove bacon and place on paper toweling. To the bacon drippings in the skillet add the vinegar, water, sugar, and salt. Bring to a boil. Beat egg until light. Add milk or sour cream. Pour boiling liquid over egg mixture, then pour back into skillet and cook over low heat until slightly thickened. Pour over lettuce and onion. Toss lightly until thoroughly mixed. Serves 4.

MEXICAN SALAD

¼ cup salad oil
1 clove garlic
1 cup soft bread cubes
½ cup celery, sliced thin
1 pimiento, cut in strips
1 cup cooked potatoes, diced
½ cup onion, grated

½ cup carrot, grated
2 tablespoons green pepper,
    minced
1 teaspoon salt
1 teaspoon chili powder
2 tablespoons vinegar

Heat oil in skillet. Sauté garlic and bread cubes until bread cubes are quite crisp. Remove garlic. Combine bread with remaining ingredients which have been placed in a salad bowl. Serves 4-6.

TREAT: Top salad with strips of salami or boiled ham and serve as a main course.

POTATO SALAD NO. 1

3 cups potatoes, diced
1 medium onion, diced fine
1 cup celery, diced fine
¼ cup olive oil
1 teaspoon salt

1 teaspoon dry mustard
½ cup nippy mayonnaise (page
    207)
2 hard-cooked eggs

Cook potatoes with skins on. Cool. Peel potatoes and dice in ¼-inch cubes. The potatoes must be diced fine for this mixture. Slice onion very fine. Add onion and diced celery to potatoes. Blend carefully, using a fork. Pour olive oil over potato mixture. Place in refrigerator and allow to stand at least 4 hours. About an hour before ready to serve, add salt and dry mustard to mayonnaise.

Blend through salad. Garnish the salad with slices of hard-cooked eggs. Serves 4-6.

TRICK: Add a little dried tarragon to water while cooking potatoes for unusual flavor.

POTATO SALAD NO. 2

3 cups cooked potatoes, diced
2 hard-cooked eggs, sliced
1 cucumber, diced
1 tablespoon onion, finely chopped
1½ teaspoons salt

¼ teaspoon black pepper
½ teaspoon celery seed or 1 cup chopped celery
¾ cup boiled dressing (page 211)

Combine all ingredients and chill for several hours. Serves 4-5.

HOT POTATO SALAD

4 slices bacon, diced
½ cup vinegar
½ cup water
1 tablespoon sugar
½ teaspoon dry mustard

4 steaming hot potatoes
1 medium-sized onion, chopped
2 tablespoons parsley, chopped
2 teaspoons salt
¼ teaspoon black pepper

Fry bacon until crisp. Remove from skillet and set aside. Add vinegar, water, sugar, and mustard to bacon drippings and bring to a boil. Slice hot potatoes into a bowl. Sprinkle with onion, parsley, salt, pepper, and bacon which has been crumbled fine. Pour hot vinegar mixture over potatoes. Toss carefully with a fork. Serve hot. Serves 4-6.

TOMATO AND COTTAGE CHEESE SALAD

4 medium-sized tomatoes
1 cup seasoned cottage cheese
Lettuce or other salad greens

½ cup mayonnaise (page 207)

Scald tomatoes and peel. Chill. Cut tomatoes into wedges, being careful not to cut all the way through. Spread gently and fill centers with ¼ cup cottage cheese. Serve on lettuce leaf. Top with mayonnaise. Serves 4.

STUFFED TOMATO SALAD

4 tomatoes
½ cup cucumber, diced
½ cup cooked chicken, diced
¼ cup nut meats, chopped
½ cup mayonnaise (page 207)

½ teaspoon salt
⅛ teaspoon pepper
Lettuce
Paprika

Scald tomatoes and peel. Prepare as directed for stuffed tomatoes (page 189). Chill. Cut tomatoes down from top about 1 inch, forming a tomato rose of about 6 petals. Mix all ingredients together excepting the lettuce and paprika. Reserve 2 tablespoons of the mayonnaise to use as a topping for the salad. Push petals of tomato open, being very careful not to break tomato apart. Fill cavity with chicken mixture. Arrange on lettuce leaf. Top with small amount of mayonnaise. Sprinkle paprika over top. Serves 4.

How to Prepare Tomatoes for Stuffing

Select medium-sized, smooth tomatoes. Scald, remove skin. Cut a slice from top, and with a spoon, carefully remove some of the pulp. Place tomatoes, cut side down, on a plate. Place in refrigerator thirty minutes to chill.

CHICKEN, MEAT, AND SEA FOOD SALADS

CHICKEN SALAD

2 cups cooked chicken, diced
3 hard-cooked eggs, chopped
1 cup celery, chopped
¼ cup slivered, salted toasted almonds

2 tablespoons sweet pickle, chopped
½ teaspoon salt
1 teaspoon onion juice
½ cup mayonnaise (page 207)

Lightly toss ingredients together. Place in refrigerator and chill for several hours. Pile high in lettuce cups. Serve immediately. Serves 4-6.

CHICKEN SWEETBREAD SALAD

2 cups cooked chicken, cut in chunks
2 cups cooked sweetbreads, cut in chunks (to cook see page 56)
1 teaspoon salt
1 teaspoon monosodium glutamate

1 cup celery, cut in ½-inch pieces
¼ cup stuffed olives, sliced
½ cup mayonnaise (page 207)
   Lettuce
½ cup shredded almonds
2 hard-cooked eggs, sliced
¼ cup French dressing (page 204)

Combine chicken and sweetbreads. Sprinkle salt and monosodium glutamate over top. Toss lightly with a fork. Add celery, olives, and mayonnaise. Toss lightly with a fork. Cover and store in refrigerator at least 3 hours. Serve in lettuce cups and garnish with slivered almonds and hard-cooked egg slices. Just before serving, spoon 1 teaspoon French dressing over each salad. Serves 6.

HAM AND CABBAGE TOSSUP

1 can (12 ounces) spiced meat	1 green pepper, diced
1 cucumber	2 tomatoes, cut in wedges
1 Bermuda onion	½ cup French dressing (page 204)
4 cups cabbage, shredded	¼ cup mayonnaise (page 207)

Cut meat in fine strips. Wash cucumber, score, and slice. Slice onion thin and separate rings. Toss all ingredients together with French dressing which has been mixed with mayonnaise. Serve at once. Serves 8.

TRICK: Remember to add beauty to your salad by scoring cucumber, page 179.

SALAD CRAB LOUIE

2 cups fresh or canned crab meat	1 small onion, chopped
2 tablespoons lemon juice	½ cup mayonnaise (page 207)
3 cups lettuce, shredded	2 hard-cooked eggs, sliced
½ cup celery, chopped	1 pimiento, cut in strips
½ cup fresh tomato, chopped	

Place crab meat in bowl and sprinkle lemon juice over it. Toss lightly with a fork. Add shredded lettuce, celery, tomato, onion, and mayonnaise. Toss carefully with a fork. Place on lettuce leaf. Garnish with hard-cooked egg slices and strips of pimiento. Serves 4-6.

TRICK: This salad makes an excellent luncheon. Serve with Melba toast or hot buttered English muffins.

SALMON SALAD

1 can (1 pound) salmon	2 hard-cooked eggs, sliced
1 sour pickle, chopped	½ cup mayonnaise (page 207)
1 cup cabbage or celery, chopped	

Flake the salmon, removing the skin and bones. Add chopped pickle, cabbage or celery, and eggs. Add mayonnaise and toss together lightly, using a fork. Serves 4-6.

FRUIT SALADS

There is no limit to what may be done with fruit salads. Orange and grapefruit segments may be served on a lettuce leaf and used as a "pepper-upper" to a simple meal. Or, the fruit salad may be more elaborate, with orange and grapefruit segments plus avocado pear strips, pineapple wedges, and so forth.

A fruit salad is just as easy to make during winter months as it is during the summer, when the majority of the fruits are in season. A salad of cooked prunes, with seed removed and stuffed with cottage cheese, nuts, or stuffed olives, is a wonderful way to intrigue the family into eating prunes. Canned Royal Ann or Bing cherries, with pits removed and stuffed with nuts or small bits of candied ginger, make an easy salad that is also delicious.

During the season when the beautiful big persimmons are available, combine slices of the persimmon with grapefruit segments and several strips of avocado pear. Serve this with a snappy Roquefort cheese dressing, and you really have a conversation salad.

Fruit plates are frequently served as the main part of the meal, when you will be wise to offer a choice of dressing. Some folks like a tart French dressing, while others prefer a sweeter dressing, such as the cooked fruit salad dressing on page 210. During hot summer months the poppy-seed dressing (page 211) is popular.

Fruit plates almost always have grapefruit and orange segments, plus other fruit in season, such as juicy ripe pears, pineapple wedges, melon balls or chunks, red-skinned apples with the skin left on, grapes, peach halves, bananas, and, if available, several strips of avocado pear to add color to the plate. Cottage cheese is frequently piled in the center of the fruit plate, while a center of orange, pineapple, or lemon sherbet is delicious.

Garnishes for fruit salads may be water cress, strawberries with stems left on, pomegranate seeds sprinkled over the top, stuffed prunes, and the good old standby, maraschino cherries.

When using canned fruit for salads, drain fruit carefully. Otherwise the salad will look sloppy and uninteresting. Save the juice, for it may be used in many ways. One good way is to give it to the family to drink.

CINNAMON APPLE SALAD

1½ cups water
½ cup sugar
½ cup red cinnamon drops
6 whole cloves
6 good-sized apples
1 cup cottage cheese

4 tablespoons nut meats,
    chopped
⅓ cup mayonnaise (page 207)
Salt to taste
Lettuce

Combine water, sugar, cinnamon drops, and cloves. Boil until all cinnamon drops are dissolved and the sirup is red in color. Peel apples and cut out core, cutting away a hole about an inch in diameter. Drop apples in sirup and boil slowly, turning frequently, until apples are tender and well colored. Drain and chill.

Combine cottage cheese and nuts and moisten with mayonnaise. Season to taste. Stuff the apples with cheese mixture. Serve on lettuce leaf or any greens available. This makes a beautiful salad for Valentine's Day or Christmas. Serves 6.

CELERY AND APPLE SALAD

2 cups apples, cubed
¾ cup celery, chopped
¼ cup nuts, chopped

¼ cup mayonnaise (page 207)
¼ teaspoon salt
Lettuce

Combine all ingredients. Cover. Place in refrigerator to chill for at least an hour before serving. Serve on crisp lettuce leaf, or garnish with a small spray of celery leaves. Serves 4-5.

TREATS: Substitute ¼ cup seedless raisins and 6 marshmallows, cut in small pieces, for the celery and nuts.

Substitute ½ cup chopped dates for nut meats and add 1 tablespoon prepared horse-radish.

COTTAGE CHEESE AND APPLE SALAD

3 apples, diced
1 cup celery, diced
½ cup cucumber, diced
¼ cup tart French dressing
    (page 204)
Lettuce

1 pint cottage cheese
½ cup salted peanuts, chopped
⅓ cup mayonnaise (page 207)

Wash and dice unpeeled apples. Toss apples, celery, and cucumber with French dressing until well coated. On each plate place crisp lettuce leaves. Then, with a spoon, shape ⅓ cup cottage cheese into a ring. Fill each ring with apple mixture and sprinkle chopped peanuts over top. Top with mayonnaise. Serves 6.

COTTAGE CHEESE AND PRUNE SALAD

Remove pits from cooked or canned prunes. Fill with seasoned cottage cheese. Finely cut nuts may be added, if desired. Serve on crisp lettuce leaf, with topping of mayonnaise.

CHEDDAR CHEESE AND PEAR SALAD

4 pear halves, fresh or canned	¼ cup French dressing (page 204)
¾ cup Cheddar cheese, grated	Lettuce leaves

If you are using fresh pears, better dip them in lemon juice to prevent discoloration. If canned pears are used, be sure to drain thoroughly. Grate the cheese on small shredder. Fill pear cavity with grated cheese and carefully pour French dressing through the cheese. Serve on lettuce leaf. Serves 4.

COTTAGE CHEESE AND PEACH SALAD

4 large peach halves, canned preferable	¼ cup toasted almonds slivered
1 cup cottage cheese	¼ cup French dressing (page 204)
1 tablespoon chives, finely chopped	Lettuce cups

Drain peaches carefully. Mix cottage cheese with chopped chives. If chives are not available, use 1 teaspoon onion juice. Fill center of peach with cottage cheese mixture. Sprinkle almonds over top, then dribble French dressing through the cottage cheese. Serve in lettuce cups. Serves 4.

CITRUS SALAD BOWL

3 cups Chinese celery cabbage, shredded	2 oranges, sectioned
1 grapefruit, sectioned	¼ cup French dressing (page 204)

Toss all ingredients together and mix with French dressing just before serving. Serves 6.

EASTER SALAD

2 cups lettuce, finely shredded	10 ½-inch balls cream cheese
2½ cups carrots, grated	⅓ cup French dressing (page 204)
5 pear halves	
10 ½-inch balls of American cheese	

Arrange shredded lettuce on salad plate. In center of lettuce make a nest of the grated carrots. Place a pear half in each nest and arrange balls of cheese inside the pear. Serve with French dressing. Serves 5.

TREAT: Roll the cottage cheese balls in finely chopped parsley. Very pretty touch.

GOLDEN SALAD

2 cups lettuce or cabbage, shredded
1½ cups orange sections
1½ cups raw carrot, shredded

½ cup seedless raisins
Salt to season
¼ cup French dressing (page 204)

Place shredded lettuce or cabbage on salad plate. Toss remaining ingredients together and serve on shredded lettuce or cabbage. Serves 4-5.

ORANGE AND GREENS SALAD

3 cups salad greens, lettuce, endive, water cress, etc., coarsely shredded
¼ cup stuffed olives, sliced
1 cup orange sections, diced

½ cup green pepper, chopped
1 tablespoon onion, finely chopped
¼ cup French dressing (page 204)

Combine salad greens, olives, orange sections, green pepper, and onion. Toss French dressing through the mixture. Serves 4-6.

PEAR AND GRAPE SALAD

4 pear halves, fresh or canned
½ pound Tokay grapes
1 package cream cheese

1 tablespoon thick cream or mayonnaise
4 grape leaves

If fresh pears are used, be sure they are very ripe. Dip in lemon juice immediately after peeling to prevent discoloration. If canned pears are used, drain thoroughly. Cut grapes in half and remove the seeds. Mix the cream cheese with cream or mayonnaise. Place pear half, cut side down, and spread cream cheese over it. Cover entire surface of pear with grapes which have been cut in half and are placed cut side down on the pear. Place grape leaf on salad plate and put pear, cut side down, on grape leaf. The finished pear resembles a bunch of grapes. Top with mayonnaise, if desired. Serves 4.

PINEAPPLE TOSSED SALAD

1 cup pineapple chunks, fresh or   3 cups lettuce, shredded
     canned   ¼ cup poppy-seed dressing
1 cup Early Thompson seedless   (page 211)
     grapes

If canned pineapple chunks are used, drain thoroughly. Combine all ingredients and carefully toss poppy-seed dressing through until all particles are well coated. Serves 4.

MOLDED SALADS

Molded salads have a great advantage in that they can be made in advance and unmolded just before serving.

Tricks with Molded Salads

Before pouring gelatin mixture into mold, rinse mold with cold water. When gelatin is firm, dip individual molds quickly into hot water. Have the desired garnish on salad plate. Invert mold on garnish. Give the mold a quick tap with a knife, and the salad should drop out. If it is a little stubborn, dip a clean dish cloth in hot water. Squeeze all moisture out and place on top of mold for about a minute.

Some people like to grease the mold first, but that has always seemed to me to be an unnecessary amount of work.

To make very sure the salad will come out of the mold, run the point of a paring knife around the upper edge of the mold before placing in the hot water. However, this is a bit tricky, because sometimes the salad comes out quicker than you expect and lands where it isn't wanted.

Large salad molds require a few extra steps. Dip a spatula in hot water and run the spatula around the congealed mixture, loosening it slightly from the pan. Do this around the outer and inner edge of the mold. Dip in hot water and unmold on garnished serving tray or plate. Or, after running the spatula around the edges, turn onto garnished serving tray or plate and lay a clean tea towel, which has been dipped in hot water and wrung out, over top of mold. Shake mold gently, lift up one end, insert spatula, and allow air to enter. Then turn mold back onto serving tray, give mold a shake or two, and, presto, the beautiful concoction is right where you want it.

How to Dissolve Unflavored Gelatin

Unflavored gelatin must always be softened in a cold liquid. If the recipe states "Dissolve over hot water," place dish containing softened gelatin in a pan of hot water. Keep water hot over low heat. Stir until gelatin is dissolved.

How to Whip Gelatin Mixtures

To whip satisfactorily the gelatin must be partially congealed. Use an electric mixer if possible, and set it at highest speed. Have both the mixer bowl and beaters thoroughly chilled. Whip until mixture is fluffy.

GOLDEN GATE SALAD

1-quart mold or 6 individual molds

1 tablespoon unflavored gelatin	1 cup canned pineapple
¼ cup cold water	crushed or finely cut,
1¼ cups pineapple juice	well drained
½ teaspoon salt	1 cup raw carrots, grated
¼ cup lemon juice	Lettuce
2 tablespoons sugar	¼ cup mayonnaise (page 207)

Soak gelatin in cold water for 5 minutes. Dissolve over hot water. Add pineapple juice, salt, lemon, and sugar. Place in refrigerator to chill. When partially set, fold in the pineapple and carrots. Turn into mold or molds. Serve on lettuce with a topping of mayonnaise. Serves 6.

JELLIED BEET RING

8-inch ring mold

1 tablespoon unflavored gelatin	3 tablespoons vinegar
¼ cup cold water	2 tablespoons lemon juice
1 cup hot water, part beet juice	1 cup celery, diced
1 tablespoon sugar	1 cup cooked beets, diced
½ teaspoon salt	Lettuce
3 tablespoons prepared	Coleslaw (page 184)
horse-radish	¼ cup mayonnaise (page 207)

Soften gelatin in cold water. Add hot liquid and stir until dissolved. Add sugar, salt, horse-radish, vinegar, and lemon juice. Place in refrigerator to chill. When mixture begins to thicken, stir in celery and beets. Pour into a ring mold. Chill until firm. Unmold on lettuce-garnished plate or tray. Fill center with coleslaw. Top with mayonnaise. Serves 6.

TRICK: If pickled beets are to be used, use beet juice for part of water and eliminate both the vinegar and lemon juice.

IMPERIAL SALAD
6 individual molds

1 package lemon-flavored gelatin	3 slices pineapple, cubed and drained
1 cup boiling water	1 cup cucumber, diced
1 cup pineapple juice	Lettuce
1 tablespoon vinegar	¼ cup mayonnaise (page 207)

Dissolve gelatin in boiling water. Add pineapple juice and vinegar. Place in refrigerator to chill. When slightly thickened, add pineapple and cucumber. Fill molds. Chill until firm. Serve on lettuce with a topping of mayonnaise. Serves 6.

JEWEL SALAD
1-quart mold or 6 individual molds

1 tablespoon unflavored gelatin	½ cup celery, diced
¼ cup cold water	½ cup beets, diced
1¼ cups boiling water	½ cup cabbage, finely shredded
1 teaspoon horse-radish	1 tablespoon onion, finely chopped
2 tablespoons lemon juice	
2 tablespoon vinegar	Lettuce
2 tablespoons sugar	¼ cup mayonnaise (page 207)
½ teaspoon salt	

Soften gelatin in cold water and dissolve in hot water. Add horseradish, lemon juice, vinegar, sugar, and salt. Place in refrigerator to chill. When mixture begins to thicken, fold in vegetables. Pour into mold or molds. Chill. When firm, unmold on lettuce leaf and top with mayonnaise. Serves 6.

SOUR-CREAM CUCUMBER SALAD
6 individual molds

1 package lime-flavored gelatin	1 cup unpeeled cucumbers, finely chopped
¾ cup hot water	
¼ cup lemon juice	Lettuce
1 teaspoon onion juice	¼ cup mayonnaise (page 207)
1 cup sour cream, whipped	

Dissolve gelatin in hot water. Add lemon juice and onion juice. Place in refrigerator to chill. When partially set, fold in whipped sour cream and cucumbers. Pour into molds and chill until firm. Unmold on lettuce leaf. Top with mayonnaise. Serves 6.

SUNSHINE SALAD

1 package orange-flavored gelatin
1¾ cups boiling water
2 tablespoons vinegar
⅛ teaspoon salt
½ cup celery, chopped
½ cup carrots, shredded

2 or 3 medium-sized green peppers
Lettuce
¼ cup mayonnaise (page 207) or French dressing (page 204)

Dissolve gelatin in boiling water. Add vinegar and salt. Place in refrigerator to chill. When partially congealed, add celery and carrots. Wash green peppers, slice off top, and remove center core and seeds. Set green peppers upright in a cup. Fill peppers with gelatine mixture. Return to refrigerator until set. To serve, slice green pepper, crosswise in half, and arrange on lettuce leaf. Serve with topping of mayonnaise or French dressing. Serves 4-6, depending upon size of green peppers.

SUNSET SALAD

1-quart mold or 8 individual molds

1 tablespoon unflavored gelatin
¼ cup cold water
1 egg yolk
½ teaspoon salt
1 cup pineapple juice
2 tablespoons lemon juice
½ cup evaporated milk, whipped (see page 206)

2 cups cabbage, shredded
1 cup canned pineapple, cut fine
½ cup carrots, shredded
Lettuce
¼ cup mayonnaise (page 207)

Soak gelatin in cold water for at least 5 minutes. Beat egg yolk and add salt, pineapple juice, and lemon juice. Place in saucepan. Bring to a boil, stirring constantly. Remove from heat, add gelatin, and stir until gelatin has dissolved. Place in refrigerator to chill. When gelatin mixture has thickened, whip the evaporated milk and fold the gelatin mixture into the whipped milk. Pour into mold or molds. Unmold on lettuce leaf. Top with mayonnaise. Serves 8.

PERFECTION SALAD

1-quart mold or 6 individual molds

1 tablespoon unflavored gelatin	½ cup cabbage, shredded
¼ cup cold water	2 tablespoons green pepper,
1 cup boiling water	chopped
¼ cup sugar	1 pimiento, chopped
½ teaspoon salt	Lettuce
¼ cup vinegar	¼ cup mayonnaise (page 207) or
1 tablespoon lemon juice	French dressing (page 204)
1 cup celery, chopped	

Soak gelatin in cold water, add boiling water, and stir until gelatin has dissolved. Add sugar, salt, vinegar, and lemon juice. Mix well. Place in refrigerator to chill. When partially set, add vegetables and pour into mold or molds. When firm, unmold on lettuce leaf and top with either mayonnaise or French dressing. Serves 6.

PINEAPPLE PARTY SALAD

1 can (No. 2½) crushed	¼ teaspoon salt
pineapple	1 cup dry cottage cheese
1 package lemon-flavored	1 cup mayonnaise
gelatin	½ cup blanched and chopped
1 package lime-flavored gelatin	almonds

Drain sirup from pineapple. Add enough water to sirup to make 2 cups. Heat to boiling point. Dissolve lemon and lime gelatin in boiling liquid. Add salt. Cool until slightly thickened. When beginning to congeal, fold in cottage cheese, mayonnaise, crushed pineapple, and nuts. Pour into mold, or 9-inch square pan. Place in refrigerator to chill and set. Serve on lettuce leaf, topped with a touch of mayonnaise. Serves 10-12.

TOMATO CHEESE RING

7- or 8-inch ring mold

3 cups tomato juice	1 cup mayonnaise (page 207)
2 packages lemon-flavored	Chicken salad (page 189)
gelatin	Lettuce or greens
2 packages cream cheese	

Heat tomato juice. Dissolve gelatin in hot juice. Place in refrigerator to chill. When partially set, mix cream cheese with mayonnaise and fold into tomato mixture. Pour into ring mold. Chill. When set, unmold on tray or plate. Fill center with chicken salad. Garnish with any greens available. Stuffed green olives would also make an attractive garnish. Serves 8.

TOMATO ASPIC

This excellent salad will enhance any meal. When molded in a ring mold, the center may be filled with cottage cheese, chicken salad, or a cooked vegetable salad. If a ring mold is not available, pour mixture into a utility pan and cut into 2-inch squares. Cottage cheese, chicken salad, and so forth may be served on top of the squares.

2 tablespoons unflavored gelatin	1 teaspoon sugar
¼ cup cold water	½ teaspoon salt
4 cups tomato juice	¼ cup lemon juice
1 onion, chopped	Lettuce
½ cup celery, chopped	½ cup mayonnaise (page 207) or
4 whole cloves	French dressing (page 204)
6 peppercorns	

Soak gelatin in cold water 5 minutes. Cook tomato juice with onion, celery, cloves, and peppercorns for about 10 minutes. Strain and add to the soaked gelatin, stirring until gelatin has dissolved. Add sugar, salt, and lemon juice. Pour into mold or molds. Place in refrigerator to chill until set. May be served on lettuce leaf with mayonnaise or French dressing. Serves 8.

JELLIED CHICKEN SALAD

Small mold or 6 individual molds

1 package lemon-flavored gelatin	½ cup celery, chopped
2 cups chicken stock	1½ cups cooked chicken, cut into medium chunks
½ cup cooked peas	Lettuce
½ cup raw carrots, grated	

Dissolve gelatin in hot chicken stock. Let cool until slightly thickened. Combine the other ingredients and add to the gelatin mixture. Pour into mold or molds. Chill. Serve on lettuce leaf with mayonnaise. Serves 6.

TRICK: Cook the chicken bones for your chicken stock. Season well. Or use 4 chicken bouillon cubes and 2 cups boiling water.

MOLDED TUNA FISH SALAD

1-quart mold or 8 individual molds

1 package lemon-flavored gelatin
2 cups hot water
2 tablespoons vinegar
½ teaspoon salt
1 cup tuna fish, flaked

1 cup celery, chopped
2 tablespoons pimiento, chopped
½ cup nut meats, chopped
½ cup mayonnaise (page 207)
Lettuce

Dissolve gelatin in hot water. Add vinegar and salt. Chill. When slightly thickened, add the other ingredients except lettuce, mixing well. Turn into mold or molds. Chill. Unmold. Serve on lettuce leaves. Serves 6-8.

TUNA VEGETABLE SALAD MOLDS

4 individual molds

1 tablespoon unflavored gelatin
¼ cup lemon juice
1 can condensed cream of chicken soup
1 can (7 ounces) tuna fish, flaked

½ cup celery, chopped
¼ cup cucumber, chopped
¼ cup mayonnaise (page 207)
Salad greens

Soften gelatin in lemon juice. Heat soup over low heat. Then blend in the gelatin, stirring until dissolved. Mix in remaining ingredients. Prepare salad molds by rinsing them with cold water. Pour the salad mixture into the molds. Chill until firm in the refrigerator. Unmold and serve on crisp salad greens. Serves 4. If desired, molds may be garnished with a thick slice of tomato, hard-cooked egg, cut in quarters, and 2 slices of cucumber.

FROZEN FRUIT SALAD NO. 1

8x10-inch utility dish

3 ripe bananas
1 cup canned pineapple, diced
1 cup canned pears, diced
1 dozen maraschino cherries, thinly sliced

1 cup fruit salad dressing (page 210)
1 cup heavy cream, whipped
Lettuce

Mash bananas to a smooth pulp, then add pineapple, pears, and cherries. Add fruit salad dressing, then cream, whipped until stiff. Pour in utility dish which has been lined with waxed paper. Place in freezer or freeze chest of refrigerator and freeze until firm. Cut into squares. Serve on lettuce leaf with a topping of dressing. Serves 12.

FROZEN FRUIT SALAD NO. 2

1 package cream cheese
2 tablespoons cream
2 tablespoons lemon juice
1 cup pineapple chunks, fresh, frozen, or canned
1 cup orange sections, broken
½ cup Royal Ann cherries, seeded

½ cup maraschino cherries, chopped
½ cup nut meats, chopped
¼ cup mayonnaise (page 207)
1 cup heavy cream, whipped
2 tablespoons sugar
Lettuce

Mix cheese with cream and lemon juice. Add fruit, nut meats, and mayonnaise. Whip cream and add sugar and fold into fruit mixture. Pour into freezing tray of your refrigerator and freeze. It is not necessary to stir. Serve on lettuce leaf. Serves 6-8.

FROZEN CRANBERRY SALAD

1 package cream cheese
½ cup jellied cranberry sauce
2 tablespoons lemon juice
⅛ teaspoon salt

1 cup heavy cream, whipped
Lettuce
¼ cup fruit salad dressing (page 210)

Beat cheese until smooth. Add cranberry sauce, lemon juice, and salt. Whip until thoroughly mixed. Fold in whipped cream. Place in ice cube tray, or comparable small pan. Freeze in freeze chest of refrigerator or home freezer. Cut in squares and serve on lettuce leaf with a topping of fruit salad dressing. Serves 4.

PIQUANT HAM RING

7-inch ring mold

1 package lemon-flavored gelatin
1½ cups hot water
3 tablespoons vinegar
⅛ teaspoon salt
1 teaspoon onion juice
⅓ cup sweet pickle, chopped
1½ tablespoons pimiento, diced

⅓ cup mayonnaise (page 207)
2 tablespoons milk
1 cup ground, cooked ham, firmly packed
½ cup celery, diced
½ teaspoon Worcestershire sauce

Dissolve gelatin in hot water. Add vinegar, salt, and onion juice. Measure 1 cup into small bowl and chill. When slightly thickened add pickles and pimiento. Turn into small ring mold. Chill until firm. Meanwhile, chill remaining gelatin until slightly thickened. Beat until fluffy and thick like whipped cream. Combine mayonnaise and milk and fold into whipped mixture. Add remaining ingredients. Turn into mold on top of firm gelatin. Chill until firm. Unmold on garnished plate. Serves 8.

TREAT: Fill the center of the mold with tossed salad or coleslaw —both pretty and delicious.

FROSTED MEAT LOAF SALAD

Large ring mold

1½ tablespoons unflavored gelatin	½ cup sour cream
¼ cup tomato juice	¼ cup mayonnaise (page 207)
1¾ cups tomato juice	2 cups cooked veal, shredded or cut very fine. (If veal has to be cooked, it may be roasted with a bit of garlic.)
1 teaspoon grated onion	
2 tablespoons lemon juice	
⅛ cup horse-radish	

Soften gelatin in ¼ cup of tomato juice. Bring remaining tomato juice to boiling point. Add onion and lemon juice to tomato juice. Add gelatin to hot mixture and stir until gelatin has dissolved. Chill. Combine horse-radish, sour cream, and mayonnaise and add to chilled tomato juice mixture. Chill. When slightly thickened, add meat and pour into ring mold. Chill.

Frosting for Meat Loaf

½ tablespoon unflavored gelatin	½ cup cucumber, finely chopped
3 tablespoons cold water	Salt and pepper to taste
½ pound cottage cheese	½ green pepper, chopped
½ cup sour cream	1 tablespoon parsley, chopped

Soak gelatin in cold water, then dissolve over hot water. Combine cheese, sour cream, cucumber, and seasonings. Add gelatin. Beat thoroughly. Pour on top of congealed mixture in ring mold. Chill until very firm. When ready to serve, unmold on garnished platter or tray. Serves 10-12.

TREAT: For a very special party or buffet supper, you could fill the center with chicken or veal salad (page 189).

SALAD DRESSINGS

FRENCH DRESSINGS

Any of these dressings are excellent on any vegetable or leafy salad. Just pick the one you like best.

FRENCH DRESSING NO. 1

½ teaspoon salt
¼ teaspoon pepper
½ teaspoon dry mustard

Dash of white pepper
¼ cup vinegar
¾ cup salad oil

Place dry ingredients in jar. Add vinegar and salad oil. Shake jar until ingredients are well blended. Chill in refrigerator before using. Serves 8.

FRENCH DRESSING NO. 2

1 teaspoon salt
½ teaspoon black pepper
½ teaspoon paprika
¼ teaspoon dry mustard
1 tablespoon onion, chopped
2 teaspoons Worcestershire
  sauce

1 tablespoon tarragon vinegar
2 tablespoons cider vinegar
¼ cup sugar
½ cup garlic vinegar
5 drops Tabasco sauce (optional)
1 tablespoon lemon juice
2 cups salad oil

Place all ingredients in bowl of mixer and mix well. Pour into quart jar and chill in refrigerator until ready to use. Makes 1 quart.

EASY FRENCH DRESSING

1 teaspoon sugar
½ teaspoon salt
⅛ teaspoon paprika

1 tablespoon vinegar
3 tablespoons salad oil

Mix ingredients in order given. Shake well. Serves 2.

EGG FRENCH DRESSING

3 hard-cooked eggs (separate
  yolks from whites)
½ teaspoon salt
½ teaspoon sugar
½ teaspoon dry mustard

⅛ teaspoon cayenne pepper
¼ teaspoon paprika
1 cup salad oil
¼ cup lemon juice

Place hard-cooked egg yolks in mixing bowl. Add salt, sugar, mustard, pepper, and paprika. Mix and beat thoroughly. Gradually add the oil and lemon juice, beating constantly until dressing is of a rich creamy consistency. Cover and place in refrigerator until ready to use. Serves 4-6.

HONEY FRENCH DRESSING

½ cup honey
1 cup salad oil
½ teaspoon salt
⅓ cup chili sauce

½ cup vinegar
1 medium onion, grated
1 tablespoon Worcestershire
   sauce

Place all ingredients in quart jar and shake well. Chill before serving. Makes 1 pint.

LEMON FRENCH DRESSING

½ cup lemon juice
½ cup salad oil
1 teaspoon salt
1 teaspoon paprika

2 tablespoons sugar
½ teaspoon celery seed
1 clove garlic, grated

Put all ingredients in quart jar and shake well. Makes 1 cup.

SPECIAL FRENCH DRESSING

1 clove garlic, grated fine
1 small onion, grated fine
½ cup sugar
⅓ cup tarragon vinegar

1 teaspoon Worcestershire sauce
⅔ cup tomato catchup
1 teaspoon salt
1 pint salad oil

Combine ingredients in bowl of electric mixer and beat until well blended and fairly thick. Store in quart jar in refrigerator. Makes 1 quart.

CELERY SEED DRESSING

5 tablespoons sugar
½ teaspoon dry mustard
½ teaspoon salt

2 tablespoons vinegar
½ cup salad oil
1½ teaspoons celery seed

Blend the sugar, mustard, salt, and 1 tablespoon of the vinegar. Gradually add the oil, beating constantly with electric or rotary egg beater. Add remaining tablespoon vinegar and the celery seeds. Chill before using. Serves 4-6.

CHEESE SALAD DRESSING

⅓ cup olive oil
⅓ cup vegetable oil
½ cup lemon juice
¼ cup Parmesan cheese, grated
½ cup crumbed Roquefort, Bleu,
  or Gorgonzola cheese
6 anchovies, cut fine
1 raw egg, beaten

1 clove garlic, peeled and halved
1 tablespoon Worcestershire
  sauce
½ teaspoon monosodium
  glutamate
¼ teaspoon salt
¼ teaspoon black pepper

Combine all ingredients in a jar or mixing bowl. Beat or shake until well blended. Cover tightly and store in refrigerator for several hours before using. Just before using, shake or mix thoroughly and remove garlic. Serve on green salad. Serves 6.

EVAPORATED MILK DRESSING—Particularly good on cabbage slaw.

½ cup sugar
⅓ cup vinegar

½ cup evaporated milk
½ teaspoon salt

Add sugar to vinegar and stir until sugar has dissolved. Beat in milk until mixture thickens. Pour over cabbage. Use a fork to blend dressing through cabbage. Serves 4-6.

PARISIENNE DRESSING

1 teaspoon salt
1 teaspoon dry mustard
1 teaspoon sugar
1 teaspoon paprika

2 tablespoons catchup
¼ teaspoon cayenne pepper
1 cup salad oil
3 tablespoons vinegar

Mix first six ingredients together. Add 1 tablespoon salad oil at a time, beating briskly. Add vinegar last and beat thoroughly. Makes about 1¼ cups.

ROQUEFORT CHEESE DRESSING

½ cup Roquefort or bleu cheese
½ cup salad oil
6 tablespoons wine vinegar
¼ teaspoon salt

½ teaspoon pepper
½ teaspoon paprika
¼ teaspoon celery salt

Place cheese in bowl and mash with a fork. Work in the oil. Add vinegar a little at a time. If you prefer your dressing a little sharper, add another tablespoon vinegar. Blend in seasonings. Chill before serving. Makes about 1 cup.

TWO-MINUTE SALAD DRESSING

¼ cup lemon juice
¼ cup salad oil
½ teaspoon salt
⅔ cup condensed milk

1 egg yolk, beaten
1 teaspoon dry mustard
Dash cayenne pepper

Place all ingredients in quart jar and shake until well blended. Chill before serving. Makes about 1¼ cups.

MAYONNAISE AND VARIATIONS

Mayonnaise is excellent on vegetable salads, and may also be used on fruit and molded salads, whenever its creamy texture seems to make it more desirable than the more pungent French dressing.

MAYONNAISE

1 teaspoon salt
¼ teaspoon sugar
1 teaspoon dry mustard
¼ teaspoon paprika

2 egg yolks
2 tablespoons vinegar
2 cups salad oil
2 teaspoons lemon juice

Mix salt, sugar, mustard, and paprika into egg yolks. If you have an electric mixer, use small bowl of mixer. If not, use a mixing bowl and a good rotary beater. If you have neither, better buy the mayonnaise. Do not beat the egg too much or the oil will not blend satisfactorily. Add vinegar. Blend quickly. Pour oil slowly onto egg yolk mixture. A pitcher is a fine thing to use. Beat briskly all the time the oil is being added. When 1 cup of the oil has been added, add lemon juice and immediately add the remainder of the oil. Makes about 1 pint.

TRICK: If you were unlucky, and the oil did not blend with the egg yolk, take another egg yolk, beat it lightly, then slowly add the mixture into it, beating briskly.

NIPPY MAYONNAISE

½ cup mayonnaise
1½ teaspoons prepared
    horse-radish

1½ teaspoons prepared mustard
1 small sweet pickle, chopped

Combine ingredients. Mix thoroughly. Chill before serving. Makes about ¾ cup or 4 servings. Especially good on tomato salad or head lettuce.

GREEN GODDESS DRESSING

1 cup mayonnaise
½ cup heavy cream
1 small jar anchovy paste
2 tablespoons tarragon vinegar

2 tablespoons garlic vinegar
2 tablespoons herb vinegar
1 teaspoon dried parsley
1 small onion, grated

Place ingredients in bowl. Mix well. Chill before serving. Makes about 2 cups.

LAMAZE DRESSING

This is the famous dressing served at the Claridge Hotel, Atlantic City. It is used on either cold shrimp, crab meat, or lobster.

1 pint mayonnaise
1 pint chili sauce
½ cup India relish, chopped
1 hard-cooked egg, chopped
1 teaspoon chives, chopped
1 pimiento, chopped
½ green pepper, chopped

2 tablespoons celery, chopped
1 tablespoon prepared mustard
1 tablespoon Worcestershire
   sauce
⅛ teaspoon paprika
⅛ teaspoon salt
Black pepper

Mix well. Chill and serve. Makes 1 quart. Serves about 12.

THOUSAND ISLAND DRESSING

1 cup mayonnaise
2 tablespoons chili sauce
2 tablespoons green pepper,
   chopped

2 tablespoons pimiento, chopped
2 tablespoons sweet pickle,
   chopped

Blend all ingredients together. Chill before serving. Serves 4.

RUSSIAN DRESSING

1 cup mayonnaise
2 tablespoons chili sauce

1 teaspoon onion juice

Blend all together. Chill before serving. Serves 4.

CUCUMBER DRESSING

1 package cream cheese
½ cup mayonnaise
½ teaspoon onion juice

¼ teaspoon salt
⅛ teaspoon paprika
¼ cup cucumber, diced

Mash cream cheese. Beat in mayonnaise until smooth. Add remaining ingredients. Mix well. Chill before serving. Especially good on tomato wedges or slices. Serves 4.

BACON DRESSING

4 slices bacon, diced fine
½ small onion, chopped
¼ cup vinegar

1 tablespoon sugar
1 teaspoon salt

Fry bacon until crisp, add onion, and cook over low heat until onion is tender but not brown. Add remaining ingredients. Bring to steaming point and pour over leaf lettuce or spinach. Serves 4.

EGG DRESSING

½ cup mayonnaise

2 hard-cooked eggs, chopped
    medium fine

Combine mayonnaise and hard-cooked eggs. Chill before serving. Excellent on leaf lettuce or spring salad. Serves 4.

YOGHURT DRESSING

1 cup yoghurt
1 hard-cooked egg, chopped
½ teaspoon salt
¼ teaspoon celery seed

¼ teaspoon prepared mustard
1 tablespoon lemon juice
1 teaspoon sugar (optional)

Mix all ingredients and chill for at least 1 hour before serving. Excellent on head lettuce. Serves 4.

SOUR-CREAM DRESSING

1 teaspoon salt
1 teaspoon sugar
⅛ teaspoon cayenne pepper

1 tablespoon lemon juice
2 tablespoons vinegar
1 cup thick sour cream

Place salt, sugar, and pepper in mixing bowl. Blend thoroughly. Add lemon juice and vinegar. When mixture is perfectly smooth, fold in the cream. Stir well and store in covered container in refrigerator. Excellent on coleslaw. Serves 4.

GUACAMOLE (Pronounced Wah-Ka-Mo'Lay)

2 avocado pears
1 tablespoon lime or lemon
    juice
1 teaspoon salt
1½ teaspoons onion, finely
    grated

2 small tomatoes, chopped
3 or 4 canned chili peppers,
    chopped, or a few drops
    Worcestershire sauce
1 clove garlic

Mash avocado pears very fine. Add lime or lemon juice, salt, onion, tomato, chili peppers or Worcestershire sauce. Rub bowl with clove of garlic, cut in half. Place mixture in bowl and chill for at least 1 hour before serving. Serves 4-5. Delicious on head lettuce of tomato slices or wedges.

TRICK: For variety, add ¼ teaspoon curry powder, or 2 tablespoons crumbled Roquefort cheese, or ¼ cup sherry. Try it simply as a dip for potato chips or crackers, too.

COOKED SALAD DRESSING

8 egg yolks or 4 eggs	2 tablespoons all-purpose flour
½ cup sugar	½ cup cream, sweet or sour
½ teaspoon dry mustard	¾ cup cider vinegar
1 teaspoon salt	¼ cup water

Place eggs in mixing bowl and beat slightly. To them, add the sugar, mustard, salt, and flour. Beat until light and fluffy. Add cream and beat again. Place vinegar and water in saucepan and heat. When hot, slowly add egg mixture, stirring constantly. Continue beating until mixture thickens. This is a rich salad dressing, delicious on cabbage slaw or potato salad. Makes about 1½ pints.

DRESSINGS PARTICULARLY GOOD ON FRUIT SALADS

SPECIAL FRUIT-SALAD DRESSING

¼ cup sugar	2 tablespoons vinegar
½ teaspoon salt	¾ cup pineapple juice
1½ tablespoons all-purpose flour	
1 egg	

Mix ingredients in order given, stirring well after each addition. Cook over low heat until thick and smooth, stirring constantly. Chill thoroughly before serving. Excellent on molded fruit, frozen fruit, or just fruit salad. Makes about 1 cup.

LIME DRESSING

3 tablespoons lime juice	½ cup heavy cream, whipped
½ cup honey	stiff
2 eggs, well beaten	

Mix lime juice, honey, and eggs. Place in saucepan and cook over low heat until thickened, stirring constantly. Cool. Fold in stiffly beaten cream. Makes about 1½ cups.

POPPY-SEED DRESSING

1½ cups sugar
  2 teaspoons dry mustard
  2 teaspoons salt
  ⅔ cup vinegar

2 teaspoons onion juice
2 cups salad oil
1 tablespoon poppy seed

Combine and beat first four ingredients. Add onion juice and beat. Then add salad oil slowly. When thick, add 1 tablespoon poppy seed. Chill before serving. Makes about 3 cups.

BOILED DRESSING

  4 tablespoons sugar
  1 teaspoon dry mustard
  1 teaspoon salt
  2 tablespoons cornstarch
  2 tablespoons vinegar

3 tablespoons lemon juice
1½ cups boiling water
2 tablespoons butter or
    margarine
2 egg yolks

Mix dry ingredients. Add vinegar, lemon juice, water, and butter or margarine. Cook over low heat until thickened, stirring frequently. Add beaten egg yolks, cook 1 minute longer. Remove from heat. When cool, place in covered jar and keep in refrigerator. Thin as needed with cream, plain or whipped. Makes 1 pint.

Fruits

Fruits play an important part in our diet. All fruits, fresh, canned, dried, or frozen, are important for their vitamin and mineral contribution to our health. Almost everyone is fond of fruits, but we are apt to forget the important role they play in our daily diet, and we therefore are prone to overlook them.

While fruits are not listed under desserts, they really should be included in the dessert classification. In fact, there is such a wide variety of fruits available today, they can be served for breakfast, lunch, and dinner, with no repeats of the same fruit, and, therefore, no one grows weary of seeing them appear regularly at mealtime.

How to Serve Raw Fruits

A bowl filled with fresh, cold fruit makes wonderful eating. Many folks enjoy eating apples, pears, in fact almost any fruit, with a bit of sharp cheese.

However, wash the fruit carefully before serving. Fruit growers are forced to use so many sprays in order to grow fruit, that it now is essential to wash carefully any fruit which is eaten raw. Even though you serve the fruit with fruit knives, in case anyone cares to peel the fruit, it is advisable to wash it before serving.

Several years ago some extensive research was done on the best temperature for serving fruit. The conclusion was that all fruit should be chilled in the refrigerator before serving. Chilling seems to make the fruit juicier and better in flavor.

Bananas are the one exception to this rule. Bananas should never be placed in the refrigerator. They do not ripen properly, and therefore the best flavor is not developed.

How to Serve Frozen Fruits

Frozen fruits should be thawed in the container in which they are packaged. This prevents discoloration or oxidation of the fruit. They should completely thaw, but should be served just as the last ice crystals are disappearing. It requires about 2 hours at room temperature to thaw a package of frozen fruit.

Frozen fruit collapses after it has thawed and loses some of its flavor and texture. Therefore, only thaw as much frozen fruit as will be served at the meal, or used at once.

For a real treat in serving frozen peaches, strawberries, or raspberries, remove frozen fruit from carton to serving dishes. (Do not thaw first.) Cover with 2 tablespoons heavy cream. The cream prevents the fruit from oxidizing as it thaws. If served in this way, only about 20 minutes is required for the frozen fruit to be at eating temperature.

APPLESAUCE

8-10 cooking apples   ½ cup sugar
½ cup water

Wash, pare, and core apples. Cut into quarters. Place in saucepan with cover. Add water. Cover and cook over medium heat until apples are soft. Remove from heat, but allow apples to cool in covered saucepan. Serves 6.

SUMMER APPLESAUCE

Duchess, Melba, and Early Transparent are all good summer apples. Wash carefully. Cut in quarters. Remove stem and blossom ends. Place in saucepan with water to cover. Cook over medium heat until apples are mushy. Put through a medium-fine sieve. Return to saucepan. Add about ¼ cup sugar to each cup apple pulp. Cook over low heat until sugar has dissolved. 2 pounds of blemish-free apples will serve 4.

TREAT: Some cooks like to add a thin peel of lemon to the apples while cooking. Others prefer a dash of cinnamon or nutmeg.

AVOCADOS (Also known as Alligator Pears.)

Many folks like to make a deep cut to the seed, separate the halves, and eat the fruit from the shell, seasoning with salt and pepper. A sprinkle of lemon juice also makes a fine seasoning.

When used in salads, avocados are usually peeled and sliced.

The center may be filled with Chicken à la King (page 86) and either placed under the broiler or heated in the oven for a short time. Avocados prepared in this manner make an excellent luncheon dish.

BANANAS

For eating, they are best when flecked with brown. If they are to be cooked, they should be slightly green at the tip. Do not refrigerate.

CRANBERRY SAUCE

2 cups sugar
2 cups water

4 cups cranberries

Place sugar and water in saucepan with cover. Wash and pick over cranberries. When sugar and water come to boiling point, and sugar has dissolved, add cranberries. Cover. Cook until all the skins pop open, which usually requires about 5 minutes. Remove from range, and allow sauce to remain in saucepan (covered) until cool. Makes about 1 quart sauce.

CRANBERRY JELLY

4 cups cranberries
3 cups water

Sugar

Cook cranberries with water in covered saucepan until soft. Strain through a fine strainer or jelly bag. Measure juice and allow ¾ cup sugar to each cup juice. Place juice in saucepan, bring to boiling point, then add the sugar, and stir until sugar has dissolved. Cook rapidly for about 5 minutes, or until a drop jells on a cold plate. Pour into sterilized glasses, cool, and cover with paraffin. Or, pour into an 8x8-inch square pan and cut jelly in cubes for serving. Makes about 4 glasses or 16 small cubes.

SPECIAL CRANBERRY JELLY

3 cups cranberries
1 cup water

12 saccharine tablets (¼ gr.)

Cook cranberries and water in covered saucepan until all skins pop open. Remove from heat and put through a sieve. Dissolve saccharine tablets in small amount of hot cranberry juice. Combine with sauce and chill. Makes about 1 cup.

STEWED CHERRIES

4 cups sour cherries   ¾ cup sugar
1 cup water

Wash and pit cherries. Place water and sugar in saucepan and allow to boil for about 3 minutes. Add cherries. Cover. Cook slowly for another 5 minutes. Serves 4-5.

CURRANTS

Currants may be cooked or eaten raw. Remove fruit from stem, making sure the blossom and stem ends are brushed off. If cooked, make a sirup of 1 cup water and ½ cup sugar, boil for about 3 minutes, then add 4 cups currants and cook slowly until currants are tender.

If served raw, prepare as above, sprinkle with sugar, about 2 tablespoons to each cup of currants, chill, and serve. Currants are delicious when mixed in equal parts with either red or black raspberries.

GRAPEFRUIT

Grapefruit is seldom cooked. It is best eaten from the shell, loosening fruit from the membrane with a sharp knife. The center may be loosened by cutting with sharp kitchen scissors. Be sure to remove all seeds.

Grapefruit may be brushed with melted butter or margarine, a tablespoon of cointreau or rum poured over fruit, and placed under broiler for a few minutes. Or, brown sugar may be substituted for the wine.

Or, the grapefruit may be peeled, the white outer membrane cut off, and the fruit sectioned (page 181). This is most generally done when using grapefruit in salads.

ORANGES

Oranges may be juiced, cut in half and served from the shell, or peeled and sliced. Many fine hotels feature sliced oranges as a breakfast treat. When serving oranges sliced, you may sweeten them with confectioners' sugar and add grated coconut.

PINEAPPLE

An easy way to remove the rough outer rind from pineapple is to stand it upright on a cutting board. Grasp the top of the pineapple with one hand, and with a sharp paring knife cut downward, from the top to the bottom. When the outer rind is removed, lay the pineapple on its side and cut in slices. These slices may vary from ½ to ¾ inch, depending upon how you wish to use them. With a sharp knife, remove eyes from the outside of the slice. These are bitter and must all be removed. Serve either in slices or dice, according to your wishes.

Add very little sugar to the pineapple before serving, since it is usually very sweet and juicy. Not more than a tablespoon of sugar per serving is necessary.

Some folks prefer to lay the uncut pineapple on its side on a cutting board and cut across in slices. Then remove the outer rind and eyes.

Suit yourself as to the method used for preparing the pineapple, but be sure to remove the center core. It is woody and has little or no flavor.

A tablespoon of kirsch poured over fresh pineapple slices or cubes, just before serving, adds a glamorous touch to the fruit when served as a dessert. Use 1 tablespoon kirsch per serving.

POMEGRANATES

The seed is the most delicious part of this beautiful fruit, although some folks enjoy cutting the fruit in half and spooning out the small portion of pulp with the seeds.

An interesting way to serve pomegranates is to remove the seeds, mix with a small amount of honey, and serve as a dessert with a sharp Cheddar cheese.

The seeds are wonderful to use as a garnish on salads, or fruit cups, or any colorless dessert that you wish to pep up with a dash of brilliant color.

RASPBERRIES

Raspberries are a perishable fruit which should be emptied from the box in which they were bought onto a platter or dish of comparable size. The fruit must not be piled. Place in food compartment of refrigerator, uncovered, and do not wash until ready to serve.

Add only a small amount of sugar, about 1 tablespoon per serving, because the fruit is sweet from its own delicious nectar.

STRAWBERRIES

Store in refrigerator the same as raspberries. Do not remove hulls before washing, and do not wash until ready to serve. The hulls protect the sweetness of the fruit.

RHUBARB

When buying rhubarb, select firm stalks, with fresh-looking leaves. Do not peel. Cut off stem ends and leaves. Wash carefully and cut in about 1-inch lengths. Place in saucepan. To 4 cups prepared rhubarb, add ½ cup water. Cover. Bring to a full rolling boil, then reduce heat. Cook on simmer heat for about 5 minutes. Then add from ½ to ¾ cup sugar, depending upon your own taste. Allow to simmer for 5 minutes, keeping saucepan covered. Remove from heat. Allow rhubarb to cool in container in which it was cooked. 2 pounds of rhubarb will make approximately 4 cups in cut lengths and will serve 4.

If you should have the oven going, place rhubarb in casserole, add ½ cup water, and ½ to ¾ cup sugar. Cover. Cook at 350° F. until tender, or for about 30 minutes. Many homemakers prefer this method for cooking rhubarb, feeling that it maintains its delicate pink color much better.

DRIED FRUITS

The dried fruits most commonly used are prunes, apricots, peaches, and figs. Pears and apples are used in certain parts of the United States and are delicious.

Unless the fruit has been tenderized, which most of it is today, it must be soaked overnight before cooking. To do this, wash fruit carefully and cover with cold water. The following morning cook in the water in which it was soaked.

Tenderized and soaked dried fruits are cooked slowly. Place in saucepan with cover. Cover with water. Cover saucepan. Bring slowly to the steaming point and allow to simmer for 45-50 minutes. When fruit is tender, add ½ cup sugar for each pound of dried fruit. Cover. Allow to simmer for 5 minutes. Remove from heat and cool in saucepan in which it was cooked, keeping saucepan covered. Many people feel the dried fruit is sufficiently sweet without adding any sugar.

Dried fruits are wonderful served for a breakfast fruit, or a luncheon, or dinner dessert. For a dinner dessert, serve a mixture of thoroughly chilled apricots, prunes, and peaches, and to each serving, add 1 tablespoon cointreau or maraschino. It is an easy dessert to prepare, and one that folks enjoy as much as many desserts which take a far longer time to prepare.

Fried Foods

Years ago most people thought that deep-fat-fried foods were unhealthy, and so, though they yearned for the crunchy tastiness of these foods, they tried not to eat them too often. Today we know that deep-fat frying, or French frying, as it is sometimes called, can be a healthful way to cook foods as long as the fat does not become too hot so that it makes the foods indigestible, nor too cool, so that it soaks into the food. With the help of today's accurate fat thermometers, and the miraculous deep-fat fryers, we are now able to eat these wonderful foods with a hearty appetite and an undisturbed conscience.

Type of Fat to Use for Deep-Fat Frying

You can pretty well take your choice on this score. Some prefer a good quality vegetable shortening. Peanut oil is a favorite with others. Salad oils made from cottonseed or corn are also excellent. Leaf lard has long been the favorite of many, and the very fine new product which is a mixture of fine leaf lard and vegetable shortening does a wonderful job of deep-fat frying.

How to Care for Fat Which Has Been Used for Deep-Fat Frying

Although there is a variance of opinion on this subject, one of our largest manufacturers of shortening recommends that the fat be strained as soon after using as possible, poured back into the original can and kept in the refrigerator. The fat may be used over and over again, but, since a small amount is used up in any frying job, it may be necessary occasionally to add a small amount of fresh shortening to the frying kettle.

An easy way to strain the used fat is to place a piece of cheesecloth in a wire mesh strainer. Put strainer over the container in which the fat is to be stored. The cheesecloth collects any small particles of food which might be left in the fat after frying.

Necessary Equipment

Today the necessary equipment is much simplified, because there are many fine deep-fat fryers on the market. Most of these are thermostatically controlled, so a thermometer is not essential. If you do not have one of these appliances, but do considerable deep-fat frying, then you probably should invest in a thermometer.

By all means have a supply of paper toweling, since all fried foods should be drained on absorbent paper as soon as they are removed from the fry kettle.

Deep-Well Cooker

If you have a deep-well cooker on your range, this is splendid to use. Some deep-well cookers are thermostatically controlled, which makes deep-fat frying very simple.

Amount of Fat to Use

Always use sufficient fat so the food being fried will be completely immersed. Also, use a kettle large enough so the fat or oil will not bubble over when food is put in.

3 pounds of fat is, in general, about the right amount for most frying.

Approximate Temperatures for Frying Foods

350° F.—Young chicken.

375° F.—Doughnuts, fritters, small whole fish, fillets, oysters, clams, breaded chops, twice-fried potatoes, croquettes.

390° F.—French-fried potatoes.

DOUGHNUTS

SWEET-MILK DOUGHNUTS

Frying temperature—375° F.

3½ to 4 cups all-purpose flour,
    sifted before measuring
  4 teaspoons baking powder
  ¼ teaspoon cinnamon
  ¼ teaspoon nutmeg, grated

1½ teaspoons salt
  1 cup sugar
  4 tablespoons shortening
  3 eggs
  1 cup sweet milk

Sift flour with baking powder, spices, and salt. Cream sugar and shortening together until light and fluffy. Add unbeaten eggs, one at a time, beating thoroughly after each addition. When eggs are completely blended, add milk and 3½ cups of the flour alternately to mixture—first adding half the flour, then half the milk, the remaining flour and remaining milk. The mixture may need more flour, so add whatever is necessary from the ½ cup flour remaining. Set dough in refrigerator for 1 hour to become thoroughly chilled. Roll only half the dough at a time, sprinkling rolling board and rolling pin generously with flour. Roll dough ¼ to ⅜ inch thick. Cut with doughnut cutter. Fry about 5 doughnuts at a time. When one side is brown, which should take about 2 minutes, turn doughnut with a long-handled fork. When doughnuts are fried, lift from hot fat with long-fork. Drain on paper toweling. Makes about 30 doughnuts.

TRICK: Better get your doughnuts all rolled out and cut before you start frying. It will save you a lot of time and considerable nervous energy.

BUTTERMILK DOUGHNUTS NO. 1

Frying temperature—375° F.

½ cup shortening
1 cup sugar
½ teaspoon salt
2 eggs
1 cup hot mashed potatoes
4 cups all-purpose flour, sifted
  before measuring

3 teaspoons baking powder
½ teaspoon nutmeg
½ teaspoon soda
1 cup thick buttermilk

Blend shortening and sugar, salt, and eggs together until light and fluffy. Stir in freshly cooked, hot mashed potatoes. Sift flour with baking powder, nutmeg, and soda and add alternately with butter-

milk to first mixture. Blend ingredients together thoroughly. Place
in refrigerator to chill for 1 hour. Roll to about ¼ to ⅜ inch on board
which has been lightly floured. Only roll half the dough at a time.
Cut with doughnut cutter. Fry. As soon as doughnuts rise to surface and are brown on underside, turn with a long-handled fork.
To remove doughnuts from hot fat, use long-handled fork. Drain
on absorbent paper. Makes about 30 doughnuts.

BUTTERMILK DOUGHNUTS NO. 2

Frying temperature—375° F.

4 cups all-purpose flour, sifted before measuring	1 teaspoon nutmeg
	¾ cup sugar
3 teaspoons baking powder	⅓ cup shortening
1 teaspoon baking soda	3 eggs, beaten
1 teaspoon salt	1¼ cups thick buttermilk

Sift flour with baking powder, soda, salt, nutmeg, and sugar. To
this, add the shortening and cut it in until mixture has the appearance of corn meal. Combine eggs and buttermilk. Work liquid
into mixture. Knead for about 1 minute. Divide dough into two
parts—you'll find it much easier to handle. Roll out dough until
it is about ¼ inch thick. Cut with doughnut cutter. Fry the "holes,"
too. Youngsters love them. When doughnuts rise to the surface of
the fat and are brown on underside, turn them with a long-handled fork. When doughnuts are fried, remove with long-handled
fork and place on absorbent paper to drain. If you fry the "holes,"
you can remove them most easily with a whisk egg beater. Makes
about 30 doughnuts.

RICH BUTTERMILK DOUGHNUTS

Frying temperature—350° F.

6 cups all-purpose flour, sifted before measuring	1 teaspoon salt
	6 tablespoons softened butter or margarine
2 cups granulated sugar	
1 teaspoon baking soda	2 eggs, well beaten
1 teaspoon baking powder	1½ cups sour milk or buttermilk

Sift dry ingredients into large bowl. Cut butter or margarine into
the dry ingredients until mixture resembles corn meal. Combine
beaten eggs with buttermilk or sour milk and add to dry ingredients. Blend together thoroughly. Roll out dough in small portions on well-floured board or pastry cloth to about ½ inch in thick-

ness. Cut with doughnut cutter. Fry, turning when underside is brown. It will require 3 or 4 minutes to brown both sides of the doughnut. Drain on absorbent paper. Dust with powdered or granulated sugar. These are crusty, rich doughnuts, and very delicious. Makes about 4½ dozen.

RAISED DOUGHNUTS
Frying temperature—375° F.

1¼ cups sweet milk	3 tablespoons butter or
1 cake quick-acting yeast	margarine
¾ cup sugar	1 egg, well beaten
4½ cups all-purpose flour, sifted	1½ teaspoons nutmeg
before measuring	1 teaspoon salt

Scald the milk, turn into a medium-sized bowl, and cool to lukewarm. Crumble yeast and add with 1 tablespoon sugar to lukewarm milk. Stir until dissolved. Add 1½ cups of the flour, beat well, cover with a clean towel and let mixture rise in a warm place about 1 hour. Cream the butter or margarine, add remaining sugar, and continue creaming until mixture is light and fluffy. Add the egg, nutmeg, and salt. Blend thoroughly, then stir into yeast mixture. Add the remaining 3 cups of flour, stir vigorously. Cover with clean towel and allow mixture to rise until doubled in bulk. This will take a little over an hour. Then turn out on a floured board and roll about ½ inch thick. Cut with floured doughnut cutter and let rise until doubled in size. Better look at doughnuts in about 30 minutes. Fry. When doughnuts are brown on underside, which will take about 2 minutes, turn with a long-handled fork and fry on other side. When doughnuts are fried, remove with long-handled fork to absorbent paper and drain. Makes about 30 doughnuts.

TREAT: Shake warm doughnuts in paper bag in which you have put either confectioners' sugar or granulated sugar. For something a little different, add 1 tablespoon cinnamon to ½ cup granulated sugar, place in bag, and shake warm doughnuts in this mixture. If you want to be extra fancy, you can ice them with confectioners' icing.

DROP DOUGHNUTS
Frying temperature—375° F.

If you are in a hurry, you can drop doughnuts from a teaspoon. Scoop enough of the dough onto a teaspoon to make a doughnut about 2 inches in diameter. Push the dough from the teaspoon with the help of a rubber spatula. Drop doughnuts are just as good to eat and do save quite a bit of time. Sprinkle with sugar just as the other doughnuts.

FRENCH-FRIED BISCUITS
Frying temperature—375° F.

Use your favorite biscuit recipe or use a can of the prepared biscuits that are ready for baking. If prepared biscuits are used, remove from can and separate. You may fry the biscuits whole or cut in half. Fry. Drain on absorbent paper. While biscuits are hot, shake in bag containing granulated sugar and cinnamon (page 225). Wonderful quick treat for children.

FRENCH-FRIED DOUGHBOYS
Frying temperature—375° F.

Make your favorite sweet-roll recipe (page 321). Roll dough about ⅛ inch thick and cut into strips 2½ inches wide. Cut strips into squares or diamond shapes. Cover. Let stand for about 15 minutes. Fry the same as you would doughnuts. Drain. Serve in place of hot rolls with a meal, or serve with maple sirup at breakfast, or even as a dessert. Different and delicious.

TRICK: If you don't want to use the entire recipe this way, make part of the recipe into rolls and fry what portion of the recipe you think your family will eat. Probably the next time you'll reserve more dough for French-fried doughboys, for you will find that they are popular with almost everyone.

FRITTERS—FRUIT AND VEGETABLE

PLAIN FRITTERS
Frying temperature—375° F.

1 cup all-purpose flour, sifted before measuring	2 eggs, beaten
	1 tablespoon melted shortening
½ teaspoon salt	½ cup milk
1 teaspoon baking powder	

Sift flour with salt and baking powder. Mix together the well-beaten eggs, melted shortening, and milk and add to flour mixture. Mix together thoroughly. Dip batter by teaspoons and slide into heated shortening. Do not drop batter from any height into heated shortening, or your hand might be burned from the spattering. Fry until golden brown, 2 or 3 minutes. Remove from shortening with whisk egg beater and drain on absorbent paper. Serve hot with lemon sauce (page 251). Makes 12-15 fritters.

FRUIT FRITTERS

Frying temperature—375° F.

Prepare fruit and then make plain fritter batter (on page 226). Dip fruit into batter and lift out with a long-handled fork. Allow excess batter to drain off. Lower fruit fritter into hot fat and fry until delicately brown, 3 to 5 minutes. Remove from fat with long-handled fork or whisk egg beater. Drain on absorbent paper. Sprinkle with powdered sugar or serve with lemon sauce (page 251).

APPLE FRITTERS

Peel and core apples and cut in ½-inch slices. Dip in batter. Fry.

BANANA FRITTERS

Peel bananas, cut in half crosswise, then in half lengthwise. Sprinkle with lemon juice and sugar. Dip in batter. Fry.

PEACHES, APRICOTS, PINEAPPLE, AND OTHER FRUIT

Drain canned fruit. Cut into bite-sized pieces and sprinkle lightly with flour. Dip in batter. Fry.

VEGETABLE FRITTERS

Frying temperature—375° F.

Dip bite-sized chunks of cooked vegetables such as carrots, eggplant, sweet potato, and so forth, into plain fritter batter (page 226). Fry as for plain fritters.

CORN FRITTERS

Frying temperature—375° F.

1 cup fresh or canned corn	½ teaspoon salt
1 egg yolk, beaten	½ teaspoon baking powder
½ cup and 2 tablespoons	Dash of paprika
all-purpose flour	1 egg white, beaten stiff

Chop the corn. Drain. Add beaten egg yolk. Sift the flour with the salt, baking powder, and paprika. Stir into corn mixture. Fold in the stiffly beaten egg white. Dip batter by teaspoonfuls and slide it into the heated shortening. Fry until golden brown, from 3 to 5 minutes. Drain. Serve immediately. Serves 4.

FRENCH-FRIED VEGETABLES

FRENCH-FRIED ONION RINGS

Frying temperature—375° F.

Peel large mild onions and cut crosswise in ¼-inch slices. Separate onion rings. Dip each ring in plain fritter batter (page 226), using a long-handled fork. Carefully drop into hot fat. Fry. Drain on absorbent paper. Serve piping hot with broiled steaks, liver, and so forth. 1 large onion will make enough rings for 4 servings.

POTATO PUFFS

Frying temperature—375° F.

2 cups mashed potatoes	½ cup cheese, grated
1 egg	½ teaspoon salt
⅛ teaspoon pepper	1 cup fine bread crumbs

Combine all ingredients except bread crumbs. Form into balls. Roll in fine bread crumbs. Fry. If the fry kettle has a fry basket, here is a good place to use it. Otherwise, lift potato puffs out of hot fat with a whisk egg beater. Drain on absorbent paper. Serve piping hot. Serves 4.

FRENCH-FRIED ASPARAGUS

Frying temperature—375°F.

1 can green tipped asparagus, or freshly cooked asparagus	½ cup finely rolled bread crumbs
	1 teaspoon salt
1 egg	½ cup Parmesan cheese
2 tablespoons cold water	¼ teaspoon paprika

Drain freshly cooked or canned asparagus. Beat egg slightly and to it add the cold water. Mix fine bread or cracker crumbs with salt, Parmesan cheese, and paprika. Dip asparagus in bread crumb mixture, then egg, then bread crumb mixture. Chill for about an hour. Chilling makes the crumbs stay on better during the frying process. Just before ready to serve, fry. Drain on absorbent paper. Serve piping hot. Serves 4-6.

FRENCH-FRIED CUCUMBERS

Frying temperature—375° F.

Wash cucumber and cut in ½-inch slices. Dip in crumbs, egg, and then crumbs as given in recipe for French-fried asparagus, above. Fry. Serves 4.

FRENCH-FRIED EGGPLANT

Frying temperature—375° F.

Wash and peel eggplant. Cut in ½-inch slices, or better yet, cut in julienne strips—long slender slices, about 3 inches long, ¼ inch wide, and ¼ inch thick. Dip in plain fritter batter (page 226) or dip in crumbs, eggs, and crumbs as given in French-fried asparagus recipe, above. Many people consider this the most delicious way to eat eggplant. Serves 4-6.

FRENCH-FRIED GREEN PEPPERS

Frying temperature—375° F.

Wash green pepper. Remove stem and blossom ends. Scoop out core and seeds. Cut in ⅛-inch rings, then cut each ring in half or thirds, depending upon the size. Dip in crumbs, egg, and crumbs, as given in French-fried asparagus recipe, above. Fry. Drain. Delicious to serve as a canapé at cocktail parties.

FRENCH-FRIED PARSNIPS

Frying temperature—375° F.

Prepare parsnips as instructed on page 161. When cooked, cool and drain. Cut into 3-inch lengths, about ½ inch wide, and ¼ inch deep. Dip in plain fritter batter (page 226). Fry. Drain. Serve with tomato sauce (page 245). Serves 4.

FRENCH-FRIED POTATOES NO. 1

Frying temperature—390-400° F.

Choose long, thin, firm potatoes. Wash and pare them. Cut lengthwise into strips the length of the potato, about ⅜ inch deep and ⅜ inch wide. If you have a special cutter, that is better yet. Cover with slightly salted ice water and let stand for about ½ hour. Remove from ice water only the amount that is to be fried at one time, usually about ¾ pound. Dry potatoes in a clean tea towel. Place potatoes in fry basket and lower into hot fat. Fry until crisp and browned to your taste, usually about 8-10 minutes. Drain on absorbent paper. Salt and serve at once. If you fry about ¾ pound at one time, it usually will serve 4. Or, you can count on 1 medium-sized potato per serving. If you need more than that amount for serving, place the fried potatoes in a shallow pan, place in oven at about 300° F., and leave oven door slightly ajar. They will stay hot while you continue to fry the remainder.

TWICE-FRIED POTATOES

First frying—375° F. . . . Second frying—400° F.

Six large potatoes, washed, pared, and cut in lengthwise strips, the length of the potato and about ⅜ inches wide and ⅜ inches deep. Dry peeled, sliced potatoes in clean tea towel. Divide potatoes in three equal amounts. Place in fry basket and lower into hot fat. Fry until potatoes are tender but not brown, about 3 minutes. Drain on absorbent paper. Cook remaining lots in the same manner. Place in refrigerator until ready to use. To brown potatoes at serving time, reheat fat. Place one half the potatoes in fry basket and carefully lower into fat. Fry until crisp and brown, about 2 minutes. Brown remaining potatoes in same manner. Drain on absorbent paper, sprinkle with salt. Serve immediately. Serves 4-6.

Many people prefer this method, since it saves considerable last-minute confusion.

OTHER FRENCH-FRIED FOODS

SNOWFLAKES

Frying temperature—375° F.

6 egg yolks	1¼ cups sifted all-purpose flour
1 egg white	½ teaspoon salt
1 teaspoon sugar	2 tablespoons sherry

Beat egg yolks until thick and lemon colored. Beat egg white until stiff. Add sugar to the egg white, then fold it into the beaten egg yolks. Sift together the flour and salt and add to the eggs. Add wine. Knead dough a few times on floured board, then divide into 3 parts. Roll out paper-thin. Cut in diamond shapes and, with a knife, cut a slit in center of each diamond. Draw one corner through slit and fry in deep fat as for doughnuts, turning over when one side is golden brown and browning the other side. Drain on absorbent paper and sift powdered sugar over before serving. Makes about 2 dozen.

TRICK: An easy way to cut diamonds is to cut diagonally across dough, making strips 2 inches apart. Then cut across opposite way. If you are still confused, turn to baked ham recipe on page 32 and follow directions for scoring.

FRENCH TOAST

Frying temperature—375° F.

2 eggs, slightly beaten
½ teaspoon salt
1 tablespoon sugar

¼ teaspoon nutmeg
⅓ cup milk
6 slices bread

Beat eggs in a shallow dish. Add salt, sugar, nutmeg, and milk. Blend well. Cut bread slices in half. Dip into egg mixture, turning so both sides are coated. Fry. When toast is brown on underside, turn and brown other side. Drain on absorbent paper. Serve piping hot with sirup, jelly, or powdered sugar. Serves 4 to 6.

TACOS

Frying temperature—375° F.

1 onion, finely chopped
2 tablespoons butter or
    margarine
1 cup tomato juice
2 peeled green chilis, minced

1 cup shredded chicken
⅛ teaspoon thyme
½ teaspoon salt
12 to 16 tortillas
Guacamole sauce (page 209)

Sauté onion in butter or margarine until golden in color. To this, add the tomato juice, chilis, chicken, thyme, and salt. Simmer until the mixture is fairly thick. Place mixture in center of tortillas. Roll so edges overlap and fasten together with toothpicks. Fry. When nicely browned, remove from fat. Drain. Remove toothpicks. Stack on hot platter. Serve with Guacamole sauce (page 209). Must be served very hot. Serves 6-8.

CHILI RELLANOS

Frying temperature—375° F.

½ pound Jack cheese (page 284)
1 can (4 ounces) roasted and
    peeled long green chilis
1 egg yolk

1 teaspoon flour
½ teaspoon salt
1 egg white

Cut cheese into oblongs about 1 inch wide, 2 inches long, and ½ inch thick. Wrap strip of peeled green chili around each piece. Beat egg yolk, add flour and salt, and beat vigorously. Beat egg white until stiff but not dry. Fold egg yolk mixture into egg whites. Dip cheese and pepper carefully into batter. Do not dip more than one at a time. Put in fry kettle with a whisk egg beater. Fry until golden brown. Drain. Serve at once. Serves 2.

HUSH PUPPIES

Frying temperature—375° F.

1 cup coarse yellow corn meal	2 tablespoons onion, minced
½ cup sifted all-purpose flour	1 egg
1½ teaspoons baking powder	⅔ cup milk
¾ teaspoon salt	

Sift dry ingredients together. Add onion. Beat egg, add milk, and add to sifted dry ingredients. Drop by teaspoonfuls into hot fat. Fry until golden brown and serve hot with fried fish. Makes about 48 small balls. A packaged hush puppy mix may also be purchased in some parts of the country. Follow directions on box.

FRENCH-FRIED CHICKEN

Frying temperature—350° F.

2 young, tender broilers	Plain fritter recipe (page 226)

Split young, tender broilers or cut in quarters. Sprinkle with salt and pepper. Dip in plain fritter batter and fry until golden brown for a total time of 15-20 minutes. Serves 4.

Other Methods

Split young chicken in half or quarters. Or, if you prefer, cut up as you would any chicken for frying. Dip each piece of chicken in water, then roll in flour which has been seasoned with salt, pepper, and paprika. Another easy method is to dip each piece in water, then roll in a prepared pancake flour. In either case, fry until golden brown, remove from hot fat, drain on absorbent paper. Serve at once. Many people prefer this method of cooking chicken because the outside of the chicken becomes crisp and crunchy.

TRICK: If your chicken is a bit older than a springer, clean carefully and cut into serving pieces. Then steam until just tender. After that you may follow any of the methods given under French-fried chicken.

FRENCH-FRIED FROGS' LEGS

The hind legs of the frog are the part of the body most generally eaten. They are usually sent to the market cleaned and skinned, ready to cook. Better allow 4 to 5 pair frogs' legs per person, especially if they are the luscious small legs.

To prepare the frogs' legs yourself, loosen the skin around the thigh, using a sharp paring knife. Then pull the skin down off the legs. Remove legs from body, then remove the feet. Soak for about ½ hour in salted water.

Frying temperature—350° F.

16 pairs frogs' legs	1½ cups fine bread or cracker
1 teaspoon salt	crumbs
¼ teaspoon pepper	2 eggs, slightly beaten
2 tablespoons lemon juice	4 tablespoons cold water

Place frogs' legs in shallow dish. Mix the salt, pepper, and lemon juice and brush over frogs' legs. Place in refrigerator and allow to marinate for 1 or more hours. When ready to use, drain, dip in crumbs, then in egg which has been mixed with water, then again in crumbs. Fry until golden brown, about 3 minutes. Serve with tartar sauce (page 245). Serves 4.

Method No. 2

Some people prefer to roll the frogs' legs in seasoned flour, or ready-mixed pancake flour and fry them as directed above. Either way is delicious.

FRENCH-FRIED HOT DOGS
Frying temperature—375° F.

1 cup ready-mix pancake	1 tablespoon sugar
flour	⅔ cup water
2 tablespoons corn meal	10-12 frankfurters

Combine dry ingredients. Add water and beat thoroughly. Dip frankfurters in batter, holding frankfurters with a kitchen fork. Drain excess batter over bowl. Fry in wire basket if one is available, until golden brown, about 3 minutes. Remove from hot fat, drain on absorbent paper. Serve piping hot. Serves 4.

DEEP-FAT-FRIED FISH AND SHELLFISH

Many of the fish and shellfish are spectacularly good when deep-fat fried. Following are some of the recipes we particularly enjoy.

CLAMS
(From Maine comes this recipe for clams fried in batter.)

Frying temperature—375° F.

2 egg yolks, beaten	¼ teaspoon salt
½ cup milk	1 tablespoon lemon juice
1 teaspoon olive oil	2 egg whites
1 cup all-purpose flour, sifted	1 pint small clams, fresh or
before measuring	canned

Beat egg yolks until thick and lemon colored. Add milk, olive oil, all-purpose flour, salt, and lemon juice. Fold in the egg whites which have been beaten until they will hold a peak. Fold in the clams. Place mixture in refrigerator and allow to stand at least 2 hours. Drop by spoonfuls and fry until a golden brown. Drain on absorbent paper. Serves 4.

CLAMS NO. 2
Frying temperature—375° F.

1 pint soft-shelled clams   Plain fritter batter (page 226)

Clean and dry clams. Dip in fritter batter. Fry. Drain on absorbent paper. Serve piping hot. Makes about 2 dozen fritters. Serves 4.

LOBSTER
Frying temperature—375° F.

Maine's favorite recipe is as follows:

Cook lobster according to directions on page 122. Cut lobster meat in pieces the size of a small egg. Roll lightly in a mixture of flour, salt, and pepper, then dip in beaten egg. Roll again in fine toasted bread or cracker crumbs. (*Note:* A prepared pancake mix may be used for this final rolling.) Fry. Drain on absorbent paper. Serve piping hot, with tartar sauce (page 245). Serves 4-6.

TRICK: To utilize the tail of the lobster, do this: break tail from body, cut the last joint from tail, then run a sharp knife around inside of the tail shell, and the meat will drop from the body end of the tail.

FRESH SHRIMP NO. 1
Frying temperature—375° F.

1 pound fresh shrimp in shell, or   1 egg beaten
    ½ pound cooked and peeled   2 tablespoons milk
    shrimp   1 cup fine cracker or bread
4 tablespoons lemon juice   crumbs
    Salt and pepper to season

Turn to page 119 for directions for cooking the fresh shrimp. Be sure to score down the back and remove the black vein. Shrimp bought already cooked and peeled usually have the vein removed. Dip the prepared shrimp in lemon juice, then sprinkle with salt and pepper. Beat egg, add milk to egg. Dip shrimp in egg mixture, then in fine cracker or bread crumbs. Shake shrimp to remove excess crumbs. Fry until golden brown. Remove from fry kettle and drain on absorbent paper. Serve piping hot. Serves 4.

FRESH SHRIMP NO. 2

Follow same procedure given above for either frozen or fresh shrimp. Dip in plain fritter batter (page 226) and fry.

TREAT: Prepare shrimp in advance, then sprinkle lemon juice over them, place in refrigerator, and allow to marinate for two or three hours. Then dip in batter or crumbs, as preferred.

FROZEN PREPARED SHRIMP

Frying temperature—375° F.

There are very fine frozen shrimp on the market, which are precooked and breaded, ready to fry in the hot fat. Do not defrost them. Carefully separate each shrimp and place in fry basket. One package of frozen prepared shrimp may be fried at one time. Fry only 2 or 3 minutes. Serves 2-3.

FRENCH-FRIED FILLETS OF MACKEREL OR OTHER FISH

Frying temperature—375° F.

1½ pounds fillets of mackerel
2 tablespoons olive or salad oil
1 teaspoon vinegar
1 teaspoon onion, grated
½ teaspoon salt
1 teaspoon paprika

⅛ teaspoon pepper
½ cup all-purpose flour
2 eggs, beaten
1 cup fine cracker or bread crumbs

Wipe fillets of mackerel with damp cloth. Place on deep plate or platter. Pour over them a dressing made by mixing together the olive or salad oil, vinegar, grated onion, salt, paprika, and pepper. Allow to marinate at least 2 hours, turning occasionally. When ready to cook, lift from dish, drain, and roll in flour, then dip in beaten egg, and roll in fine cracker or bread crumbs. Fry to a golden brown, remove from fat, drain on absorbent paper, and serve piping hot. Serves 4.

(*NOTE:* Allow ⅛ pound fish per serving.)

FRENCH-FRIED SCALLOPS

Frying temperature—375° F.

1 pound scallops	2 eggs, beaten
½ cup all-purpose flour	4 tablespoons milk
1 teaspoon salt	1 cup fine bread or cracker
½ teaspoon paprika	crumbs

Wash scallops in cold water, drain, and dry thoroughly. If the scallops are large, cut into cubes of about ¾ inch. Roll in flour seasoned with salt and paprika, then dip in beaten egg to which the milk has been added. Roll in fine bread crumbs. A good trick is to mix the bread crumbs half and half with flour. This mixture seems to cling to scallops better than plain bread or cracker crumbs. Place only a single layer in a fry basket, so the scallops will brown evenly all over. Fry. Drain on absorbent paper. Serve piping hot with tartar sauce (page 245). Serves 4.

CROQUETTES

SALMON CROQUETTES

Frying temperature—375° F.

1-pound can pink or red salmon	1 egg
1 teaspoon lemon juice	1 cup fine cracker crumbs
1 recipe for white sauce	

Drain juice from salmon and save. It may be used as part of the liquid for making the white sauce. Remove bones and skin from salmon. Break into medium-sized pieces. Add lemon juice. Combine salmon mixture with white sauce. Place in refrigerator to chill for at least 2 hours. Shape croquettes by placing a tablespoon of the mixture in the palm of the hand and quickly molding it. Place each mound on a plate. Return to refrigerator to chill for about 1 hour. Just before serving, roll in fine crumbs, then in egg which has been slightly beaten, and again in crumbs. Fry in hot fat, using a basket if you have one. Fry until golden brown, about 3 minutes. Drain on absorbent paper and serve at once. Serves 4.

White Sauce

This white sauce is used as the foundation for all fish or meat croquettes. Croquettes are an excellent way to use odds and ends of meat, rice, or vegetables.

2 tablespoons butter or
  margarine
⅓ cup all-purpose flour
1 cup milk, or use juice drained
  from salmon, and enough
  milk to make 1 cup

1 teaspoon salt
¼ teaspoon pepper

Melt butter or margarine in small saucepan. Add flour, blend thoroughly. Add milk and cook over medium heat until thick. Add salt and pepper. Cool thoroughly. White sauce should be made several hours before needed for croquettes.

FISH BALLS

Frying temperature—375° F.

6 medium-sized potatoes
2 cups salt fish, shredded
2 eggs, beaten
1 tablespoon softened butter or
  margarine

Pepper to taste
1 cup fine cracker crumbs

Peel potatoes and cut in quarters. Place in saucepan. Place salt fish on top. Add only enough water to cover bottom of saucepan. Cover. Cook until potatoes are soft. Drain and mash the potatoes and fish together. To this mixture add the eggs, butter or margarine, and pepper to season. Make into balls or oblong rolls. Roll in cracker crumbs and place in refrigerator to chill about 2 hours. Fry. Drain on absorbent paper. Serve piping hot. Serves 4-6.

CHICKEN BALLS

Frying temperature—375° F.

2 tablespoons butter or
  margarine
3 tablespoons all-purpose flour
1 cup milk, or chicken broth
2 cups cooked chicken, chopped

1 tablespoon parsley, chopped
Salt and pepper to taste
1 egg, beaten
6-8 slices day-old white bread

Melt butter or margarine in saucepan. Add flour, stir until well blended, then slowly add the milk or chicken broth. Cook over medium heat until thickened, stirring frequently. Cool. Add the chopped chicken and seasonings. Place in refrigerator to chill for 2 or 3 hours. Shape into large balls. Roll in beaten egg, then in bread. To prepare the bread, remove crusts and pull the bread into ½-inch cubes with your fingers. Return to refrigerator and let stand 2 or 3 hours, or until egg and bread coating has dried. Fry in hot fat. Drain on absorbent paper. Serve piping hot with mushroom sauce (page 244). Serves 4-6.

Sauces

In many ways, sauces represent the most difficult challenge that any cook must face; and yet, at the same time, they also offer the greatest satisfaction to those cooks who are willing to experiment.

The honor in which sauces are held by the cooking profession is evidenced by the fact that, in any hotel or restaurant kitchen, the sauce chef is the cock of the walk. He is the acknowledged king of the chefs, and with reason, for his sauces can make or break any meal that the restaurant serves.

You will not want to serve a sauce with every dish that you cook, of course, but you will find that an unusual sauce can stir up new enthusiasm for an accustomed food, or coax your family to try some new dish they might otherwise refuse.

There are many different kinds of sauces which you may purchase, and many of them may be used just as they come from the bottle or can, while others may be improved with a bit of experimenting on your part.

Whether you buy them ready-made, mix them up from the recipes that appear here, or experiment with new combinations on your own, remember that sauces can enhance any food that you serve and make you a real "king of the chefs" as far as your own family is concerned.

SAUCES FOR FISH, MEATS, AND VEGETABLES

BARBECUE SAUCE FOR BEEF

1 medium-sized onion, chopped fine

1 clove garlic, minced

2 tablespoons butter, margarine, or oil

2 tablespoons brown sugar

⅛ teaspoon cayenne pepper

½ tablespoon dry mustard

1 teaspoon salt

½ cup celery, or 1 tablespoon celery salt

1 tablespoon horse-radish

2 tablespoons vinegar

4 tablespoons lemon juice

1 cup catchup

3 tablespoons Worcestershire sauce

1 cup water

Cook onion and garlic in melted butter, margarine, or oil until lightly brown. Add dry ingredients and blend in. Then add remainder of ingredients. Simmer for 10 or 15 minutes. Pour over meat and baste occasionally with sauce.

BARBECUE SAUCE FOR POULTRY

¼ cup cooking oil, or melted butter or margarine

¾ cup white table wine

1 clove garlic, minced fine

1 large onion, minced fine

1 teaspoon salt

1 teaspoon celery salt

⅛ teaspoon cayenne pepper

¼ teaspoon black pepper

⅛ teaspoon dried tarragon

¼ teaspoon dried thyme

1 tablespoon parsley, chopped

Mix all ingredients thoroughly. Let stand overnight, if possible. Use for barbecuing chicken. Especially fine to brush over young chickens when broiling. If you are using on broiled chicken, let chicken marinate in sauce for an hour or so before broiling.

BLACK BUTTER SAUCE FOR FISH

¼ cup butter, margarine, or cooking oil

1 tablespoon lemon juice

Salt and pepper

Add butter, margarine, or oil to drippings left in skillet after frying fish. Stir until a dark brown. Add lemon juice and seasonings.

BROWN BUTTER FOR VEGETABLES

Put ¼ cup butter or margarine in small skillet or saucepan. Melt. Stir until a deep brown. Pour over cooked and drained snap beans, broccoli, carrots, or almost any vegetable.

HERB BUTTER FOR BAKED POTATOES, LAMB CHOPS, HOT FRENCH BREAD

¾ cup sweet butter
1 tablespoon parsley, finely chopped
1 teaspoon lemon juice

1 tablespoon chive or onion tops, finely chopped
½ teaspoon dried basil

Cream butter until smooth. Add remaining ingredients and blend thoroughly.

PARSLEY BUTTER FOR FISH

¼ cup butter or margarine
1 teaspoon lemon juice
1 tablespoon parsley, finely chopped

½ teaspoon salt

Cream butter or margarine, add lemon juice, parsley, and salt. Blend thoroughly.

MUSTARD BUTTER FOR SANDWICHES OR STEAK

¼ cup butter or margarine

2 tablespoons prepared mustard

Cream butter or margarine and mustard together.

CELERY SAUCE FOR FISH

1 can condensed cream of celery soup
1 teaspoon prepared mustard

¼ cup milk
3 tablespoons sweet pickle relish
1 hard-cooked egg, chopped

Empty soup into a saucepan. Blend in remaining ingredients. Heat over low heat. Serve piping hot on any kind of sea food. Especially good on fish cakes.

COCKTAIL SAUCE FOR SHRIMP AND CRAB MEAT

½ cup chili sauce
1 cup catchup
¼ cup prepared horse-radish
Dash of Tabasco sauce
1 tablespoon Worcestershire sauce

½ teaspoon celery salt
1 teaspoon green pepper, finely chopped

Mix all ingredients and chill before serving on shrimp, crab meat, or other shell sea foods.

CREOLE SAUCE

¼ cup onion, finely chopped
¼ cup green pepper, finely
    chopped
2 tablespoons drippings
½ cup water

1 can condensed cream of tomato
    soup
1 teaspoon vinegar
⅛ teaspoon black pepper
Dash of Tabasco sauce

Cook onion and green pepper in drippings. Add remaining ingredients. Cook over low heat for 10 minutes. Excellent on rice, omelets, sea food, or pot roasts.

TREAT: Add ½ cup canned mushrooms.

CUCUMBER CREAM SAUCE FOR FISH

½ cup heavy cream
2 tablespoons tarragon vinegar
¼ teaspoon salt

Dash cayenne pepper
1 medium-sized cucumber, pared,
    chopped, and drained

Whip cream, add vinegar, beating constantly. Fold in seasonings and well-drained cucumber.

TREAT: Try substituting sour cream for the sweet cream, but if you do, better use only 1 tablespoon vinegar.

CURRANT-HORSE-RADISH SAUCE FOR HAM OR TONGUE

⅓ cup prepared horse-radish
1 glass (6 ounces) currant jelly

Mix horse-radish and jelly together until thoroughly blended.

EGG SAUCE FOR FISH

2 tablespoons butter or
    margarine
2 tablespoons all-purpose flour
1 cup milk
½ teaspoon salt

⅛ teaspoon pepper
2 hard-cooked eggs, diced
1 tablespoon parsley, finely
    chopped

Melt butter or margarine in saucepan, blend in flour, add milk slowly, stirring constantly. When thickened, remove from heat, add seasonings, hard-cooked eggs, and parsley. Serve hot.

HOLLANDAISE SAUCE FOR ASPARAGUS, BROCCOLI

½ cup butter or margarine
2 egg yolks
1 tablespoon lemon juice

¼ teaspoon salt
Few grains cayenne pepper

Must use double boiler, or better yet, a heavy crockery bowl which will fit in a pan of water. Hollandaise must cook over hot, but never boiling, water.

Divide butter or margarine into three pieces. Put one piece in bowl or top of double boiler with egg yolks and lemon juice. Cook, stirring constantly with wire whisk or wooden spoon until butter melts. Add second piece of butter. Keep on stirring until mixture thickens. Then add last piece of butter. Remove from heat and beat until mixture is thick and glossy. Season with salt and pepper.

TRICK: If mixture separates, it's because water was too hot and the sauce cooked too rapidly. Stir in a little boiling water, drop by drop, beating vigorously.

MOCK HOLLANDAISE NO. 1

2 packages (3 ounces) cream
    cheese
2 egg yolks

2 tablespoons lemon juice
½ teaspoon salt

Soften cream cheese. Add egg yolks, one at a time, blending thoroughly after each addition. Add lemon juice and salt. Place over hot, not boiling, water until sauce is heated through.

MOCK HOLLANDAISE NO. 2

3 egg yolks
¼ teaspoon salt
    Few grains cayenne pepper
1 tablespoon lemon juice

½ cup butter or margarine,
    melted
3 tablespoons hot water

Beat egg yolks until smooth. Add seasonings and lemon juice. Stir in melted butter or margarine. Add hot water. Set over hot, but not boiling, water and do not allow pan in which you are cooking the sauce to touch the water. Stir until thick. You can set this aside until ready to use and reheat over hot water.

HORSE-RADISH SAUCE NO. 1 FOR HAM OR TONGUE

½ cup heavy cream
½ teaspoon salt

¼ cup prepared horse-radish
1½ tablespoons tarragon vinegar

Beat cream until stiff. Fold in remaining ingredients.

HORSE-RADISH SAUCE NO. 2

½ cup chilled evaporated milk
⅓ cup mayonnaise
¼ cup prepared horse-radish

1 tablespoon sugar
1 teaspoon salt
Tabasco sauce (optional)

Whip the chilled evaporated milk (page 247). Fold in remaining ingredients.

MINT SAUCE FOR LAMB

½ cup mild vinegar
4 tablespoons powdered sugar

¼ cup fresh mint leaves, finely chopped

Heat vinegar and sugar. Put chopped mint in bowl and pour hot vinegar over leaves. Let stand at least one hour in warm room before using.

MUSHROOM TOMATO SAUCE FOR BEEF AND RICE

4 tablespoons shortening
1 can (4 ounces) mushrooms (save liquid)

1 onion, finely minced
1 can (8 ounces) tomato sauce

Melt shortening in saucepan. Brown mushrooms and onions slowly, about 5 minutes. Add liquid from mushrooms and tomato sauce. Simmer, uncovered, about 10 minutes.

MUSHROOM CHEESE SAUCE

1 can condensed cream of mushroom soup

¾ cup shredded cheese
⅛ teaspoon pepper

Combine soup and cheese. Heat slowly. Add pepper. Serve on rice or almost any vegetable.

MUSTARD SAUCE FOR FISH, BEEF, AND HAM

1 cup top milk or evaporated milk
¼ cup sugar
2 tablespoons dry mustard

1 tablespoon all-purpose flour
¼ teaspoon salt
1 egg yolk, beaten
¼ cup hot vinegar

Heat ¾ cup milk over low heat. Mix sugar, mustard, flour, and salt together and blend with remaining ¼ cup milk. Pour over beaten egg yolk. Add to heated milk. Stir and cook until thickened. Remove from heat. Stir in vinegar.

RAISIN SAUCE FOR BAKED HAM

2 tablespoons drippings from ham
2 tablespoons all-purpose flour
½ teaspoon dry mustard

1 cup pineapple juice or cider
½ cup seedless raisins
¼ cup sherry (optional)

Blend drippings, flour, and mustard. Slowly add fruit juice or cider. When boiling, add raisins and simmer 10 minutes. Add sherry just before serving.

TARTAR SAUCE FOR FISH

1 cup mayonnaise
2 tablespoons pickles, finely
    chopped, or 1 tablespoon
    chopped pickles and 1
    tablespoon chopped olives

1 teaspoon onion, finely chopped
1 tablespoon parsley, finely
    chopped
1 tablespoon green pepper,
    finely chopped

Blend all ingredients together.

TOMATO SOUP SAUCE

Heat 1 can condensed cream of tomato soup. Season to taste. Use as a sauce for chops, stuffed green peppers, meat loaf, croquettes, etc.

TOMATO SAUCE

4 tablespoons shortening
4 tablespoons all-purpose flour
2 cups tomato juice
1 teaspoon salt
1 teaspoon sugar

1 teaspoon parsley, chopped
    fine
1 small onion, chopped fine
¼ teaspoon dried celery leaves

Melt shortening and stir in flour. When well blended, add tomato juice, stirring until thickened. Add remaining ingredients. Simmer for 5 minutes.

TOMATO CURRY SAUCE FOR CHICKEN, FISH, RICE

1 can (8 ounces) tomato sauce
1 medium onion, finely chopped
1 tart cooking apple, peeled and
    finely chopped
1 teaspoon salt
1 tablespoon curry powder

1 bay leaf, crushed
2 tablespoons butter or
    margarine
1 clove garlic, finely chopped
½ teaspoon dry ginger

Empty tomato sauce in saucepan. Fill can with water and add to sauce. Add remaining ingredients and cook over low heat 20-30 minutes.

WHITE SAUCE

4 tablespoons butter or
    margarine
4 tablespoons all-purpose flour
    Dash of pepper

½ teaspoon salt
2 cups milk

Melt the butter or margarine. Stir in flour and seasonings, add cold milk, then cook on medium heat until mixture thickens. Stir occasionally. This recipe makes a medium white sauce.

To prepare a thin white sauce, use *one* tablespoon butter or margarine and *one* tablespoon flour to each *cup* of milk or liquid. For medium white sauce, use two tablespoons flour, two tablespoons butter or margarine to one cup milk or liquid. For thick white sauce, three tablespoons flour and three tablespoons butter or margarine to one cup milk or liquid.

TREATS: To change the flavor of white sauce, add a sprinkling of celery salt, a teaspoon of onion juice, or 2 tablespoons of chopped parsley.

To make cheese sauce, add 1 cup shredded cheese to 2 cups of white sauce.

To make curry sauce, add 1 teaspoon finely minced onion, 1 teaspoon curry powder, and 1 teaspoon lemon juice to each cup of white sauce.

To make brown sauce, brown the butter and flour to a deep golden brown before adding the milk. Add 3 tablespoons of horseradish for a good meat sauce.

Here is a variation that is especially good with corned beef hash or fish. To each cup of white sauce, add 2 hard-cooked eggs, chopped fine, and 1 teaspoon prepared mustard.

WINE SAUCE FOR BAKED HAM

4 tablespoons butter or margarine	¾ cup brown sugar
	1 tablespoon dry mustard
1 can (No. 2) crushed pineapple	1½ cups sherry

Melt butter or margarine in saucepan over low heat. Add pineapple, brown sugar, and mustard. Cook slowly until ingredients are thoroughly blended. Remove from heat. Add sherry.

BROWN SAUCE OR GRAVY

2 tablespoons drippings	1 cup water or stock
1 small onion, chopped fine	½ teaspoon salt
2 tablespoons all-purpose flour	⅛ teaspoon pepper

Melt drippings in saucepan, add onions, blend in the flour. Stir until flour and onion are a rich brown. Add liquid slowly, stirring constantly. Add seasonings and cook until thickened and smooth.

TREAT: Try adding ½ teaspoon Worcestershire sauce to give this sauce extra tang.

GIBLET GRAVY

Giblets of one fowl	¼ cup drippings from roasting
2¾ cups water	fowl
1 teaspoon salt	4 tablespoons all-purpose flour
1 onion, sliced fine	
Several celery leaves	

Wash giblets carefully. Place in saucepan; add water, salt, onion, and celery leaves. Cover. Bring to a boil, then simmer slowly until giblets are tender. Remove giblets. Strain broth. There should be 2 cups. Chop giblets or cut into small pieces. Blend drippings and flour together. Add broth. Cook until thickened, stirring frequently. Add chopped giblets to thickened gravy. Serve piping hot.

DESSERT SAUCES

A good sauce can make or break a dessert. A good rule to follow is to serve a light sauce on a rich dessert and a rich sauce for a plain dessert.

If fruit juice is used as the liquid in the sauce, better use cornstarch for the thickening so the finished sauce will be clear.

Always add liquor or flavoring to cooked sauces after the sauce has cooled, in order to get full benefit of flavoring.

Generally hot sauces are served piping hot with hot desserts, and thoroughly chilled cold sauces with cold desserts.

How to Whip Cream

Have bowl and beaters very cold. If you have room in the freeze chest of your refrigerator, put them in freeze chest for about an hour before using. Be sure the cream is cold, but let it remain in food compartment of your refrigerator. If you are using an electric mixer, use medium-high speed. Add sugar and flavoring just when cream begins to thicken. Don't let the cream begin to look lumpy. The next step after those lumps will be butter.

If you are beating cream by hand, use a rotary egg beater. Better have a "relief" near by. Beating cream by hand gets monotonous.

How to Prepare Evaporated Milk for Whipping

There are several ways to do this. Whipped evaporated milk makes a fine substitute for whipping cream. Much cheaper, too.

1. Pour milk from can into freezing tray of refrigerator. Let stand until just about ready to freeze. Whip until stiff.

2. Place unopened can of milk in saucepan. Cover with water. Bring to boiling point, let boil 5 minutes. Put in freeze chest of your refrigerator to chill thoroughly. Empty contents of can in bowl and whip until stiff.

3. Empty milk into saucepan and heat slowly to boiling point. Then pour into freezing trays and chill. Whip until stiff.

4. Place unopened can in freezing compartment. When ready to use, empty contents of can into bowl and whip until stiff.

NOTE: Be sure bowl, milk, and beaters are very, very cold.

CUSTARD SAUCE—SERVE CHILLED

3 egg yolks	¼ teaspoon salt
1 tablespoon cornstarch	2 cups milk, scalded
3 tablespoons sugar	1 teaspoon vanilla

Beat egg yolks. Mix cornstarch, sugar, and salt together and add to egg yolks. Slowly add to scalded milk, stirring constantly. Cook over low heat until mixture coats spoon. Remove from heat, pour into bowl or jar to cool. Cover to prevent scum from forming. Add flavoring after custard has chilled. Store in refrigerator as soon as transferred from saucepan to bowl or jar.

BUTTERSCOTCH SAUCE—SERVE HOT OR COLD

1½ cups light brown sugar	⅛ teaspoon salt
⅓ cup butter or margarine	1 cup light cream or
¾ cup light corn sirup	evaporated milk

Cook sugar, butter or margarine, corn sirup, and salt together. Stir constantly until sugar is dissolved. Add cream very slowly, stirring constantly, and cook until sirup thickens. If you have a candy thermometer, the sirup should come off at 228° F., which is slightly below the soft-ball stage. Will keep in covered container in refrigerator indefinitely.

HARD SAUCE—SERVE COLD ON HOT DESSERTS

6 tablespoons butter or margarine	1 tablespoon boiling water
	⅛ teaspoon salt
1 cup powdered sugar	1 teaspoon vanilla

Cream butter or margarine and sugar together until creamy. Add boiling water, salt, and vanilla. Beat until creamy. Shape into molds or balls, or press firmly in small pan and cut into squares. Chill in refrigerator.

TREATS: Fluffy hard sauce is made by folding a stiffly beaten egg white into hard sauce. Use sherry for flavoring.

Golden hard sauce. Add a well-beaten egg yolk to hard sauce. Use rum for flavoring.

Fold ⅛ cup heavy cream whipped stiff into hard sauce. Use 1 tablespoon grenadine plus a dash of curaçao for flavoring.

CHOCOLATE SAUCE NO. 1—SERVE HOT OR COLD

8 squares bitter chocolate	¼ teaspoon salt
1¾ cups boiling water	1 teaspoon vanilla
2½ cups granulated sugar	

Place chocolate in saucepan. Add boiling water. Cook over medium heat for 5 minutes, stirring constantly. Remove from heat and beat until chocolate is thoroughly blended with water. Add sugar and salt. Return to range and continue cooking over medium heat for 5 minutes, stirring constantly. Remove from heat. Cool. Add vanilla. Store in covered glass jar in refrigerator, and this sauce will keep for months, provided the family will leave it alone. Makes about 1 quart.

CHOCOLATE SAUCE NO. 2—SERVE HOT OR COLD

3 squares bitter chocolate, or	½ cup granulated sugar
¾ cup cocoa	½ cup corn sirup
⅔ cup water	½ teaspoon vanilla

Place chocolate or cocoa and water in saucepan. Cook over low heat until well blended, stirring frequently. Add sugar, bring to a boil, and boil gently for two minutes, stirring constantly. If thicker sauce is desired, boil for 4 minutes. Add corn sirup and bring to boil again. Cool. Add vanilla. Store in covered jar in refrigerator. Makes 1½ cups sauce.

EGGNOG SAUCE—SERVE COLD

2 egg yolks	2 tablespoons rum or sherry
½ cup confectioner's sugar	½ cup heavy cream

Beat egg yolks until thick and lemon colored. Add sugar and continue beating. Add flavoring. Whip cream until stiff and fold into creamed mixture.

CARAMEL SUNDAE SAUCE—SERVE HOT OR COLD

2 cups granulated sugar	3 tablespoons heavy cream
1 cup boiling water	½ teaspoon vanilla

Melt sugar in skillet, stirring constantly. When sugar has dissolved, continue to heat until it is amber in color. Stir constantly, or the sugar will burn. Add 1 cup boiling water slowly, stirring until well blended. If you use an electric range, turn heat to "Off" and cook for 2 or 3 minutes, or until mixture is consistency of a medium sirup. Remove from heat, stir in cream and vanilla. Cool slightly. Serve over ice cream. Makes about 2 cups.

PINEAPPLE SAUCE—SERVE COLD

2 tablespoons cornstarch
½ cup sugar
⅓ cup lemon juice
1 cup pineapple juice

Mix cornstarch and sugar together. Add lemon and pineapple juice and cook until thickened. Cool before serving. Will serve 6 to 10 depending upon size of serving.

STERLING SAUCE—SERVE COLD

½ cup butter or margarine
1 cup light brown sugar (free from lumps)
2 tablespoons heavy cream
1½ tablespoons sherry
1 tablespoon brandy

Cream butter or margarine with light brown sugar until very creamy. Then slowly add the cream, beating vigorously. Add sherry and brandy slowly, beating continuously. Serves 6-8.

TREAT: Add 2 tablespoons finely chopped nuts and 2 table-spoons finely cut dates. This is particularly good on suet pudding (page 333).

FOAMY SAUCE—SERVE HOT

½ cup butter or margarine
1 cup powdered sugar
Dash of salt
2 egg yolks, well beaten
1 teaspoon vanilla or sherry to taste

Cream butter or margarine, add sugar, salt, egg, and flavoring. Place in double boiler or pan set in hot water. Beat with rotary egg beater until light and fluffy, about 6-7 minutes. Keep over hot water until time to serve. Serves 8.

TREAT: If no one is watching calories, fold in ½ cup heavy cream, whipped stiff, just before serving.

SIRUP FOR PANCAKES AND WAFFLES—SERVE HOT

¾ cup granulated sugar
1 cup honey
1 cup evaporated milk

Boil all ingredients together for 5 minutes. Makes about 2 cups.

ALMOND SAUCE—SERVE COLD

3 egg yolks
½ cup sugar
½ cup orange juice or sherry
1 tablespoon orange rind,
   grated

1 cup heavy cream
½ cup almonds, blanched,
   shredded and toasted

Beat egg yolks with sugar until thick and lemon colored. Add orange juice or sherry. Place in top of double boiler, or in saucepan set in pan of water. Stir constantly until mixture thickens. Just keep the water hot, not boiling. Stir in grated orange rind. Cool. Fold in stiffly beaten cream and toasted almonds. For a rush job you could use moist, shredded coconut instead of the almonds. Wonderful on sponge cake (page 402). Serves 8.

HONEY BUTTER SAUCE—SERVE COLD

⅔ cup butter or margarine   2½ cups honey

Let butter or margarine stand at room temperature until soft enough to blend. Add honey and stir until well mixed. Place in jar with tight-fitting lid and keep in refrigerator at least 2 days before using. This mixture is delicious on toast, hot biscuits, or hot gingerbread. Makes about 1½ pints.

CRANBERRY BUTTER SAUCE—SERVE HOT

1 can (No. 2) whole cranberry
   sauce

¼ cup butter or margarine
¼ cup light brown sugar

Combine cranberry sauce, butter or margarine, and brown sugar in small saucepan. Bring to boiling point. Serve hot on pancakes or waffles. Makes about 2 cups.

LEMON SAUCE—SERVE HOT

⅔ cup granulated sugar
1 tablespoon cornstarch
1 cup boiling water
2 tablespoons lemon juice

1 teaspoon lemon rind
2 tablespoons butter or
   margarine
Few grains salt

Mix cornstarch and sugar. Add to boiling water, stirring vigorously. Cook over medium heat until thickened. Remove from heat. Stir in lemon juice and rind, butter or margarine, and salt. Serves 8.

VANILLA SAUCE

In place of lemon juice and rind, use 1 tablespoon vanilla and a dash of nutmeg.

RUM SAUCE—SERVE HOT

½ cup butter or margarine	½ cup boiling water
1 cup brown sugar	⅓ to ½ cup rum
1 tablespoon all-purpose flour	

Place butter or margarine, brown sugar, and flour in saucepan. Blend thoroughly. Add boiling water and cook over low heat until mixture is clear. Remove from heat. Add rum. Fine for plum pudding (page 334). Serves 8.

BRANDY SAUCE—SERVE HOT

¼ cup butter or margarine	½ cup light cream
1 cup powdered sugar	2 egg whites, beaten stiff
2 egg yolks, well beaten	¼ cup brandy

Cream butter or margarine with powdered sugar. Add egg yolks and light cream. Cook over hot water until thickened. Pour slowly over stiffly beaten egg whites. Add brandy. Wonderful on plum pudding (page 334). Serves 8.

BING CHERRY SUNDAE SAUCE—SERVE COLD

6 cups Bing cherries, chopped	1 cup granulated sugar

Pit and chop cherries coarsely. Stir in sugar and continue stirring until sugar is dissolved. Place in freezer bags or cartons and freeze in your home freezer or freeze chest of your refrigerator. Serve on ice cream. Makes about 3 pints.

TRICK: The crushed fruit must be prepared and frozen with a minimum of delay to avoid color and flavor changes. Let frozen fruit stand at room temperature for about 1 hour before serving.

CREAM CHEESE TOPPING—SERVE COLD

1 package (3 ounces) cream cheese	½ teaspoon vanilla
¼ cup sugar	⅛ teaspoon nutmeg
	2 tablespoons light cream

Mash cream cheese with a fork. Add all ingredients and beat well. Excellent on hot gingerbread, apple or pumpkin pie. Serves 4.

Macaroni, Spaghetti, Noodles and Rice

These foods should be the economy-minded homemaker's best friends. They are inexpensive and filling, and, if properly used, can add variety and flavor to your meals. But remember that they need particularly loving care, for their flavor will depend completely upon the foods and sauces that accompany them. Never serve them simply as a "filler," but rise to the challenge they offer and make each filling dish a tasty triumph in its own right.

How to Buy

Usually 2 ounces per serving is sufficient, so the ordinary 8-ounce package will serve a family of four.

Remember that macaroni and spaghetti double in bulk when cooked; noodles stay the same; while one cup of uncooked rice will equal four cups when cooked.

How to Cook

3 quarts water   8-ounce package spaghetti,
1 teaspoon salt   macaroni, or noodles

Select a large kettle, remembering that these foods have a tendency to boil over easily.

Add salt to water and bring to a rapid boil. Break macaroni or spaghetti into desired lengths, if necessary, and add to water. Do this slowly so that water will maintain its rapid boil.

Cook, uncovered, stirring occasionally with a long-handled fork so that the food will not stick to the bottom of the kettle. Cook until tender (about 10-15 minutes). Drain through a colander. Rinse with hot water.

TRICK: If you are cooking macaroni or spaghetti in long lengths, place one end in water, and as sticks soften, shape softened portion in a circle like movement in water. By doing this, the lengths are kept separate and become completely submerged in the boiling water.

When you are cooking spaghetti to use with a sauce, such as Italian spaghetti, cook a whole clove of garlic with spaghetti. Garlic peps up the bland flavor of the spaghetti.

MACARONI

MULLIGAN

Large skillet with cover . . . Cooking time—about 45 minutes

1 package (8 ounces) macaroni, cooked as directed on page 253	1 onion, grated or chopped fine
	1 pound ground beef
	1 can (No. 2½) tomatoes
½ pound ground fresh pork	1 tablespoon chopped parsley
1 tablespoon bacon drippings or shortening	2 teaspoons salt
	⅛ teaspoon pepper

Brown the pork in the bacon drippings or shortening. Add chopped onion, then the ground beef, and stir until mixture is a golden brown. Add cooked macaroni, tomatoes, parsley, and seasonings. Cover and bring to steaming point, then reduce heat to simmer, and continue cooking. Serves 6.

MACARONI AND CHEESE

3-quart uncovered casserole . . . Preheated oven—350° F. . . . Baking time—1 hour

1 package (8 ounces) macaroni, cooked as directed on page 253	2 tablespoons all-purpose flour
	½ teaspoon salt
	2½ cups milk
3 tablespoons butter or margarine	½ pound sharp cheese, grated or cut in small pieces

Place butter or margarine in skillet. When melted, add flour and salt. Stir until blended. Add milk to flour mixture, stirring constantly until ingredients are well blended. Cook until thickened. Add cheese and immediately remove from range. Stir until cheese has melted. By making a sauce first, you have a much more delicious concoction. Grease casserole and place macaroni in casserole. Pour cheese sauce over macaroni. Bake. Serves 4-6.

TREAT: For something different and delicious, add ½ cup leeks or spring onions, cut fine.

MACARONI WITH TOMATO CHEESE SAUCE

2-quart uncovered casserole . . . Preheated oven—400° F. . . .
  Baking time—20 minutes

1 package (8 ounces) macaroni, cooked as directed on page 253	½ teaspoon celery seed
	½ teaspoon salt
	2 cups Cheddar cheese, shredded
1 can condensed cream of tomato soup	2 tablespoons buttered bread crumbs
½ cup milk	

Heat soup, milk, seasonings, and 1½ cups of the shredded cheese over low heat until cheese has melted. Blend with cooked macaroni. Pour mixture into greased casserole. Top with remaining cheese and buttered crumbs (see page 131). Bake uncovered. Serves 4-6.

MACARONI FRANKFURTER LOAF

9x5x3-inch loaf pan . . . Preheated oven—375° F. . . . Baking time—
  45 minutes

1 package (8 ounces) elbow macaroni, cooked as directed on page 253	1 cup milk
	2 eggs, well beaten
	2 cups Cheddar cheese, grated or shredded
3 tablespoons butter or margarine	2 tablespoons prepared or 1 teaspoon dry mustard
3 tablespoons all-purpose flour	8 frankfurters
2 teaspoons salt	

Melt butter or margarine over medium heat. When melted, add flour and salt. Blend thoroughly. Now add the milk, stirring constantly. This makes a thick white sauce. Quickly add the eggs, remove from heat, add cheese and mustard, and stir until cheese has melted. Then combine the cooked macaroni with cheese sauce.

Put a layer of macaroni mixture in bottom of greased loaf pan. Place 4 frankfurters on top of the mixture, lengthwise of pan. Add another layer of macaroni, remainder of frankfurters, and top with another layer of the macaroni mixture. Bake. Serves 6.

MACARONI HOE (Good way to use leftover macaroni.)

2-quart uncovered casserole . . . Preheated oven—350° F. . . . Baking time—45 minutes

1 cup cooked macaroni	1 cup soft bread crumbs
1 cup Cheddar cheese, grated	1 cup milk
1 tablespoon pimiento, chopped	2 eggs, well beaten
1 tablespoon green pepper, chopped	1 teaspoon salt
1 tablespoon parsley, chopped	⅛ teaspoon pepper

Cut or chop cooked macaroni into pieces the size of a navy bean. Mix grated cheese, macaroni, pimiento, green pepper, and chopped parsley together. Soak bread crumbs in the milk for a few minutes, then add well-beaten eggs, salt, and pepper. Mix all together and pour into greased casserole. Set in pan of hot water and bake. Serves 4.

TREAT: Delicious served with mushroom sauce (page 244) or creamed chicken (page 84).

DAVY JONES MACARONI

1½- or 2-quart casserole . . . Preheated oven—350° F. . . . Baking time—30-40 minutes

1 package (4 ounces) shell macaroni, cooked as directed on page 253	1 egg, beaten
2 tablespoons butter or margarine	2 tablespoons lemon juice
	1 can (8 ounces) salmon
	1 can (8 ounces) peas
2 tablespoons all-purpose flour	½ cup celery, chopped
1¼ teaspoons salt	2 tablespoons pimiento
½ teaspoon dry mustard	¼ cup buttered bread crumbs
1½ cups liquid (use liquid from salmon and peas, plus enough milk to make required amount)	

Melt butter or margarine in saucepan. Stir in flour, salt, and mustard. Gradually add liquid and stir until thickened. Stir thickened sauce into beaten eggs. Add lemon juice, salmon, peas, celery, and pimiento. Fold in cooked macaroni. Pour into greased casserole or utility dish. Sprinkle with buttered crumbs. Bake uncovered. A fine budget meal. Wonderful to make the night before. Place in refrigerator until ready to serve. Serves 4-5.

MACARONI SALMON LOAF

9x5x3-inch loaf pan . . . Preheated oven—350° F. . . . Baking time—
45 minutes

1 package (4 ounces) macaroni, cooked as directed on page 253	1 tablespoon parsley, chopped
	1 teaspoon salt
	⅛ teaspoon pepper
1 can (1 pound) pink or red salmon, boned and flaked	1 cup broken cracker crumbs or dry bread crumbs
1 tablespoon onion, minced or grated	3 eggs, slightly beaten
	1 cup milk

To the cooked macaroni, add ingredients in order given and blend thoroughly. Place in loaf pan and bake. Serve with tomato sauce (page 245). Serves 4.

CREAMY MACARONI PATTIES

8x6x2-inch utility pan . . . Cooking time—about 15 minutes

4 tablespoons bacon drippings or shortening	1½ cups cooked macaroni
5 tablespoons all-purpose flour	1 tablespoon parsley, chopped
1 teaspoon salt	1 tablespoon onion, grated
1 cup milk	Fine dry bread crumbs
½ pound Cheddar cheese, grated	1 egg
	1 tablespoon water

Melt bacon drippings or shortening. Blend in flour. Add salt and milk and cook until thick, stirring constantly. Remove from heat and add cheese, stirring until cheese has melted. This will be a thick sauce. Chop the cooked macaroni, to which the parsley and onion have been added. To the chopped macaroni, add the cheese sauce. Blend thoroughly. Pour into well-greased pan. Chill until firm. Cut into 2-inch squares. Dip squares in bread crumbs, then in beaten egg, to which the water has been added. Then again in the crumbs. Fry in skillet in hot shortening until brown, browning first on one side, then turning and browning on second side. Serve with a topping of tomato sauce (page 245). Serves 4.

SPAGHETTI

SPAGHETTI DE LUXE

4-quart covered saucepan . . . Cooking time—3-4 hours

Sauce

¾ pound lean beef
¼ pound lean veal
½ pound lean pork
1 strip bacon
½ cup parsley
1 small stalk celery (cut off leaves)
1-pint package fresh mushrooms
2 onions

2 cloves garlic
¼ cup butter or margarine
¼ cup olive oil
1 can (6 ounces) tomato paste
2 cans (No. 2½) tomato purée
¼ teaspoon orégano
1 tablespoon salt
1 teaspoon black pepper

Grind together (medium grind) the beef, veal, pork, bacon, parsley, celery, mushrooms, onion, and garlic. Sauté this mixture in the butter or margarine and olive oil until the meat has browned. Pour into a large kettle. Add the tomato paste, tomato purée, and the seasonings. Bring to steaming point, then simmer for at least 3 hours. Keep covered during the entire cooking period.

Spaghetti

1 package (1 pound) spaghetti
1 clove garlic
2 tablespoons butter or margarine

2 tablespoons olive oil
1 cup Parmesan cheese, grated

Cook the spaghetti and a clove of garlic in boiling water until spaghetti is tender. Drain, then return to kettle. Add butter or margarine, olive oil, and about 2 cups of the sauce. Mix well. Serve in individual portions with remaining sauce on each serving. Sprinkle Parmesan cheese over top of each serving as desired. Serves 8.

QUICK SPAGHETTI MEAL

Skillet with cover . . . Cooking time—about 15 minutes

3 tablespoons shortening (drippings are excellent)
½ cup onion, finely chopped

½ pound ground beef
1 can (No. 2) spaghetti in tomato sauce

Melt shortening, add onions, and cook slowly until onions are golden brown. Then add ground beef and continue cooking until beef is brown and crumbly. Add spaghetti. Cook on simmer heat for about 15 minutes. Serves 4.

If you have your oven going, instead of simmering for 15 minutes, place mixture in 1½-quart greased casserole. Sprinkle with grated cheese and bake for 20 minutes at 375° F.

SHRIMP SPAGHETTI

Large covered skillet . . . Cooking time—about 65 minutes

3 tablespoons butter or margarine	1 teaspoon salt
	1 teaspoon Worcestershire sauce
1 medium-sized onion, chopped fine	
¼ cup green pepper, chopped	1 package (4 ounces) spaghetti
2½ cups cooked or canned tomatoes	2 cups shrimp, canned or fresh
	1 cup Cheddar cheese, grated

Melt butter or margarine in skillet. Add chopped onion and sauté until golden brown. Add green pepper, tomatoes, seasonings, and uncooked spaghetti. Cover. When vigorous steaming starts, turn heat to low setting. Cook about 45 minutes. Add shrimp and cheese and simmer slowly for 20 minutes longer. Serves 5-6.

HAM SPAGHETTI SKILLET MEAL

Large covered skillet . . . Cooking time—30-40 minutes

4 slices bacon	1 teaspoon salt (more may be necessary depending upon saltiness of ham)
½ cup onion, chopped	
¼ cup green pepper, chopped	
2 cups cooked ham, cut in cubes	⅛ teaspoon pepper
1 clove garlic, grated fine	½ cup Cheddar cheese, shredded
2½ cups cooked tomatoes	
1 cup uncooked spaghetti, broken in 1½-inch pieces	

Dice bacon. Fry until partially crisp. Drain off half the bacon drippings. Add onion, green pepper, and ham and brown slightly. Add remaining ingredients except cheese. Stir lightly. Cover. When steaming point is reached, turn heat to simmer setting for 30 minutes. Remove cover and add cheese. Continue cooking on simmer heat until cheese has melted, about 10 minutes. This is a fine way to use leftover ham. Serves 4-5.

SPAGHETTI AND MEAT SKILLET MEAL

Skillet with cover . . . Cooking time—50 minutes

2 tablespoons shortening
1 pound ground beef
1 small onion, finely chopped
1 cup uncooked spaghetti,
   broken in pieces

2 cups tomato juice
1 cup catchup
1 teaspoon salt
¼ teaspoon pepper

Melt shortening in skillet. Add meat and onion. Cook until meat loses its red color. Place spaghetti over meat and onions. Add remaining ingredients. Stir just enough to blend. Place cover on skillet. When steam escapes, turn to simmer heat and continue cooking. Serves 4.

CHICKEN OR TURKEY TETRAZZINI

3-quart casserole or 7x11x1½-inch oblong utility pan . . . Preheated oven—400° F. . . . Baking time—30 minutes

1 package (8 ounces) spaghetti
   (you may use macaroni),
   cooked as directed on page
   253
4 tablespoons butter or
   margarine, or chicken fat
½ pound fresh mushrooms, sliced,
   or 1 cup canned, broken
   mushrooms

3 tablespoons all-purpose flour
1 cup broth made from bones of
   fowl, or canned consomme,
   or 2 chicken bouillon cubes
½ cup white wine
¾ cup top milk, or light cream
3 cups turkey or chicken, cut in
   medium-sized pieces
½ cup Parmesan cheese, grated

Melt shortening in skillet. Add mushrooms and sauté slowly for about 5 minutes. To the mushrooms, add the flour and blend carefully. If you use a fork to do the blending, you won't mash the mushrooms. Add broth and cook until thickened. Remove from heat. Add wine and cream or top milk. Stir until well blended.

Place a layer of cooked spaghetti or macaroni in greased baking dish. Then a layer of chicken, next a layer of the sauce. Repeat. This time you'll use up all the chicken and sauce, but leave a little of the spaghetti, so you can top it off with a thin layer of spaghetti. Sprinkle cheese over top. Bake. Serves 6-8.

NOODLES

HOMEMADE NOODLES

2 cups (about) all-purpose flour,   3 tablespoons cold water
   sifted before measuring   1 teaspoon salt
4 egg yolks

Place sifted flour in mixing bowl. With a fork, make a well in center of flour. Beat egg yolks slightly and add water and salt to them. With the fork, start blending the ingredients together. When the fork has gone as far as it can, begin working ingredients with fingertips until ingredients are well blended. Remove dough from bowl to a floured board and knead mixture. Divide dough into 3 parts. Roll each section as thin as possible. My grandmother used to say, "No thicker than a piece of paper." When the 3 portions have been rolled, place on clean tea towel to dry. The rolled dough must not be sticky, neither must it be brittle. When partially dry, sprinkle lightly with flour and roll up like a jelly roll. Be quite gentle when you roll the dough and don't press down hard. Find a very sharp knife and cut roll into strips from $\frac{1}{16}$ inch wide up to 3 inches, depending upon how you wish to use them. Shake out each piece as you cut it. Allow to dry. You may decide it's a lot easier to buy your noodles. However, homemade ones are delicious.

GREEN NOODLES

Buy a small can of spinach. A jar of baby food is excellent. Use above recipe, substituting ⅛ cup puréed spinach for cold water. Proceed as above.

NOODLE RING

7-inch ring mold . . . Preheated oven—375° F. . . . Baking time—
   30-40 minutes, or until a silver knife plunged in center comes
   out clean

1 package (8 ounces) fine   ½ teaspoon dry mustard
   noodles, cooked as directed   1 tablespoon butter or
   on page 253   margarine, melted
3 eggs   ¾ cup light cream or top milk
   Salt and pepper to season

Beat eggs slightly, add salt, pepper, mustard, melted butter or margarine, and cream. Stir until thoroughly blended. Arrange hot noodles in greased ring mold. Pour custard mixture over noodles. Set ring mold in pan containing water at least 1 inch deep. Bake.

To remove: Loosen mixture from side of ring mold with a knife and let stand for 5 minutes. Unmold on dish you plan to use for serving. Fill center with creamed chipped beef (page 54), or creamed chicken (page 84), or creamed tuna fish. Serves 6-8.

MARZETTI

3-quart uncovered casserole . . . Preheated oven—375° F. . . . Baking time—45 minutes

1 package (4 ounces) noodles, cooked as directed on page 253
2 tablespoons shortening
1 pound ground beef
1 large onion, chopped fine
½ green pepper, chopped
1 can (8 ounces) mushrooms, juice, stems, and pieces
1 teaspoon salt
¼ teaspoon pepper
¼ teaspoon orégano
1 can condensed cream of tomato soup
1 can (6 ounces) tomato paste
⅓ cup water
1 tablespoon Worcestershire sauce
½ pound sharp cheese, grated

Melt shortening and brown the ground meat. Add onion, green pepper, and mushrooms. Cook until tender. Add seasonings. Combine tomato soup, tomato paste, water, and Worcestershire sauce. Place a layer of noodles in greased casserole, then a layer of meat, covered with sauce and half the cheese, which has been grated or shredded. Repeat. Top with cheese. Bake. Serves 6-8.

LASAGNA (Means very broad noodles.)

12x8x2-inch baking dish . . . Preheated oven—350° F. . . . Baking time—30-40 minutes

1 package (8 ounces) lasagna, cooked as directed on page 253 (Run cold water through lasagna after cooking. Each noodle must be separated.)
1 can (No. 2½) Italian-style peeled tomatoes
2 cans (6 ounces) tomato paste
1 teaspoon salt
1½ teaspoons orégano
¼ teaspoon pepper
1 teaspoon onion salt
¼ cup olive or salad oil
1 cup onions, minced
2 cloves garlic, minced fine
1 pound ground chuck or round steak
1 teaspoon salt
¾ pound Ricotta cheese
½ pound Mozzarella cheese, finely sliced
¾ cup Parmesan cheese, grated

Simmer tomatoes, tomato paste, salt, orégano, pepper, and onion salt in uncovered saucepan. Put oil in skillet. When hot, sauté finely minced onion and garlic until lightly browned. Add ground meat and salt to onion mixture and cook until crumbly and red color has gone. Add to tomato sauce. Simmer 2 to 2½ hours, or until thickened. Cover bottom of baking dish with ⅓ of the sauce. Place ½ of the lasagna crisscross over sauce. Cover noodles with ½ the Ricotta cheese, ½ the Mozzarella cheese, and ⅓ the Parmesan cheese. Repeat, ending up with sauce on top. Sprinkle remaining Parmesan cheese over top. Bake until bubbly. Let stand about 15 minutes before serving. Serves 6-8.

TRICK: If you can't find Mozzarella cheese, substitute Swiss cheese.

If you can't find Ricotta cheese, substitute cottage cheese.

FRIED NOODLES

1 package (8 ounces) thin noodles, cooked until soft enough to bend but not thoroughly cooked, about 5 minutes. Rinse in cold water.

Drain. Spread on dry cloth until noodles are dry. With a long-handled fork, pick up a forkful of the dry noodles. Dip in deep fat, 375° F., and fry until brown, about 2-3 minutes. Drain. Serve hot. These are not as good as regular Chinese noodles, but may be used as a substitute.

EPICURE'S NOODLE RING

7-inch ring mold . . . Preheated oven—350° F. . . . Baking time— 45-50 minutes

1 package (4 ounces) thin noodles, cooked as directed on page 253	1 tablespoon onion, grated
	¼ cup melted butter or margarine
	¼ teaspoon salt
2 eggs, separated	½ cup thick sour cream
¼ teaspoon paprika	

Separate eggs. To the egg yolks, add the paprika, grated onion, and melted butter or margarine. Blend these ingredients through the hot, cooked noodles. Better use a table fork to do the blending.

Whip egg whites and salt until stiff. Then carefully fold the sour cream into the stiffly beaten egg whites, and fold this mixture carefully into the noodle mixture. If you have a slotted wooden spoon, it will be useful for folding noodle mixture and egg-white mixture together. Pour into well-greased ring mold. Set ring mold into pan which has at least 1 inch of water in it. Place in oven and bake. Don't overcook, or the ring mold will be curdly. When baked, remove from oven, run knife around sides, let stand for about 5 minutes, then invert on dish you will use for serving. Serves 4-6.

Fill center with creamed chicken (page 84), tuna fish, or Chicken à la King (page 86).

MOCK CHICKEN NOODLES

4-quart covered saucepan . . . Cooking time—about 1½ hours

½ pound veal shoulder	2 tablespoons onion, minced
¼ pound pork shoulder	1 package (4 ounces) noodles
4 cups water	3 teaspoons salt
1 cup celery, diced	¼ teaspoon pepper
1 carrot, diced	2 tablespoons butter or
1 tablespoon parsley, minced	margarine

Cut uncooked veal and pork in 1-inch cubes. Add water, celery, carrot, parsley, and onion. Simmer until nearly tender, about 1½ hours. Add noodles, salt, and pepper. Cook 15 minutes. Add butter or margarine and serve. Serves 4.

LYDIA'S SOUR-CREAM NOODLES

2-quart uncovered casserole . . . Preheated oven—350° F. . . . Baking time—45-50 minutes

1 package (8 ounces) noodles, cooked as directed on page 253	1 cup sour cream
	1 cup sharp Cheddar cheese, grated
2 eggs	1 teaspoon salt

Place cooked noodles in greased casserole. Beat eggs and add to sour cream. Add cheese and salt. Blend thoroughly. Pour over noodles in casserole. Place casserole in pan containing 1 inch of water. Bake. Serve as a vegetable with chicken, pork, or beef. Serves 6-8.

RICE

White rice may be bought in long, medium, or short grains. The long grain is considered by many to be the best.

Brown rice is the natural color of rice and retains some of the bran. It has more food value than white rice, and a nutty, pleasing flavor.

Wild rice is the seed of a marsh grass. It is especially fine served with game, provided your budget can afford it, for it is very expensive.

How to Cook Rice (Brown and White)

Most rice is packaged, and usually the directions on the box advise you against rewashing it, since most rice is washed before being packed.

If you do need to wash rice, however, place it in a colander and allow cold water to run through it 3 or 4 minutes. One cup uncooked rice will serve 4 when cooked. To cook, use:

2 cups cold water	1 cup rice
1 teaspoon salt	

Place water, salt, and rice in saucepan. Cover. Cook on high heat until steaming, then reduce heat to a simmer setting. Cook 20-25 minutes.

MINUTE RICE—Follow directions on package.

WILD RICE

1 cup uncooked wild rice equals 3 cups of cooked rice. Cook as follows:

4 cups water	1 cup wild rice
1 teaspoon salt	

Wash and carefully pick over wild rice. Place water in large saucepan. Add salt and rice. Cover. Cook over high heat until water is steaming. Then reduce heat to simmer setting. Cook 40-45 minutes.

RICE AND BACON

Skillet with cover . . . Cooking time—about 30 minutes

¼ pound or 6 strips bacon, diced	2 teaspoons salt
½ cup onion, chopped	1 teaspoon Worcestershire sauce
1 cup green pepper, chopped	1 cup uncooked rice
2 tablespoons pimiento, diced	3 cups water

Fry bacon until half done. Drain off most of the grease. Add onion and continue frying until bacon is crisp and onion is yellow in color. Add remaining ingredients. Bring to steaming point, then reduce heat so mixture will simmer. Cover. Fluff with a fork before serving. Tomato juice may be used instead of water. Serves 4-5.

PILAF

Skillet with cover . . . Cooking time—about 40 minutes

2 tablespoons shortening
⅔ cup uncooked rice
1 cup onion, finely chopped

4 cups cooked tomatoes
1 teaspoon salt
¼ teaspoon pepper

Put shortening in skillet. When hot, add rice and stir until rice is light brown in color. Add onions and tomatoes. Season with salt and pepper. Cover. When mixture reaches steaming point, reduce heat to simmer and cook until rice is soft. If you find it necessary to stir mixture, better use a fork so you won't mash the rice. For extra flavor, add 2 tablespoons finely chopped celery or finely chopped celery leaves. Serves 4.

SPANISH RICE

Skillet with cover . . . Cooking time—about 1 hour

4 tablespoons shortening
1 cup onion, chopped
2 cloves garlic, chopped fine
1 cup uncooked rice
2 cups cooked tomatoes
1 cup water or consommé

1 can (4 ounces) pimiento, chopped
1 teaspoon paprika
2 teaspoons salt
¼ teaspoon pepper

Place shortening in skillet. When hot, add onion and garlic and cook to a light, golden brown. Add rice, tomatoes, water or consommé, pimiento, and seasonings. Stir until ingredients are well blended. Cover. When mixture reaches steaming point, reduce heat to simmer setting. It may be necessary to add more water. Cook until mixture has thickened and rice is tender. Serves 5-6.

RICE MILANESE

Skillet with cover . . . Cooking time—about 40 minutes

2 tablespoons shortening
½ cup onion, chopped
1 cup uncooked rice
3½ cups chicken broth

½ cup Parmesan cheese, grated
1 teaspoon salt
1 teaspoon paprika
Chopped parsley

Heat shortening in skillet. When shortening is hot, add onions and sauté to a golden brown. Add rice and chicken broth. Stir. Cover. When mixture begins to steam, reduce heat to simmer setting and continue cooking until rice is tender. Add cheese and seasonings. Stir and continue simmering until cheese has melted. Sprinkle with chopped parsley just before serving. Serves 4.

GOLDEN RICE CASSEROLE

3-quart uncovered casserole . . . Preheated oven—350° F. . . .
Baking time—about 30 minutes

1 cup rice, cooked as directed on page 265	⅛ teaspoon pepper
	1 tablespoon all-purpose flour
3 tablespoons shortening	¾ cup milk
½ cup onion, chopped	1½ cups Cheddar cheese
¾ teaspoon salt	

Melt shortening. When shortening is hot, add onion and seasonings. Sauté to a golden brown. Add flour. Blend through onions,
then add milk, stirring until mixture has thickened. Remove from
heat, add cheese, and stir until cheese has melted. Add cooked
rice and blend together, using a fork so as not to mash rice. Pour
into greased casserole. Bake. Serve with buttered green beans or
carrots. Serves 5-6.

DEVILED RICE CROQUETTES

4 tablespoons shortening	1 cup Cheddar cheese, grated
5 tablespoons all-purpose flour	1 cup cooked rice
1 cup sweet milk	1 cup dry bread crumbs
1 teaspoon salt	1 egg
⅛ teaspoon cayenne pepper	1 tablespoon cold water
¼ teaspoon mustard	⅓ cup shortening, melted

Melt the 4 tablespoons shortening. Stir in flour. Add milk and stir
constantly until thickened. Add salt, cayenne pepper, mustard,
cheese, and rice and stir with a fork until cheese has melted. Pour
into a shallow pan. Place in refrigerator 3 or 4 hours, or until mixture is thoroughly cold. Shape into croquettes with a tablespoon.
Roll first in crumbs, then in egg beaten with water, then in
crumbs again. Heat shortening in skillet and pan-fry croquettes,
turning until all sides are golden brown. May be served with
tomato sauce (page 245). Serves 5-6.

GREEN RICE RING

8-inch ring mold . . . Preheated oven—350° F. . . . Baking time—
30 minutes

2 cups cooked rice	½ cup melted butter or margarine
1 cup parsley, chopped	3 eggs, separated
2 tablespoons green onion tops, chopped	

Combine all ingredients but eggs. Separate eggs, beat egg yolks, then add to rice mixture. Beat egg whites until stiff and fold into the above mixture. Pour into a greased ring mold. Place in pan of hot water to bake. To remove from mold, run knife around edge of mold. Invert on serving plate. Serves 6-8.

JAMBALAYA

8-inch skillet with cover . . . Cooking time—about 40 minutes

2 tablespoons shortening
1 pound ground beef
½ cup onion, chopped
⅓ cup green pepper, chopped
1 clove garlic, finely minced
2 teaspoons salt

⅛ teaspoon black pepper
¼ teaspoon thyme
1 can cream of tomato soup, diluted with 1 can water
⅔ cup uncooked rice

Heat shortening in skillet, add ground beef, and cook until red color disappears. Add all remaining ingredients at one time. Stir thoroughly. Cover skillet. When mixture starts steaming, turn heat to simmer setting and cook for 35 minutes. Stir well before serving. Serves 4-6.

GNOCCHI WITH CHEESE SAUCE

Gnocchi

½ cup quick-cooking wheat cereal
3 cups boiling water

1 teaspoon salt
¼ cup butter or margarine
1 egg, slightly beaten

Cook cereal in boiling salted water for 5 minutes. Add butter or margarine and beaten egg. Pour into greased shallow pan, 7x11 inches. Let stand until thoroughly cold. Cut into squares, place squares on a shallow pan, 10x14 inches, and cover with cheese sauce. Just before serving, place under broiler for about 5 minutes, or until delicately browned. Serves 6.

Cheese Sauce

4 tablespoons butter or margarine
4 tablespoons all-purpose flour
1 teaspoon dry mustard

1 teaspoon salt
2 cups milk
2 cups cheese, shredded

Place butter or margarine in saucepan. Melt over medium heat. Add flour, mustard, and salt. Blend thoroughly. Add milk, stirring constantly until mixture has thickened. Remove from heat. Add cheese, stirring until cheese has melted.

VACATION CASSEROLE

2-quart casserole . . . Preheated oven—350° F. . . . Baking time—
45 minutes

- 2 tablespoons butter or margarine
- 2 cups hot, cooked rice
- ½ pound Cheddar cheese, grated
- 1 cup evaporated milk or cream
- ½ teaspoon salt
- 1 teaspoon Worcestershire sauce

- 1½ cups cooked chicken or leftover meat, diced
- 1 cup cooked peas, drained
- 1 can (4-ounces) mushrooms, drained
- 1 cup buttered crumbs or potato chips, rolled fine

Add butter or margarine to hot rice. Stir with a fork until well blended. Combine cheese, cream or evaporated milk, salt, and Worcestershire sauce. Cook over low heat until cheese has melted. Place a layer of rice in greased casserole, next a layer of chicken, then peas, mushrooms. Repeat, ending with a layer of rice. Pour cheese mixture over all. Top with buttered crumbs or potato chips. Bake. Remove from oven and allow to stand about 10 minutes before serving. Serves 6-8.

TRICK: This casserole will keep hot at least an hour if wrapped in several layers of newspaper. Wonderful for church suppers or picnics.

Eggs

There is a famous couplet written by Oliver Goldsmith that you very probably know. It goes:

> And still they gazed, and still the wonder grew
> That one small head could carry all he knew.

I often think of these lines when I see a bowl of eggs and I am tempted to paraphrase those lines and say:

> And still they gazed, and still the wonder grew
> That these small spheres can do all that they do!

For eggs are perhaps one of the most adaptable and valuable foods that we have. They add incomparable nutritional values to any meal or dish of which they are a part; they add lightness to cakes and body to sauces; they add flavor to any meal of the day; and, in general, they would be almost impossible to do without! The following pages will give you a few suggestions for egg dishes that may suit your needs, but, as you know, recipes that call for eggs will be found throughout the book. Try these recipes and then experiment with some combinations of your own, for you will find that eggs may serve you in many more ways than you imagine.

How to Buy

Eggs are graded on the basis of outside appearance, weight, and interior quality. They come in several official sizes:

Extra large ....27 ounces, or 1 pound, 11 ounces, per dozen
Large ....24 " " 1 " 8 " " "
Medium ....21 " " 1 " 5 " " "
Small ....18 " " 1 " 2 " " "

The smaller eggs are usually more plentiful in late summer or early fall. The size never affects the quality of the eggs, but it does affect the price, with the smaller eggs, naturally, costing less.

High *quality* eggs should be used when you plan to cook them in the shell, poach, or fry them. For general cooking, however, lower quality eggs may be economically used. The grades are divided in this way:

Fancy grade .... top grade, usually unavailable in markets.

Grade A .... the only grade legally entitled to be termed "fresh." These are high quality eggs, and expensive.

Grade B .... containing the same nutritive values as the Grade A eggs, these Grade B are suitable for baking, frying, poaching, use in omelets, and so on. In short, they are considered satisfactory for almost any use.

Grade C .... these eggs are suitable for ordinary cooking uses, but not for poaching, and so on.

The shells of eggs vary in color from white to deep brown. The color in no way affects the flavor, nutritive value, or cooking performance. Nor is the shell's color a guide to the color of the yolk, which may vary from light to deep yellow. The yolk color is determined, however, entirely by the ingredients of the feed given the hens, and does not affect the food values of the egg.

Care and Storage

Try to buy eggs from a store where they are kept in a refrigerator.

If the eggs are dirty, wipe them off but do not wash them. They have a protective coating that you do not want to disturb. Remove from the paper egg cartoon and place in a covered container in the refrigerator.

If you have egg yolks, or egg whites, to keep, store them by placing in a tightly covered clean container such as a small mayonnaise jar. If an airtight container is used, it will not be necessary to cover the egg yolks with water, as many people do.

Beating Egg Whites

Whites from freshly laid eggs do not beat to a good volume.

Allow egg whites to stand at room temperature for about 30 minutes before beating for greater volume.

How to Cook

Always use low-temperature cooking for eggs. Too much heat toughens the whites and they are not as digestible.

SOFT-COOKED EGGS IN THE SHELL

Method No. 1

Have enough water in saucepan to cover eggs. Bring water to boiling point. Place egg on a tablespoon and lower into boiling water. Turn heat to simmer. DO NOT ALLOW EGGS TO BOIL. Cover.

Soft-Cooked Eggs.............	3 to	5 minutes
Medium-Cooked Eggs.........	7 to	8 minutes
Hard-Cooked Eggs............	25 to	30 minutes

TRICK: If you are hard-cooking the eggs, as soon as they are cooked remove from hot water and plunge into cold water. This prevents egg yolk from discoloring, and the eggs shell more easily.

Method No. 2

Place eggs in saucepan. Cover with cold water. Cover saucepan. Place over low heat and bring slowly to boiling point.

For soft-cooked eggs, remove as soon as water has reached boiling point, or for a firm white, allow to stay in water just below boiling point for about 3 minutes.

Hard-cooked eggs should simmer for 15 to 20 minutes after boiling point is reached.

FRIED EGGS

Break eggs into a skillet containing a little heated shortening. Bacon drippings are excellent, or butter may be used. If you are frying eggs just after frying bacon, pour some of the bacon grease from the skillet before starting to fry the eggs. Too much grease will spoil flavor.

Fry eggs over a low heat, or you won't get the full food value from them. Although some like their eggs fried in very hot grease, so the white bubbles up, this is a colossal waste of the health value of the eggs and makes them indigestible as well. The skillet may either be covered or uncovered, but covered is better.

When eggs begin to set, add 1 tablespoon water, cover tightly, cook to taste. If eggs are cooked uncovered, dip fat over top of eggs as they cook. For eggs to be fried well done, flip over when yolk is thoroughly set and beginning to harden.

BACON AND EGGS

If you want delicious bacon, fry on medium heat. This may take a little longer, but it's worth it. After the bacon has fried to desired crispness, remove bacon and drain on paper toweling. Pour off at least half the bacon grease. Then fry the eggs as above.

POACHED EGGS

Poaching is a method of cooking the egg, without a shell, in water or steam. As in all egg cookery, the most important rule to remember is to cook them just under the boiling point. A skillet is handy for poaching eggs. Fill half full of water. Add 1 teaspoon salt and 1 tablespoon vinegar to each quart of water used. The vinegar helps hold the white in place so it won't be so difficult to remove the egg from the water. Let water come to boiling point, then reduce heat so water stays just under boiling. Drop in required number of eggs. Cover pan and allow eggs to remain in water 3 minutes, or longer, depending on how firm the eggs are to be cooked. Lift eggs out with a skimmer or perforated spoon.

POACHED EGG ON HAM TOAST

2 tablespoons butter or margarine	½ cup milk
1½ teaspoons all-purpose flour	1 cup cooked ham, ground
1 teaspoon dry mustard	6 slices bread
1½ teaspoons prepared horse-radish	6 poached eggs

Melt butter or margarine, blend in flour, mustard, and horse-radish. Add milk and cook until thick. Add ham. Toast one side of bread under broiler. Spread untoasted side with ham mixture. Return to broiler, ham side up, until hot and beginning to brown.

To serve: Top each slice of ham toast with a poached egg. To poach eggs, see page 274. Serves 6.

CREAMED TOAST WITH POACHED EGGS

4 tablespoons butter or   ⅛ teaspoon pepper
    margarine   5 slices toast
4 tablespoons all-purpose flour   5 poached eggs
2 cups milk   Chopped parsley
½ teaspoon salt

Melt butter or margarine. Add flour and blend. Add milk and stir constantly until sauce thickens. Add salt and pepper. Toast bread and keep warm until eggs are poached (page 274). Lay slices of toast on serving platter, pour hot sauce over toast, then place one poached egg on each piece of toast. Sprinkle with chopped parsley and serve at once. Serves 4-5.

SHIRRED EGGS

Preheated oven—350° F. . . . Baking time—about 15 minutes

When shirring eggs, which is another way of saying, "baking eggs," use individual baking dishes, such as custard cups or ramekins, or a shallow baking dish large enough to hold the number of eggs to be cooked. Grease the dish or dishes generously. Bake until eggs are set, but not hard.

For Individual Dishes

Grease the individual custard cups, break 1 egg in each cup, sprinkle with salt and pepper, dot with butter or margarine. If you are confused about "dotting," a good rule is to use ¼ teaspoon butter or margarine for each egg. Spoon 1 tablespoon light cream over each egg. Bake until eggs are set but not hard.

For Larger, Shallow Baking Dish

Grease dish generously as directed above. Break desired number of eggs into dish. Season with butter or margarine, salt, and pepper and add 1 tablespoon light cream for each egg in dish. Bake as directed above.

SCRAMBLED EGGS

6 eggs, slightly beaten   2 tablespoons butter or
½ cup milk   margarine
1 teaspoon salt

Beat eggs slightly. Add milk and salt. Heat butter or margarine in skillet. When melted, add egg mixture. Cook over low heat until of creamy consistency, constantly stirring and scraping from bottom and sides of skillet. Do not overcook. Ham or bacon drippings may be used instead of butter or margarine. Serves 4.

TREATS: Instead of butter or margarine, use 2 strips of bacon cut into ½-inch pieces. Put bacon into cold skillet, heat, and fry slowly until bacon is crisp. Pour off all but 2 tablespoons of the drippings. Add beaten egg mixture. Follow directions for scrambled eggs.

Or, try sour or sweet cream in place of milk for a special treat.

Or, add 1 tablespoon Worcestershire sauce for a tangy flavor.

SCRAMBLED EGGS AND SPINACH

4 slices bacon, diced
2 cups cooked spinach, drained and chopped

6 eggs, slightly beaten
Salt to taste
Pepper to taste

Fry bacon in skillet until crisp, add spinach, and heat. Add eggs and stir until eggs are set. Add salt and pepper. Serve immediately. Serves 6.

SCRAMBLED EGGS WITH HERBS

6 eggs, beaten
¼ cup cream
½ teaspoon salt
Dash of pepper
2 tablespoons butter or margarine

⅛ teaspoon thyme
1 tablespoon chives or onion, chopped
1 pound little link sausages
1 tablespoon parsley, chopped

Beat eggs and combine with cream and seasonings. Heat butter or margarine in skillet. Pour in egg mixture and cook slowly until partially set, stirring lightly. Add thyme and chopped onion or chives. Cook until set. Serve with little pork sausages. Garnish with parsley. Serves 4.

CHINESE OMELET

9½x13½-inch oblong pan . . . Preheated oven—350° F. . . . Baking time 30-40 minutes

½ cup uncooked rice
4 tablespoons butter or margarine
4 tablespoons all-purpose flour
2 cups milk

3 eggs, separated
¼ teaspoon paprika
1¼ teaspoons salt
⅛ teaspoon dry mustard
4 tablespoons cheese, grated

Cook rice until tender (page 265). Rinse with hot and then cold water. Make sauce of butter or margarine, flour, and milk. Cook until thickened. Beat egg yolks and add rice, sauce, seasonings, and cheese to them. Fold in stiffly beaten egg whites. Pour into a greased, shallow pan. Bake. Wonderful to serve with creamed chicken (page 84). Serves 6.

FRENCH OMELET

6 eggs, slightly beaten	4 tablespoons milk
½ teaspoon salt	3 tablespoons butter, margarine,
⅛ teaspoon pepper	or drippings

Beat eggs only until yolks and whites are blended. Add seasonings and milk. Heat butter or margarine, or drippings, in skillet until moderately hot.

The trick in making French omelet is in not allowing the shortening to become too hot. When shortening is hot, add eggs. Cook slowly, lifting the mixture very gently with a fork or spatula as it cooks on the bottom. Also, gently tip the skillet so the uncooked egg mixture runs under. Do not cut through the mixture or stir it. You want one nice large mass of softly cooked eggs. When bottom is brown and mixture firm, fold in half. Serve at once with Spanish omelet sauce. Serves 4.

Spanish Omelet Sauce

2 tablespoons butter or margarine	¼ cup celery, chopped fine
	½ teaspoon salt
1 tablespoon onion, chopped fine	Dash of cayenne pepper
	1¾ cups cooked tomatoes
½ medium-sized green pepper, chopped fine	

Make the sauce before you make the omelet. Heat butter or margarine in saucepan or skillet, add onion, green pepper, celery, and seasonings and sauté until golden brown. Then add tomatoes and cook slowly until mixture has thickened. Before folding omelet, place ¼ cup tomato mixture in center of omelet, fold, place on hot serving plate, and pour remainder of sauce over and around omelet.

FOAMY OMELET

4 eggs, separated	4 tablespoons milk
½ teaspoon salt	1 tablespoon shortening
Pinch of pepper	

Beat yolks of eggs, add seasonings and milk. Beat whites until stiff but not dry. Place shortening in skillet. Just as soon as shortening has melted, reduce heat. Have bottom and sides of skillet well greased. Fold the stiffly beaten egg whites into yolk mixture. By this time the skillet should be very hot (about 5 minutes from time skillet was placed on unit). Pour in omelet, spread evenly, reduce heat, and cook slowly until omelet is set. Then place omelet in oven, which has been preheated to 375° F., so that omelet will dry slightly on top. Fold. Turn out and serve at once. Finely minced ham, grated cheese, or finely chopped parsely may be folded into mixture, if desired. Serves 4.

COUNTRY OMELET

2 cups cooked potatoes, diced
3 slices bacon, diced
¼ cup onion, minced
4 eggs, separated
2 tablespoons top milk

1 teaspoon salt
¼ teaspoon pepper
1 tablespoon parsley, chopped
1 tablespoon drippings

Brown potatoes, bacon, and onion together in skillet. Cool. Beat egg yolks slightly. Add milk, salt, pepper, and chopped parsley. Blend into the potato mixture. Beat egg whites until stiff; fold potato mixture into beaten egg whites. Heat 1 tablespoon drippings in skillet. Pour in omelet. Cook over low heat until lightly browned on the bottom (about 10 minutes). Brown top slowly under broiler and serve. Serves 5.

MUSHROOM OMELET

Follow recipe for either foamy omelet (page 277) or French omelet (page 277).

Sauté 1 cup chopped mushrooms in 3 tablespoons butter or margarine and place on ½ the omelet before folding.

EGG FOO YUNG

8 eggs, beaten slightly
½ pound fresh or canned shrimp, cut fine
½ cup green onion, chopped

1 teaspoon sugar
2 teaspoons Soy Sauce
½ teaspoon salt
4 tablespoons salad oil

Beat eggs slightly. Add all ingredients except oil. Place oil in skillet, and when hot, fry mixture as you would pancakes, putting mixture in hot oil by spoonfuls and turning when underside is brown. Serve with special sauce. Serves 6.

Special Sauce

1 beef bouillon cube	⅛ teaspoon pepper
1 tablespoon Soy Sauce	2 tablespoons all-purpose flour
1 cup water	2 tablespoons water
½ teaspoon salt	

Heat bouillon cube and Soy Sauce in the water. Add salt and pepper. Thicken slightly with a paste made of flour and water.

BAKED EGGS IN TOAST CUPS

Custard cups . . . Preheated oven—400° F. . . . Baking time—15-20 minutes

6 slices bread	6 eggs
¼ cup butter or margarine, melted	Salt and pepper

Cut crust from slices of bread, brush with melted butter or margarine, and gently press into greased custard cups. The four corners of the bread will extend up to the tops of the custard cup, forming a bread cup. Break an egg into each cup. Season, dot with butter or margarine, and bake until eggs are set and bread corners toasted. Serves 6.

BAKED EGGS IN RICE NESTS

8x8-inch square baking dish . . . Preheated oven—350° F. . . . Baking time—25-30 minutes

1 cup uncooked rice	6 eggs
1 cup leftover vegetables, diced	Salt and pepper
1 cup cheese, grated	Paprika
2 tablespoons butter or margarine	

Cook rice as directed on page 265. Combine with vegetables, cheese, and butter or margarine. Pour into greased, shallow baking dish. With the back of a large spoon form 6 rice nests. Break an egg into each nest, sprinkle with salt and pepper, and bake. Dust with paprika before serving. Serves 4-6.

DEVILED EGGS

6 hard-cooked eggs, shelled	½ teaspoon Worcestershire sauce
1 tablespoon cream or mayonnaise	¼ teaspoon salt
1½ teaspoons vinegar	Dash of pepper
¾ teaspoon prepared mustard	

Cut hard-cooked eggs in half lengthwise. (To cook, see page 273.) Remove yolks and put through a sieve. Add seasonings and beat until smooth and fluffy. Refill whites of eggs.

TREATS: Garnish top with a dash of paprika, a sprig of parsley, or chopped chives. Other seasonings such as onion juice, ham, sardine, or cheese may be added to the yolk mixture.

CURRIED EGGS

6 hard-cooked eggs
2 tablespoons butter or margarine
1 small onion, chopped fine
1 apple, chopped fine
¼ cup blanched almonds
1¾ cups milk or chicken stock

½ teaspoon salt
Dash of pepper
1½ teaspoons cornstarch
1½ teaspoons curry powder
¼ cup milk
½ teaspoon paprika

Prepare hard-cooked eggs as directed on page 273. Heat butter or margarine in skillet. When hot, sauté onions, apples, and almonds until golden brown. Add milk or chicken stock and simmer gently for about 10 minutes. Add salt and pepper. Dissolve cornstarch and curry in milk. Add to mixture in skillet. Cook until slightly thick. Add eggs which have been shelled and cut in ¼-inch slices. Heat thoroughly. Serve on hot buttered English muffins or hot buttered toast. Sprinkle with paprika. Serves 4.

EGG CUTLET

8-inch skillet . . . Cooking time—about 15 minutes

3 tablespoons butter or margarine
4 tablespoons all-purpose flour
1 cup milk
1 teaspoon salt
Dash of pepper
¼ teaspoon paprika

6 hard-cooked eggs, chopped
2 tablespoons parsley, chopped
1 cup fine, dry bread crumbs
1 egg, slightly beaten
1 tablespoon water
4 tablespoons shortening

Melt butter or margarine, blend in flour, slowly add milk. Cook over medium heat, stirring constantly until thick. Add seasonings, eggs, and chopped parsley. Pour into 8-inch square pan which has been lined with waxed paper. Chill 3 hours. Loosen edges, turn out on waxed paper, peel off paper from bottom, cut into 8 equal portions. Roll in bread crumbs and shape into cutlets. Dip in slightly beaten egg to which water has been added. Dip again in crumbs. Fry on both sides in hot shortening. Serve piping hot. Serves 8.

SCALLOPED EGGS

Utility dish . . . Preheated oven—400° F. . . . Baking time—25 minutes

2 tablespoons butter or margarine	⅛ teaspoon pepper
	¼ teaspoon paprika
2 tablespoons all-purpose flour	1 tablespoon parsley, chopped
2 cups milk	6 hard-cooked eggs, sliced
2 teaspoons salt	½ cup buttered bread crumbs

Melt butter or margarine and stir in the flour. Add the milk and bring slowly to a boil, stirring constantly until thick and smooth. Add salt, pepper, paprika, and chopped parsley. Place a layer of sliced egg in a greased utility dish, cover with half of the sauce, then put another layer of eggs, cover with remaining sauce, then top with buttered bread crumbs (see page 131). Bake. Serves 4-5.

CREAMED EGGS ON TOAST

4 hard-cooked eggs	1 teaspoon salt
3 tablespoons butter or margarine	1½ cups milk
	Toast as required
3 tablespoons all-purpose flour	

Hard-cook eggs (page 273). If you have difficulty removing shell, it is probably because you didn't cool the egg immediately after removing from hot water by plunging in cold water. Also, it helps if you break the shell first on the large end of the egg.

Quarter the eggs lengthwise for creaming.

Melt butter or margarine. Add flour and salt to melted butter or margarine, then milk, stirring constantly. Cook until thick. Add eggs, but take care not to break them. Leftover vegetables such as celery, carrots, or peas may be added, if desired. This will make the mixture go a little farther, one egg may then be left out. Pour over toast. Serves 4.

Cheese

Americans love cheese, and they are wise, for all cheeses, made as they are from milk and cream, are rich in nutritional values.

Milk, as we know, is perhaps the most perfect single food, but it lacks the adaptability and variety that makes cheese such a good friend to all cooks.

Do a little experimenting on your own and try out some of the cheeses that may, up to now, have been unfamiliar to you. You will find that each cheese has a personality and flavor that is completely its own, and you may find that some varieties you never tried before will turn out to be your favorites.

Varieties of Cheese

There is a great variety of both domestic and imported cheeses available in most markets. However, thy fall in about three general classifications: hard, semi-hard, and soft.

Hard Cheese

Caciocavallo: an Italian cheese, white in color. Must be grated. Used in soups, sphagetti, and many comparable foods.

283

Parmesan: an Italian cheese, also made in the United States. Creamy in color. Must be grated. Used in soups, spaghetti, and salads.

Gorgonzola: an Italian cheese. Marbled and sharp in flavor. Must be grated. Excellent to use in salads.

Pineapple cheese and Hard Cheddar: sharp in flavor. Must be grated. Excellent to use in salads.

Romano: another Italian cheese. Must be grated. Used in preparing many foods which require cheese.

Provolone: an Italian cheese, somewhat smoky in flavor. Must be grated. Excellent to use in stews.

Semi-Hard (Used in cooking, and also for eating without cooking)

American or Cheddar, cheese: ranges in flavor from mild to very sharp. Jack cheese, sometimes called Monterey cheese, of California; Tillamook, of Oregon; Coon, of Wisconsin are varieties of Cheddar cheese. Long Horn and Daisy are also Cheddar cheese.

Processed cheese: made of blended cheeses pressed into brick form.

Cheshire cheese: an English cheese. Sharp in flavor.

Bel Paese: an Italian cheese. Mild in flavor.

Bleu: an American cheese. Marbled in texture; strong, salty flavor.

Gouda: comes from Holland. Mild in flavor.

Gruyère: from both France and Switzerland. With eyes regularly distributed. Mild in flavor and yellow in color.

Oka or Trappest: from Canada. Moderately sharp in flavor. Strong odor.

Roquefort: originally from France. Strong in flavor and pungent.

Stilton cheese: from England. Somewhat like Roquefort or Bleu.

Swiss, and American Swiss cheese: irregular eyes, white to pale yellow in color. Mild in flavor.

Scandinavian-type cheese: include Gzedost, Primost, Nokkelost. Sandy in texture, and range from mild to pungent. All delicious.

Soft Cheese

Brie: soft, almost liquid center. The thick, moldy crust should be removed before eating, or dip center out with a spoon.

Camembert: a French cheese. Soft, almost liquid center. Sharp in flavor. A thin, edible crust covers this cheese.

Cottage cheese: mild in flavor. Used in many ways.

Cream cheese: mild in flavor. Used in many ways.

Liederkranz—an American cheese: sharp in flavor and pungent.

Limburger: from both Belgium and Germany. Also made in America. Slightly sharp in flavor and very pungent.

Neufchâtel: a French cheese, somewhat sharper than cream cheese, but similar in texture.

Tricks in Cooking Cheese

1. Remember that cheese becomes tough and rubbery when cooked at too high a heat. For best results, therefore, always cook cheese at a low temperature.

2. The hard cheeses must be grated before they are used in a recipe. For best flavor, grate just before use. You will find that some of these hard cheeses, such as Parmesan, Romano, Gruyère, and so on, may be bought already grated. Some cooks believe that these pre-grated packages lack flavor, but they do offer convenience in the kitchen.

The semi-hard cheeses, such as soft cheddar or the processed cheeses, should be shredded, rather than grated, before you add them to the rest of the ingredients. That is, simply slice the cheese into small bits which will melt easily. Or, if you have a coarse grater, use it for shredding the cheese.

You will not use the soft cheeses, such as Camembert, cottage cheese, and cream cheese, quite so often in your cooking, and yet, if you have limited your eating of these cheeses to cracker spreads, you may be surprised at how well they adapt themselves to cooked dishes.

To Store Cheese

Wrap in aluminum foil and store in a cool place. Your refrigerator is excellent. Or, wrap in a cloth moistened with vinegar.

To Serve

Cheese should stand at room temperature several hours before serving. Camembert and Brie should be kept in a slightly warmer place so the soft center will be almost liquid.

CHEESE SOUFFLÉ

3-quart casserole . . . Preheated oven—300° F. . . . Baking time—
1-1½ hours

4 tablespoons butter or margarine	½ teaspoon salt
	⅛ teaspoon cayenne pepper
4 tablespoons all-purpose flour	2 cups cheese, shredded
1½ cups milk	6 eggs, separated

Melt butter or margarine over medium heat. Add flour and blend.
Add milk and seasonings. Cook until smooth and thickened, stirring frequently. Add grated cheese. Stir until cheese is smooth
and melted. Pour slowly over the well-beaten egg yolks. Mix well.
Cool. When cool, fold into stiffly beaten egg whites. Pour into
greased casserole. Bake. Serve immediately after removing from
oven. For smaller families, divide recipe in half and use a 2-quart
casserole. Serves 6-8.

EASY CHEESE SOUFFLÉ

3-quart casserole . . . Preheated oven—300° F. . . . Baking time—
1-1¼ hours

1 can condensed cream of asparagus soup	1 cup cheese, shredded
	6 eggs, separated

Heat soup slowly over medium heat. (Cream of mushroom soup
may be used instead of asparagus soup.) Add cheese and cook,
stirring constantly until cheese has melted. Add slightly beaten egg
yolks. Cool. Fold stiffly beaten egg whites into soup mixture. Pour
into greased casserole. Bake. Serve immediately. Serves 6.

CHEESE SCOTCH WOODSTOCK

2-quart casserole . . . Preheated oven—350° F. . . . Baking time—
15-20 minutes

4 eggs, hard-cooked (page 273)	1 cup Cheddar cheese, shredded
4 tablespoons butter or margarine	2 teaspoons Worcestershire sauce
4 tablespoons all-purpose flour	1 cup chipped dried beef or leftover ham
2 cups milk	

Peel and cut hard-cooked eggs in half lengthwise. Lay, cut side
down, in greased casserole. Melt butter or margarine, blend in
flour, add milk, and cook until thickened, stirring frequently. When
thickened, remove from heat, add remaining ingredients. Pour
over eggs. Bake. Serve hot on toast. Serves 4.

CHEESEBURGER LOGS

1 pound ground beef	Dash of pepper
½ cup crisp rice cereal	1 egg
½ cup dry bread crumbs	¼ pound sharp cheese
¼ cup catchup	8 frankfurter buns
½ teaspoon salt	

Combine and mix well all ingredients except the cheese and buns. Form into 8 logs to fit the buns. Make a groove in the meat the full length of the log. Cut cheese into narrow strips, press into groove, and shape log again to hide cheese. Broil 7 to 8 minutes on each side, or until done. Split frankfurter buns and place a log in each bun for serving. Buns may be heated, if desired. Serves 4-8.

CHEESE FONDUE

2-quart casserole . . . Preheated oven—350° F. . . . Baking time— 30-40 minutes

1 cup cheese, shredded	½ teaspoon salt
1 cup soft bread crumbs	3 eggs, separated
1 cup milk	
1 tablespoon butter or margarine	

Place cheese, bread crumbs, milk, butter or margarine, and salt in saucepan and cook over low heat until mixture is smooth and cheese melted. Remove from heat, add well-beaten egg yolks. Stir until thoroughly blended. Fold in the stiffly beaten egg whites. Pour into casserole. Bake. Serve at once. Serves 4.

TRICK: An easy way to tell when fondue is done is to insert a silver knife in center of baking mixture. If knife comes out clean, it is done.

CHEESE DREAMS

1 cup cheese, shredded	¼ teaspoon Worcestershire sauce
¼ teaspoon dry mustard	1 egg, beaten
½ teaspoon salt	8 slices bread
Pepper to taste	Softened butter or margarine

Add cheese, dry ingredients, and Worcestershire sauce to beaten egg. Mix thoroughly. Spread on 4 slices of bread and top with remaining four slices of bread. Spread softened butter or margarine on outside of slices of bread. Place on preheated griddle. Brown both sides of sandwich to a rich golden brown. Serve hot. Serves 4.

TRICK: These may also be toasted under broiler, turning once.

SUPER CHEESE SANDWICHES

6 slices of cheese
12 slices of bread, buttered on
   one side

6 slices of tomato, which have
   been pan-fried
Mushroom sauce (page 244)

Place slices of cheese on unbuttered side of bread. Place pan-fried tomatoes on top of cheese. Lay second slice of bread on top, buttered side up. Toast under broiler, or fry a golden brown on hot skillet. Serve hot with mushroom sauce.

TREAT: To make this extra special, add a few fried onion rings on top of the tomato.

CHEESE PUDDING

3-quart baking dish . . . Preheated oven—325° F. . . . Baking time—
   50-60 minutes

¼ cup soft butter or margarine
6 slices bread, toasted
2½ cups cheese, shredded
3 eggs, slightly beaten
1 can condensed cream of
   tomato soup

1 can condensed cream of
   mushroom soup
¼ teaspoon mustard
¼ teaspoon salt

Spread butter or margarine on toasted bread. Cut each slice into six squares. Into a greased casserole place alternate layers of toast squares and cheese, ending with cheese. Combine eggs, soups, mustard, and salt. Pour over bread and cheese layers. Bake. Serve piping hot. Serves 6.

DANISH CHEESE SOUFFLÉ

3-quart casserole . . . Preheated oven—300° F. . . . Baking time—
   1 hour

2 cups milk
2 tablespoons onion, grated
3 cups bread cubes
   Dash of Tabasco

½ teaspoon dry mustard
3 cups cheese, shredded
4 eggs, separated

Place milk and onion in saucepan. Slowly bring to scalding point. Add bread cubes, seasonings, and cheese. Remove from heat, add slightly beaten egg yolks. Blend all ingredients thoroughly. Cool.

Pour cooled mixture over stiffly beaten egg whites. Pour into casserole. Bake. Serve immediately after removing from oven. Serves 4-6.

ENGLISH MONKEY

1 cup stale bread crumbs
1 cup milk
1 tablespoon butter or
   margarine
½ cup mild cheese, cut in small
   pieces

1 egg, slightly beaten
½ teaspoon salt
¼ teaspoon dry mustard
Few grains cayenne pepper

Soak bread in milk about 15 minutes. Melt butter or margarine over low heat with cheese. When cheese has melted, add soaked bread crumbs, egg, and seasonings. Cook over low heat until thickened. Serve over toasted bread or crackers. Serves 3-4.

OPEN-FACED CHEESE SANDWICH

Toast bread. Butter one side. Cover buttered side with medium-thin slices of sharp cheese. Place sandwich under broiler so it is about 5 inches from heat. Broil slowly until cheese is soft and melted.

TREAT: Spread buttered bread with prepared mustard before putting on cheese.

QUICK PIZZA

3 9-inch pie pans . . . Preheated oven—425° F. . . . Baking time—30 minutes

1 package hot-roll mix
1 can condensed cream of
   tomato soup
1 small clove garlic, chopped
   fine
¼ teaspoon orégano

2 tablespoons oil or melted
   shortening
¾ pound sharp Cheddar
   cheese, sliced
Crushed red pepper (optional)

Prepare a dough from roll mix according to directions on package. Let rise until double in bulk. Meanwhile, combine soup, garlic, and orégano and let stand to blend flavors. Divide risen dough into 3 parts. Roll or pat into a circle about ⅛ inch thick. Place each in lightly greased 9-inch pie pan. Brush dough with oil or melted shortening. Pour ⅓ mixture into each. Place cheese slices on top. Bake. Serve hot. Serves 6.

WELSH RAREBIT

1 tablespoon butter or
   margarine
½ pound semi-soft cheese, grated
   or cut in small pieces
½ teaspoon dry mustard

Few grains cayenne pepper
Salt and pepper to taste
½ cup evaporated milk or cream
1 egg, slightly beaten

Melt butter or margarine on medium-low heat. When melted, add cheese and seasonings and turn heat to a low setting. As cheese melts, gradually add milk, stirring constantly. Then add the slightly beaten egg. Cook until mixture thickens, about 2 minutes. Serve on toast squares or toasted crackers. Serves 4.

BEER RAREBIT

Omit milk. Use beer or ale instead.

QUICK WELSH RAREBIT

1 can condensed cream of celery
   soup
½ cup milk
1 cup sharp Cheddar cheese,
   shredded

½ teaspoon dry mustard
2 eggs, well beaten

Combine ingredients in order given. Heat over low heat, stirring frequently until cheese has melted and mixture has thickened. Serve on toast or crackers. Serves 4-6.

RINKTUM DITTY

1 can condensed cream of
   tomato soup
2 cups Cheddar cheese,
   shredded

¼ teaspoon dry mustard
1 egg, slightly beaten
6 pieces toast

Heat soup slowly over low heat. Add cheese; stir until melted. Add mustard and egg. Mix and heat thoroughly. Serve on toast. Serves 6.

Sandwiches, Canapés

A sandwich may be anything from the thick, hearty meal-in-one sandwiches that you will pack in lunch pails, to the dainty and attractive creations you will serve at a bridge party. Although every family has its favorite sandwiches, you may find that new combinations and unusual fillings will perk up a schoolchild's appetite or a workingman's energy.

HEARTY SANDWICHES

Always use fresh bread when making sandwiches, remembering that there are many varieties of bread, such as whole wheat, rye, brown bread, and nut bread, which offer a variety of flavors.

Be generous with the butter or margarine when making hearty sandwiches and spread it clear to the edge of the bread. Not only will the sandwiches taste better, but the filling will not be so apt to soak through.

Lettuce should not be used in making sandwiches, unless the sandwich is to be eaten immediately. If you are making sandwiches for a lunch pail, wrap the lettuce separately in a piece of waxed paper or foil so it may be put in just before eating. Lettuce becomes limp very quickly when placed in sandwiches, particularly if the sandwiches are wrapped and carried in a lunch pail. Unfortunately, the limper the lettuce, the tougher it becomes.

Leave the crusts on your sandwiches, unless the owner of the lunch pail objects too strenuously, for the crusts will help keep the bread moist. And, for the same reason, you will find it is wiser not to cut lunch-pail sandwiches in half, for the whole sandwich will stay much fresher when uncut.

If you have a lunch pail to pack every day, and are fortunate enough to own a home freezer, make up a variety of sandwiches, wrap in moisture-vapor proof packaging material, and freeze them. Of course you should wrap each separately and label it. When packing the lunch pail, take from the freezer the desired number of frozen sandwiches and place in lunch pail. By lunchtime the sandwich will be completely thawed and will taste as though it were freshly made.

Cooked Meat for Sandwiches

When you are making hearty sandwiches, you may use any kind of cooked meat. Leftover roasts, chicken, turkey, all make wonderful sandwiches. Or, you can buy corned beef, liverwurst, or any of the cooked and packaged meats. If the leftover supply isn't sufficient to make the desired number of sandwiches, grind the meat with sweet or sour pickles, or hard-cooked eggs, and moisten with mayonnaise.

Cooked Fish for Sandwiches

For a pleasing variation, fish, such as sardines, shrimp, tuna fish, or lobster make wonderful hearty sandwiches. Any of these may be mixed with finely chopped celery, ground cheese, or chopped peanuts, and moistened with mayonnaise or lemon juice. A small amount of prepared horse-radish, mustard, curry, or a bit of powdered tarragon added to any of the above sandwiches makes interesting variations.

Egg and Cheese Sandwiches

Don't overlook eggs as a sandwich filler. Hard-cooked eggs are perfect for sandwiches that must be carried in a lunch pail. They should be chopped and mixed with either cream or mayonnaise.

Eggs scrambled with a bit of cheese, bacon, or sausage make a wonderful late in the evening snack, or a perfect luncheon sandwich.

Toasted cheese sandwiches may be broiled in the oven, or on a regular sandwich grill. These are always in great demand. Or, cheese may be ground with hard-cooked eggs, green pepper, or pickle and made into a delicious sandwich spread.

Some people are especially fond of cream cheese and jelly, and usually this combination is preferred on whole wheat or dark bread. Don't overlook crackers. They are delicious with a topping of cheese.

Vegetable Sandwich Spreads

If the sandwich is to be eaten as soon as it has been made, there is nothing better than a tomato sandwich. However, tomato sandwiches are not satisfactory to carry in the lunch pail, unless you spread the bread with butter or margarine and put the tomato in separately, allowing the person to prepare his own sandwich.

Baked beans, navy, kidney, or lima, make wonderful sandwiches. Mash them fine, blend with a little mayonnaise, and spread on the bread reasonably thick.

If you have never tried putting carrots and raisins through a food grinder and mixing with mayonnaise, you have missed a real treat.

Here are a few suggestions for making hearty sandwiches:

PORK AND EGG SANDWICH FILLING

1 can Junior Pork
1 hard-cooked egg, finely chopped
1 teaspoon mayonnaise
Salt to taste

Blend ingredients and chill. Makes 3 sandwiches.

BACON-CHEESE SANDWICH SPREAD

1 package (3 ounces) cream cheese
¼ cup cooked bacon, chopped
½ teaspoon prepared horse-radish
½ teaspoon Worcestershire sauce
1 tablespoon milk

Blend all ingredients thoroughly. Store in refrigerator until used. Makes 2-3 sandwiches.

CHEESE AND DRIED BEEF SANDWICH SPREAD

½ pound Cheddar cheese
½ cup drained, canned, or freshly cooked tomatoes
¼ cup butter or margarine
¼ pound dried beef, chopped
1 teaspoon onion juice

Melt the cheese over low heat. Add tomatoes gradually, stirring constantly. Add the butter or margarine and blend thoroughly. Add the dried beef and mix well. Store in refrigerator. Makes about 2 cups sandwich spread.

COTTAGE CHEESE SANDWICH SPREAD

1 cup well-seasoned cottage cheese
1 cup peanuts, finely chopped

1 tablespoon mayonnaise
½ teaspoon paprika

Combine all ingredients. Store in refrigerator. Makes about 1½ cups.

DEVILED CHEESE SANDWICH SPREAD

½ pound mild cheese
1 small onion
½ cup green pepper or 3 canned pimientos

3 hard-cooked eggs
¼ teaspoon salt
½ teaspoon paprika
4 tablespoons mayonnaise

Grind the cheese, onion, and green pepper. Add the chopped eggs, seasonings, and mayonnaise. Mix well. Store in refrigerator. Makes about 2 cups.

DEVILED EGG SANDWICH SPREAD

6 hard-cooked eggs
½ teaspoon salt
Dash of pepper

¼ teaspoon dry mustard
2 tablespoons vinegar
2 tablespoons mayonnaise

Remove shells from eggs. Separate yolks from whites. Mash the yolks fine and add the salt, pepper, mustard, vinegar and mix well. Cut whites of egg with fork. Combine the two mixtures and add the mayonnaise. Mix well. Store in refrigerator. Makes 4 sandwiches.

CORNED-BEEF SANDWICH SPREAD

4 tablespoons sharp cheese
2 tablespoons mayonnaise
¼ pound cooked corned beef, chopped
6 tablespoons sweet pickle, minced

2 teaspoons onion, finely minced
1 teaspoon prepared mustard
¼ teaspoon salt
⅛ teaspoon pepper

Cut cheese into small pieces and blend thoroughly with mayonnaise until smooth and soft. Add remaining ingredients. Mix until all ingredients are well blended. Store in refrigerator. Makes 12 sandwiches.

RED KIDNEY OR LIMA BEAN SANDWICH SPREAD

2 cups cooked beans, well drained and pressed through a sieve

2 tablespoons pickle relish

1 teaspoon salt

½ teaspoon paprika

1 tablespoon mayonnaise

Combine all ingredients and mix thoroughly. Store in refrigerator. Makes about 8 sandwiches.

LIVER SANDWICH SPREAD

⅔ pound pork liver

2 hard-cooked eggs

1 small onion, chopped

1 tablespoon shortening

½ cup cream or top milk

Salt

Pepper

Few drops Tabasco sauce

Steam liver 25 minutes. Cool. Put through food grinder. Chop eggs coarsely. Brown onions in shortening until a light, golden brown. Mix all ingredients. Store in refrigerator. Makes about 2 cups.

FLAKED-FISH SANDWICH SPREAD

1 cup canned fish flakes, or cooked leftover fish

1 tablespoon celery, chopped

1 tablespoon pickle, chopped (sweet or sour)

3 tablespoons mayonnaise

½ tablespoon catchup

1 teaspoon prepared mustard

¼ teaspoon salt

½ teaspoon pepper

Place all ingredients in a bowl and mix well. Store in refrigerator. Makes 4 sandwiches.

PEANUT BUTTER-BACON SANDWICH SPREAD

¼ cup peanut butter

2 strips bacon, crisply fried

1 tablespoon mayonnaise

Combine peanut butter and finely broken, crisply fried bacon. Moisten with mayonnaise. Makes 2 sandwiches.

TRICK: Store peanut butter lid side down. This will prevent the oil from separating.

GREEN-TOMATO SANDWICH SPREAD

2 cups ground green tomatoes

2 red peppers

2 green peppers

1 teaspoon salt

6 medium-sized sweet pickles

Grind tomatoes. Drain. There must be 2 cups of tomatoes after the liquid has been drained off. Grind red and green peppers. Sprinkle salt over mixture and let stand 15 minutes. Again drain off all liquid. Add ground sweet pickles to mixture and cook over medium heat for 10 minutes.

Dressing

1 cup granulated sugar	2 tablespoons all-purpose flour
1 cup sour cream	2 tablespoons prepared mustard
3 eggs, well beaten	½ cup cider vinegar

Mix all ingredients together and bring to a boil, stirring frequently. Add tomato-pepper-pickle mixture and cook over medium heat, stirring constantly to prevent mixture from sticking. Cook about 10 minutes after boiling point has been reached. Put in sterilized jars and seal. Delicious during winter months. Makes about 3 pints.

LUNCHEON SANDWICH SUGGESTIONS

BACON CHEESE TREAT

2 tablespoons pimiento, chopped	3 tablespoons prepared mustard
4 tablespoons parsley, chopped	6 slices bread, toasted on one side
4 tablespoons onion, chopped	4 slices bacon, cut in small pieces
2 packages (3 ounces) cream cheese	

Blend pimiento, parsley, onion, cheese, and mustard together. Spread on the untoasted side of bread. Sprinkle bacon pieces over cheese mixture. Place on broiler rack and broil about 4 minutes. Keep the broiler pan at least 4 inches from broiler unit. Otherwise the cheese mixture will be apt to burn. Serves 4-6.

TRICK: If you do not have the prepared mustard, mix 1 tablespoon dry mustard with 1½ tablespoons mayonnaise.

CRUNCHY FRIED SANDWICHES

2 eggs, slightly beaten	12 slices bread
½ teaspoon salt	½ cup peanut butter
½ cup milk	¼ cup shortening

Combine eggs, salt, and milk. Spread 6 slices of bread with peanut butter. Top with remaining slices of bread and cut in half diagonally. Dip sandwiches in egg mixture and fry on preheated, well-greased griddle until golden brown on both sides. Serve hot with jelly. Serves 4-6.

PARTY SANDWICHES OR CANAPÉS

If canapés are to be served untoasted, be sure to make them from fresh bread. They may be open canapés, or topped with a second round of bread. Canapés are usually cut round, or in fancy shapes. It will make the tray look more interesting if you vary the shapes.

It isn't much of a trick to make rolled canapés, but it will be much easier to roll them if the average-sized slice of bread is cut into 2 thin slices. There is a fine little gadget on the market that cuts the regulation slice of bread in half, and if you anticipate making canapés which require thinly sliced bread, it might be worth while to invest in one of these. It looks something like an old-fashioned toaster. The bread is placed between two metal covers, and with a special knife which comes with the set, the bread is easily and quickly cut in half.

However, in some localities, bakers are now cutting bread extra thin. If such bread is available, the gadget mentioned above will not be necessary.

Dainty canapés always need garnishing. Very small bits of parsley, water cress, stuffed olives, cut in thin slices, and radishes, cut thin, all make interesting bits of decoration.

Canapés should always have a thin layer of butter or margarine or mayonnaise spread over the top. When using butter or margarine, soften it for easy spreading.

Some recipes for easy, inexpensive canapés follow:

CUCUMBER-RADISH CANAPÉ

This is particularly good during hot summer months. Slice radishes paper thin. Do not peel them. Cut the bread in rounds. If you do not own a round cooky cutter, the top of a baking powder can will make a fair substitute. Spread rounds with softened butter or margarine, or mayonnaise. Place a thin slice of crisp cucumber in the center of the round of bread. Then arrange paper-thin slices of radishes around the outer edge. The bit of red on the radish makes a wonderful garnish. Top with just a mere suggestion of mayonnaise, and if you wish, sprinkle paprika over top.

TRICK: You can have your bread all prepared, but don't put the cucumber and radish on canapé until shortly before guests arrive. Both radishes and cucumber must be crisp.

WATER CRESS-CHEESE CANAPÉ

Remove leaves from the stems of water cress. Chop leaves very fine. Mix with a 3-ounce package cream cheese which has been mixed with ½ teaspoon Worcestershire sauce and moistened either with coffee cream or mayonnaise. Blend thoroughly. Spread, not too thick, on rounds or fancy cuts of bread.

CORNUCOPIA OR LILY SANDWICHES OR CANAPÉS

One of the prettiest canapés of all is the lily canapé. You will need fresh bread for this. Remove crusts from all four sides. Mix cream cheese with a dash of Worcestershire sauce and about ¼ teaspoon prepared horse-radish and spread over slices of bread. Roll two opposite corners toward center to form a cornucopia. Overlap edges and hold them in place by spreading a bit of softened butter or margarine on the edges of the bread. Press gently with the finger. As the butter or margarine hardens, it holds the edges in place. Insert a very narrow strip of carrot in each "lily" for the stamen. The strip of carrot should be match thick and about 1½ inches long. A 3-ounce package of cream cheese will make about 12 lilies.

PINWHEEL CANAPÉS

Remove crusts from bread. Spread with cream cheese and water cress mixture. Roll like a jelly roll (page 316). Cut each roll in 2 or 3 slices just before serving. If you can buy unsliced bread, remove crusts from bread and cut in thin slices across the loaf of the bread. Spread with any desired filling, and cut in about ½-inch slices just before serving.

TRICK: Spread the ends of bread with softened butter or margarine just before finishing the roll. This will keep the edge in place and make a perfect pinwheel when cut.

CHECKERBOARD CANAPÉS

You will need a loaf of whole wheat and a loaf of white bread. Remove crusts from bread. Spread each slice with softened butter or margarine. Or, if you prefer, make a filling of cream cheese, flavored with onion juice, or prepared horse-radish. Start with a slice of whole wheat, on top of it place a slice of white bread, then another slice of whole wheat. Start all over again, using white bread for the starter slice. Trim each pile evenly and cut in 3 or 4 strips. Brush these strips with softened butter or margarine, then place them on top of each other, so that a white-centered block will alternate with a whole wheat center block. Wrap each little loaf in waxed paper and store in refrigerator until ready to use. Slice in about ¼-inch slices before serving.

CREAM PUFF CANAPÉS

Prepare standard cream puff batter. Unless you need a great many canapés, use only half the recipe. The whole recipe will make about 60 bite-sized canapés.

To bake, use a teaspoon and drop about ½ teaspoon cream puff batter on greased cooky sheet. Bake according to directions. These should come out about the size of a small walnut. Just before serving, fill with chicken salad, tuna fish salad, lobster, or shrimp salad. You'll find these recipes in the salad section (pages 177-211).

TOASTED CANAPÉS

Use day-old bread for toasted canapés. Cut slices of bread into rounds or fancy shapes. Brush one side with softened butter or margarine. Toast unbuttered side to a golden brown. Just before serving, spread filling on untoasted side. These may be browned quickly under broiler, or served plain.

TRICK: If you have a home freezer, these may be made in advance, spread with desired filling, wrapped carefully, and frozen. They will defrost in about 15 minutes.

FILLINGS FOR TOASTED CANAPÉS

Clam dip (page 303) may be varied with shredded crab, lobster, or shrimp in place of the clam. Also, a tablespoon prepared horseradish may be used instead of the lemon juice.

HAM CANAPÉS

Cooky sheet . . . Preheated oven—400° F. . . . Baking time—10 minutes

¼ pound processed cheese, grated	¼ teaspoon monosodium glutamate
¼ cup deviled ham spread	6 tablespoons all-purpose flour
2 tablespoons cornstarch	½ teaspoon Worcestershire sauce

Mix all ingredients thoroughly. Pinch off bits and shape into balls ½ inch in diameter. Place on ungreased cooky sheet and flatten with a fork dipped in flour to about 1½ inches in diameter. Cover with waxed paper. Chill 1 hour. Bake. Makes 20-24 small canapés.

TRICK: May be frozen for as long as several weeks before baking.

PAPRIKA CHEESE ROLL

½ pound sharp Cheddar cheese
½ pound pimiento cheese
2 packages (3 ounces each)
     cream cheese
½ teaspoon Tabasco sauce
1 tablespoon Worcestershire
     sauce

1 teaspoon onion, finely minced
½ clove garlic, finely minced
     Mayonnaise to moisten
⅓ cup paprika

Put Cheddar cheese and pimiento cheese through food chopper.
This is essential for a smooth roll. Add cream cheese and seasonings, excepting paprika. Blend thoroughly. Add just enough mayonnaise to moisten and still make the mixture easy to handle. Chill
mixture for at least an hour in the refrigerator. Sprinkle a sheet
of waxed paper with paprika. Shape cheese into 2 rolls and wrap
in waxed paper which has been generously sprinkled with paprika. Chill. When ready to serve, place on platter or tray, surrounded with crackers, potato chips, or even very thin slices of
crisp carrots.

CHEESE WAFERS

Cooky sheet . . . Preheated oven—375° F. . . . Baking time—10-15
  minutes

½ pound Cheddar cheese,
     grated
¼ pound butter or margarine

1½ cups all-purpose flour
1 teaspoon salt
     Few grains cayenne pepper

Cream the cheese with butter or margarine. Add flour, salt, and
cayenne pepper. Mix well. Place in refrigerator to chill. Shape into
roll; wrap in waxed paper and chill for 2 or 3 hours. Slice very thin
and bake. Makes about 4 dozen wafers.

HAM CHEESE PUFFS

Ham Mixture

1 cup cooked ham, ground
2 teaspoons prepared mustard
½ teaspoon Worcestershire sauce

¼ cup mayonnaise
1 teaspoon onion, finely grated
1 teaspoon baking powder

Combine ham, mustard, Worcestershire sauce, mayonnaise, onion,
and baking powder. Mix well.

Cheese Mixture

¾ cup Cheddar cheese, grated
1 egg, beaten
1 teaspoon onion, grated

1 teaspoon baking powder
18 2-inch bread rounds, or
     1½-inch strips

Combine cheese, beaten egg, onion, and baking powder. Toast bread on one side. Spread untoasted side with ham mixture and top with cheese mixture. Broil until topping puffs and is brown. Serve at once. Makes 18 canapés.

TRICK: These may be prepared in advance and frozen. Do not remove from freezer until ready to broil for serving. Broil from frozen state.

SNAPPY CHEESE BALLS

Cooky sheet . . . Preheated oven—375° F. . . . Baking time—10-15 minutes

1 package (6 ounces) snappy cheese   ½ cup all-purpose flour
¼ cup butter or margarine   Dash of Worcestershire sauce

Blend all ingredients until smooth. Shape into small round balls. Place on cooky sheet and bake. Serve hot or cold. Makes about 1½ dozen.

DEVILED HAM CANAPÉS

Cooky sheet . . . Preheated oven—425° F. . . . Baking time—18-20 minutes

1 recipe for pie crust (page 365)   2 cans (3¼ ounces) deviled ham

Divide dough into 2 equal parts and roll each into rectangular shape, about ¼ inch thick. Drop deviled ham by scant teaspoonfuls, about ½ inch apart, on one rectangular-shaped piece. Place second rectangle over the one which is covered with ham. Cut into squares with a pastry wheel or square biscuit cutter. Seal edges as for pastry (page 366). Prick top surface of canapés and bake. Makes about 2 dozen small canapés.

CHEESE AND TOMATO CANAPÉS

1 package (3 ounces) cream cheese   ½ teaspoon Worcestershire sauce
⅛ teaspoon salt   3 or 4 small tomatoes
1 teaspoon onion juice   Mayonnaise
    1 can anchovies (rolled)

Have cream cheese at room temperature. Add salt, onion juice, and Worcestershire sauce. Spread rounds of bread with cheese mixture. Cut the bread with a cutter about the size of the tomato you will use, and not more than 1½ inches across. Place thin slice of tomato on each round, then a small amount of mayonnaise in center of tomato, and place an anchovy on top of mayonnaise.

TRICK: These are still better if the bread rounds are brushed with butter or margarine, and placed on cooky sheet to brown in oven. Preheat the oven to 425° F. About 5 minutes and the rounds are ready to come out. Then proceed as above.

CHEESE CUP CANAPÉS

Cooky sheet ... Preheated oven—425° F. ... Baking time—5 minutes

1 package (8 ounces) cream cheese	2 egg yolks
1 tablespoon onion juice	Salt and pepper to season
1 teaspoon Worcestershire sauce	Bread cups
½ teaspoon prepared horse-radish	½ cup melted butter or margarine

Have cream cheese at room temperature. Mix all ingredients together until well blended.

To prepare bread cups: Use unsliced bread and slice ¾ to 1 inch thick. Cut each slice in 4 pieces and remove crusts. Trim corners to make each piece round. This is simpler than attempting to cut these thick pieces with a round cutter. Remove centers of bread with a sharp knife, being careful not to go through bottom of bread. Brush entire surface inside and out with melted butter or margarine. Fill with cheese filling. May be placed in refrigerator overnight, or may be frozen for a period not longer than 2 months. If canapés have been refrigerated or are being used directly after making, bake just before serving. If canapés are frozen, remove from freezer, unwrap, and let stand on cooky sheet at least 20 minutes. Then bake. Makes 20-24 canapés.

TRICK: 1 jar (12 ounces) Welsh rarebit may be used instead of the cheese filling above.

CHEESE BALL SPREAD

2 packages (3 ounces each) cream cheese	½ cup sherry
1 pound bleu or Roquefort cheese	1 teaspoon Worcestershire sauce
¼ pound butter or margarine	1 teaspoon poppy seed
1 large clove garlic, grated fine	1 teaspoon mixed herb salt

Place cheese, butter or margarine, and grated garlic in mixing bowl. Beat, while gradually adding sherry. Add Worcestershire sauce, poppy seed, and herb salt. Beat thoroughly. This mixture will be slightly soft. Place in refrigerator to chill until mixture can be handled easily. Shape into medium-sized balls and wrap in waxed paper or foil, preferably the foil. Keep in refrigerator at least a week before serving. Serve on platter, or tray, surrounded by crackers, potato chips, or very thin toast. Let each guest cut off desired amount.

SARDINE ROLLS

2 cans sardines	8 thin slices bread
4 teaspoons lemon juice	Melted butter or margarine
¾ teaspoon prepared horse-radish	

Drain oil from sardines. Mash sardines and mix with lemon juice and prepared horse-radish. Spread on thin slices of bread. Roll each slice like a jelly roll (page 316). Brush with melted butter or margarine. Place under broiler and brown. Serve hot. Serves 8.

SUGGESTIONS FOR DIPS

GUACAMOLE DIP

Make Guacamole (page 209), but use ¼ to ½ cup sherry to make it of dipping consistency.

CLAM DIP

1 package (3 ounces) cream cheese	2 teaspoons onion, grated
1 tablespoon mayonnaise	2 teaspoons parsley, chopped
1 can (8 ounces) minced clams, drained	1½ teaspoons lemon juice
¼ teaspoon Worcestershire sauce	¼ teaspoon salt
	3 drops Tabasco sauce

Have cheese at room temperature. Mix with mayonnaise. Add remaining ingredients and blend thoroughly. Allow mixture to chill for about an hour so all flavors will blend. Serve with crackers or potato chips. Makes about ¾ cup.

Variations

Substitute about ¼ cup prepared horse-radish for clam. May need a little additional cream or mayonnaise.

Use shredded lobster or crab meat instead of clam.

Use bleu or Roquefort cheese instead of cream cheese. Or, mix half cream cheese with bleu cheese.

HORS D'OEUVRES

Wrap a stuffed olive or sweet gherkin in a half slice lean bacon. Spear with toothpick and broil until bacon is crisp. Serve hot.

Cut a stuffed olive in half crosswise. Place a small cube of sharp cheese between each half. Spear on toothpick.

Marinate cubes of canned, frozen, or fresh pineapple in French dressing, then roll in chopped mint or finely grated coconut. Spear with a toothpick.

Have salami cut in ½-inch slices. Cut these slices in ½-inch cubes. Spear on toothpick. Serve with clam dip or cocktail sauce.

Scoop out center of radishes, tiny cooked beets, or the small Italian tomatoes. Stuff center with Roquefort or bleu cheese. Spear with toothpick. Stuffed olives may be stuffed with Roquefort or bleu cheese. Remove pimiento and press cheese in cavity. Rather tedious work, but awfully good to eat.

Marinate banana slices cut about ¼-inch thick in pineapple juice. Just before serving, drain and top generously with crisp bacon bits. Spear with toothpick.

Quick Breads

Hot muffins can turn the simplest meal into a delight, for there is something about a muffin, oozing with melting butter, that can perk up the dullest appetite and please almost every palate.

There is one rule, however, that you must *always* follow no matter how rushed you may be. And that is that the muffins you serve must be brought to the table *piping hot*. It is better not to cook them at all than to serve them cold! Here are some more tricks you might like to try.

Tricks in Muffin Cooking

Never overbeat your muffin batter. If you are fortunate enough to have an electric mixer, remember that you must curb its efficiency when you make muffins, for overbeating makes tough muffins.

If you have too many muffin cups for the amount of batter you have mixed, fill empty cups about ⅛ full of water. This will save you a stubborn dishwashing job.

Always be sure to remove muffins from pan immediately after baking.

If the oven will be in use until mealtime, do a little advance work. Sift all dry ingredients together. Measure the liquid, and should any creaming of shortening and sugar be necessary, do that. Grease muffin cups.

Just before you remove the food from the oven, mix the muffin batter, put in muffin cups, and as soon as food has been removed, pop the muffins in the oven. You may need to increase the oven temperature, but that won't delay activities too much. The muffins will be ready to serve by the time the food has been dished out and the family gathered at the table.

Or, bake them in advance. When baked, loosen muffins and set them sidewise in muffin cup. Then, just before ready to serve, return them to oven, and they will be hot in about 5 minutes.

Or, if you have a home freezer, bake the muffins, cool, wrap in freezer foil. When needed, remove from freezer. Do not remove foil. Place in oven along with rest of food. Takes about 45 minutes to get these piping hot, but they taste like freshly baked ones.

PLAIN MUFFINS

Muffin pans or cups . . . Preheated oven—425° F. . . . Baking time —15-20 minutes

2 cups all-purpose flour, sifted before measuring	1 cup sweet milk
2 teaspoons baking powder	1 egg, well beaten
⅔ teaspoon salt	4 tablespoons butter or
4 tablespoons sugar	margarine, melted

Sift flour, baking powder, salt, and sugar. Combine milk, beaten egg, and melted butter or margarine. Combine the liquid ingredients with the dry ingredients. Stir only until all dry ingredients are moist. The secret of good muffins is not to stir them too much. Never beat. Pour into greased muffin pans or cups. Yields 10-12 muffins.

BLUEBERRY MUFFINS

Follow recipe above. At the last, blend in carefully 1 cup well-drained, fresh blueberries or ¾ cup well-drained, canned or frozen blueberries.

PRUNE MUFFINS

Add ¼ teaspoon nutmeg to flour mixture. At the last, blend in ¾ cup well drained, cooked, coarse-chopped prunes.

DATE OR RAISIN MUFFINS

At the last, add 1 cup finely cut dates or raisins.

BRAN MUFFINS

Muffin pans or cups . . . Preheated oven—400° F. . . . Baking time
—25-30 minutes

¼ cup sugar or molasses
2 tablespoons shortening
1 egg, well beaten
1 cup All-Bran
¾ cup milk

1 cup all-purpose flour, sifted
　before measuring
2½ teaspoons baking powder
½ teaspoon salt

Blend sugar or molasses and shortening. Add well-beaten egg.
Stir in All-Bran and milk. Let soak until most of moisture is taken
up, about 10 minutes. Sift flour with baking powder and salt. Add
to first mixture. Stir only until all ingredients are combined. Fill
greased muffin pans or cups ⅔ full. Bake. Yields 8 muffins 2¼ inches
in diameter or 12 small ones.

CORN MUFFINS (MEXICAN)

Muffin pans or cups . . . Preheated oven—400° F. . . . Baking time
—25-30 minutes

1 egg, well beaten
1¼ cups milk
3 tablespoons shortening
1 cup whole kernel corn
1½ cups all-purpose flour, sifted
　before measuring

3½ teaspoons baking powder
1 teaspoon salt
3 tablespoons sugar
1 cup yellow corn meal

Mix together thoroughly the beaten egg, milk, melted shortening,
and corn. Sift together flour, baking powder, salt, sugar, and corn
meal. Sift again into the liquid mixture and stir just enough to
moisten flour. Fill well-greased muffin pans or cups ½ to ⅔ full. Bake.
Makes 12 medium-sized muffins.

CORN BREAD

9¾x14¾-inch oblong pan . . . Preheated oven—425° F. . . . Baking
time—25-30 minutes

1 cup all-purpose flour, sifted
　before measuring
¾ cup corn meal
2 tablespoons sugar
¾ teaspoon salt

3 teaspoons baking powder
1 cup sweet milk
1 egg, well beaten
2 tablespoons shortening, melted

Sift flour with corn meal, sugar, salt, and baking powder. Gradually add milk, beaten egg, and melted shortening. Pour into hot, greased pan. Bake. Serves 5-6.

You may make this corn bread into muffins, if you wish. Will make 10-12 medium-sized muffins.

TRICK: Use bacon drippings for shortening. Wonderful for greasing pans, too.

CORN-MEAL SQUARES WITH CREOLE SAUCE

Oblong utility pan . . . Preheated oven—350° F. . . . Baking time—25-30 minutes

4 cups milk	1 cup cheese, shredded
1 cup corn meal	½ teaspoon dry mustard
1½ teaspoons salt	Creole sauce (page 242)

Scald 3 cups of the milk. Mix remaining cup of milk with the corn meal and stir into scalded milk. Add salt. Stir vigorously. Cover. Reduce heat to simmer and cook for 30 minutes. Remove from heat. Add cheese and mustard. Stir until cheese has melted. Pour into a greased 8-inch square pan. Cool. Cut into 2-inch squares. Place squares in oblong baking dish. Cover with Creole sauce (page 242). Bake. Serve piping hot. Serves 6-8.

Tricks in Biscuit Making

1. Cut shortening into flour with pastry blender, if you have one. If not, you can use a fork, or two silver knives.
2. Don't work the shortening and dry ingredients too long. Leave some chunks of shortening about the size of a pea.
3. Use an oval-shaped bowl.
4. When you have finished blending the shortening, take a table fork and push the flour mixture until there is a small hole in center of ingredients. Then dump all the milk in that empty space, begin stirring, working from the center, until all ingredients are blended.
5. Turn the mass of dough on a lightly floured kneading board and knead the dough for about one minute.
6. Roll or pat out the dough about ½ inch thick. It's easier to roll the dough away from you than toward you, but remember not to press down as you roll. Cut with biscuit cutter and bake. You will have delicious biscuits.

BAKING-POWDER BISCUITS

10x14-inch cooky sheet . . . Preheated oven—450° F. . . . Baking
time—12-14 minutes

2 cups all-purpose flour, sifted before measuring	1 teaspoon salt
	4 tablespoons shortening
4 teaspoons baking powder	¾ cup milk

Sift flour, baking powder, and salt. Cut in shortening with pastry
blender or fork until mixture has the appearance of coarse corn
meal, working mixture for as short a time as possible. Add milk,
stirring only enough to combine ingredients. Turn out on floured
board, knead until smooth, for about a minute. Pat or roll out ½
inch thick and cut with biscuit cutter. Place on cooky sheet. Bake.
Yields about 18 small biscuits.

ORANGE BISCUITS

If you want to be a little fancy, follow recipe for biscuits, but add
grated rind of 1 orange to flour mixture.

After the biscuits have been cut, press a small cube of sugar
which has been dipped in orange juice into top of each biscuit.

CHEESE BISCUITS

Follow biscuit recipe, but add ½ cup grated, dry, sharp cheese to
flour and shortening mixture. Wonderful way to use odds and ends
of dry cheese.

HOMEMADE BISCUIT MIX

8 cups all-purpose flour, sifted before measuring	4 teaspoons salt
	⅔ cup dry milk
¼ cup baking powder	1½ cups shortening

Sift dry ingredients together. Cut in shortening until mixture has
a fine, even crumb. Keep in covered container in refrigerator.

How to Use Biscuit Mix

1 cup mix	¼ cup water

Stir until blended. Turn out on lightly floured board. Knead for
about a minute. Pat to desired thickness, about ½ inch. Cut and
place on ungreased baking sheet. Bake in preheated oven, 450° F.,
for 12-14 minutes. Yields about 8 biscuits.

DROP BISCUITS

Follow recipe above for baking-powder biscuits, using a full cup
of milk rather than ¾ of a cup. Drop from spoon onto greased

pan. Taste and flavor will be the same as in ordinary biscuits but they will cook in irregular shapes.

SHORTCAKE OR RICHER BISCUITS

Follow recipe for biscuits (page 309), substituting ½ cup of shortening for the 4 tablespoons of shortening and using only ⅔ cup of milk. If at least half of the shortening you use is butter, it will make the shortcake particularly good. Cut biscuits a little larger than usual. (A doughnut cutter with the center removed would be just right.) Bake. While hot, break in half. Spread lightly with butter and cover with strawberries or any other suitable fruit. Serve while biscuits are hot.

It's better to mash most of the strawberries and add the necessary sweetening beforehand, while biscuits are baking. Sweeten to taste. Sometimes you may want to let the natural sweetness of the fruit stand alone, but usually a bit of extra sugar will improve the flavor. Save a few of the biggest and prettiest berries to put on top as a garnish.

Raspberries, peaches, or sliced oranges will all make wonderful shortcake desserts.

QUICK CINNAMON ROLLS

Follow the recipe for biscuits (page 309), but make the dough richer, just as for shortcake. Roll dough ¼ inch thick into a rectangle 7 x 16 inches. Spread with 3 or 4 tablespoons softened butter or margarine. Mix ½ cup sugar and 1½ teaspoons cinnamon together. Sprinkle this over the buttered dough. Roll up as for jelly roll, but start at the wide side. When it has been rolled, pinch the edges of dough so all the goodness will stay inside. Cut into 1-inch slices, placing, cut side down, on greased baking sheet. Bake at 425° F. for about 15 minutes, or until browned. Serve hot.

GRIDDLECAKES

1½ cups all-purpose flour, sifted
    before measuring
3½ teaspoons baking powder
¾ teaspoon salt
3 tablespoons sugar

1 egg, beaten
1¼ cups sweet milk
3 tablespoons shortening, melted

Sift flour together with baking powder, salt, and sugar. Combine egg, milk, and shortening and add to dry ingredients. Stir until smooth. Drop by tablespoonfuls onto hot griddle. Cook on one side until puffed and full of bubbles. Turn and cook on other side. Serves 4.

TRICKS: Be sure the griddle is hot, but not so hot that it will burn the pancakes.

Always try the water test. Sprinkle a few drops of water on griddle. If bubbles dance around, heat is just right. If they do not dance, you know that the griddle is either too hot or not hot enough.

Batter poured from tip of large spoon or a pitcher works fine. Be sure to leave space between each pancake, since they spread as they cook.

The above recipe makes a rather thick pancake. If your husband likes them thin, add another ¼ cup milk.

TREATS: Make the pancakes large. As soon as they are brown on both sides, place on a warm plate, slather with butter and a little brown sugar. Place in oven that is barely warm. Fry the next pancake and repeat. When all the batter has been fried, cut the stack of pancakes in wedge shapes, as you would a pie. Serve hot. Maple sirup tastes wonderful on these.

BUCKWHEAT GRIDDLECAKES

6 tablespoons shortening	2 eggs, separated
2 cups buckwheat flour	1 tablespoon sorghum molasses
1½ teaspoons salt	2¼ cups sweet milk
4 teaspoons baking powder	

Cut shortening into blended dry ingredients. Combine the slightly beaten egg yolks with molasses and milk. Add to dry ingredients, mixing just enough to moisten. Fold in stiffly beaten egg whites. Drop mixture on hot griddle. Cook on one side until puffed and full of bubbles. Turn and cook on other side. Serves 4-5.

POPOVERS

Iron popover pans or ovenproof glass custard cups . . . Preheated oven—450° F. . . . Baking time—45 minutes

2 cups all-purpose flour, sifted before measuring	1 cup sweet milk
	1 cup water
1 teaspoon salt	4 eggs, beaten
2 tablespoons sugar	

Grease pans or cups and put them into oven while it is preheating. If custard cups are to be used, place them on a cooky sheet. Sift flour once together with salt and sugar. Add milk and water gradually to make a smooth batter. Beat whole eggs until light and add to mixture. Then beat for 6 or 7 minutes if an electric mixer is used, longer if a hand beater is used. Pour into hot custard cups or hot iron popover pans. Bake. At end of baking time, open oven door and let popovers remain in oven to dry a few minutes. Makes 10-12.

WAFFLES

2 cups all-purpose flour, sifted before measuring

4 teaspoons baking powder

1 teaspoon salt

6 tablespoons shortening

2 tablespoons sugar

1½ cups milk

3 eggs, separated

Sift dry ingredients together. Blend shortening into flour, as you would when making biscuits (page 309), working the ingredients until they resemble corn meal. Beat egg yolks and add milk. Beat together thoroughly. Then add to dry ingredients and beat only until liquid and other ingredients are thoroughly blended. Fold in the stiffly beaten egg whites. Preheat waffle baker and bake 4 to 5 minutes, or until signal light goes out. This recipe will make enough for 4 people.

TRICK: If your family is particularly fond of waffles, you may want to keep frozen waffles on hand. Bake as described above, then cool waffles. Wrap the baked waffles in aluminum foil and place in freezing compartment of refrigerator. When you want waffles in a hurry, remove wrapping from frozen waffles and drop sections in an electric toaster. Set toaster on "Light" setting and put the waffles through twice.

DUMPLINGS FOR STEWS

1½ cups all-purpose flour, sifted before measuring

2 teaspoons baking powder

¾ teaspoon salt

¾ cup milk

Sift dry ingredients together. Add milk and stir only until well blended.

Drop by spoonfuls into boiling stew. Dip your spoon first into hot stew mixture and then in dumpling batter. This will make the batter slide easily off the spoon. Cook 12 minutes in a tightly covered kettle. Be sure the stew mixture is steaming briskly. Do not peek while dumplings are cooking.

TREAT: Add 3-4 tablespoons finely chopped parsley or chives to the sifted dry ingredients.

CORN-MEAL DUMPLINGS

1 cup corn meal
1 teaspoon salt
1⅓ cups boiling water
½ teaspoon onion, minced

1 teaspoon parsley, chopped
2 eggs, slightly beaten
¼ cup all-purpose flour

Combine corn meal and salt. Gradually add to boiling water, stirring constantly. Remove from heat and stir until smooth. Cool. Add remaining ingredients except flour. Mix thoroughly. Drop by spoonfuls onto floured waxed paper. Roll around on the flour to form balls. Drop into boiling meat or chicken stew. Cover tightly. Steam 10 minutes. Serves 6.

OATMEAL BREAD

2¾x5x9¼-inch loaf pan . . . Preheated oven—350° F. . . . Baking time—1 hour

2 cups all-purpose flour, sifted
  before measuring
1 teaspoon salt
1 teaspoon baking powder
1 teaspoon baking soda
⅓ cup sugar
2 cups quick-cooking oatmeal,
  ground

½ cup sorghum molasses
2 tablespoons shortening, melted
2 cups sour milk, or 1⅔ cups
  sweet milk with 1 tablespoon
  vinegar added
1 cup raisins

Sift flour, salt, baking powder, soda, and sugar together. Grind quick-cooking oatmeal or crush with a rolling pin. Add to the other dry ingredients. Add molasses, melted shortening, and milk. Mix thoroughly and add raisins. Pour into greased loaf pan. Let stand 20 minutes, then bake. Remove from pan immediately after baking. Cool on cake rack. Makes 1 loaf.

DATE-NUT BREAD

2 bread pans or 4 small loaf pans . . . Preheated oven—350° F. . . .
  Baking time—45 minutes-1 hour, depending upon size

2 cups boiling water
4 cups dates, cut up
4 cups cake flour, sifted before
  measuring
1 teaspoon salt
½ cup shortening

1½ cups brown sugar, firmly
  packed
2 eggs
2 teaspoons soda
2 cups nut meats, broken

Pour boiling water over dates. Sift cake flour with salt. Cream shortening and brown sugar together until light and fluffy. Add eggs. Beat thoroughly. Add soda to date mixture, then stir the date mixture and the flour into the creamed mixture. Lastly stir in nuts. Pour into well-greased and floured pans. Bake. Remove from pan immediately after baking. Cool on cake rack.

NUT BREAD

Glass, tin, or aluminum bread pan . . . Preheated oven—350° F. . . .
  Baking time—60-70 minutes

3 cups all-purpose flour, sifted before measuring	¼ cup shortening
	1¼ cups milk
1 cup sugar	1 egg
1½ teaspoons salt	1 cup nut meats, coarsely
4 teaspoons baking powder	chopped

Sift flour, sugar, salt, and baking powder into large mixing bowl. Add shortening and mix with a fork or pastry blender until ingredients have appearance of coarse corn meal. Add milk and slightly beaten egg. Add nuts last. Pour into well-greased loaf bread pan and let stand 20 minutes. Bake. When baked, turn on rack to cool.

Yeast Breads

One sure way to create pleasurable excitement at your house is to surprise the family one day and bake some bread. There is nothing so completely wonderful as the aroma of homemade bread baking in the oven.

You may feel a little timid about trying your hand at baking homemade bread, but there is nothing to it, provided you remember to follow a few simple tricks such as those you will see below.

Trick No. 1

Be careful about the temperature of the liquid used. Yeast should not be placed in any liquid hotter than 85° F. Test the temperature of the milk by dipping a drop or so on your wrist. If you feel no sensation of heat, it is just right.

Remember how you test the temperature of a bottle of milk for the baby? The same rule applies here, and for much the same reason, for neither yeast nor babies enjoy too-hot milk.

Trick No. 2

Use fresh yeast. You can buy the quick-acting granular yeast or compressed yeast. Either one is suitable.

Trick No. 3

Keep the bread dough away from drafts. Yeast doesn't react well to cold any more than to heat. A temperature between 80° F. and 85° F. is ideal.

Trick No. 4

If the house is chilly, try this easy trick, provided your range is electric. After you have finished kneading the dough and have placed it in the bowl for rising, turn your electric oven on for one minute, no longer. Turn it off. Then place bowl of dough in oven to rise. If you have a gas oven with automatic lighter, better not try this trick. The pilot light sometimes causes too much heat, and the yeast is killed.

Trick No. 5

Be sure you have a bowl sufficiently large so that the dough can rise without cascading over the sides.
Be accurate. Follow recipe.
Be sure to sift flour before measuring.
Be sure to use an all-purpose flour, never cake flour.
Good luck!

General Instructions for Shaping Dough Like a Jelly Roll

Roll dough about ½ inch thick into a rectangular shape, about 9x18 inches. Brush generously with melted butter or margarine. At this point you can make cinnamon rolls or Swedish tea ring. Usually one half of sweet-roll dough recipe (page 321) makes all you need, unless the family is large, or especially fond of cinnamon rolls.

WHITE BREAD—STRAIGHT DOUGH METHOD

Tin or aluminum bread pans . . . Preheated oven—375° F. . . . .
    Baking time—1 hour

2 cakes quick-acting yeast	5 teaspoons salt
1 cup lukewarm water	About 13 cups all-purpose
5 tablespoons sugar	flour, sifted before measuring
4 cups lukewarm milk	5 tablespoons shortening

Dissolve yeast in 1 cup lukewarm water, and to it add 1 teaspoon sugar. The sugar makes the yeast plant grow more quickly. Let stand for 10 minutes.

Place lukewarm milk in bowl in which you expect to mix dough. To the milk, add the remaining sugar and salt. Add dissolved yeast to milk mixture. Next, add all but 1 cup of the flour and the shortening. Start mixing with a spoon, but as the flour and liquid become blended, you will need to finish the mixing with your hands. Add remaining cup of flour, but only if needed. Bread dough that is too stiff never makes quite such good bread.

When all ingredients have been mixed and the dough begins to leave the sides of the bowl, turn dough out on lightly floured board.

Knead until dough becomes elastic and does not stick to board. Place in greased bowl, cover, allow to rise until double in bulk, then punch down. Allow to rise a second time until double in bulk. Remove dough from bowl, punch down, and cut into four equal-sized loaves. Recipe makes approximately 4 1½-pound loaves. Shape and allow to stand 20 minutes. Then flatten out each loaf and again reshape.

Place in greased pans. Allow to rise until double in bulk, or until imprint does not disappear when pressed with a finger. Just before placing in oven sprinkle a little cold water over raised dough.

Bake. Remove from pans as soon as baked. Cool on wire cake rack.

OATMEAL BREAD

Tin or aluminum bread pans . . . Preheated oven—350° F. . . . Baking time—1 hour

Sponge

4 cups boiling water	2 packages quick-acting yeast
3 cups quick-cooking oatmeal	2 cups all-purpose flour, sifted
½ cup lukewarm water	before measuring
1 teaspoon sugar	

Pour the boiling water over the oatmeal, cover, and let stand until lukewarm. Mix the lukewarm water, sugar, and yeast together. Let stand until yeast is softened and bubbly. When the oatmeal mixture is lukewarm, add softened yeast and the flour. Beat well. Let rise in a warm place until light.

Dough

6 teaspoons salt	7 cups all-purpose flour, sifted
½ cup sorghum molasses	before measuring
4 tablespoons melted shortening	

When the oatmeal mixture is light and bubbly, stir in the salt, molasses, and melted shortening. Add about 6 cups of the flour, blend well, and if not stiff enough to knead, add remaining flour. Knead until smooth and elastic. Let dough rise in a warm place until double in bulk. Divide and make into 3 loaves. Place in greased pans and let double in size. Bake. Remove from pans as soon as baked. Cool on wire cake rack.

PLYMOUTH BREAD

Glass tin, or aluminum bread pans . . . Preheated oven—350° F. . . . Baking time—1 hour

½ cup yellow corn meal	2 teaspoons salt
2 cups boiling water	1 cake quick-acting yeast
2 tablespoons butter or	½ cup lukewarm water
margarine	4¾ cups all-purpose flour, sifted
½ cup sorghum molasses	before measuring

Stir corn meal very slowly into boiling water, stirring constantly. Boil 5 minutes, add butter or margarine, molasses, and salt. Cool. Do not cover. When lukewarm, add the yeast which has been softened in the lukewarm water. Add flour. Knead well and let rise until double in bulk. Shape into 2 loaves, place in well-greased pans, again let rise until double in bulk. Bake. Remove from pans as soon as baked. Cool on wire cake rack.

Note: This bread makes wonderful tea sandwiches.

FRENCH BREAD

Cooky sheet . . . Preheated oven—350° F. . . . Baking time—1 hour

2 cups hot water	2 packages quick-acting yeast
2 teaspoons salt	7-8 cups all-purpose flour, sifted
1 tablespoon sugar	before measuring
2 tablespoons shortening	½ cup yellow corn meal

Put hot water in large bowl. Add salt, sugar, and shortening. When liquid has cooled to lukewarm, add yeast. If dry yeast is used, sprinkle over top of liquid. If compressed yeast is used, crumble over liquid. Stir briskly until yeast has dissolved. Add 4 cups sifted, all-purpose flour and beat until smooth. You can use your electric mixer up to this point. Add 3 more cups of flour. This must be a stiff dough, so possibly you will need to add slightly more flour. Turn dough out on lightly floured kneading board. Knead until smooth and elastic. Put in a greased bowl (you can use the one you mixed in, provided you wash it). Cover with a warm, slightly dampened cloth. Let rise until double in bulk. This will take from 1½ to 2 hours. Turn out on slightly floured board, divide into 2 equal parts, using either a sharp knife or scissors. Shape into long, slender loaves. Place on an ungreased cooky sheet which has been sprinkled with corn meal. Brush with the following mixture, and let rise until *very* light.

½ teaspoon salt	1½ teaspoons cornstarch
½ cup cold water	

Combine ingredients and cook until clear. Cool.

If the dough seems to get a little dry while it is rising, brush again with the cornstarch mixture.

Just before putting bread in oven, cut diagonal slashes on top of the dough, about ¼ inch deep and about 2 inches apart. Be sure to use very sharp scissors or a razor blade.

Put a bread pan ¾ full of boiling water in oven beside cooky sheet or on the upper shelf in oven. This bread needs to bake in steam. Yields 2 loaves.

TRICK: Hard dinner rolls may be made from same dough. Shape either round or oblong. Brush with cornstarch mixture. When *very* light, slash with razor blade. Bake 45 minutes in steam in preheated oven, 350° F.

GARLIC BREAD

10x13-inch cooky sheet . . . Preheated oven—350° F. . . . Heating time—20 minutes

1 loaf French bread	⅓ cup butter
1 clove garlic	

Slice bread, but not through the bottom crust. Crush garlic in saucepan, add the butter, and heat slowly. Remove the garlic. Brush the slices (tops and sides) of bread lightly with garlic butter. Set loaf on cooky sheet. Bake. Serve hot.

PARTIAL WHOLE-WHEAT BREAD

Tin or aluminum bread pans . . . Preheated oven—350° F. . . . Baking time—1 hour

2 cakes quick-acting yeast	About 6 cups all-purpose flour,
1 cup lukewarm water	sifted before measuring
6 tablespoons sugar or molasses	About 6 cups whole wheat flour,
3 cups milk	sifted before measuring
4 teaspoons salt	4 tablespoons shortening

Dissolve yeast in cup of lukewarm water. Add 1 teaspoon sugar or molasses. Allow to stand 10 minutes. Scald milk and to it add remainder of sugar or molasses, and salt. When milk has cooled to lukewarm, add yeast mixture. Mix the two flours together, and add all but about 1 cupful to the liquid. Some flours do not require as much liquid as others, so it is advisable not to add all the flour until needed. Then add softened shortening. Mix well.

Turn out on floured board and knead until dough becomes elastic and does not stick to board. Place in greased bowl, cover, allow to rise until double in bulk. Remove from bowl and shape into loaves. Makes 4 medium-sized loaves. Place in greased pans which are sufficiently large so pans will be ⅔ full when loaves are first molded. Let loaves rise to top of pan, or until, when pressed with a finger, imprint does not disappear. Bake. Remove from pans immediately after baking. Cool on wire cake rack.

REFRIGERATOR ROLLS—WITHOUT EGGS

Baking sheet or pan . . . Preheated oven—425° F. . . . Baking time—15-20 minutes

1 quart sweet milk	8 cups all-purpose flour + 1
1 cup sugar	cup, sifted before measuring
1 cup shortening	1 tablespoon salt
1 cake quick-acting yeast	1 teaspoon soda
¼ cup lukewarm water	2 teaspoons baking powder

Scald milk with sugar and shortening. Cool to lukewarm, then add yeast dissolved thoroughly in ¼ cup lukewarm water. Add the 8 cups of flour. Beat thoroughly. Let rise until double in bulk, then add salt, soda, and baking powder. Add enough flour (about 1 cup) to make soft dough. Place in bowl, grease surface of the dough, cover, and place in refrigerator. Make rolls as wanted. Bake on any type baking sheet or in muffin cups. Dough will keep for a week or ten days. Makes about 4 dozen.

TREAT: Slice or grate an onion quite fine. Sauté in butter, but do not brown. Sprinkle over top of yeast rolls just before placing rolls in oven to bake. Makes a pleasing topping for hot rolls. If you wish to "up" the flavor, you can use garlic, but better grate it pretty fine. No one enjoys an overdose of garlic.

Directions for Shaping Rolls

All rolls are brushed lightly with melted butter or margarine as soon as shaped. Use a pastry brush—it simplifies the job.

SWEET-ROLL DOUGH

Baking sheet or pan . . . Preheated oven—425° F. . . . Baking time—
15-20 minutes

2 cakes quick-acting yeast	3 teaspoons salt
¼ cup sugar	6 to 6½ cups all-purpose flour,
¼ cup lukewarm water	sifted before measuring
2 eggs	¼ cup shortening, melted
2 cups lukewarm milk	

Soften yeast with sugar in ¼ cup lukewarm water. Beat the eggs, add the lukewarm milk, add yeast-sugar mixture, salt, half the flour, then mix thoroughly. Add the melted shortening and beat well. Add balance of flour, or enough to make a soft dough. Turn out on a floured board. Knead until smooth and elastic without sticking to board. Place in a well-greased bowl. Grease top of dough. Cover. Let rise until double in bulk. Knead down. Then let rise 45 minutes. Use for rolls. Bake on any type baking sheet or pan, or use muffin pans and make cloverleaf rolls. Makes about 3 dozen.

CLOVERLEAF ROLLS

Take small chunks of dough. Size depends somewhat upon muffin cup, but each chunk should usually be about the size of a walnut.

You can either squeeze the chunks of dough off or cut them off with a sharp knife. To save time, shape in balls with the fingertips, tucking the edges under. This makes a nice smooth top. Put three little balls in a muffin cup, brushing melted butter between them. Let rise until double in size. Bake 15-20 minutes in preheated oven, 400° F. Remove from pan at once and cool on cake rack.

How to Roll Dough

Lift the dough out of the bowl, putting the bottom of the dough next to the lightly floured board. Without handling the dough at all, put the rolling pin in the middle of the dough, and, with short, firm strokes, roll the pin over to one edge. Then return to middle of dough and roll the other side. Lift the dough to allow it to relax or shrink.

PARKER HOUSE ROLLS

Roll dough about ½ inch thick. Cut with a 2½-inch biscuit cutter, brush with melted butter or margarine. Let rest about 10 minutes (that is, just leave the little rounds of dough alone for about 10 minutes). Make a deep crease, a bit off-center, with the back of a knife handle. Fold dough over, so top half slightly overlaps. Place close together in greased pan or cooky sheet. Let rise until double in bulk. Bake in preheated oven, 425° F., for 15-20 minutes. Remove from pan at once and cool on cake rack.

BUTTER FLAKES

Roll dough about ¼ inch thick. Brush with melted butter or margarine. Cut into strips about 1½ inches wide and 7 inches long. Stack 5 or 6 strips evenly on top of each other. Cut into 2-inch pieces and place, cut side down, in greased muffin cups. Let rise until double in bulk. These are conversation rolls. Easy to do, too. Bake in preheated oven, 400° F., for 20 minutes. Remove from muffin cups at once and cool on wire rack.

BUTTERHORNS—PLAIN

Roll dough about ¼ inch thick (don't make it more than ¼ inch, less if possible) into a 9-inch circle. Brush with melted butter or margarine. Cut in 12 to 16 pie-shaped pieces. This takes a little figuring. It might be a good idea to make a paper pattern first. Sharp kitchen scissors would be helpful, too. Roll each wedge, starting from rounded edge and rolling to point. Place on buttered cooky sheet or pan, point edge under. To make crescents, roll as above, but shape in a curve when putting on pan. Let rise until double in bulk. Bake in preheated oven, 425° F., for 15-20 minutes. Remove from pan at once and cool on cake rack.

BUTTERHORNS—OUT OF THIS WORLD

10x14-inch cooky sheet . . . Preheated oven—325° F. . . . Baking time—30 minutes

4 cups all-purpose flour, sifted before measuring	1¼ cups butter or margarine
	½ cup sour cream
1 teaspoon salt	5 egg yolks
1 cake compressed yeast	1 teaspoon vanilla

Sift flour and salt together. Add yeast which has been crumbled into small bits and butter or margarine. Blend together with pastry blender or tips of fingers until mixture resembles fine corn meal. Combine sour cream, egg yolks, and vanilla. Add to flour mixture and mix thoroughly. Divide the dough into six portions and roll out each into a 9-inch circle. Divide filling into 6 equal portions and spread on circles of dough. Cut each circle into 12 pie-shaped wedges and roll each one from the outside to the pointed end. Arrange on baking sheet with point end under. Bake immediately. Makes 6 dozen butterhorns.

Filling

5 egg whites	½ teaspoon almond extract
1 cup granulated sugar	1 cup nut meats, ground
1 teaspoon vanilla	

Beat egg whites until stiff. Add sugar gradually while still beating. Do this beating in a vigorous, wholehearted manner. Carefully fold in vanilla, almond extract, and ground nut meats.

SNAILS

Take a narrow roll of dough 6 to 8 inches long. Twist and hold one end down on greased baking sheet. Wind narrow roll of dough around and around, keeping it flat. Let rise until double in bulk. Bake in preheated oven, 425° F., for 12-15 minutes. Remove from pan and cool on cake rack.

CINNAMON ROLLS

Prepare ½ sweet-roll dough recipe (page 321). Roll dough about ½ inch thick. Brush rolled dough with melted butter or margarine and sprinkle with a generous amount of brown sugar and cinnamon which have been mixed together. You can vary the amount of cinnamon to suit your own taste, but usually 1 cup of brown sugar and 1 tablespoon cinnamon is the accepted amount. White sugar may also be used. Roll dough carefully, beginning at wide side and working away from you (see page 321). Carefully seal by pinching edges of roll together. Cut roll in 1-inch slices. Cover the bottom of greased pan with cooled sirup (below) and place slices, cut side down, in pan. Do not crowd them or they will pop up in the middle. Don't cut too thick, either, because then it takes too long to bake them and the sirup may burn. Bake in preheated oven, 375° F., for 20-25 minutes. When removed from oven, let stand in pan for about 5 minutes. Then invert on cake cooler. The reason it's a good idea to let them stand about 5 minutes is to give the sticky sirup a chance to thicken. You may use muffin cups if you prefer, but they make dishwashing more of a chore.

Sirup for Cinnamon Rolls

1 cup light brown sugar	2 tablespoons corn sirup
¼ cup butter or margarine	¼ cup water

Cook ingredients until sugar has completely dissolved, stirring most of the time. Cool before placing cut dough in sirup.

For something extra special, put a few chopped pecans on top of sirup before placing the sliced dough on top of the sirup mixture.

SWEDISH TEA RING

Follow directions for cinnamon rolls, except sprinkle about ¾ cup seedless raisins over sugar and cinnamon. Roll as for cinnamon roll. Place on greased cooky sheet and join two ends, sealing together by pressing. Be sure the rolled, sealed ends are underneath. With scissors, make cuts ⅔ of the way through ring at about 1-inch intervals. Turn each cut section on its side. Let double in bulk. Bake in preheated oven, 375° F., for about 30-40 minutes. Remove from pan and cool on wire cake rack.

ORANGE ROLLS

Use ½ basic sweet-roll dough recipe (page 321). Divide dough into 3 or 4 parts. Follow directions given for rolling dough (page 321). Divide orange filling (below) in equal parts and spread on dough. Roll as for jelly roll (page 316). Then cut in pieces about 1 inch thick. Place in a well-greased 8-inch square pan, cut side down, or in well-greased muffin pans. Bake in preheated oven, 375° F., for 15-20 minutes. Let stand a few minutes before removing from pan. Cool on wire cake rack.

Orange Filling for Rolls

½ cup butter or margarine	Grated rind of 3 oranges
1 cup sugar	3 tablespoons orange juice

Melt butter or margarine. Add remaining ingredients. Bring to full, rolling boil, stirring constantly. Then boil one minute. Cool until of spreading consistency.

SUGAR BUN LOAF

Large angel food cake pan . . . Preheated oven—350° F. . . . Baking time—1 hour

1 cup warm potato water or milk	2 packages quick-acting yeast
2 teaspoons salt	½ cup lukewarm water
6 tablespoons shortening	2 eggs, well beaten
¼ cup sugar	6¼ cups all-purpose flour, sifted before measuring

If potato water is used, drain hot water from cooked potatoes. Add salt, shortening, and the ¼ cup sugar. If milk is used, scald and proceed as above. Cool to lukewarm. Dissolve yeast in the lukewarm water; let stand 5 minutes, then add to first mixture. Add eggs, well beaten. Add flour gradually, beating vigorously. When all flour has been added, turn onto lightly floured board and knead until smooth and elastic. Place in a greased bowl, cover, and let rise until double in bulk. Shape dough as for cloverleaf rolls (page 321), only make them larger, about 2 inches in diameter.

Dressing for Rolls

1½ cups sugar
1½ cups pecans, cut fine
1½ tablespoons cinnamon

¾ cup butter or margarine, melted

Combine sugar, pecans, and cinnamon. Dip each ball into the melted butter or margarine, then roll in sugar mixture. Place in well-greased, large angel food cake pan or spring mold. Cover, let rise until double in bulk. Bake. Remove from pan immediately. Cool on wire cake rack.

HERB PICNIC BUNS—HAMBURGER AND FRANKFURTER BUNS

Baking sheet or pan . . . Preheated oven—400° F. . . . Baking time —15 minutes

½ cup scalded milk
¼ cup shortening
1 tablespoon sugar
1½ teaspoons salt
½ cup cold water
1 package quick-acting yeast, dissolved according to directions on package

1 egg
1 teaspoon celery seed
½ teaspoon onion salt
½ teaspoon dry mustard
3 cups all-purpose flour, sifted before measuring

Combine scalded milk, shortening, sugar, and salt. Cool by adding the cold water. When lukewarm, add yeast which has been dissolved according to directions on package. Mix well. Blend in egg and add celery seed, onion salt, and dry mustard. Add the 3 cups of flour gradually. Mix until dough is well blended and soft. Place in greased bowl and cover. Store dough immediately in refrigerator for 2 hours, or until well chilled. Roll out chilled dough for hamburger buns to ¼-inch thickness and cut with a round 3½-inch cutter. For buns, divide dough into 12 balls, then shape into long, narrow buns. Bake. Remove from pan and cool on wire cake rack.

HOT CROSS BUNS

9x9x1½-inch pan . . . Preheated oven—400° F. . . . Baking time—15 minutes

1 cup scalded milk	1 egg, beaten
¼ cup shortening	½ cup seedless raisins
⅓ cup granulated sugar	1 teaspoon cinnamon
½ teaspoon salt	¼ teaspoon allspice
1 teaspoon granulated sugar	3½ to 4 cups all-purpose flour,
1 cake compressed yeast or	sifted before measuring
quick-acting granular yeast	1 egg white
2 tablespoons lukewarm water	

Combine milk, shortening, ⅓ cup sugar, and salt. Cool to luke-warm. Mix the 1 teaspoon sugar with yeast that has been softened in lukewarm water and add to lukewarm milk mixture. Add egg, raisins, cinnamon, allspice, and as much sifted all-purpose flour as can be stirred into the dough. Place in a greased bowl, cover, and let rise in a warm place until double in bulk. Knead, shape into 2-inch balls, and arrange on greased pan. Brush each bun with egg white, cover, and let rise until double in bulk. Snip a deep cross in the top of each with scissors. Bake. Remove from pan immediately. Cool on wire cake rack. When cool, fill the cross on top of each with powdered sugar icing. Makes 2 dozen buns.

EASTER NESTS

Baking sheet . . . Preheated oven—400° F. . . . Baking time—15 minutes

⅓ recipe for hot cross buns	¼ pound colored jelly beans
Plain confectioners' icing	

Roll dough to ½-inch thickness. Cut with a 2½-inch doughnut cutter. Put on greased baking sheet and allow to rise until light. Bake. Remove from baking sheet. When slightly cooled, frost with plain icing and arrange 3 or 4 jelly beans in the center of each bun. Makes about 1 dozen.

Desserts

You will find that the desserts you choose to serve can do more than supply a pleasant ending to your meals, for they will also help you to balance your menu, and so give added value to the whole meal.

A dessert may be anything from a simple platter of cheese and apple slices to an elaborate Baked Alaska. It can buoy up a too-light meal, or add a light fillip to an overly solid dinner. It may be tart or sweet—solid or airy—thinning or flattening! In short, a dessert may serve as a kind of counterweight to keep your meal from veering too much in one direction or another.

You will be a wise—and a popular—cook if you take the extra trouble and provide suitable desserts for your meals. Remember that a good dessert, well chosen, can add beauty, flavor, and balance to every meal you serve.

CUSTARD AND PUDDING DESSERTS

BAKED CUSTARD

3-quart greased casserole or individual custard cups . . . Cold or preheated oven—325° F. . . . Baking time—50-60 minutes

6 eggs	4 cups milk, scalded
¾ cup sugar	½ teaspoon vanilla
½ teaspoon salt	Nutmeg

Beat eggs slightly. Add sugar, salt, milk, and vanilla. Mix thoroughly. Pour into greased casserole and sprinkle top with nutmeg. Place casserole in a pan which contains enough water to come halfway up the sides of the casserole. Test a baked custard by inserting knife in center of pudding. If knife is only slightly coated, remove custard. The heat of the casserole will finish the cooking. If baked custard is overcooked it becomes watery. You may also use individual custard cups. The recipe will make at least 8. Place custard cups in pan of water, too. May be served hot or cold. Serves 6-8.

TREATS: Add ½ cup shredded coconut to mixture before baking.

Put 2 tablespoons maple sirup in bottom of each individual custard cup. Cool before serving, then unmold to serve.

Melt 2 squares of shaved, unsweetened chocolate in milk while it is scalding. Stir thoroughly before combining with egg mixture.

TRICK: Use 8 or 9 egg yolks in place of whole eggs. Just as good, and a thrifty way to use leftover egg yolks.

FLOATING ISLAND

¼ cup granulated sugar	2 egg yolks
1 tablespoon cornstarch	1 teaspoon vanilla
¼ teaspoon salt	2 egg whites
2 cups milk	¼ cup granulated sugar

Thoroughly mix sugar, cornstarch, and salt. Add milk gradually. Cook in double boiler, or over hot water, stirring constantly until slightly thickened. Beat egg yolks. Add hot milk mixture. Return to double boiler, stirring constantly until mixture coats a spoon. Cool. Add vanilla. Chill. Place custard in serving dish.

To make "islands": Beat egg whites until stiff but not dry, adding sugar gradually as the egg whites are beating. Place ½ cup water in a 2-quart saucepan which has a cover. Bring water to boiling point. Then reduce heat, so water stays just below boiling point. Drop beaten egg white onto the water. A tablespoon is excellent for doing this. There should be 6 mounds of egg whites. Return cover and allow egg whites to steam for 2-3 minutes. Lift from saucepan and place over custard. Serve one mound of egg whites with each serving of custard. Rather an old-fashioned dessert, but delicious, inexpensive, and healthful.

PLAIN SOFT CUSTARD

Use the above recipe, but do not separate the eggs. Beat the eggs lightly and add to hot milk.

CORNSTARCH PUDDING

3 tablespoons cornstarch
¼ cup sugar
¼ teaspoon salt
¼ cup cold milk

1¾ cups scalded milk
1 teaspoon vanilla
2 egg whites, beaten stiff

Mix cornstarch, sugar, and salt with cold milk. Add scalded milk to this mixture. Cook over medium heat until thickened, stirring frequently. Turn to simmer heat and continue cooking. Cool slightly. Add vanilla and egg whites. Mix thoroughly. Pour into mold and chill. Serve with custard sauce (page 248). Serves 4.

CARAMEL PUDDING

½ cup granulated sugar
½ cup boiling water
2 cups milk
⅓ cup granulated sugar
3 tablespoons all-purpose flour

¼ teaspoon salt
1 egg, beaten
1 tablespoon butter or margarine
1 teaspoon vanilla

Caramelize the ½ cup sugar in heavy saucepan or skillet. Add boiling water and stir until sugar is melted and a sirup is formed. Cool. Scald milk. Blend sugar, flour, cornstarch, and salt. Add the cooled, caramelized sirup gradually. Be sure all lumps are gone. Then add gradually to scalded milk, stirring constantly. Cook until thickened. To the beaten egg, add a small amount of the custard mixture. Pour into hot custard and cook 2 minutes longer. Remove from heat, add butter or margarine, and vanilla. Stir until butter or margarine has melted. Chill. Serve with whipped cream or top milk. Serves 4-6.

To Caramelize Sugar

Rub a heavy pan or skillet lightly with butter or margarine. Add granulated sugar and place utensil over moderate heat. Stir constantly until sugar melts and becomes golden brown in color.

To Make a Caramel Sirup

Caramelize sugar, then add water very slowly, stirring constantly until all sugar has dissolved.

DATE AND NUT PUDDING

8x12-inch baking pan . . . Preheated or cold oven—350° F. . . .
Baking time—1 hour

1 cup sugar	3 eggs, separated
4 tablespoons sifted cake flour	1 cup dates, chopped
2 teaspoons baking powder	½ cup nut meats, chopped
4 tablespoons fine cracker crumbs	

Combine sugar, flour, baking powder, and cracker crumbs. Add
egg yolks, beaten until thick and lemon colored, dates, and nuts.
Fold in stiffly beaten egg whites, then pour into greased pan. Do
not cover. Bake. Serve hot or cold with whipped cream. Serves 5-6.

COTTAGE PUDDING

8x8-inch square pan . . . Preheated oven—350° F. . . . Baking time—
35-45 minutes

1¾ cups all-purpose flour, sifted before measuring	1 cup sugar
½ teaspoon salt	1 egg
2½ teaspoons baking powder	½ teaspoon lemon flavoring
¼ cup shortening	⅔ cup sweet milk

Sift flour with salt and baking powder. Thoroughly cream shortening and sugar. Add egg and flavoring. Beat vigorously. Add
sifted dry ingredients alternately with milk. Pour into well-greased
pan. Bake. Serve warm with lemon sauce (page 251), chocolate
sauce (page 249), butterscotch sauce (page 248), or with top
milk. Serves 4-5.

TAPIOCA CREAM PUDDING

1 egg yolk	⅛ teaspoon salt
2 cups milk	1 egg white
3 tablespoons quick-cooking tapioca	2 tablespoons sugar
3 tablespoons sugar	½ teaspoon vanilla

Mix egg yolk with 2 tablespoons of the milk. Place remainder of
milk in saucepan, add tapioca, sugar, and salt. Heat slowly to boiling point. Then add egg yolk and cook until mixture thickens
slightly, stirring frequently. Beat egg white until stiff, add sugar,
and beat until egg white holds a stiff peak. Pour hot mixture over

beaten egg white. The hotter the tapioca mixture and the faster it is blended in, the thicker the custard will be. Add vanilla. Cool. Stir once after 15 or 20 minutes. Serves 4.

TREAT: Top with grated coconut or crushed fresh fruit.

LEMON SPONGE CUPS

8 small baking cups ... Preheated oven—350° F. ... Baking time—
   45 minutes

2 tablespoons softened butter or margarine	5 tablespoons lemon juice Grated rind of lemon
1 cup sugar	3 eggs, separated
4 tablespoons all-purpose flour	1½ cups milk
¼ teaspoon salt	

Cream butter or margarine, add sugar, flour, salt, lemon juice, and lemon rind. Add the well-beaten egg yolks which have been mixed with the milk. Lastly, add the stiffly beaten egg whites. Pour into greased custard cups. Set cups in a pan of water and bake. When done, each cup will contain lemon custard at bottom of cup and sponge cake on top. Cool. Unmold. May be baked in a 2-quart baking dish. Serves 8.

RICE PUDDING

2-quart casserole ... Preheated oven—350° F. ... Baking time—
   15 minutes

2 eggs, separated	¼ teaspoon salt
2 cups milk	½ cup sugar, or ¼ cup sugar and
½ cup raisins	¼ cup honey
1 teaspoon vanilla	¼ teaspoon cinnamon or nutmeg
1 cup cooked rice	4 tablespoons sugar

Separate whites and yolks of eggs. Add 2 tablespoons milk to yolks. Place remainder of milk in saucepan over low heat. Wash raisins and add to milk. Cook until raisins are soft. Add vanilla and rice. Cook 5 minutes longer. Then stir in egg yolks, salt, sugar, and spice. Stir well. Remove from heat. Pour into greased casserole. Beat egg whites until stiff, and slowly add the 4 tablespoons sugar. Lightly cover pudding with beaten egg whites. Place in oven until egg whites are golden brown. Serve cold. Serves 6-8.

CARAMEL RICE PUDDING

Uncovered 2-quart baking dish . . . Cold or preheated oven—
300° F. . . . Baking time—3 hours

⅓ cup uncooked rice	1 teaspoon vanilla, or dash of
4 cups milk	nutmeg or grated lemon rind
½ teaspoon salt	½ cup seedless raisins
⅔ cup sugar	

Add rice to milk with salt, sugar, and flavoring. Pour into greased
casserole. Bake uncovered for 3 hours. During first hour of baking
stir mixture with a fork 3 or 4 times to prevent rice from settling
to bottom of baking dish. Stir in raisins after first hour. Serve warm
or cold. Very delicious. Serves 4-5.

LEMON CREAM RICE

2-quart casserole . . . Preheated oven—350° F. . . . Baking time—
15 minutes

4 cups milk	¾ teaspoon salt
½ cup uncooked rice	2 eggs, separated
½ cup sugar	2 tablespoons powdered sugar
1 tablespoon grated lemon rind	¼ teaspoon lemon extract
2 tablespoons lemon juice	

Scald the milk, add the rice, and cook in saucepan over low heat
until rice is soft. Add sugar, lemon rind, lemon juice, salt, and
beaten egg yolks. Stir gently and cook until thickened. Turn into
buttered casserole and cool. Beat egg whites stiff, but not dry, and
gradually add the powdered sugar and lemon extract and pile
over pudding. Brown in preheated oven. When cool, place in
refrigerator and serve after thoroughly chilled. Serves 8.

STEAMED PUDDING DESSERTS

Steamed puddings are excellent winter desserts. If a recipe calls
for suet, it may be bought at the meat market. In preparing suet,
be sure you separate it carefully and discard the tissuelike film
which separates the sections of suet.

To Fill Molds

You do not need elaborate molds. Use coffee cans, baking-powder
cans, or even straight-sided glass jars. You can cover these con-
tainers with aluminum foil, fastened down with string or rubber
bands. This will work just as satisfactorily as a lid.

Grease the mold and fill only ⅔ full. Remember, the pudding
will expand as it steams.

To Steam

You will need a large kettle with a cover. If the kettle has a rack, that is even better. Fill the kettle with enough water to come half-way up the sides of the mold. Place mold on rack. Make sure the water boils steadily, but not vigorously.

If you have a deep well cooker on your range, that is a perfect place to steam puddings.

You can also steam in a double boiler, but check water in lower part occasionally to guard against boiling dry.

STEAMED CARROT PUDDING

1 cup all-purpose flour, sifted
    before measuring
1 teaspoon baking powder
½ teaspoon soda
½ teaspoon nutmeg
½ teaspoon cloves
½ teaspoon cinnamon

1 cup raw carrots, ground
1 cup raw apples, ground
1 cup seedless raisins
½ cup brown sugar
½ cup molasses
½ cup bread crumbs
1 cup suet, ground

Sift flour with baking powder, soda, and spices. Mix remaining ingredients with suet, then blend dry ingredients through suet mixture. Pour into greased mold. Cover. Steam 2 hours. Serve hot with hard sauce (page 248) or vanilla sauce (page 251). Serves 6.

SUET PUDDING

3 cups all-purpose flour, sifted
    before measuring
1 teaspoon soda
1½ teaspoons salt
½ teaspoon each ginger, cloves,
    and nutmeg

1 teaspoon cinnamon
1 cup suet, chopped fine
1 cup molasses
1 cup sweet milk
1½ cups raisins

Sift dry ingredients. Add suet, molasses, milk, and raisins. Pour into well-greased pudding mold. Cover. Steam 3 hours. Serve with sterling sauce (page 250) or hard sauce (page 248). Serves 12.

SPICY OATMEAL PUDDING

1 cup all-purpose flour, sifted
    before measuring
¾ cup sugar
¾ teaspoon salt
1⅛ teaspoons soda
1 teaspoon cinnamon
1 cup quick-cooking oatmeal

¾ cup dates or raisins, chopped
3 tablespoons shortening,
    melted
1⅛ cups thick sour milk or
    buttermilk
1½ teaspoons vanilla

Sift flour, sugar, salt, soda, and cinnamon. Add oatmeal and dates or raisins. Add melted shortening to buttermilk or sour milk and add to the dry ingredients. Add vanilla. Pour into well-greased pudding pan or squat coffee can. Cover with waxed paper and tie securely. Steam for 1½ hours. Serve pudding with lemon sauce (page 251). Serves 6.

QUAKER PUDDING

2¼ cups all-purpose flour, sifted before measuring

1½ teaspoons soda

1 teaspoon salt

1½ cups thick buttermilk

1 cup suet, ground

1 cup molasses

1 cup raisins (dates or candied fruit may be substituted)

¾ cup quick-cooking oatmeal

Sift flour with soda and salt. Add other ingredients and mix thoroughly. Pour into greased mold. Cover. Steam 3 hours. Serve with foamy sauce (page 250). Serves 8-10.

ENGLISH PLUM PUDDING

½ pound suet, chopped fine

1½ cups seeded raisins

1½ cups currants

½ pound mixed candied fruit peel, chopped

2 cups all-purpose flour, sifted before measuring

1½ cups brown sugar

½ teaspoon nutmeg

½ teaspoon allspice

½ teaspoon salt

½ teaspoon soda

3 eggs, well beaten

Mix the suet, raisins, currants, and chopped peel with half the flour. Mix together remaining flour, sugar, spices, salt and soda. Add the well-beaten eggs. Stir the fruit and suet mixture into the flour, sugar, and spice mixture. Blend thoroughly. Pour into well-greased molds. Cover and steam for 3 hours. Serve with hard sauce (page 248). Serves 12.

FLUFFY FIG PUDDING

1 pound dried figs

1¾ cups milk

1½ cups suet, ground

1½ cups fresh bread crumbs, without crusts

3 eggs, beaten

1½ cups all-purpose flour, sifted before measuring

2½ teaspoons baking powder

1 cup sugar

1 teaspoon nutmeg

1 teaspoon cinnamon

¾ teaspoon salt

3 tablespoons orange rind, grated

Snip stems off the dried figs with scissors. Cut the figs into small bits and put them in a pan with the milk. Cook over medium heat for 20 minutes. Combine the suet, bread crumbs, and the beaten eggs. Add the cooked fig mixture, the sifted dry ingredients, and the orange rind to suet mixture. Mix and turn into a very thoroughly and generously greased 2-quart pudding mold. Cover the mold tightly. Steam for 2 hours. Unmold after the pudding has cooled for 2 minutes. Serve hot with your favorite pudding sauce. Serves 8-10.

FONDUE AND SOUFFLÉ DESSERTS

All soufflés must be steam baked. This means that the baking dish must be set in a pan of hot water. Though this seems simply to be extra trouble, you will find that it is necessary if these delicate and delicious puddings are to turn out as they should.

QUICK CHOCOLATE SOUFFLÉ

8 custard cups . . . Preheated oven—350° F. . . . Baking time—30 minutes

1 package chocolate pudding	1 teaspoon vanilla
Dash of salt	3 egg yolks
2 cups milk	3 egg whites

Put contents of package pudding and salt in 2-quart saucepan. Slowly stir in the milk. Cook and stir over medium heat until mixture comes to a boil and thickens. Remove from heat. Add vanilla and slightly beaten egg yolks, stirring well. Cool. When mixture is cool, beat egg whites until they stand in peaks. Gently fold in the cooled pudding. Pour into well-greased custard cups. Place custard cups in a pan of hot water. Bake. Serve hot with coffee cream. Leftover pudding is good served cold. Serves 8.

LEMON SOUFFLÉ

6x10-inch utility dish . . . Preheated oven—325° F. . . . Baking time —50 minutes

2½ cups sugar	2 cups milk
5 tablespoons all-purpose flour	¾ cup lemon juice
¼ teaspoon salt	Grated rind of 3 lemons
5 tablespoons softened butter	1 cup dates, chopped
or margarine	¾ cup nut meats, broken
6 eggs, separated	

Blend sugar, flour, salt, and softened butter or margarine until ingredients are thoroughly mixed. (When softened shortening is indicated, never melt. Simply soften at room temperature.) Beat egg yolks until light and lemon colored. Add milk to beaten egg yolks, then mix with sugar and flour mixture. Blend in lemon juice and grated rind. Beat egg whites until stiff. Fold into sugar and flour mixture. Add chopped dates and nut meats. Pour into lightly greased utility dish or casserole. Set dish in pan of hot water. Bake. Chill before serving. Serves 10-12.

PRUNE WHIP

2-quart casserole . . . Preheated oven—300° F. . . . Baking time—
1½ hours

1 cup stewed prunes, pitted	1 teaspoon lemon rind
½ cup sugar	4 egg whites
1 tablespoon all-purpose flour	½ teaspoon cream of tartar
1 tablespoon lemon juice	¼ cup sugar

Rub prunes through sieve, add sugar, and cook slowly until mixture is consistency of marmalade. Cool. Add flour, lemon juice, and rind to prune mixture. Stir until well blended. Beat egg whites until foamy, add cream of tarter, and continue beating until egg whites stand in peaks. Add sugar slowly and carefully fold into beaten egg whites. Lastly, fold prune mixture into egg whites. Pile lightly into casserole. Place casserole in pan of hot water. Bake. Serve cold with custard sauce (page 248) or whipped cream. Serves 4-5.

TORTES

A torte is a dessert consisting of very delicate cake, made with eggs, nuts, and very little flour. Or, very fine bread or cracker crumbs may be used instead of flour. Tortes are usually served with whipped cream or a topping of fruit.

DATE TORTE

8x8-inch cake pan . . . Preheated oven—325° F. . . . Baking time—
45 minutes

About 18 dates, pitted	1 teaspoon baking powder
1 cup nut meats	½ cup sugar
2 eggs, separated	1 teaspoon vanilla
1 tablespoon all-purpose flour	½ cup whipping cream (optional)
¼ teaspoon salt	

Cut pitted dates and nut meats into small pieces. Beat egg yolks until very creamy. Then beat the whites until light and stiff. Sift the flour, salt, baking powder, and the sugar together. Fold the yolks into the beaten whites and very slowly add the sifted dry ingredients. Fold as for an angel food cake. Then add the vanilla, dates, and nuts. Bake in well-greased pan. Serve hot or cold with whipped cream, if desired. Serves 6-8.

OLD-FASHIONED NUT TORTE

8x8-inch cake pan . . . Preheated oven—325° F. . . . Baking time—
   40-50 minutes

½ cup all-purpose flour, sifted before measuring	¼ teaspoon salt
	3 eggs, separated
½ teaspoon baking powder	¾ cup sugar
1½ cups walnuts, or other nut meats, chopped	½ teaspoon vanilla

Sift flour with baking powder. Add nuts to flour mixture. Add salt to egg whites and beat until stiff but not dry. Gradually beat in half the sugar. Beat the egg yolks with remaining sugar until thick and yellow, add vanilla, and fold in the nut mixture. Last, fold in beaten egg whites. Pour into a greased square pan and bake. Cool and cut in squares. Split the squares and serve with whipped cream in center and on top. Or, cut into bars and roll pieces in confectioners' sugar. Serves 8.

RAISIN PRUNE TORTE

8x8-inch cake pan . . . Preheated oven—400° F. . . . Baking time—
   30 minutes

Filling

1½ cups dried prunes, cooked and drained	¾ cup seedless raisins
	1 cup prune juice
⅔ cup sugar	1 teaspoon lemon juice

Crust

1 cup all-purpose flour, sifted before measuring	1 cup quick-cooking oatmeal
	⅓ cup butter or margarine, melted
1 teaspoon soda	½ cup brown sugar
½ teaspoon salt	½ teaspoon vanilla

Pit prunes and chop. Combine with sugar, raisins, prune juice, and lemon juice. Cook over medium heat for 20 minutes, stirring occasionally. Cool. Sift flour, soda, and salt together. Add oatmeal. Combine butter or margarine with sugar and vanilla. Add to flour mixture. Press ½ of the mixture firmly into bottom of an 8x8-inch pan. Spread filling on bottom crust and sprinkle remaining crust mixture over top. Press crust lightly on top and around edges of pan to seal in fruit filling. Serve with soft custard (page 329). Serves 8.

MOCHA TORTE

2 8-inch cake pans . . . Preheated oven—325° F. . . . Baking time—30 minutes

4 eggs, separated	1 teaspoon baking powder
1 cup sugar	½ teaspoon salt
1 tablespoon butter or	1 cup ground nuts
margarine, melted	½ teaspoon vanilla
½ cup all-purpose flour, sifted	
before measuring	

Beat egg yolks and add sugar gradually. Beat until light and thick. Beat in melted butter or margarine. Add flour which has been sifted with baking powder and salt. Beat egg whites until stiff. Add ground nuts and vanilla. Combine egg yolk mixture with egg white mixture. Bake in two well-greased and floured cake pans.

Filling

½ pint heavy cream, whipped	1 tablespoon powdered sugar
1 tablespoon instant coffee	

Whip the cream, sift together the coffee and powdered sugar, and fold into cream. When cool, place filling between the cake layers. Serves 8.

DATE APPLE TORTE

8x8-inch cake pan . . . Preheated oven—400° F. . . . Baking time—40 minutes

4 cups apples, diced	1 tablespoon butter or
1 cup sugar	margarine, melted
½ cup all-purpose flour, sifted	1 teaspoon vanilla
before measuring	½ cup nuts, chopped
2 teaspoons baking powder	½ cup dates, cut small
1 beaten egg	

Peel apples, then dice. Mix all ingredients thoroughly. Pour into greased pan. Bake. Serve hot or cold with cream, whipped cream, or ice cream. Serves 6 or 8.

CRACKER NUT TORTE

8-inch pie pan . . . Preheated oven—325° F. . . . Baking time—30 minutes

3 egg whites	¾ cup nut meats, chopped
1 cup sugar	½ teaspoon vanilla
½ teaspoon baking powder	1 pint ice cream
1 cup cracker crumbs, rolled very fine	

Beat egg whites until stiff. Mix sugar and baking powder and add gradually to egg whites. Continue beating until egg whites hold a stiff peak. Fold in cracker crumbs, nut meats, and vanilla. Use a wire whisk egg beater to do this. Pour into greased pan which has been lightly dusted with flour. Bake. When cool, cut in pie-shaped sections. Serve topped with ice cream and crushed fruit, if desired. Serves 6-8.

FRUIT DESSERTS

APPLE TAPIOCA—BAKED

2-quart covered casserole . . . Preheated oven—375° F. . . . Baking time—20-30 minutes

2½ cups thickly sliced tart apples	1 cup light brown sugar, firmly packed
3 tablespoons butter or margarine	3 cups water
¼ teaspoon mace or cinnamon	¾ teaspoon salt
½ cup quick-cooking tapioca	2 tablespoons lemon juice

Grease casserole. Place sliced apples in casserole, dot with butter or margarine, and sprinkle with mace or cinnamon. Place tapioca, sugar, water, salt, and lemon juice in saucepan. Bring to boiling point over medium heat, stirring as needed. Pour over apples in casserole. Cover. Bake. Serves 6.

BAKED APPLES

Varieties of apples suitable for baking are Fall Pippin, Rome Beauty, Baldwin, Spitzenburg, and Jonathan.

Select good-sized apples, wash, remove core, and pare down

about one-third from stem end. Place in deep baking pan. In center of each apple place 2 tablespoons brown sugar, and 1 teaspoon butter or margarine. Pour 1 cup water around apples, cover, and bake at 375° F. until tender. Baking time depends upon apple. Usually 45 minutes is about right. If baking dish cannot be covered, baste two or three times while baking.

TREAT: For something special, fill apple centers with chopped dates or raisins, while mincemeat makes a delicious treat.

BAKED APPLES IN CREAM

Peel and core as many apples as needed. Roll in melted butter or margarine, then in sugar and cinnamon which has been mixed together, then in buttered crumbs. Place apples in shallow baking dish. Fill centers with sugar and cinnamon. Add dots of butter or margarine. Bake at 400° F. When apples have baked about 20 minutes, add ½ cup light cream. Continue baking until apples are tender.

CINNAMON APPLES

1 cup granulated sugar	1½ cups water
3 tablespoons red cinnamon drops	6 apples
	12 whole cloves

Boil sugar, cinnamon drops, and water together. Stir occasionally so red color will be thoroughly distributed. Pare and core apples. Place 2 whole cloves in each apple. Add apples to boiling sirup, reduce heat and cook slowly until apples are tender. It will be necessary to baste apples frequently with sirup in pan. Chill before serving.

TRICK: Cinnamon apples may be used as garnish on plate when serving roast pork.

APPLE ROLL

6x10-inch utility pan . . . Preheated oven—450° F. . . . Baking time 20-25 minutes

Sirup

1 cup sugar	2 cups apples, finely chopped
1 cup water	

Boil sugar and water together to make a thin sirup. Peel and chop apples.

Dough

1 cup all-purpose flour, sifted before measuring	1 tablespoon sugar
	3 tablespoons shortening
2 teaspoons baking powder	⅓ cup milk
½ teaspoon salt	1 teaspoon cinnamon

Sift flour, baking powder, salt, and sugar together. Cut in shortening, add milk, and blend through flour mixture to make a soft dough. Roll out on floured board in rectangular shape to about ¼-inch thickness. Spread chopped apples over dough and roll like cinnamon roll (page 323). Cut in 1-inch pieces and place, cut side down, in greased pan. Sprinkle with cinnamon, pour hot sirup over rolls, and bake. Serve hot. Serves 4-6.

APPLE DUMPLINGS

6x10-inch shallow baking pan . . . Preheated oven—425° F. . . .
Baking time—45-50 minutes

4-5 good-sized baking apples, peeled and cored	2 tablespoons butter or margarine
¼ cup brown sugar	Cinnamon and raisins, if desired

Dough

2 cups all-purpose flour, sifted before measuring	¾ teaspoon salt
	6 tablespoons shortening
1 teaspoon baking powder	6 tablespoons cold water

Sauce

1 tablespoon cornstarch	3 tablespoons butter or margarine
1 cup brown sugar	
1½ cups water	

Blend cornstarch and sugar. Add water and butter or margarine. Cook until thickened. Cool.

Make dough according to recipe for biscuits (page 309). Roll out ¼ inch thick. Cut in 7-inch squares.

Place peeled and cored apple in center of each square. Fill centers of apples with brown sugar, butter or margarine, and cinnamon and raisins, if desired. Fold dough over the apples, moisten corners, and pinch together so whole apple is covered. Place in greased pan, folded side down. Prick dough with fork. Pour cooled sauce over apples. Bake. Serves 4-5.

TRICK: Brush top of dumpling with white of egg slightly beaten and sprinkle with powdered sugar before putting in oven.

TREAT: Serve hot with hard sauce (page 248).

DUTCH APPLE CAKE

7x11-inch shallow pan . . . Preheated oven—400° F. . . . Baking time—30-35 minutes

1½ cups all-purpose flour, sifted before measuring	1 egg, well beaten
½ teaspoon salt	4 large, sour apples, peeled and cut into eighths
2 teaspoons baking powder	
1 tablespoon sugar	2 tablespoons brown or granulated sugar
4 tablespoons shortening	
½ cup milk	1 teaspoon cinnamon

Sift flour with salt, baking powder, and sugar. Cut in the shortening. Add milk to beaten egg. Stir into flour mixture. This will make a soft dough. Spread dough in greased pan. Arrange apples, pointed sides down, in parallel rows on dough. Mix sugar and cinnamon together and sprinkle over top. Bake. Serve hot with lemon sauce (page 251), or top milk. Serves 4-6.

ENGLISH APPLE PIE

2-quart casserole . . . Cold or preheated oven—375° F. . . . Baking time—45-55 minutes

6-8 apples, peeled and sliced medium thick	1 cup light brown sugar
	¾ cup all-purpose flour, sifted before measuring
½ cup butter or margarine	

Place peeled and sliced apples in greased baking dish. Blend together the butter or margarine, sugar, and flour as for making pie dough. Work until crumbly, then pack firmly over the apples. If apples are very mealy, it may be necessary to add 2 tablespoons water. Bake. Serve warm with whipped cream, top milk, or lemon sauce (page 251). Good when served cold. Serves 4-5.

BROWN BETTY

Greased 2-quart covered casserole . . . Preheated oven—350° F. . . . Baking time—1 hour

1½ cups dry bread cubes	1 teaspoon cinnamon
¼ cup butter or margarine, melted	¼ teaspoon salt
	⅓ cup water
4 cups tart apples, diced or sliced	2 tablespoons lemon juice
¾ cup brown sugar, or ½ cup honey	

Mix bread cubes with melted butter or margarine. Combine apples, sugar or honey, cinnamon, and salt. Mix water and lemon juice together.

Place part of bread cubes in greased casserole. Add layer of apples alternately with bread cubes, ending with bread cubes on top. Pour water and lemon juice mixture carefully through bread cubes and apples. Cover and bake. Take off cover the last half hour. Serve hot or cold with cream or top milk or custard sauce (page 248). Serves 4-5.

APRICOT TAPIOCA

1 cup water	¼ cup quick-cooking tapioca
¼ cup sugar	½ cup cooked apricot pulp
¼ teaspoon salt	1 tablespoon lemon juice

Combine water, sugar, salt, and minute tapioca. Cook over medium heat until mixture is transparent, stirring frequently. Remove from heat. When cool, add apricot pulp and lemon juice. Serve with cream. Serves 4.

TRICK: Buy a can of baby-food apricots, which will be just the right amount for this recipe.

APRICOT SQUARES

11x7-inch utility pan ... Preheated oven—350° F. ... Baking time —30 minutes

Filling

1 cup water	¾ cup honey or ½ cup sugar
½ pound dried apricots	

Add water to apricots. Cover. Cook over medium heat until boiling, then reduce heat to simmer and cook until tender. Add honey or sugar. Stirr thoroughly. Chill.

Dough

1 cup all-purpose flour, sifted before measuring	½ cup brown sugar
	1 cup quick-cooking oatmeal
½ teaspoon soda	½ cup shortening
¼ teaspoon salt	

Sift flour together with soda and salt. Add brown sugar and oatmeal. Cut shortening in until the mixture is a crumbly mass.

Put ⅔ of the mixture in bottom of pan, pat down, and spread apricot mixture over bottom mixture. Cover with remaining crumbs. Bake. Cut in squares while warm. Serve with custard sauce (page 248), top milk, or whipped cream. Serves 6-8.

BLUEBERRY TURNOVERS

10x14-inch cooky sheet . . . Preheated oven—400° F. . . . Baking time—20-25 minutes

1 shortcake recipe (page 346)   ¼ cup sugar
2 tablespoons butter or   1 tablespoon flour
   margarine, melted   1 tablespoon lemon juice
1 cup blueberries

Prepare shortcake dough. Roll out ¼ inch thick. Brush with melted butter or margarine. Cut into 3-inch squares.

  Mix blueberries, sugar, flour, and lemon juice together. Place a generous tablespoon of this fruit mixture on each square. Moisten edge of dough with water. Fold dough over to form a triangle. Seal edges with tines of a fork. Prick dough. Place on greased cooky sheet. Bake. Serve with cream. Serves 8.

  TRICK: Use any leftover fruits or berries you may have. All will make delicious turnovers.

FRUIT COBBLER (BASIC RECIPE)

2-quart casserole or utility dish . . . Preheated oven—400° F. . . . Baking time—25-30 minutes

1 cup sugar (if canned fruit is   2 cups canned fruit with ¾ cup
  sweetened, use only ¼ cup   juice, or 3 cups fresh fruit,
  sugar)   such as cherries, peaches,
4 tablespoons all-purpose flour   berries
½ teaspoon cinnamon   ½ recipe for shortcake (page 346)

Mix sugar, flour, and cinnamon and blend with fruit (and juice, if canned fruit is used). Pour into greased casserole or utility dish. Roll shortcake dough ½ inch thick. Fit over top of fruit. Prick with fork. Bake. Serve hot. Serves 4.

UPSIDE-DOWN CAKE

10-inch heavy skillet or 9-inch square pan . . . Preheated oven—350° F. . . . Baking time—45 minutes

⅓ cup butter or margarine   1 small jar maraschino cherries
½ cup brown sugar   ¼ pound whole pecans
1 can (No. 2½) peaches or   1 can moist coconut
  pineapple

Melt butter or margarine in skillet. Do not overheat. Sprinkle brown sugar over butter or margarine. Arrange drained canned fruit over the sugar mixture. Place sliced pineapple or peaches over sugar mixture, filling center with maraschino cherry, and filling in between circles of fruit with pecans. Sprinkle moist coconut over all. If you use peaches, place cherry in center of each peach and lay peach cut side down. Fill in with nuts and cover with coconut. Pour cake batter over all. Bake.

Cake Batter

2 eggs, beaten	1 cup cake flour, sifted before
⅔ cup sugar	measuring
6 tablespoons fruit juice	1 teaspoon baking powder
1 teaspoon vanilla	¼ teaspoon salt

Beat eggs until fluffy, then add sugar, and beat until thick and lemon colored. Beat the fruit juice and vanilla all at once. Sift cake flour, baking powder, and salt together and beat into egg mixture.

When cake has baked, immediately turn upside down on serving plate. Keep pan on cake for few minutes, so that brown sugar mixture will run down over cake instead of sticking to pan. Serve warm or cold, though you may decide it tastes a little better served warm with plain or whipped cream. Serves 6-8.

HUNGARIAN PLUM CAKE

6x11x2-inch pan . . . Preheated oven—400° F. . . . Baking time—
30-35 minutes

Batter

½ cup shortening	1 teaspoon baking powder
½ cup sugar	½ teaspoon salt
2 eggs	1 teaspoon cinnamon
1 cup all-purpose flour, sifted	½ teaspoon lemon extract
before measuring	

Topping

10 canned plum halves, drained	1 tablespoon cinnamon
½ cup sugar	

Cream shortening, add sugar, and beat until light and fluffy. Add eggs one at a time, beating well between each addition. Sift flour with baking powder, salt, and cinnamon. Add flavoring. Pour into well-greased pan. Then put on topping by pressing plum halves into batter. Sprinkle sugar and cinnamon, which have been mixed together, over top. Bake. Serve hot or cold with cream or top milk. Serves 6.

OATMEAL PEACH CRUMBLE

Shallow baking dish ... Preheated oven—350° F. ... Baking time 45 minutes

2 cups canned sliced peaches	⅔ cup all-purpose flour, sifted
2 tablespoons lemon juice	before measuring
¼ teaspoon cinnamon	⅛ teaspoon salt
1 tablespoon butter or margarine	¼ teaspoon soda
¼ cup shortening, melted	⅔ cup quick-cooking oatmeal
⅓ cup brown sugar	½ teaspoon vanilla

Arrange peaches in greased baking dish, sprinkle with lemon juice and cinnamon, and dot with butter or margarine. Combine melted shortening and brown sugar. Sift flour, salt, and soda together and mix with the oatmeal. Blend with the sugar mixture, crumbling well. Add vanilla. Spread over peaches and bake. Serve with warm custard sauce (page 248) or top milk. Serves 4-5.

SHORTCAKE (BASIC RECIPE)

10x14-inch cooky sheet ... Preheated oven—425° F. ... Baking time—depends upon size

2 cups all-purpose flour, sifted	¾ cup sweet milk
before measuring	2 tablespoons butter or
4 teaspoons baking powder	margarine
½ teaspoon salt	Fruit—strawberries, peaches,
2 tablespoons sugar	etc.
½ cup shortening	

Sift dry ingredients together and work in shortening until mixture is a crumbly mass. Add milk, and when all ingredients are well blended, toss on floured kneading board. Knead gently for a minute or so, then pat to ½-inch thickness. Bake either as a large shortcake or cut into individual-sized shortcakes. When done, take a fork and carefully split in two parts. Spread lower half with butter or margarine, place half of sweetened fruit on bottom layer, then put on top layer, and cover with remaining fruit. Serve with or without cream. Serves 6-8.

SPECIAL STRAWBERRY SHORTCAKE

Use basic recipe (page 346), reducing shortening to ¼ cup and adding 2 well-beaten eggs and 1 cup of orange juice instead of the milk. This makes a softer dough. Do not knead. Can be baked in 9-inch round or square greased cake pan.

GELATIN DESSERTS

Unflavored gelatin must always be dissolved first in a little cold water, about 2 tablespoons water to 1 tablespoon gelatin. 1 tablespoon gelatin is sufficient to use with 2 cups liquid. Do not add hot liquid until gelatin has softened.

To speed the setting, heat only half the liquid, stir until gelatin has dissolved, then add remainder of liquid, cold.

Fresh pineapple should never be used in gelatin desserts. This fruit must first be scalded because fresh pinapple contains an enzyme which prevents gelatin from setting.

Flavored gelatins have flavoring, coloring, and sugar added to them. The liquid used may be water or fruit juice and must always be hot to dissolve the gelatin. All gelatin desserts will set more quickly if placed in the refrigerator.

Molded gelatin desserts are easily removed by first running knife around top edge. Then quickly dip the mold in hot water. Then place serving dish on top of the mold. Turn upside down, and be sure you hold serving dish tightly to mold. Give mold a shake. Lift one end of mold gently. If dessert does not seem inclined to budge, dip a clean cloth in hot water, squeeze out water, and lay hot cloth over top of mold. Then give mold a hearty bang with the handle of the knife. Now lift corner of mold. If dessert is loosening, carefully raise mold; if it still sticks, use cloth again.

Usually a very fine recipe folder comes with the package of unflavored or flavored gelatin desserts. You will find it worth saving.

How to Whip Gelatin Desserts

Better not attempt this unless you have an electric mixer. When gelatin is partially set, but not firm, beat until light and fluffy. Then put in mold or pile lightly in serving dish.

How to Make Gelatin Sponges

When gelatin mixture begins to congeal, fold beaten egg whites into it, beating mixture vigorously. Use 3 egg whites to 2 cups gelatin mixture. Beat until mixture holds its shape.

How to Dissolve Unflavored Gelatin

Unflavored gelatin must always be softened in a cold liquid. If the recipe states "Dissolve over hot water," place dish containing the softened gelatin in a pan of hot water. Keep water hot over low heat. Stir until gelatin is dissolved.

CRANBERRY ANGEL WHIP

1 teaspoon unflavored gelatin
2 tablespoons cold water
1 cup jellied cranberry sauce
¼ cup powdered sugar

2 egg whites
½ cup heavy cream, whipped
½ teaspoon vanilla

Soften gelatin in cold water. Heat ½ cup cranberry sauce and dissolve gelatin in it. Cool. Add powdered sugar and remaining cranberry sauce. Fold in stiffly beaten egg whites and whipped cream to which vanilla has been added. Chill. Serve with whipped cream or custard sauce (page 248). Serves 4.

DIVINITY REFRIGERATOR CAKE

9-inch square cake pan

1 package orange-flavored
    gelatin
¾ cup boiling water
¾ cup evaporated milk
2 egg yolks, well beaten
¼ teaspoon salt

1½ cups frozen, fresh, or canned
    peaches, sliced and well
    drained
1 cup vanilla wafer crumbs
2 egg whites
¼ cup sugar

Dissolve gelatin in boiling water. Scald milk. Remove from heat and slowly stir into well-beaten egg yolks to which salt has been added. Stir dissolved gelatin into egg mixture. Cool. Add ¾ cup of the peaches to cooled gelatin mixture. Chill until mixture begins to thicken. Grease pan, arrange remaining peaches in bottom. Roll vanilla wafers into fine crumbs. Beat egg whites until stiff and slowly add sugar to them. Fold into gelatin mixture. Spread over peaches. Top with vanilla wafer crumbs. Chill until firm. Cut in squares to serve. Sliced canned pineapple or bananas may be used. Serves 6.

SPANISH CREAM

1 tablespoon unflavored gelatin
¼ cup cold water
3 cups scalded milk

3 eggs, separated
½ cup sugar
1 teaspoon vanilla

Soften gelatin in cold water 5 minutes, then dissolve in scalded milk. Combine egg yolks and sugar, add gelatin mixture, and cook over low heat 5 minutes, stirring constantly until sugar has dissolved. Cool and then chill until slightly thickened. Add vanilla and fold in stiffly beaten egg whites. Turn into mold, chill until firm, unmold. Chocolate sauce (page 249) or caramel sauce (page 249) may be served over this. Serves 5-6.

GELATIN PRUNE WHIP

1 package orange-flavored gelatin	¼ teaspoon orange rind, grated
1 pint hot water	4 tablespoons sugar
¼ teaspoon salt	1½ cups cooked prunes, chopped

Dissolve gelatin in hot water. Add salt and orange rind. Chill until cold and sirupy. Place in bowl of cracked ice and water and whip with rotary beater or electric beater until fluffy and thick like whipped cream. Add sugar to the prunes and fold into whipped gelatin. Pile lightly in sherbet glasses or mold. Chill until firm. Serve with whipped cream or custard sauce (page 248). Serves 4-5.

PINEAPPLE BAVARIAN CREAM

1-quart mold

1 cup pineapple juice	¼ teaspoon salt
1 tablespoon unflavored gelatin	1 cup cooked pineapple, crushed
2 tablespoons cold water	1 tablespoon lemon juice
½ cup sugar	1 cup heavy cream

Heat pineapple juice. Soften gelatin in cold water. When softened, add to hot pineapple juice. Add sugar, salt, crushed pineapple, and lemon juice. Blend thoroughly. Remove from heat. Cool. Stir occasionally until mixture is partially set. Then fold in stiffly beaten cream. Pour into mold; chill at least 4 hours. Or, may be molded in individual molds or custard cups. Serves 8.

TREAT: Substitute strawberries or raspberries for pineapple.

SNOW PUDDING

1 tablespoon unflavored gelatin	¼ cup lemon juice
¼ cup cold water	1 tablespoon lemon rind, grated
1 cup boiling water	2 egg whites
¾ cup sugar	¼ teaspoon salt

Soak gelatin in cold water about 5 minutes. Dissolve in boiling water. Add sugar, lemon juice, rind, and salt. Cool. When mixture becomes quite thick, beat vigorously with an electric mixer or rotary egg beater. Beat egg whites until stiff. Add to gelatin mixture and continue beating until mixture is stiff enough to hold its shape. Turn into mold. Chill. Serve with custard sauce (page 248). Serves 5-6.

LEMON DESSERT

6x10-inch utility dish

1 can (13 ounces) evaporated milk	¾ cup boiling water
	24 graham crackers
3 lemons, juice and rind	4 tablespoons butter or
1 cup sugar	margarine, melted
1 package lemon-flavored gelatin	

Boil unopened can of evaporated milk for at least 1 hour. Keep can covered with boiling water. Chill overnight in refrigerator. Next day, open can and pour contents into mixing bowl and beat until stiff. Add juice and rind of lemons, and sugar and beat thoroughly. Dissolve gelatin in boiling water. Let cool but not congeal. Beat this into evaporated milk mixture. Pour into pan which has been lined with waxed paper. Roll graham cracker crumbs until fine and mix with melted butter or margarine. Sprinkle over top. Cool 5 to 6 hours in refrigerator. Serves 6.

REFRIGERATOR DESSERTS

LEMON REFRIGERATOR CAKE

Bake chiffon cake (page 401), or sponge cake (page 402).

Filling

½ pound butter or margarine	⅓ cup lemon juice
2¼ cups sugar	8 eggs, separated
1½ teaspoons vanilla	1 cup heavy cream
1 tablespoon lemon rind	

Cream the butter or margarine and sugar well, add the vanilla, grated lemon rind, and lemon juice. Add the egg yolks one at a time and beat well after each addition. Fold in the stiffly beaten egg whites and the whipped cream. Cut cake in three horizontal slices. Line a utility pan with heavy waxed paper. Lay slices of cake for bottom layer. Then a layer of the filling, and so on until all is used, having filling on top. Place in refrigerator for 24 hours before serving. Serves 16-20.

PINEAPPLE ANGEL FOOD DESSERT

1 cup heavy cream
1 cup granulated sugar
1/3 cup lemon juice

1 cup top milk
Leftover angel food cake

Whip cream until thick. Add sugar slowly and mix thoroughly. Fold in lemon juice, a tablespoon at a time, then slowly fold in top milk. Slice leftover cake about 1 inch thick. Line bottom of refrigerator trays with cake. Pour cream mixture over top. Place in refrigerator and allow to set for 4-6 hours before cutting into squares. Serve with pineapple sauce (page 250). Serves 10-12.

CHOCOLATE DELIGHT

1/2 cup butter
1 cup powdered sugar, sifted
3 eggs, separated
2 squares unsweetened chocolate
1/2 teaspoon vanilla

1/2 cup nuts, chopped
1 cup crushed vanilla wafers, or
    whole wafers, chocolate or
    vanilla

Cream butter, gradually add sugar, and continue beating. Add egg yolks and blend well. Melt chocolate over hot water and add vanilla and nuts. Fold in stiffly beaten egg whites. Line a refrigerator tray with waxed paper. Spread one half of the crushed or plain wafers in the bottom of the tray. Pour in the chocolate mixture and sprinkle remaining wafers on top. Top layer of wafers should not be thick. Place in refrigerator overnight. Serves 10-12.

SNOWBALL DESSERT

2 cups dates, chopped, or 1 cup
    dates and 1 cup prunes,
    chopped
1/2 cup water
1/8 teaspoon salt

1/2 cup nut meats, chopped
24 vanilla wafers
1 cup heavy cream
1 cup coconut, grated

Cut or chop the fruit, add water and salt. 1/8 cup sugar may be added if a sweeter dessert is desired. Cook until thickened over low heat. Take from range and add chopped nut meats. Put between vanilla wafers, pile 3 or 4 wafers high. Let stand in refrigerator overnight. Next day cover with whipped cream and top with coconut. Serves 8.

VANILLA REFRIGERATOR DESSERT

½ cup butter
1 cup powdered sugar
3 eggs

½ teaspoon vanilla
½ cup English walnuts, broken
2¼ cups vanilla wafers, rolled

Cream the butter and sugar together thoroughly. Add eggs one at a time, beating well after each addition. Add vanilla, nut meats, and ¾ cup of wafer crumbs and beat together. Butter an 8-inch square pan, spread ¾ cup of the crumbs over the bottom, spread the creamed mixture evenly over the crumbs. Sprinkle the remaining ¾ cup of the crumbs over the top. Let stand overnight in refrigerator. Serve with whipped cream. Serves 10-12.

FROZEN DESSERTS

LEMON PIE (FROZEN)

2 eggs, separated
⅓ cup lemon juice
1 tablespoon lemon rind, grated
½ cup sugar
1 cup evaporated milk, whipped,
    or 1 cup heavy cream,
    whipped

½ cup graham crackers or cake
    crumbs

Beat egg yolks, add lemon juice, grated rind, and all but 2 tablespoons of the sugar. Cook over low heat, stirring constantly. Cool. Beat egg whites and remaining 2 tablespoons of sugar until stiff. Fold into cooked mixture. Fold in whipped evaporated milk, or cream. Line dessert tray with waxed paper. Sprinkle with ¼ cup of crumbs. Pour in lemon mixture, sprinkle with remaining crumbs. Set control dial on your refrigerator at "Coldest" and freeze until firm. To serve, cut across tray diagonally to make pie-shaped pieces. Serves 5-6.

CRANBERRY PARFAIT

1 can (1 pound) jellied or whole
    cranberry sauce
2 tablespoons sugar

1 cup heavy cream
½ teaspoon almond extract

If jellied cranberry sauce is used, crush with a fork. Combine with sugar. Whip cream, add almond extract, and fold into the cranberry mixture. Spoon into a shallow freezing tray and cover with gingersnap topping. Freeze until firm.

Topping

¾ cup gingersnap crumbs   2 tablespoons butter, softened
1 tablespoon sugar

Combine gingersnap crumbs and sugar. Blend in butter thoroughly with pastry blender or fork. Sprinkle as topping over parfait. Serves 6.

BISCUIT TORTONI

1 cup macaroon crumbs   2 egg whites
¾ cup top milk   1 cup heavy cream
¼ cup sugar   ½ teaspoon vanilla
⅛ teaspoon salt   ½ teaspoon almond extract

Mix together ¾ cup of the crumbs, top milk, sugar, and salt and let stand for 1 hour. Beat egg whites until stiff. Pour cream into chilled mixer bowl and whip until stiff. Add the whipped cream to the stiffly beaten egg whites. Add this mixture gradually to the macaroon crumbs and flavor with vanilla and almond extract. Pour into individual paper cups and sprinkle with remaining crumbs. Freeze until firm. Serves 6.

FROZEN CAKE BALLS

Shape ice cream in round balls with an ice cream scoop. Roll ice cream balls in stale cake crumbs. Return to home freezer or freeze chest of your refrigerator until ready to serve. Serve with hot caramel sundae sauce (page 249).

FROZEN CHEESECAKE

½ pound dry cottage cheese   2 eggs, separated
1 package (3 ounces) cream   1 cup heavy cream
    cheese   1 teaspoon vanilla
½ cup sugar   1 cup graham crackers, rolled

Cream cottage cheese and cream cheese together. Add sugar gradually and beat until creamy. Add egg yolks, one at a time, beating well after each addition. Beat egg whites until stiff. Whip cream and combine with egg whites. Add to first mixture, folding carefully. Add vanilla. Sprinkle half of graham cracker crumbs in bottom of refrigerator tray. Add cheese mixture and top with remaining crumbs. Freeze in evaporator of refrigerator. Serves 8-10.

BAKED ALASKA

Preheated oven—450° F. . . . Baking time—5 minutes

1 sponge cake (page 402)	5 egg whites
1½ quarts ice cream, brick or bulk	½ teaspoon cream of tartar
	⅔ cup sugar

Bake sponge cake. Cool. Then slice in half lengthwise. Use the bottom half. Cover a bread board large enough to hold the sponge cake with white paper or aluminum foil. Place the cut sponge cake on the paper. Then pile ice cream on cake. Make sure the sponge cake extends about one inch beyond the ice cream.

Just before serving, beat egg whites until foamy, then add cream of tartar. Beat until stiff. Gradually add the sugar. Continue beating until meringue is stiff and glossy.

Completely cover ice cream and sides of cake with a thick covering of the meringue. Place in preheated oven. Just as soon as meringue is golden brown, remove.

Slip dessert from bread board to serving platter and serve immediately. This will serve about 12 persons and must be eaten at once.

TRICK: For a small group, cut 3-inch squares of sponge cake, one for each guest. You can make ice cream into balls (page 353), place on cake, and cover with meringue. You will need more meringue this way, so allow one egg white for each individual serving, and 3 tablespoons sugar per egg white.

CHOCOLATE CUP ALASKAS

10 large muffin cups . . . Preheated oven—375° F. . . . Baking time —12 minutes

⅓ cup butter or margarine	1 teaspoon vanilla
2 squares bitter chocolate	1 quart ice cream (vanilla, chocolate, or mint)
¼ teaspoon salt	
½ cup brown sugar	4 egg whites
⅓ cup all-purpose flour, sifted before measuring	½ cup sugar
	½ teaspoon vanilla
1 cup quick-cooking oatmeal, uncooked	

Melt butter or margarine and chocolate in double boiler. Remove from heat. Mix salt, sugar, flour, and oatmeal and blend into melted chocolate mixture. Add vanilla. Pack into well-greased muffin cups, covering the bottom and extending two-thirds up the sides of the muffin cups. Bake. When you remove them from the oven they will look fluffy. Take a glass custard cup which has been slightly greased on the outside and press down into the baked mixture. Give the muffin cup a slight twist and lift chocolate cups out. The baked mixture will not stick to the cup but will be shaped into little cups. Cool.

Just before serving, fill cups with ice cream and cover with meringue. To make meringue, beat egg whites until frothy, then begin slowly to add the sugar, beating at high speed. Continue beating even after sugar has been added, until whites stand in peaks. Add vanilla and beat until well blended. Spread meringue over top and sides of ice cream cups, completely covering the ice cream. Place at least 4 inches below broiler unit. Turn broiler on and heat until meringue is golden brown. This requires about 2-3 minutes. Serve at once. Serves 10.

TRICK: If you have a freezer, fill chocolate cups with ice cream and place in freezer until time to serve. Saves last-minute confusion.

ICE CREAM AND SHERBETS

Ice cream is a favorite dessert. Many prefer to buy ice cream, but there still are those who like occasionally to have some good home-made ice cream.

To Make Ice Cream at Home

Method No. 1: Using An Ice Cream Freezer

A 2-quart freezer is a good size for the average family. Usually sufficient ice can be frozen in the freeze chest of your refrigerator to take care of the ice needs, or you can buy crushed ice at most ice-making companies. Use coarse salt for mixing with the ice. Table salt will not do.

Fill the freezer can only about two thirds full of mixture to be frozen. Ice cream expands as it freezes. When freezer can is in place, put crank on freezer. Then fill about one third full of crushed ice, add salt, and continue until freezer is filled with ice mixed with salt. Use about 4 parts crushed ice to 1 part coarse salt.

Be sure the mixture to be frozen is very cold. Let the ice cream enthusiasts do the turning of the crank. They'll want to lick the dasher, anyway, so let them work for it.

After the ice cream has frozen, drain off water, then lift out dasher. Pack mixture down solidly, using a spoon. Repack. Cover freezer with newspapers or heavy cloth.

Method No. 2: Refrigerator Ice Cream

You can use ice cream mixes, in which case follow the directions on the package of mix. Freeze in refrigerator trays. Follow refrigerator manufacturers' instructions for setting temperature control of refrigerator.

When you are freezing ice cream in your refrigerator, corn sirup is used for part of the sugar. The mixture freezes better.

How to Beat Ice Cream When Frozen in Freeze Chest of Refrigerator

First, place the bowl and beaters in refrigerator to chill.

Freeze the mixture in dessert tray until there are no soft spots. A good way to tell whether the mixture is sufficiently hard is to tip the dessert tray carefully. When there is no oozing of liquid on the side of tray and tray can be turned upside down, mixture is sufficiently frozen. Cut frozen mixture from tray, place in chilled bowl. Add unbeaten egg whites and beat quickly with electric mixer or large rotary egg beater. Beat only until egg whites are well blended and mixture is free from frozen lumps. STOP BEATING BEFORE MIXTURE BECOMES SOFT AND MUSHY. Pile in dessert tray, do not spread smooth. The dessert tray will not be completely filled, but the consistency of the frozen dessert is much better if mixture is piled in rather than spread over entire tray.

BASIC CUSTARD ICE CREAM—FOR THE ICE CREAM FREEZER

2 cups whole milk	2 eggs, well beaten
2 tablespoons cornstarch	1 quart light cream
1 cup sugar	2 teaspoons vanilla
⅛ teaspoon salt	

Scald milk. Mix cornstarch, sugar, and salt together and add to scalded milk, stirring vigorously. Cook until thickened. Remove from heat. Slowly add the eggs, which have been beaten until thick and lemon colored, stirring vigorously as the eggs are added. Cool. Add cream and vanilla. Freeze. Serves 6 to 8.

CHOCOLATE ICE CREAM—FOR THE ICE CREAM FREEZER

2 squares bitter chocolate, or ¼   ¼ teaspoon salt
   cup cocoa   1 quart light cream
1 cup sugar   1 tablespoon vanilla
½ cup hot water

Melt chocolate (if using cocoa, stir in with sugar) and to it add the sugar, hot water, and salt. Beat vigorously until all ingredients are well blended. Cool. Then add cream and vanilla. Freeze. Serves 6.

ECONOMY ICE CREAM—FOR THE REFRIGERATOR

2 eggs   1 cup top milk
6 tablespoons sugar   1 cup light cream
4 tablespoons white corn sirup   1 teaspoon vanilla

Beat egg yolks, sugar, and corn sirup until thick and lemon colored. Add milk, cream, flavoring. Pour into refrigerator dessert tray. Freeze until firm with control dial set at "Coldest." Remove to chilled bowl, add unbeaten egg whites, and beat until fluffy. Return to freeze chest for 20 to 25 minutes, or until frozen. Serves 5.

Economy Ice Cream Variations

Chocolate

Cook 2 ounces shaved chocolate with sugar and milk of previous recipe, stirring constantly until chocolate has melted. Chill, add 1 teaspoon vanilla, then proceed as above.

Maplenut

Add 6 drops maple flavoring and ½ cup chopped walnuts to the basic recipe.

Peanut Brittle

Substitute 1 cup crushed peanut brittle for sugar. Add 1 teaspoon vanilla. Proceed as instructed for basic recipe.

Peach

Crush peaches through a sieve and substitute 1 cup of pulp for 1 cup of milk. Add ¼ cup sugar and ½ teaspoon almond extract. Proceed as instructed for basic recipe.

Strawberry

Substitute 1 cup finely sieved strawberries for 1 cup of milk. Add ¼ cup sugar. Combine as shown for basic recipe.

Peppermint

Substitute ⅛ pound crushed peppermint sticks for the sugar in basic recipe.

Coffee

Dissolve 1 tablespoon instant coffee in 1 teaspoon boiling water. Add to basic recipe before freezing.

BUTTER CRISP ICE CREAM—FOR THE REFRIGERATOR

1 tablespoon unflavored gelatin	⅛ teaspoon salt
1½ cups whole milk	2 teaspoons vanilla
2 eggs	1 cup heavy cream
½ cup granulated sugar	

Soak gelatin in 2 tablespoons of the whole milk. Scald remaining milk over low heat. Beat eggs until light and lemon colored, add sugar, salt, and vanilla. Continue beating until ingredients are thoroughly mixed. Add milk slowly to sugar and egg mixture and, lastly, add soaked gelatin. Cool. When mixture is completely chilled, add cream which has been whipped stiff. Place in refrigerator dessert tray on bottom shelf of freezing compartment, turn control dial to "Coldest," and freeze until firm. Remove to a chilled bowl, beat in half the butter crisp mixture. Return to freezing tray, sprinkle remainder of butter crisp mixture on top. Return to freezing compartment and continue freezing until firm. Serves 8.

Butter Crisp Mixture

1 tablespoon melted butter	2 tablespoons brown sugar
¼ cup corn flakes, finely crushed	¼ cup chopped nut meats

Blend all ingredients, place in shallow pan, and bake at 375° F. for 10 minutes. Stir several times.

FRUIT WHIP ICE CREAM

1 package strawberry-flavored gelatin	1 pint vanilla ice cream
2 cups hot water	1 cup strawberries

Dissolve gelatin in hot water. Chill until partially set. Beat in ice cream with electric or rotary beater. Fold in berries. (*Note:* Any fruit, raspberries, blackberries, peaches, etc., may be used.) Serve at once. Garnish with whole or cut-up fruit used in dessert. Serves 6.

GRAPENUT ICE CREAM

½ cup granulated sugar

½ cup hot water

1⅔ cups evaporated milk

1 egg, beaten

½ cup cold water

¼ teaspoon salt

1 tablespoon unflavored gelatin

2 tablespoons cold water

½ cup grapenuts

1 teaspoon vanilla

Caramelize sugar to light brown (page 329). Add hot water slowly, stirring constantly until sugar has dissolved. Mix ⅔ cup of the milk, the beaten egg, cold water, and salt together and add to sugar mixture. Cook, stirring constantly until mixture coats a spoon. Remove from heat, add gelatin which has been soaked for 5 minutes in cold water. Cool. Soak grapenuts in remaining 1 cup milk. When cooked mixture is cool, add grapenuts, milk, and vanilla. Pour in refrigerator dessert tray. Freeze. When frozen, remove from refrigerator, put in bowl, and beat thoroughly. Return to freeze chest. Serves 6-8.

SHERBETS

How to Beat Sherbets When Freezing in Refrigerator

Let the mixture freeze until firm. Then cut the semi-solid mass in squares. Place in bowl of electric mixer. Add unbeaten egg whites and beat until fluffy. Do not allow mixture to become watery or soft. Return to refrigerator and continue freezing until firm.

MILK SHERBET

1 tablespoon unflavored gelatin

2 cups whole milk

1 cup sugar

6 tablespoons lemon juice

2 egg whites, unbeaten

Soak gelatin in 2 tablespoons of the milk. Dissolve gelatin by placing dish in pan of hot water. Mix sugar and lemon juice very thoroughly. Stir in the dissolved gelatin. Slowly add the milk to lemon and gelatin mixture. Pour in refrigerator dessert tray. Place on bottom shelf of freezing compartment and turn control dial to "Coldest." Freeze until firm. Then transfer mixture to bowl, add unbeaten egg whites, and beat until light and fluffy. Return to refrigerator and continue freezing until firm. Serves 6.

APRICOT SHERBET

2 cups dried apricots
2 cups water (additional water may be needed)

1½ cups sugar
½ cup orange juice
2 egg whites

Wash apricots and cook slowly in 2 cups of water until tender. Drain cooked apricots. Add enough water to apricot juice to make two cups and heat with 1½ cups sugar until sugar has thoroughly dissolved. Chill. Press apricots through a sieve. Add orange juice. Add to sirup. Pour in refrigerator dessert tray with control dial set at "Coldest." Freeze until firm. Remove to a chilled bowl, add unbeaten egg whites, and beat until fluffy. Return to freezing compartment and continue freezing until firm. Serves 6.

PINEAPPLE SHERBET

2 cups buttermilk
⅔ cup sugar
4 tablespoons white corn sirup
1 can (9 ounces) crushed pineapple

1 teaspoon vanilla
1 egg white, unbeaten

Combine buttermilk, sugar, corn sirup, pineapple, and vanilla. Pour in refrigerator dessert tray. Freeze until firm with control dial set at "Coldest." Remove to chilled bowl, add unbeaten egg white, and beat until fluffy. Return to freeze chest for 20 to 25 minutes, or until frozen. Serves 5.

CRANBERRY SHERBET

1 pound cranberries
3 cups water
1½ cups sugar
1 tablespoon unflavored gelatin

¼ cup cold water
Juice of 1½ lemons and enough orange juice to make 1 cup
2 egg whites, unbeaten

Cook cranberries with 3 cups water until berries are tender. Strain through purée strainer, then add sugar, and stir until sugar has dissolved. To this hot mixture, add gelatin which has been soaked in ¼ cup cold water and then add fruit juices. Stir until well dissolved. Allow to cool, then pour into refrigerator dessert tray. Set control at "Coldest." Freeze until firm. Then place frozen mixture in mixer bowl, add unbeaten egg whites. Beat until light and fluffy. Return to tray and finish freezing until firm. Wonderful to serve with turkey. Serves 8.

LEMON SHERBET

2 teaspoons unflavored gelatin	1 cup water
2 tablespoons cold water	¾ to 1 cup lemon juice
1⅔ cups basic sugar sirup (recipe below)	2 egg whites, unbeaten

Soak gelatin in 2 tablespoons cold water, then dissolve in hot sirup. Cool sirup, then add water and lemon juice. Place in refrigerator dessert tray on bottom shelf of freezing compartment. Set control dial to "Coldest." Freeze until firm. Remove to a chilled bowl, add unbeaten egg whites, and beat until fluffy. Return to freezing compartment for about 30 minutes, or until sufficiently firm to serve. Serves 8.

Basic Sugar Sirup

1 cup sugar	½ cup white corn sirup
1 cup warm water	

Dissolve the sugar in warm or hot water and boil 5 minutes. Add corn sirup and chill before using for sherbets or punches. This sirup may be made in quantity and stored in the refrigerator. Recipe makes 1⅔ cups.

Pastry

A favorite nephew of mine once said that he really only cared for two kinds of pie. This seemed a little unusual, since pie is a favorite with most men. When questioned as to the two kinds he liked he said, "One crust and double-crust pies."

Most husbands seem to feel the same way—they'll eat anything so long as it's pie—and yet pastry making seems to be a culinary hurdle for many homemakers. There are a few golden rules in pie making, however, that will make that hurdle disappear. Armed with these, you can make pastry fit for a king—or a husband.

Tricks in Pastry Making

1. Sift the flour before measuring.

2. Be *extra* careful in the accurate measurement of your shortening.

3. Be very careful to use only the right amount of water and not a drop more. A heavy hand with water has ruined many a potentially fine pie crust.

What Type Flour to Use

An all-purpose flour makes wonderful pastry, but many cooks, especially in the south, where soft wheat flour is more commonly used, prefer to make their pie crusts with pastry or cake flour.

What Type Shortening to Use

There are many fine pastry makers who refuse to use anything but lard. Lard makes a fine flaky pie crust, but make certain it is not rancid or strong flavored, because, if so, your pastry will not taste good. Leaf lard is excellent to use.

Other cooks prefer to use a hydrogenated shortening, which also makes excellent pastry, while salad oils are preferred by others. Butter is rarely used. It has a tendency to make a flaky, but rather tough, pastry.

Recipes for all these different shortenings will be given, and you may take your choice.

Mixing and Blending

If you have never used your electric mixer to mix your pie crusts, you better begin right now, for it does a wonderful job of blending and mixing all ingredients.

You'll need few utensils for your pastry making, but a pastry blender is a gadget which will be of great help. The pastry blender consists of eight or ten fairly heavy wires, bowed and caught at both ends in a wooden handle, which becomes a chopper, so that one downward stroke of the blender really performs a number of cutting operations.

In lieu of a pastry blender, take two table knives and chop through the shortening and flour. A table fork is wonderful for blending water into the flour mixture. Don't use a heavy hand. Work with a light touch.

How to Roll the Dough

It is not necessary to chill the dough before rolling, though some pastry cooks believe chilling makes the crust more flaky. It certainly does no harm. In fact, unbaked pastry may be rolled into a ball, wrapped in waxed paper, and kept in the refrigerator for a week or longer. When you are ready to use the pastry, remove from refrigerator and let stand until it is about room temperature.

Use either a clean table top surface, or a pastry board. If you are using a pastry canvas, better anchor it down, or it will keep sliding.

Another trick is to buy an infant's stocking, cut off the foot, and slip it over the rolling pin. Be sure to flour both the canvas and the rolling pin before starting to roll the crust.

Before starting to roll, divide the dough into two equal parts, if you are making a double-crusted pie. Dough is usually rolled about ⅛ inch thick and always rolled from the center out to the edge.

When you are ready to fit crust in pie pan, fold dough in half and lift into the pie pan. Fit the dough into the pan, paying special attention to the junction of the sides and bottom of the pan. Bubbles of air between paste and pan will cause the pie crust to buckle.

Trim around the edge of the pastry, leaving about ½ inch overlapping. This will be used later for sealing the pie. Kitchen shears are fine for trimming the pastry, or a good sharp kitchen knife may be used.

Directions for forming double-crust pies will be found on page 366.

PASTRY MADE WITH LARD . . . ONE-CRUST PIE . . . 9-INCH PIE PAN

¾ teaspoon salt	½ cup lard
1½ cups all-purpose flour, sifted before measuring	2½ tablespoons water

Add salt to flour and sift into a mixing bowl. Add lard, not chilled, and blend with pastry blender until the mixture resembles coarse meal. Sprinkle water over the surface of the flour and mix gently by blending the mixture together with a fork. Dough will hold together and should be dry enough to handle. Shape portion to be rolled into a ball, place on lightly floured canvas, and roll lightly, rolling from center of dough to edge. Turn the dough around as you roll it, so it will form a circle. Roll about 1 inch larger than the pan to be used. Fold, or roll around a rolling pin, and transfer to pan, pressing dough into place.

How to Bake a Single Crust

A single crust may be baked either over the back of pie pan or fitted inside the pan. Crimp edges, prick liberally with tines of a fork (so pastry will not bubble up), and bake at 425° F. for 12-15 minutes.

Or, if you have two pie pans the same size, fit the dough into the pan, just as for making a double-crust pie. Crimp edges, then place second pan inside. This weighs the dough down and prevents dough from bubbling.

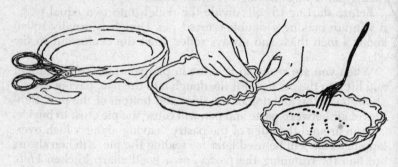

1. Fitting in pan.   2. Crimping edges.   3. Pricking crust.

TWO-CRUST PIE

1 teaspoon salt
2 cups all-purpose flour, sifted
    before measuring

⅔ cup lard
3½ to 4 tablespoons water

Use same method for mixing as given above under one-crust pie.

PASTRY MADE WITH HYDROGENATED SHORTENING—
TWO-CRUST PIE

Pastry may be made with shortening of this kind in exactly the same way as when using lard. However, the following recipe is almost foolproof, and the pastry is flaky and tender:

2 cups all-purpose flour, sifted
    before measuring
1 teaspoon salt

¼ cup water
¾ cup shortening

Sift flour and salt into a bowl. Take out ⅓ cup of this flour and mix with the ¼ cup water to form a paste. Cut shortening into remaining flour until the pieces are the size of small peas. Add flour paste to blended shortening and flour mixture. Mix with a fork until the dough comes together and can be shaped into a ball. Divide in half, roll out both crusts about ⅛ inch thick.

If you are making a one-crust pie by this method, use 1½ cups all-purpose flour, sifted before measuring, ½ teaspoon salt, ½ cup shortening. Take out ¼ cup flour and blend with 3 tablespoons water. Proceed as above.

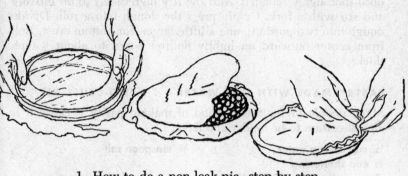

1. How to do a non-leak pie—step by step.

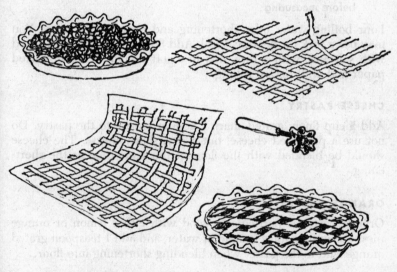

2. How to do lattice pies—step by step.

PASTRY MADE WITH OIL . . . TWO-CRUST PIE

1 teaspoon double-action baking powder	⅓ cup ice water
1 teaspoon salt	½ cup salad oil
2 cups all-purpose flour, sifted before measuring	

Add baking powder and salt to flour and sift into a bowl. Combine ice water with salad oil and beat with a fork or rotary egg beater until thoroughly blended. Add the dry ingredients to oil mixture and stir with a fork. Gently press the dough into a roll. Divide dough into two portions, one a little larger, for bottom crust. Roll from center outward on lightly floured board to about ⅛ inch thick.

PASTRY MADE WITH HOT WATER . . . TWO-CRUST PIE

Many people prefer this method of making pastry because it is almost certain to be tender and flaky.

⅓ cup boiling water   ¾ teaspoon salt
⅔ cup shortening
2 cups all-purpose flour, sifted
   before measuring

Pour boiling water over shortening and beat until creamy. You may use a fork for beating. Cool. Add flour which has been sifted with salt and, with a fork, mix to a soft dough. Wrap in waxed paper and chill before rolling.

CHEESE PASTRY

Add ½ cup finely grated sharp Cheddar cheese to the pastry. Do not use a packaged cheese, but a dry, sharp cheese. The cheese should be blended with the flour at the same time as the shortening.

ORANGE PASTRY

Orange pastry is particularly good with either lemon or orange pies. Use orange juice instead of water, and add 1 teaspoon grated orange rind to the pastry when blending shortening into flour.

SWEET PASTRY . . . ONE-CRUST PIE

1½ cups all-purpose flour, sifted   2 tablespoons sugar
   before measuring   ½ cup shortening
1 teaspoon baking powder   1 egg yolk
½ teaspoon salt   4 tablespoons ice water

Sift dry ingredients together. Add shortening and cut in with pastry blender. Add egg to ice water and beat with a fork. Then add to dry ingredients. Knead lightly. Chill in refrigerator before rolling.

PEANUT BUTTER PASTRY . . . ONE-CRUST PIE

1½ cups all-purpose flour, sifted   ½ cup shortening
    before measuring   2 tablespoons peanut butter
¼ teaspoon salt   3½ tablespoons water

Sift flour and salt into a bowl. Cut shortening and peanut butter
into flour, leaving pieces of shortening the size of a pea. Sprinkle
water over flour, blending ingredients together with a fork. Work
dough only enough to gather together into a smooth dough. Especially good with banana cream or custard pie.

Sweet Crumb Pastry

If you feel you simply cannot make the regular pastry, why not
try a crumb crust. The following recipe for graham cracker crust
may be used, substituting vanilla wafers, thin chocolate wafers, or
zwieback for the graham crackers.

GRAHAM CRACKER CRUST

9-inch pie pan . . . Preheated oven—375° F. . . . Baking time 8-10
minutes

1⅔ cups crumbs or about 20   ¼ cup softened butter or
    graham crackers, rolled   margarine (do not melt
    fine   butter or margarine)
¼ cup granulated sugar

Thoroughly blend together the crumbs, sugar, and softened butter
or margarine. Press firmly into an even layer against bottom and
sides of pie plate. Bake. If chocolate crumbs are used, bake at
350° F. instead of 375° F. Cool before filling. May be filled with
ice cream or custard fillings.

CHOCOLATE-COCONUT CRUST

2 squares Baker's unsweetened   ⅔ cup confectioners' sugar,
    chocolate   sifted
2 tablespoons butter   1½ cups coconut, cut, toasted or
2 tablespoons hot milk or water   plain

Melt chocolate and butter in top of double boiler, stirring until
blended. Combine the milk or water and sugar. Add to chocolate
mixture, stirring well. Add coconut and mix well. Spread on bottom and sides of greased 9-inch pan. Chill until firm. Fill with ice
cream, cream pie filling, or chiffon filling.

How to Make Meringue

A pie topped with a fluffy, golden meringue is a beautiful sight. Some homemakers feel a meringue is difficult to make. Perhaps the following suggestions for making meringue will be helpful.

1. For a fluffy, generous meringue, allow 3 egg whites for a 9-inch pie.

2. Use 2 level tablespoons sugar for each egg white.

3. Beat egg whites stiff before adding sugar. They should be glossy on top, and when you invert the bowl, they should remain in place.

4. Fold in sugar gradually. Use a folding motion. Do not beat sugar in.

5. When putting meringue on pie, be sure you seal it carefully all around the crust edge of the pie. A good way to do this is to pile the meringue in the center of the pie, then work out toward the edges.

6. Bake at 350° F. for 18 minutes.

A meringue made as given above should not "weep" or become tough and sticky when cutting.

MERINGUES

10x14-inch cooky sheet . . . Preheated oven—250° F. . . . Baking time—25-30 minutes

¾ cup egg whites   1 teaspoon vanilla
2 cups granulated sugar

Put all ingredients in large bowl of mixer. Beat 10 minutes on low speed, 10 minutes on middle speed, and a final 10 minutes on high speed. Spoon, in any desired shape or size, onto slightly greased cooky sheet, allowing 2 inches between meringues. Bake until a very light crust has formed on the outside. These meringues will be white in color and very delicate. Let cool slightly before removing from pan. Makes 12 medium-sized meringues.

ANGEL PIE

10x14-inch cooky sheet . . . Preheated oven—275° F. . . . Baking time—1 hour

Meringue Shell

4 egg whites	1 teaspoon vanilla extract
½ teaspoon cream of tartar	1 cup granulated sugar
⅓ teaspoon salt	

Place egg whites in large mixing bowl. Beat until foamy. Add cream of tartar, salt, and vanilla. Beat until stiff and dry. Add sugar gradually and continue beating until sugar has dissolved. On a greased baking sheet, spoon mixture into a 9-inch round having sides at least an inch high. Bake. Turn off heat and allow to dry in oven for 10 to 15 minutes. Cool slightly before removing from pan.

Lemon Filling

2 tablespoons all-purpose flour	¼ cup lemon juice
1 cup sugar	4 egg yolks, beaten
⅓ teaspoon salt	¼ teaspoon almond extract
¼ cup water	2 cups heavy cream

Mix flour, sugar, and salt. Add water and lemon juice. Stir until smooth. Add beaten egg yolks. Mix well. Cook over low heat until mixture is thick, stirring constantly. Remove from range; add almond extract. Chill. Whip cream until stiff. Fold half of the whipped cream into the filling. Pour into meringue shell. Top with remainder of whipped cream. Let stand 24 hours in refrigerator before serving. Serves 8-10.

ONE-CRUST PIES BAKED IN THE SHELL

APPLE CHEESE PIE

9-inch pie plate . . . Preheated oven—375° F. . . . Baking time—50-60 minutes

Sweet pastry for one-crust pie (page 368)

6 tart apples, peeled and cored	½ cup thick sour cream
⅔ cup sugar	½ cup snappy cheese, finely
2 tablespoons all-purpose flour	grated
¼ teaspoon cinnamon	

Line pie plate with sweet pastry. Cut apples in eighths. Arrange apples in pastry-lined pie plate. Mix sugar, flour, cinnamon, and sour cream together. Pour mixture over apples. Sprinkle grated cheese over apples. Bake. Serves 6.

APPLE PIE DE LUXE

9-inch pie plate . . . Preheated oven—400° F. . . . Baking time—50-60 minutes

Pastry for one-crust pie (page 365)

6-7 tart apples, peeled and cored	2 tablespoons butter or
⅔ cup granulated sugar	margarine
1 teaspoon cinnamon	

Line pie plate with pastry. Cut apples in eighths. Arrange apples in pastry-lined pie plate. Mix sugar and cinnamon together. Pour over apples. Dot with butter or margarine. Cover top with crumb topping (below). Bake. Serves 6.

Crumb Topping

½ cup butter or margarine	1 cup all-purpose flour, sifted
½ cup brown sugar	before measuring

Cream butter or margarine and brown sugar together. Cut in flour.

TREAT: This pie is delicious when served slightly cool with a topping of ice cream, or with plenty of coffee cream or top milk.

BERRY PIE SUPREME

9-inch pie plate . . . Preheated oven—400° F. . . . Baking time—40-50 minutes

Pastry for one-crust pie (page 365)

4 cups fresh berries	¼ teaspoon salt
1 cup sugar	½ teaspoon cinnamon
4 tablespoons all-purpose flour	1 cup top milk or cream

Line pie plate with pastry. Add berries. Mix together the sugar, flour, salt, and cinnamon. Add cream and stir vigorously. Pour over berries. Bake. Serve slightly warm. Serves 6.

BUTTERMILK PIE

9-inch pie plate . . . Preheated oven—400° F. . . . Baking time—30-40 minutes

Pastry for one-crust pie (page 365)

1 cup sugar	Grated rind of 1 lemon
2 tablespoons all-purpose flour	¼ teaspoon salt
2 tablespoons softened butter or margarine	1½ cups buttermilk
3 egg yolks, beaten	3 egg whites for meringue (page 370)
2 tablespoons lemon juice	

Line pie plate with pastry. Combine all ingredients in order given, except the 3 egg whites for the meringue. Pour into unbaked pastry. Bake. Remove pie from oven and cool. Cover with meringue. Brown. Serves 6.

BUTTERSCOTCH SOUR-CREAM PIE

9-inch pie plate . . . Preheated oven—425° F. and 350° F. . . . Baking time—10 minutes at 425° F.; 30 minutes at 350° F.

Pastry for one-crust pie (page 365)

3 egg yolks	1 tablespoon butter, melted
1 cup thick sour cream	1 teaspoon vanilla
1 cup brown sugar	3 egg whites for meringue (page 370)
⅛ teaspoon salt	
1 tablespoon all-purpose flour	

Line pie plate with pastry. Beat egg yolks and add sour cream. Blend the brown sugar, salt, and flour, then add to beaten egg yolk and sour cream mixture. Add melted butter and vanilla. Turn into unbaked pastry. Bake 10 minutes at 425° F., then remainder of time at 350° F. Cool before covering with meringue. Brown. Serves 6.

CHESS PIE

9-inch pie plate . . . Preheated oven—350° F. . . . Baking time—50-60 minutes

Pastry for one-crust pie (page 365)

1¼ cups raisins	1 teaspoon vanilla
2 cups boiling water	¼ cup thick cream
1 cup sugar	1 cup nut meats, chopped
½ cup butter or margarine	½ cup dates, chopped (optional)
3 eggs, unbeaten	

Line pie plate with pastry. Soak raisins in boiling water for 30 minutes. Drain well on absorbent paper. Beat sugar and butter or margarine together until light and fluffy. Add whole eggs, one at a time, beating briskly after each egg has been added. Add vanilla, cream, nut meats, raisins, and dates. Pour into unbaked pastry. Bake. Serves 6.

COTTAGE CHEESE PIE

2 8-inch pie plates . . . Preheated oven—350° F. . . . Baking time—50-60 minutes

Pastry for double-crust pie (page 366)

1 pound dry cottage cheese	¼ teaspoon salt
1 can (14 ounces) evaporated milk	1 teaspoon vanilla
	½ cup seedless raisins
4 eggs, beaten	¼ teaspoon nutmeg
¾ cup granulated sugar	

Line pie plates with pastry. Mix cottage cheese, milk, eggs, sugar, salt, and vanilla together and force through a sieve. Add raisins. Pour in unbaked pastry shells. Sprinkle with nutmeg. Bake. Serves 10-12.

TRICK: If you have only 1 9-inch pie plate, use that. There will be enough filling for 2 custard cups. Set cups into pan containing hot water and bake the same as pie. Excellent dessert for children.

CUSTARD PIE

9-inch pie plate . . . Preheated oven—450° F. and 325° F. . . . Baking time—10 minutes at 450° F.; 25-30 minutes at 325° F.

Pastry for one-crust pie (page 365)

4 eggs, slightly beaten	2½ cups milk
½ cup sugar	1 teaspoon vanilla
½ teaspoon salt	¼ teaspoon nutmeg

Line pie plate with pastry. Beat eggs slightly; add sugar and salt. Next add milk and vanilla. Pour into unbaked pastry-lined shell and sprinkle top with nutmeg. Bake, remembering to reduce heat after first 10 minutes of baking, or your pie will curdle. Serves 6.

TRICK: The best way to tell when a custard pie is done is to insert a silver knife at the edge of the pie. If it comes out clean, remove pie, even though center may be slightly soft. The center will finish cooking after pie has been removed. Overcooking also causes a custard pie to curdle.

TREAT: For a delicious coconut custard pie, sprinkle ½ cup coconut over top before putting in oven to bake.

LEMON SPONGE PIE

9-inch pie plate . . . Preheated oven—425° F. and 325° F. . . . Baking time—10 minutes at 425° F.; 25-30 minutes at 325° F.

2 tablespoons softened butter or margarine	5 tablespoons lemon juice Grated rind of 1 lemon
1 cup granulated sugar	3 egg yolks
4 tablespoons all-purpose flour	1½ cups milk
¼ teaspoon salt	3 egg whites

Line pie plate with pastry. Cream butter or margarine with sugar. Add flour, salt, lemon juice, and rind and stir until ingredients are thoroughly blended. Add the well-beaten egg yolks, which have been mixed with the milk. Lastly add the stiffly beaten egg whites. Pour into unbaked pastry-lined pie plate. Bake, being sure to turn the heat back to 325° F., after 10 minutes of baking. Otherwise, the pie will curdle. Serves 6.

TRICK: You may bake this same filling in a greased casserole without pastry, if you wish.

OH-SO-GOOD PIE

9-inch pie plate . . . Preheated oven—350° F. . . . Baking time—45-50 minutes

Pastry for one-crust pie (page 365)

3 eggs, beaten	2 teaspoons vinegar
1 cup sugar	1 teaspoon vanilla
1 teaspoon cinnamon	1 cup raisins, chopped
½ teaspoon cloves	¾ cup pecan meats, chopped

Line pie plate with pastry. Beat eggs slightly, then gradually add sugar, and beat vigorously. Add remaining ingredients to egg mixture. Pour into unbaked pastry shell. Bake. Serves 6.

PEACH PIE SUPREME

9-inch pie plate . . . Preheated oven—400° F. . . . Baking time—50-60 minutes

Pastry for one-crust pie (page 365)

4 cups fresh peaches, sliced	Dash of salt
1 cup sugar	1 cup cream
4 tablespoons all-purpose flour	4 drops vanilla

Arrange sliced peaches in pastry-lined pie plate. Mix sugar, flour, and salt. Stir in cream and vanilla. Pour over peaches. Bake. If peaches are very juicy, use only ¾ cup cream. Serves 6-7.

PECAN PIE

9-inch pie plate . . . Preheated oven—350° F. . . . Baking time—50-60 minutes

Pastry for one-crust pie (page 365)

¾ cup granulated sugar	1 teaspoon vanilla
1 cup dark corn sirup	1 cup pecan meats, coarsely
3 eggs, slightly beaten	broken
4 tablespoons butter or margarine	

Line pie plate with pastry. Boil sugar and sirup together for about 2 minutes. Pour slowly over slightly beaten eggs, stirring vigorously. Add butter or margarine, vanilla, and nut meats. Pour into unbaked pastry-lined pie plate. Bake. Serves 6-8.

PINEAPPLE CUSTARD PIE

9-inch pie plate . . . Preheated oven—400° F. and 325° F. . . . Baking time—10 minutes at 400° F.; 50 minutes at 325° F.

Pastry for one-crust pie (page 365)

⅓ cup sugar	½ cup sugar
1 tablespoon cornstarch	1 teaspoon salt
1 can (9 ounces) crushed pineapple, juice and all	2 eggs
	½ cup milk
1 package (3 ounces) cream cheese	½ teaspoon vanilla
	¼ cup pecan meats, chopped

Line pie plate with pastry. Blend first three ingredients. Place in saucepan and cook over low heat until mixture is thick and clear. Cool. Blend cream cheese, sugar, and salt. Add eggs, one at a time, beating well after each egg has been added. Blend in milk and vanilla. Spread cooled pineapple mixture over bottom of un-baked pastry-lined pie plate. Pour cream cheese mixture over pineapple and sprinkle pecans over top. Bake. Be sure to watch temperature and time on this pie. Bake at 400° F. only 10 minutes, then reduce heat to 325° F. Serves 6-7.

PLUM PIE

9-inch pie plate . . . Preheated oven—375° F. . . . Baking time—
  30-40 minutes

1 recipe sweet pastry (page 368)

4 cups blue plums, peeled	3 tablespoons heavy cream
1½ cups sugar	3 egg whites for meringue
1 teaspoon cinnamon	(page 370)
3 egg yolks	

Line pie plate with sweet pastry. Peel plums, cut in half, remove pit, and lay in parallel rows on top of pastry. Mix sugar and cinnamon together, beat egg yolks, and add to cream. Then add egg yolk mixture to sugar and cinnamon. Pour over plums. Bake. Remove from oven, cool. Cover with meringue, return to oven, and brown meringue. Serves 6-7.

PUMPKIN PIE

9-inch pie plate . . . Preheated oven—450° F. . . . Baking time—
  10 minutes at 450° F.; 30 minutes at 350° F.

Pastry for one-crust pie (page 365)

½ cup brown sugar	4 egg yolks or 2 whole eggs
1 tablespoon all-purpose flour	1½ cups milk (part light cream or
½ teaspoon salt	evaporated milk makes
½ teaspoon ginger	this filling richer)
1 teaspoon cinnamon	2 tablespoons sorghum
1½ cups strained or canned	molasses
pumpkin	

Line pie plate with pastry. Mix all dry ingredients. Blend in remaining ingredients. Mix thoroughly. Pour into unbaked pastry-lined pie plate. Bake, paying particular attention to the baking temperatures and times given above. Be sure to turn heat back to 350° F. after 10 minutes' baking at 450° F. Serves 5-6.

RHUBARB CUSTARD PIE

9-inch pie plate . . . Preheated oven—400° F. . . . Baking time—
50-60 minutes

Pastry for one-crust pie (page 365)

3 cups rhubarb, cut in 1-inch pieces	3 tablespoons all-purpose flour
2 eggs, beaten	¼ teaspoon salt
2 tablespoons whole milk	¼ teaspoon nutmeg
1½ cups sugar	1 tablespoon butter or margarine

Line pie plate with pastry. Place rhubarb in bowl. Combine beaten
eggs with milk, sugar, flour, salt, nutmeg, and mix with rhubarb.
Pour into unbaked pastry-lined pie plate. Dot butter or margarine
over top. May be covered with lattice top, or leave uncovered, or
top with crumb topping (see apple pie de luxe, page 372). Bake
Serves 6.

SOUR-CREAM PIE

9-inch pie plate . . . Preheated oven—350° F. . . . Baking time—
50-60 minutes

Pastry for one-crust pie (page 365)

3 eggs, beaten	2½ teaspoons cinnamon
1½ tablespoons all-purpose flour	½ teaspoon cloves
1 cup sugar	1⅓ cups thick sour cream
½ teaspoon salt	1 cup seedless raisins

Line pie plate with pastry. Beat eggs until light and fluffy. Mix
flour, sugar, salt, and spices together and add to egg mixture,
blending well. Fold in the cream and raisins. Pour into unbaked
pastry-lined pie plate. Bake. Serves 6.

ONE-CRUST PIES IN BAKED SHELLS

ALMOND SPONGE PIE

8-inch pie plate . . . Preheated oven—325° F. . . . Baking time—
30-40 minutes

1 baked pastry shell

2 tablespoons butter or margarine	3 egg yolks
2 teaspoons lemon juice	½ teaspoon salt
Grated rind of 1 lemon	½ cup almonds, chopped
¾ cup sugar	3 egg whites

Bake pastry shell according to directions on page 365. Cool. Cream butter or margarine with lemon juice and rind. Add sugar gradually, beating until thoroughly blended. Beat egg yolks with salt. Add almonds. Combine butter or margarine mixture with egg yolk mixture. Beat egg whites until stiff and fold into mixture, blending thoroughly. Pour into baked pastry shell. Bake. Insert a knife in edge of pie, and when it comes out clean, the pie is done. Serves 5-6.

BUTTERSCOTCH CHIFFON PIE

9-inch pie plate

1 baked pastry shell

2 teaspoons unflavored gelatin	1 cup scalded milk
¼ cup cold water	½ teaspoon vanilla
3 tablespoons butter or margarine	¼ teaspoon salt
1 cup firmly packed brown sugar	4 egg whites
4 egg yolks	¼ cup granulated sugar

Bake pastry shell according to directions on page 365. Cool. Dissolve gelatin in the cold water. Melt butter or margarine in small saucepan; add brown sugar and allow to simmer until it begins to turn brown. Beat egg yolks and add slowly to scalded milk, then pour sugar and butter or margarine mixture into hot milk and place over low heat. Cook, stirring frequently until it has a custard consistency. Add gelatin. Cool. Add vanilla. Add salt to egg whites and beat until stiff. Fold in granulated sugar. Pour into baked pastry shell. Chill. Serves 6-8.

CHOCOLATE CREAM PIE

9-inch pie plate

1 baked pastry shell

1½ cups sugar	3 egg yolks
½ teaspoon salt	1 tablespoon butter or margarine
2½ tablespoons cornstarch	1½ teaspoons vanilla
1 tablespoon all-purpose flour	3 egg whites for meringue (page 370)
3 cups milk	
3 squares unsweetened chocolate, cut fine, grated, or melted over hot water	

Bake pastry shell according to directions on page 365. Cool.
Blend together in a saucepan the sugar, salt, cornstarch, and flour.
Gradually stir in the milk to which the chocolate has been added.
Cook over medium heat, stirring constantly until mixture thickens.
Remove from heat. Stir a portion of this hot mixture over the
beaten egg yolks, stirring briskly. Then blend into hot mixture,
return to heat, and continue cooking over low heat until thick,
stirring constantly. Remove from heat. Add butter or margarine
and vanilla. Cool. Pour into baked pastry shell. Top with meringue.
Serves 6-8.

COCONUT BANANA CREAM PIE

9-inch pie plate . . . Preheated oven—375° F. . . . Baking time—10
   minutes

3 tablespoons softened butter or   1 box instant vanilla pudding
   margarine   2 bananas
2 packages shredded coconut

Pat softened butter or margarine evenly on bottom and sides of
pie plate. Reserve ½ cup coconut from the two packages, then pat
the remainder evenly over the sides and bottom of pie plate. Press
the coconut firmly into the greased pie plate. Place the ½ cup of
coconut in a small shallow pan and brown it while the coconut
crust is baking. Remove from oven and cool. Prepare the instant
vanilla pudding while the shell is cooling. Fill shell and place in
refrigerator until ready to use. Just before serving, slice bananas
and arrange around edge of pie with a few slices in the center.
Fill remaining space with ½ cup browned coconut. Serves 6-8.

COCONUT CREAM PIE

9-inch pie plate

1 baked pastry shell

   ½ cup sugar   3 egg yolks, beaten
   5 tablespoons all-purpose flour   1 teaspoon vanilla
   ⅛ teaspoon salt   1 cup shredded coconut
   ¼ cup cold milk   3 egg whites for meringue
   1½ cups scalded milk   (page 370)

Bake pastry shell according to directions on page 365. Cool. Blend
sugar, flour, and salt with the cold milk. Add to scalded milk,

stirring constantly. Cook over low heat until thickened. Add beaten egg yolks. Stir thoroughly. Remove from heat. Add vanilla and coconut. Cool. Pour into baked pastry shell. Cover with meringue. Serves 6.

CRANBERRY CHIFFON PIE

8-inch pie plate

1 baked pastry shell

1 envelope unflavored gelatin	1 teaspoon lemon rind, grated
¼ cup cold water	2 teaspoons lemon juice
1 can jellied cranberry sauce	2 egg whites
⅛ teaspoon salt	2 tablespoons granulated sugar

Bake pastry shell according to directions on page 365. Cool. Place gelatin in custard cup. Add cold water. Place custard cup in pan of hot water and heat until gelatin has dissolved. Add to jellied cranberry sauce which has been crushed with a fork. Add salt, lemon rind, and lemon juice. Chill until mixture begins to set. Beat egg whites until stiff and beat in sugar. Fold into cranberry mixture. Pour filling into baked pastry shell and chill until firm. Top with whipped cream, if desired. Serves 6-8.

EGGNOG PIE

9-inch pie plate

1 baked pastry shell

1½ teaspoons unflavored gelatin	2 tablespoons milk
2 tablespoons cold water	3 egg whites
3 egg yolks	½ cup heavy cream, whipped
⅔ cup sugar	2-4 tablespoons rum (optional)
⅛ teaspoon salt	1 teaspoon nutmeg
1 teaspoon vanilla	

Bake pastry shell according to directions on page 365. Cool. Soak gelatin in cold water. Beat egg yolks, add ⅓ cup of the sugar, salt, vanilla, and milk. Cook over very low heat until thickened. Add gelatin to hot custard mixture. Stir until completely dissolved. Beat egg whites until stiff but not dry; gradually beat in other ⅓ cup of sugar. Fold the custard mixture into the egg whites. Set aside to cool. Fold in whipped cream and rum. Pour into baked pastry shell. Sprinkle top with nutmeg and place in refrigerator until firm. Serves 6-8.

LEMON PIE

9-inch pie plate

1 baked pastry shell

1½ cups sugar	4 egg yolks
4 tablespoons all-purpose flour	⅓ cup lemon juice
4 tablespoons cornstarch	Grated rind of 2 lemons
½ teaspoon salt	4 egg whites for meringue
2 cups boiling water	(page 370)

Bake pastry shell according to directions on page 365. Cool. Mix sugar, flour, cornstarch, and salt together. Add to boiling water, stirring constantly, and cook over low heat until mixture is thickened and transparent in color. Add beaten egg yolks, stir well. Remove from heat. Add lemon juice and rind. Cool. Pour lemon filling into baked pastry shell. Make meringue of the 4 egg whites and cover top of pie. Serves 6-8.

TREAT: Take 2 generous tablespoons of the meringue and fold into the lemon custard mixture before pouring mixture in pastry shell. This makes a fluffy filling. Then proceed with remaining meringue according to directions.

LEMON CHIFFON PIE

9-inch pie plate

1 baked pastry shell

1 package lemon-flavored gelatin	¼ cup sugar
1 cup boiling water	¼ cup lemon juice
¼ teaspoon salt	4 egg whites
4 egg yolks, beaten	¼ cup sugar

Bake pastry shell according to directions on page 365. Cool. Dissolve gelatin in boiling water, add salt. Beat egg yolks with sugar until light and fluffy. Gradually add hot gelatin mixture, stirring constantly. Add lemon juice. Chill until partially set. Beat egg whites until stiff and carefully fold in sugar. Be sure the sugar has all dissolved. Add to partially set gelatin mixture and pour into baked pastry shell. Chill until firm enough to cut. Serves 8-10.

LEMON LUSCIOUS PIE
9-inch pie plate
1 baked pastry shell

4 tablespoons lemon juice	3 egg yolks
4 tablespoons water	¼ teaspoon salt
25 marshmallows	3 egg whites

Bake pastry shell according to directions on page 365. Cool. Combine lemon juice and water and place in saucepan. Add marshmallows which have been cut in small pieces. Cook over low heat until marshmallows have dissolved. When marshmallows have completely melted, add beaten egg yolks. Cook over low heat until mixture has thickened, stirring constantly. Cool. Add salt to egg whites and beat until stiff. Fold egg whites into marshmallow mixture. Pour into baked pastry shell. Chill in refrigerator. May be served with whipped cream. Serves 6-8.

TRICK: To cut marshmallows easily, dip kitchen scissors in boiling water. The marshmallows will not stick to the hot metal.

MAGIC LEMON PIE
8-inch pie plate

1 baked graham cracker crust	2 egg yolks
1 can sweetened condensed milk	2 egg whites
½ cup lemon juice	2 tablespoons sugar
Grated rind of 1 lemon	

Bake graham cracker crust according to directions on page 369. Cool. Reserve a few of the graham cracker crumbs to sprinkle over top of pie. Blend together condensed milk, lemon juice, grated rind, and egg yolks which have been slightly beaten. Beat egg whites until stiff, and to them add the sugar. Fold egg whites into the first mixture. Pour into baked pastry shell. Chill before serving. Serves 6.

PINEAPPLE CHIFFON PIE
8-inch pie plate
1 baked pastry shell

1 tablespoon unflavored gelatin	½ teaspoon salt
½ cup cold water	¾ cup sugar
1 cup unsweetened pineapple juice	3 egg yolks, beaten
1 tablespoon lemon juice	3 egg whites
	½ cup heavy cream, whipped

Bake pastry according to directions on page 365. Cool. Soften gelatin in cold water. Combine pineapple juice, lemon juice, salt, and sugar and heat until sugar has dissolved, stirring occasionally. Add softened gelatin to hot pineapple mixture. Add beaten egg yolks and mix thoroughly. Chill until partially set. Beat egg whites and fold into chilled mixture. Whip the cream and fold into mixture. Pour into baked shell. Chill until ready to serve. Serves 6-8.

NESSELRODE PIE

9-inch pie plate
1 baked pastry shell

1 tablespoon unflavored gelatin	1 teaspoon lemon rind, grated
¼ cup cold milk	1 tablespoon maraschino cherry juice
1 cup scalded milk	
3 egg yolks	4 maraschino cherries, cut in small pieces
⅓ cup raisins, cut fine	
¼ cup blanched almonds, slivered and toasted	¼ teaspoon salt
	3 egg whites
1 cup macaroons, broken in small pieces	½ cup sugar

Bake pastry according to directions on page 365. Cool. Soften gelatin in cold milk, then add to scalded milk. Beat egg yolks slightly. Add gelatin mixture to egg yolks and cook over low heat until mixture coats a silver spoon. Stir constantly. Add raisins, almonds, macaroons, lemon rind, maraschino cherry juice and cherries, and salt. Chill until partially set. Beat egg whites until stiff, add sugar, and continue beating until sugar has dissolved. Fold in gelatin mixture. Pour into baked pastry shell. Chill until firm. Serves 8-10.

PUMPKIN CHIFFON PIE

9-inch pie plate
1 baked pastry shell

1 package prepared butterscotch pudding	½ teaspoon cinnamon
	¼ teaspoon salt
¼ teaspoon ginger	1¼ cups milk
½ teaspoon nutmeg	1¾ cups canned pumpkin

Bake pastry shell according to directions on page 365. Cool. Place butterscotch pudding in saucepan. Add spices and salt. Gradually add milk and cook over low heat, stirring frequently. As soon as mixture has thickened, remove from heat. Add pumpkin and stir. Pour into baked pastry shell. Cool. Serves 6-8.

RAISIN MERINGUE PIE

9-inch pie plate

1 baked pastry shell

1½ cups raisins	2 cups boiling water
1 cup sugar	4 tablespoons orange juice
4 tablespoons cornstarch	1 teaspoon orange rind, grated
½ teaspoon salt	3 egg yolks, beaten
1 tablespoon butter or margarine	3 egg whites for meringue (page 370)

Bake pastry shell according to directions on page 365. Cool. Grind or chop raisins medium fine. Combine sugar, cornstarch, salt and mix well. Add butter or margarine. Add mixture to boiling water, cooking over low heat and stirring frequently. Cook until mixture is clear. Add orange juice, rind, and chopped raisins. Bring to boiling point, stirring constantly. Mix small amount of this mixture to beaten egg yolks, then stir into hot mixture, and allow mixture to come to a boil. Remove from heat. Cool. Pour into baked pastry shell. Cover with meringue. Serves 6-8.

STRAWBERRY PIE

9-inch pie plate

1 baked pastry shell

1 teaspoon unflavored gelatin	2 tablespoons cornstarch
2 tablespoons cold water	4 tablespoons lemon juice
1 quart strawberries	1 cup heavy cream, whipped
1 cup sugar	

Bake pastry shell according to directions on page 365. Cool. Soak gelatin in cold water until softened. Wash berries before hulling, saving the best ones for garnishing top. Hull remainder. Put half the berries into a saucepan with sugar and crush them, using a pastry blender or potato masher. Combine cornstarch with lemon juice, add to strawberry mixture. Cook over low heat, stirring constantly until mixture has thickened and becomes transparent in color. Add softened gelatin to hot mixture. Stir briskly. Cool. Now add remaining berries which have been cut in half. Stir these berries in gently, using a fork so as not to crush the berries. Pour into baked pastry shell. Chill in refrigerator. Just before serving, whip the cream and spread over top of pie. Garnish with berries which you selected earlier. Serves 6-8.

RAISIN SOUR-CREAM MERINGUE PIE

9-inch pie plate

1 baked pastry shell

1½ cups raisins	1 cup sour cream
½ cup sugar	3 egg yolks
2 tablespoons cornstarch	⅓ cup milk
½ teaspoon salt	3 egg whites for meringue
1½ teaspoons cinnamon	(page 370)

Bake pastry shell according to directions on page 365. Cool. Rinse and drain raisins. Combine sugar, cornstarch, salt, and cinnamon. Mix thoroughly. Add sour cream and raisins. Stir until well blended. Cook over low heat, stirring constantly, until thickened. Remove from heat. Beat egg yolks, add to milk, then add to hot mixture. Stir briskly. Return to heat and cook about 1 minute longer, or until mixture has thickened nicely. Cool. Pour into baked pastry shell. Cover with meringue. Serves 6-8.

STRAWBERRY CHIFFON PIE

9-inch pie plate

1 baked crumb shell

2 cups strawberries, sliced	1 tablespoon lemon juice
¾ cup sugar	⅛ teaspoon salt
1 tablespoon unflavored gelatin	½ cup evaporated milk, whipped
¼ cup cold water	(see page 247)
½ cup boiling water	

Bake crumb shell according to directions on page 369. Cool. Combine berries and sugar. Let stand 20 minutes. Soften gelatin in cold water. When gelatin has softened, dissolve in boiling water. Add lemon juice and salt to gelatin mixture. Carefully stir in strawberries. Cool until partially thickened. Whip evaporated milk and fold into cooled strawberry mixture. Pour into baked crumb shell. Some of the crumbs from the pastry shell may be saved and sprinkled over top of pie, or it may be garnished with whole berries. Place in refrigerator. Serves 6.

DOUBLE-CRUST PIES

APPLE PIE

9-inch pie plate . . . Preheated oven—425° F. . . . Baking time—
45-50 minutes. Pastry for two-crust pie (page 366)

6 to 7 tart apples	1 teaspoon cinnamon
4 tablespoons all-purpose flour	1 tablespoon butter or margarine
1 to 1½ cups sugar	

Make pastry for double-crust pie. Peel apples, core, then cut in
eighths. Do not slice apples too thin. Combine flour, sugar, and cinnamon. Spread about half this mixture over unbaked bottom crust.
Place apples over sugar and cinnamon mixture, then sprinkle remaining sugar and cinnamon mixture over apples. Add butter or
margarine in small bits over apples. Add top crust and seal as
shown on page 366. Bake. Serves 5-6.

TRICK: Use Dutchess or Melba apples for pies made in the
summer months. Wealthies, Rome Beauties, and Winesaps are excellent for wintertime pies.

TREAT: Try using half granulated and half brown sugar in
apple pies for a different flavor.

BERRY PIE (Fresh)

9-inch pie plate . . . Preheated oven—425° F. . . . Baking time—
45-50 minutes. Pastry for two-crust pie (page 366)

1 cup sugar	4 cups fresh berries
5 tablespoons all-purpose flour	2 tablespoons butter or
½ teaspoon cinnamon	margarine
¼ teaspoon salt	

Make pastry for double-crust pie. Mix together the sugar, flour, cinnamon, and salt and carefully blend through the berries. Better use a fork to do this, otherwise the berries are apt to be bruised. Pour into pastry-lined pie plate. Dot with butter or margarine. Add top crust and seal as shown on page 366. Bake. Serves 5-6.

TRICK: Use 4 tablespoons quick-cooking tapioca instead of all-purpose flour.

BERRY PIE (Canned)

9-inch pie plate . . . Preheated oven—425° F. . . . Baking time—30-40 minutes

Pastry for two-crust pie (page 366)

1 can (No. 2) berries, juice and all	½ teaspoon cinnamon
¾ cup sugar	1½ tablespoons butter or margarine
4 tablespoons all-purpose flour	

Make pastry for double-crust pie. Pour contents of canned berries into a saucepan. Carefully blend together the sugar, flour, and cinnamon. Stir this into the berries. Better use a fork to do the stirring. Cook over medium heat until thickened, stirring constantly. Remove from heat. Cool and pour into pastry-lined pie plate. Dot with butter or margarine. Add top crust and seal as shown on page 366. Bake. Serves 5-6.

BERRY PIE (Frozen Fruit)

Use same method as for canned berry pie, only add 1 additional tablespoon all-purpose flour. Do not thaw fruit before cooking. Place frozen fruit in saucepan, carefully blend through the sugar and flour mixture, using a fork, and start cooking over low heat. Just as soon as the fruit has thawed, turn heat to medium setting, stirring frequently with a fork. Cool. Frozen fruits are a little juicier and that is the reason they need extra flour.

BLUEBERRY PIE

9-inch pie plate . . . Preheated oven—425° F. . . . Baking time—35-45 minutes

Pastry for two-crust pie (page 366)

1 cup sugar	2 tablespoons butter or margarine
5 tablespoons all-purpose flour	2 tablespoons lemon juice
¼ teaspoon salt	
4 cups blueberries	

Make pastry for double-crust pie. Mix sugar, flour, and salt together and carefully blend through the blueberries. Pour into pastry-lined pie plate. Dot with butter or margarine. Spoon lemon juice over top. Add top crust and seal as shown on page 366. Bake. Serve slightly warm. Serves 5-6.

CHEESE APPLE PIE

9-inch pie plate . . . Preheated oven—425° F. and 350° F. . . .
  Baking time—15 minutes at 425° F.; 30-35 minutes at 350° F.

Cheese pastry for two-crust pie (page 368)

5 cups pared apples, sliced (about 6)	½ cup cheese, grated
¾ cup sugar	1 tablespoon butter

Make pastry for double-crust pie. Line pie plate with pastry. Combine all ingredients and pour into unbaked pastry. Add top crust and seal as shown on page 366. Bake. Serves 5-6.

CHERRY PIE (Fresh)

9-inch pie plate . . . Preheated oven—425° F. . . . Baking time—
  40-50 minutes

Pastry for two-crust pie (page 366)

1½ cups sugar	2 tablespoons butter or margarine
5 tablespoons all-purpose flour	
¼ teaspoon salt	4 drops almond extract
4 cups sour, pitted cherries	(optional)

Make pastry for double-crust pie. Mix sugar, flour, and salt together and carefully blend through the pitted, sour cherries. Pour into pastry-lined pie plate. Dot with butter or margarine. Drop almond extract over top. Add top crust and seal as shown on page 366. Bake. Serve slightly warm. Serves 5-6.

CHERRY PIE (Canned)

Make the same as canned berry pie (page 388).

CHERRY PIE (Frozen)

Make the same as berry pie made from frozen fruits (page 388).

DIFFERENT CHERRY PIE

9-inch greased pie plate . . . Preheated oven—325° F. . . . Total
  baking time—35 minutes

Perhaps you will enjoy doing an out-of-the-ordinary cherry pie. Here it is in all three parts:

Pastry for One Crust

½ cup butter or margarine   1 cup all-purpose flour, sifted
½ teaspoon salt   before measuring
½ cup brown sugar

Mix butter or margarine, salt, brown sugar, and flour together with
a pastry blender. Work until the mixture resembles corn meal.
Pat into pie plate, pushing some of the pastry up the sides of the
pie plate to form a shell. Bake 15 minutes.

Filling

1 cup sugar   2 cups cherries
3 tablespoons cornstarch   2 or 3 drops almond flavoring
1 cup cherry juice

Mix sugar and cornstarch together. Add cherry juice and stir until
ingredients are well blended. Fold in cherries. Cook over medium
heat, stirring constantly, until mixture thickens. Pour into hot pie
shell.

Topping

½ cup quick-cooking oatmeal,   4 tablespoons all-purpose flour
    uncooked   5 tablespoons butter or
½ cup brown sugar   margarine

Blend oatmeal, brown sugar, flour, and butter or margarine together until crumbly in appearance. Spread over top of cherry filling. Bake 20 minutes. Serves 6-8.

DEEP-DISH CHERRY PIE

1½ quart casserole . . . Preheated oven—425° F. . . . Baking time—
45-50 minutes

Pastry for one-crust pie (page 365)

1 can (No. 2) cherries, juice and   ¼ teaspoon cinnamon
    all   ¼ teaspoon salt
1 cup sugar   2 tablespoons butter or
4 tablespoons all-purpose flour   margarine

Make pastry for one-crust pie. Roll and lay aside until ready to use.
    Pour cherries into a mixing bowl. Blend sugar, flour, cinnamon,
and salt together and carefully blend through the cherries. Pour

into casserole. Dot with butter or margarine. Place crust on top, pinching edges around crust, just as for any two-crust pie. Be sure you put some openings in top crust, otherwise crust will raise off the top. Bake. This is an excellent way to make use of a small amount of leftover pie dough. Serves 4-5.

CRANBERRY PIE

9-inch pie plate . . . Preheated oven—425° F. . . . Baking time—
35-45 minutes

Pastry for two-crust pie (page 366)

3 cups cranberries, cut in half	¼ teaspoon salt
½ cup water	½ teaspoon almond extract
1¾ cups sugar	2 tablespoons butter or
5 tablespoons all-purpose flour	margarine

Make pastry for double-crust pie. Place cranberries and water in saucepan. Bring slowly to boiling point. Mix sugar with flour and salt, and when cranberry mixture is boiling, slowly add the dry ingredients, stirring constantly. Use a fork to stir the ingredients. Cook on low heat until the mixture thickens. Remove from heat, add almond extract. Cool and pour into pastry-lined pie plate. Dot with butter or margarine. Add top crust and seal as shown on page 366. Bake. Serves 5-6.

CRANBERRY AND RAISIN PIE

9-inch pie plate . . . Preheated oven—425° F. . . . Baking time—
40-50 minutes

Pastry for two-crust pie (page 366)

3 cups cranberries, cut in half	¼ teaspoon salt
1 cup seeded raisins	½ teaspoon almond extract
1 cup water	2 tablespoons butter or
1½ cups sugar	margarine
4 tablespoons all-purpose flour	

Make pastry for double-crust pie. Place cranberries, raisins, and water in saucepan and bring slowly to boiling point. Mix sugar with flour and salt, and when cranberry mixture is boiling, slowly add the dry ingredients, stirring all the time. Cook over low heat until mixture thickens. Remove from heat. Cool. Add almond flavoring. Stir. Pour into pastry-lined pie plate. Dot with butter or margarine. Add top crust and seal as shown on page 366. Bake. Serves 5-6.

ELDERBERRY PIE

9-inch pie plate . . . Preheated oven—425° F. . . . Baking time—
45-55 minutes

Pastry for two-crust pie (page 366)

3 cups elderberries
1 to 1½ cups sugar
5 tablespoons all-purpose flour
¼ teaspoon salt

½ teaspoon cinnamon
3 tablespoons lemon juice
2 tablespoons butter or
   margarine

Make pastry for double-crust pie. Carefully remove stems from elderberries. Mix the sugar, flour, salt, and cinnamon together and carefully blend through the elderberries. Better use a fork to do this so you won't mash the berries. Pour into pastry-lined pie plate. Pour the lemon juice over the berries, then dot with butter or margarine. Add top crust and seal as shown on page 366. Bake. Serve slightly warm. Serves 5-6.

GOOSEBERRY PIE

9-inch pie plate . . . Preheated oven—425° F. . . . Baking time—
45-55 minutes

Pastry for two-crust pie (page 366)

4 cups gooseberries, with stem
   and blossom end removed
1¾ cups sugar
5 tablespoons all-purpose flour

¼ teaspoon salt
2 tablespoons butter or
   margarine

Make pastry for double-crust pie. Place gooseberries in mixing bowl. Blend sugar, flour, and salt together and mix through the gooseberries. Pour into pastry-lined pie plate. Dot with butter or margarine. Add top crust and seal as shown on page 366. Bake. Serve slightly warm. Serves 5-6.

GRAPE PIE (Concord Grapes)

9-inch pie plate . . . Preheated oven—425° F. . . . Baking time—
35-45 minutes

Pastry for two-crust pie (page 366)

6 cups Concord grapes
1¼ cups sugar
4 tablespoons all-purpose flour
2 teaspoons lemon juice

½ teaspoon grated lemon rind
⅛ teaspoon salt
2 tablespoons butter or
   margarine

Make pastry for double-crust pie. Remove and save skins from grapes. Put pulp in saucepan without water and bring to full boil.

While pulp is still hot, rub through a sieve so that all seeds will be removed. Mix the strained pulp with the skins. Mix sugar, flour, lemon juice, lemon rind, and salt together. Blend carefully through the grape mixture. Pour into pastry-lined pie plate. Dot with butter or margarine. Add top crust and seal as shown on page 366. Bake. Serve slightly warm. Serves 5-6.

MINCE PIE SUPERB

9-inch pie plate . . . Preheated oven—425° F. . . . Baking time—
35-40 minutes

Pastry for two-crust pie (page 366)

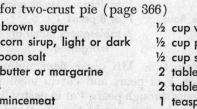

½ cup brown sugar	½ cup walnut meats, chopped
½ cup corn sirup, light or dark	½ cup pecans, chopped
½ teaspoon salt	½ cup seedless raisins
¼ cup butter or margarine	2 tablespoons orange juice
2 eggs	2 tablespoons lemon juice
½ cup mincemeat	1 teaspoon vanilla

Make pastry for double-crust pie. Combine sugar, corn sirup, salt, and butter or margarine in saucepan and slowly bring to a boil. Beat eggs, add mincemeat, nuts, raisins, fruit juices, and flavoring to beaten eggs. Pour hot sirup over egg mixture, stirring constantly. Cool. Pour into pastry-lined pie plate. Add top crust and seal as shown on page 366. Bake. Serve slightly warm.

MOCK MINCEMEAT PIE

9-inch pie plate . . . Preheated oven—425° F. . . . Baking time—
30-40 minutes

Pastry for two-crust pie (page 366)	3½ to 4 cups mock mincemeat (see below)

Make pastry for double-crust pie. Put mincemeat in pastry-lined pie plate. Add top crust and seal as shown on page 366. Bake. Serve hot or quite warm.

Mock Mincemeat

(Some people prefer this green tomato mincemeat to any other kind.)

6 pounds green tomatoes, chopped	½ pound suet, chopped fine
6 pounds tart apples, chopped	1½ tablespoons salt
2½ pounds brown sugar	1 tablespoon cloves, ground
½ pound seedless raisins	2 tablespoons cinnamon
1 pound currants	1 tablespoon nutmeg
	2 cups vinegar

Mix all ingredients in order given. Bring slowly to boiling point and simmer for 3 hours. Pour into sterilized jars. Seal and store. Makes about 6 quarts.

TRICK: Butter or margarine may be substituted for the suet.

PEAR PIE

9-inch pie plate . . . Preheated oven—425° F. . . . Baking time—
40-50 minutes

Pastry for two-crust pie (page 366)

¾ cup brown sugar	1 tablespoon lemon juice
2 tablespoons all-purpose flour	7 or 8 pears
1 teaspoon nutmeg	2 tablespoons butter or
⅛ teaspoon salt	margarine

Make pastry for double-crust pie. Mix sugar, flour, nutmeg, salt, and lemon juice together. Peel pears and cut in medium-thick slices. Blend dry ingredients through pears. Put in pastry-lined pie plate. Dot with butter or margarine. Add top crust and seal as shown on page 366. Bake. Serve slightly warm. Serves 5-6.

PEACH PIE

9-inch pie plate . . . Preheated oven—425° F. . . . Baking time—
40-50 minutes

Pastry for two-crust pie (page 366)

4 cups peaches, sliced	¼ teaspoon almond extract
¾ cup sugar	2 tablespoons butter or
4 tablespoons all-purpose flour	margarine
1 tablespoon lemon juice	

Make pastry for double-crust pie. Place sliced peaches in a mixing bowl and blend the sugar and flour, which have been mixed together, through them. Put in pastry-lined pie plate. Mix lemon juice and almond extract together and pour over the peaches. Dot with butter or margarine. Add top crust and seal as shown on page 366. Bake. Serve cold or slightly warm. Serves 5-6.

RAISIN PIE

9-inch pie plate . . . Preheated oven—425° F. . . . Baking time—
40-50 minutes. Pastry for two-crust pie (page 366)

2 cups seedless raisins	¾ cup nuts, chopped
2 cups boiling water	1 tablespoon lemon rind, grated
½ cup sugar	3 tablespoons lemon juice
3 tablespoons all-purpose flour	

Make pastry for double-crust pie. Place raisins and water in saucepan and cook until tender. Blend sugar with flour and add to raisin mixture and cook over low heat until thickened, stirring frequently. Add nuts, lemon rind, and juice. Stir. Cool and pour into pastry-lined pie plate. Add top crust and seal as shown on page 366. Bake. Serve warm. Serves 5-6.

RHUBARB PIE

9-inch pie plate . . . Preheated oven—425° F. . . . Baking time—
   40-50 minutes
Pastry for two-crust pie (page 366)

4 cups rhubarb, cut in 1-inch lengths	⅛ teaspoon salt
1¼ cups sugar	2 tablespoons butter or margarine
4½ tablespoons all-purpose flour	

Make pastry for double-crust pie. Place rhubarb in mixing bowl and blend through it the sugar, flour, and salt which have been mixed together. Put in pastry-lined pie plate. Dot with butter or margarine. Add top crust and seal as shown on page 366. Bake. Serve slightly warm. Serves 5-6.

FUDGE PIE

9-inch pie plate . . . Preheated oven—350° F. . . . Baking time—
   40-45 minutes

⅓ cup butter or margarine	¼ teaspoon salt
3 squares unsweetened chocolate	1 teaspoon vanilla
2 cups sugar	⅔ cup nut meats, chopped
	4 eggs, well beaten

Melt butter or margarine and chocolate over low heat. Beat sugar, salt, vanilla, and nuts into the eggs. Add chocolate mixture to egg mixture and blend thoroughly. Pour into greased pie plate. Bake. Cool. Before serving, top with vanilla ice cream or whipped cream. Serves 6-8.

Cakes

Years ago, the cook whose cakes always came from the oven light, fluffy, and delectable was a village heroine, very much in demand when it came time for church fairs or town picnics. But today, when modern ovens have become so completely dependable that every batch of baked goods can be uniformly successful, it is possible for every woman to be a heroine in her own kitchen. Nowadays, we cannot blame a faulty or temperamental oven if our baking fails but must admit that we ourselves have made some error in measuring or mixing. In any case, you will have no need of alibis if you follow the delicious recipes you will find in this section, which, I believe, will help make every cake a perfect cake.

Tips on Cake Baking

It's a smart idea to read your recipe over carefully, then get all ingredients out and put them on a tray. It is embarrassing to be halfway through a cake and discover you are minus something.

Measuring

Measure all ingredients accurately. Always sift flour before measuring. Be sure to use cake flour if recipe calls for it.

Possible Causes of Cake Failures

UNEVEN

Batter too stiff; uneven heat,
pan; oven too hot

HUMPED

Too much flour; oven too hot at first

TOUGH

Too little shortening or sugar;
too much flour; oven too hot

FALLEN

Too much shortening or leavening
or sugar; baked too slowly

RUNNY

Too much batter or leavening
or sugar; heat too low

BLACK BOTTOM

Darkened, warped or too deep pan

UNDERSIZED

Too little leavening; overmixed;
heat too high; pan too large

SOGGY

Heat too low; baked too slowly
or quickly; left too long in pan

The phrase "dry ingredients" means the flour, baking powder or soda, salt, etc.

Beating

Be careful not to overbeat after flour and leavening agent are added to batter.

Shortenings

Shortening is a very important ingredient in successful baking. Wherever butter or margarine is indicated in recipe, be sure to use these, because there is a reason for it. If shortening only is indicated, use whatever you prefer—butter, margarine, or any of the homogenized fats.

Utensils

Use bright, shiny pans. Discolored pans cause uneven browning. Avoid using warped pans because they will cause uneven baking.

Use the correct size pan for the batter. A cake recipe calling for 2 cups of flour should be baked in 2 8-inch round pans, 1½ inches deep. A recipe calling for 2½ to 3 cups of flour should be baked in 2 9-inch round pans, 1½ to 2 inches deep, or in 2 8-inch square pans, 2 inches deep.

Preparation of Pans

Grease cake pans thoroughly and dust lightly with flour. Shake off surplus flour before putting cake batter into pans. A clean powder puff dipped in flour is excellent for dusting cake pans.

Temperatures

Be certain oven has been preheated to correct temperature before putting cakes in to bake. Temperatures that are either too high or too low will spoil the texture. Better start preheating oven when you start mixing cake.

If glass cake dishes are used, reduce oven temperature 25° F. below temperature called for in the recipe.

If you are using an electric range, don't be a "peeping tom." Do your part accurately and your range will do the baking without assistance from you.

MOONLIGHT CAKE

10-inch tube pan . . . Preheated oven—325° F. . . . Baking time
—60-65 minutes

1 cup cake flour, sifted before measuring	10 egg whites
	1 teaspoon cream of tartar
1½ cups sugar	7 egg yolks
½ teaspoon salt	1½ teaspoons lemon extract

Sift flour five times after measuring. Sift sugar five times. Add salt
to egg whites, beat until frothy, then add cream of tartar. Continue
beating until egg whites are stiff but not dry. In another bowl beat
the egg yolks until creamy. Add to them 2 tablespoons beaten egg
whites. To whites, gradually add sugar. Combine yellow and white
mixtures. Fold in flavoring and flour. Bake. Immediately after removing from oven, invert on cake rack to cool.

TRICK: Rinse pan with cold water before putting in batter.
Cake comes out easier.

FOOLPROOF ANGEL FOOD CAKE

10-inch tube pan . . . Preheated oven—325° F. . . . Baking time
—about 65 minutes

1½ cups cake flour, sifted before measuring	½ teaspoon salt
	1½ teaspoons cream of tartar
2 cups sugar	1½ teaspoons vanilla
1½ cups egg whites	1 teaspoon almond flavoring

Sift flour once, then measure and set aside. Measure sugar and
divide into two equal parts. Add one half the sugar to the flour
and sift the two ingredients together 4 times. Sift the remaining
sugar 4 times. Do all this before starting to beat the egg whites. It
is convenient to place the sugar and flour mixture on waxed paper
until ready to use. Add the salt to egg whites, beat until foamy,
add cream of tartar, then continue beating until stiff but not dry.
Then add one half the sugar to the egg whites, 2 tablespoons at
a time. If an electric mixer is used, use low speed to do this. Use a
whisk beater if you are mixing by hand. Add the flavorings. Do not
use electric mixer from here on to add the remainder of the ingredients, but use a wire whisk egg beater. Fold in flour and sugar
mixture, adding it to egg white mixture, 2 tablespoons at a time.
Fold in with slow, careful folding strokes. Pour into ungreased pan.
Cut down through cake batter with silver knife to remove any

large air bubbles. Bake. When cake is removed from oven, invert pan on wire cake cooler until cold, then carefully remove cake from pan.

CHIFFON CAKE

10-inch tube pan or 13x9-inch oblong pan . . . Preheated oven —325° F. . . . Baking time—65-70 minutes

2¼ cups cake flour, sifted before measuring	1 cup egg whites
1½ cups sugar	½ cup cooking (salad) oil
3 teaspoons baking powder	¾ cup cold water
1 teaspoon salt	2 teaspoons lemon rind, grated
5 egg yolks, unbeaten	2 teaspoons vanilla
	½ teaspoon cream of tartar

Follow this recipe very carefully. It's a delicious cake, but it can be pretty terrible if you don't do right by it.

Sift flour, measure, then put back in sifter. Measure sugar and add to flour in sifter, also the baking powder and salt. Sift these into a bowl.

Next separate the eggs, putting 5 egg yolks in a sauce dish. (Put any leftover egg yolks in a small jar and turn to page 272 to see how to store them.) When you have a cup of egg whites, put them in a bowl and set aside. Now you are ready to proceed.

Using a spoon or rubber spatula, make a well in the center of the flour mixture. Add, in this order, the oil, egg yolks, and water, to which grated lemon rind and vanilla have been added. Beat until smooth. Add cream of tartar to egg whites and beat until they hold a *very stiff* peak. This is important and is most easily done in an electric mixer. If you are beating by hand, however, keep on beating, even though you may get tired.

Pour egg yolk mixture in thin stream over entire surface of egg whites, gently cutting and folding in with rubber spatula. Fold gently, bringing rubber spatula across bottom of bowl, up the side and over. Don't lift spatula out of mixture, but keep turning bowl and continue until egg yolk mixture and egg whites are completely blended. Do it gently and not too long, or you may break down the egg whites.

Pour mixture into ungreased angel food cake pan or oblong pan. Bake until surface springs back when lightly touched. Let hang until cold. That means, turn upside down. If cake is so high it extends above edge of cake pan, put center tube through a funnel or coke bottle to hold cake off table surface.

When cool, loosen cake from pan with knife or metal spatula. Turn pan over and hit edges sharply on table to loosen.

Delicious unfrosted or frosted, depending upon your family's likes and your own time and energy.

EGG YOLK SPONGE CAKE

9-inch tube cake pan . . . Preheated oven—350° F. . . . Baking time —45 minutes

1½ cups cake flour, sifted before measuring	6 egg yolks
2 teaspoons baking powder	1 cup sugar
½ teaspoon salt	½ cup boiling water
	1 teaspoon lemon extract

Sift flour, baking powder, and salt together. Beat egg yolks about 1 minute, then add sugar, and continue beating until thick and lemon colored. Add boiling water and lemon extract. Beat until ingredients are thoroughly blended. Add flour, all at once, and mix until well blended. For best results, this cake requires a tube pan which has been greased and lined with waxed paper. Regardless of type of baking pan used, it must always be greased and lined with waxed paper. Pour into cake pan and bake. When cake has baked, remove from pan, remove waxed paper, and cool on wire rack. An excellent way to use leftover egg yolks.

QUICK SPONGE CAKE

7x11x1½-inch oblong baking pan . . . Preheated oven—325° F. . . . Baking time—60-65 minutes

1½ cups cake flour, sifted before measuring	3 eggs
1 teaspoon baking powder	1¼ cups sifted sugar
½ teaspoon salt	½ cup cold water
	1 teaspoon vanilla

Sift flour, baking powder, salt. Beat eggs until light and fluffy. Add sugar, continue beating until mixture is thick and lemon colored. Add flour mixture, water, and vanilla, all at once. Mix until thoroughly blended. Pour into pan which has been greased and lined with waxed paper. Bake. When cake has baked, remove from pan, remove waxed paper. Cool on a wire rack.

TRICKS: Sponge cake makes a fine base for Baked Alaska (page 354).

If the family isn't dieting, you'd hunt far and wide for a better dessert than squares of sponge cake with a generous serving of whipped cream. Or try piling peaches or strawberries to make a mock shortcake.

Sponge cake does not need to be frosted.

SPONGE JELLY ROLL

10x15x½-inch jelly roll pan . . . Preheated oven—400° F. . . . Baking time—15 minutes

4 eggs	2 teaspoons baking powder
¼ teaspoon salt	1 teaspoon vanilla
1 cup granulated sugar	¼ cup hot milk
1 cup all-purpose flour, sifted before measuring	

Beat eggs and salt together until light. Add sugar and beat again. Sift flour and baking powder together and slowly add to egg mixture, blending thoroughly, but do not overmix. Add vanilla and hot milk last. Line the bottom of the jelly roll pan with greased waxed paper. Pour in batter and bake. When cake is done, turn out immediately onto towel sprinkled with sifted confectioners' sugar. Cut off crisp edges. Spread quickly and lightly with tart jelly and roll. Work quickly, or roll will crack. Whipped cream may be used instead of jelly.

PLAIN LAYER CAKE

2 9-inch round pans . . . Preheated oven—375° F. . . . Baking time —25-30 minutes

2⅔ cups cake flour, sifted before measuring	1¼ cups granulated sugar
4 teaspoons baking powder	3 eggs
¾ cup shortening	1½ teaspoons vanilla
	¾ cup sweet milk

Sift flour with baking powder. Grease cake pans and dust lightly with flour. Cream the shortening, add sugar, and beat vigorously until light and fluffy. Add the whole eggs, one at a time, beating well after the addition of each. Add vanilla to milk, then add alternately with flour to shortening mixture. Add flour first, then milk, ending with dry ingredients. Beat until smooth and thoroughly mixed. Do not overbeat. Divide evenly into two thoroughly greased and lightly floured pans. Bake. Remove from pans immediately after baking. Cool on wire cake racks.

BANANA LAYER CAKE

2 9-inch round cake pans . . . Preheated oven—375° F. . . . Baking
time—25-30 minutes

2½ cups cake flour, sifted before measuring	¼ cup thick sour milk or buttermilk
1 teaspoon soda	1 teaspoon vanilla
½ teaspoon baking powder	1¼ cups ripe bananas, mashed with potato masher, then measured
¾ cup shortening	
1½ cups sugar	
2 eggs	

Sift flour with soda and baking powder. Cream shortening, add
sugar, and cream together until light and fluffy. Add the whole
eggs, beating well after the addition of each. Add sour milk or
buttermilk and vanilla to bananas. Add the flour and banana mixture alternately to creamed shortening and sugar mixture, beginning and ending with the dry ingredients. Beat until smooth and
well blended. Do not overmix. Pour into greased and floured cake
pans. Bake. Remove from pans immediately after baking. Cool
on wire cake racks.

SPICE CAKE

8x12-inch sheet pan . . . Preheated oven—350° F. . . . Baking time—
45-50 minutes

1 cup shortening	¼ teaspoon cloves
2 cups sugar	1 teaspoon cinnamon
2 eggs	1 teaspoon allspice
3 cups all-purpose flour, sifted before measuring	2 cups buttermilk
4 teaspoons cocoa	2 teaspoons soda

Cream shortening and sugar until light and fluffy. Add eggs and
beat until thoroughly blended. Sift flour with cocoa and spices.
Add dry ingredients and buttermilk, to which the soda has been
added, to the shortening mixture. Beat only until ingredients are
well blended. Do not overbeat. Bake in well-greased and floured
pan. Remove from pan immediately. Cool on wire cake racks.

Icing for Spice Cake

6 tablespoons butter or margarine	1½ cups confectioners' sugar
½ cup brown sugar	½ teaspoon vanilla
⅓ cup milk	¼ teaspoon salt

Melt butter or margarine; add brown sugar and milk. Bring mixture to a boil and cook for 2 minutes. Remove from heat and cool. Beat in confectioners' sugar, vanilla, and salt. The texture is greatly improved by using an electric mixer.

TRICK: Use this cake for serving large groups, or for church suppers.

ONE-TWO-THREE-FOUR CAKE

2 8-inch square cake pans, or 2 9-inch round cake pans . . . Preheated oven—375° F. . . . Baking time—35-40 minutes

1 cup shortening	3 teaspoons baking powder
2 cups sugar	1 cup milk
¼ teaspoon salt	1 teaspoon vanilla
4 eggs, separated	
3 cups cake flour, sifted before measuring	

Cream shortening, sugar, and salt together until light and fluffy. Add beaten egg yolks and blend until smooth. Sift flour and baking powder together three times and add to first mixture with milk and vanilla. Fold in the stiffly beaten egg whites. Pour into greased and floured cake pans. Bake. Remove from pans immediately after baking. Cool on wire cake racks.

OLD-FASHIONED POUND CAKE

10-inch tube pan . . . Preheated oven—325° F. . . . Baking time—1¼-1½ hours

4 cups cake flour, sifted before measuring (1 pound)	2 cups sugar (1 pound)
½ teaspoon salt	10 eggs
2 cups butter (1 pound)	1 teaspoon almond extract
	1 teaspoon vanilla extract

Sift flour and salt together. Place butter and sugar in mixing bowl. Cream together until light and fluffy. Add whole eggs, one at a time. Beat thoroughly between each addition of the eggs. If an electric mixer is used, do not stop mixer while adding eggs. Add ½ the sifted flour and salt. Beat about 1 minute. Add remaining flour and flavorings. Beat about 1 minute. Use rubber spatula to collect all flour from sides of mixing bowl. Pour into a well-greased and floured tube cake pan. Bake. Remove from pan immediately after removing from oven. Cool on a cake rack.

PINEAPPLE CAKE

2 8-inch square or 2 9-inch round cake pans . . . Preheated oven—
350° F. . . . Baking time—25-30 minutes

½ cup shortening	½ teaspoon soda
1 cup sugar	½ teaspoon salt
3 eggs, separated	1 can (9 ounces) crushed
2½ cups cake flour, sifted before	pineapple
measuring	½ cup orange juice
2 teaspoons baking powder	

Cream the shortening and ¾ cup of the sugar. Add egg yolks and
beat until light. Sift dry ingredients together. Add alternately with
the pineapple and orange juice to the creamed mixture. Fold in
stiffly beaten egg whites, to which the remaining ¼ cup sugar has
been added. Pour into greased and floured pans. Bake. When
cake has baked, remove from pans immediately and cool on wire
cake racks.

WHIPPED-CREAM CAKE

2 8-inch round cake pans . . . Preheated oven—375° F. . . . Baking
time—20-25 minutes

1 cup heavy cream	1½ cups cake flour, sifted before
2 eggs	measuring
1 cup sugar	½ teaspoon salt
1 teaspoon vanilla	2 teaspoons baking powder

Whip cream until firm. Add eggs, one at a time. Beat until light
and fluffy. Add sugar, beat again. Add vanilla. Sift flour with salt
and baking powder. Fold in flour. Pour into well-greased pans,
lined with greased waxed paper. Bake. When cake has baked, remove immediately from pans and cool on wire cake racks.

BLACK WALNUT CAKE

2 8-inch square cake pans . . . Preheated oven—375° F. . . . Baking
time—25-30 minutes

1½ cups brown sugar	½ teaspoon salt
½ cup shortening	1 cup thick sour milk
2 eggs	1 teaspoon soda
2 cups cake flour, sifted before	1 teaspoon vanilla
measuring	⅔ cup black walnuts, chopped
1 teaspoon baking powder	

Cream sugar and shortening. Add eggs and beat well. Sift flour, baking powder, and salt. Add dry ingredients and sour milk, to which soda has been added, to sugar and shortening. Add vanilla and black walnuts. Grease and flour cake pans and bake. Remove from pans as soon as cake has baked and cool on wire cake racks.

LADY BALTIMORE CAKE

2 9-inch square cake pans . . . Preheated oven—350° F. . . . Baking time—30-35 minutes

¾ cup shortening	½ cup milk
2 cups sugar	½ cup water
3 cups cake flour, sifted before	½ teaspoon vanilla
measuring	½ teaspoon lemon extract
¾ teaspoon salt	6 egg whites, stiffly beaten
3 teaspoons baking powder	

Thoroughly cream shortening and sugar. Add sifted dry ingredients alternately with milk and water. Beat smooth after each addition. Add flavorings. Fold in stiffly beaten egg whites. Bake in greased and floured cake pans. Remove from pans as soon as baked and cool on wire cake racks. Put layers together with Lady Baltimore filling (below) and frost with two thirds the recipe for seven-minute frosting.

Lady Baltimore Filling

Make seven-minute frosting. To ⅓ of the frosting add ¼ cup each chopped figs, seeded raisins, candied cherries, and chopped pecans and place on top of bottom layer. Then place second layer over bottom layer and finish icing cake with remainder of seven-minute frosting.

CUPCAKES

24 muffin cups or tins . . . Preheated oven—375° F. . . . Baking time —15-20 minutes

1 cup sugar	3 teaspoons baking powder
⅔ cup shortening	¼ teaspoon salt
2 eggs	½ cup milk
2 cups cake flour, sifted before	1 can moist coconut
measuring	½ teaspoon vanilla

Cream sugar and shortening together until light and fluffy. Add eggs and beat thoroughly. Sift dry ingredients together and add alternately with the milk to the creamed mixture. Fold in one half of the can of coconut. Add vanilla. Pour batter into well-greased muffin tins. (You can use paper baking cups. If so, place on cooky sheet or flat pan for easy handling. Do not remove cake from paper cups until ready to eat.) Sprinkle remaining coconut over tops of cakes before baking. Bake. Remove from pans as soon as baked and cool on wire cake racks.

ONE-EGG CUPCAKES

Muffin cups or tins . . . Preheated oven—375° F. . . . Baking time— 20 minutes

¼ cup shortening	1¼ teaspoons baking powder
½ cup sugar	⅛ teaspoon salt
1 egg	½ teaspoon vanilla
1 cup cake flour, sifted before measuring	¼ cup milk

Cream shortening and sugar; add egg and beat well. Add flour, sifted with baking powder and salt, alternately with vanilla and milk. Fill greased muffin cups ½ full. Bake. Remove from pans as soon as baked and cool on wire cake racks. Makes about 12 cupcakes.

TREATS: Add ½ cup chocolate bits, raisins, or nuts to the above recipe.

Sprinkle tops of cupcakes with a mixture of 1½ tablespoons sugar and ½ teaspoon cinnamon.

Put a seeded, cooked prune on top of each cupcake.

1 teaspoon grated orange rind or ¾ teaspoon lemon rind may be used instead of vanilla.

HURRY-UP CAKE

2 8-inch round cake pans . . . Preheated oven—350° F. . . . Baking time—25-30 minutes

2 cups cake flour, sifted before measuring	½ cup shortening
1¼ cups sugar	1 cup sweet milk
3½ teaspoons baking powder	1 teaspoon vanilla
1 teaspoon salt	¼ teaspoon lemon extract
	3 egg whites, unbeaten

Sift flour, sugar, baking powder, and salt into mixing bowl of electric mixer. Add shortening. Add ⅔ cup of the milk and the flavorings. Beat until perfectly smooth (about 100 strokes by hand;

or, if an electric mixer is used, beat on "Medium" speed for about 2 minutes). Add unbeaten egg whites and remaining milk and beat until well blended, or for same period of time or strokes as given above. Pour into greased and floured pans and bake. Remove from pans immediately after baking. Cool on wire cake racks.

TRICK: Make cupcakes with this hurry-up cake recipe. Fill greased muffin cups or tins about ½ full. Bake 15-18 minutes at 350° F. Makes about 18 cupcakes.

GINGERBREAD

10x14-inch pan . . . Preheated oven—350° F. . . . Baking time—40-45 minutes

2½ cups all-purpose flour, sifted before measuring	½ teaspoon cloves
	½ cup shortening
1½ teaspoons soda	½ cup sugar
½ teaspoon salt	1 egg
1 teaspoon ginger	1 cup sorghum molasses
1 teaspoon cinnamon	1 cup hot water

Sift flour with soda, salt, and spices. Cream shortening and sugar until light and fluffy. Add beaten egg and molasses. Add sifted dry ingredients and hot water alternately. Beat until smooth. Pour into well-greased, floured pan. Bake. This gingerbread may be reheated to serve hot at dinner.

SPICE CAKE WITH BROILED COCONUT ICING

9x12x2-inch pan . . . Preheated oven—350° F. . . . Baking time—45-50 minutes

2½ cups cake flour, sifted before measuring	2 teaspoons baking powder
	½ teaspoon soda
¼ teaspoon each of mace, cloves, nutmeg	½ cup shortening
	1 cup brown sugar, firmly packed
½ teaspoon allspice	
1 teaspoon cinnamon	2 eggs
½ teaspoon salt	1 cup thick sour milk

Sift flour with spices, salt, baking powder, and soda. Cream shortening and sugar together until light and fluffy. Add eggs, beating well after each addition. Add sifted dry ingredients alternately with thick sour milk to creamed shortening and sugar mixture. Beat thoroughly. Bake in greased and floured pan. Let cake stand in pan while preparing icing.

Broiled Coconut Icing

4 tablespoons butter or   2 tablespoons milk
   margarine   1 cup coconut, shredded
½ cup brown sugar, firmly packed

Combine butter or margarine, brown sugar, and milk in saucepan.
Bring to a boil. Remove from range and add coconut. Pour over
warm cake. Spread evenly. Turn oven control to "Broil" position
and broil slowly until a golden brown. This takes two or three
minutes.

APPLESAUCE CAKE

8-inch square pan . . . Preheated oven—350° F. . . . Baking time—
45-60 minutes

½ cup shortening   ¼ teaspoon salt
1½ cups sugar   1 teaspoon baking powder
2 eggs, beaten   ½ teaspoon soda
1 cup thick, unsweetened   1 teaspoon cinnamon
   applesauce   ½ teaspoon cloves
2 cups all-purpose flour, sifted   1 cup seeded raisins, chopped
   before measuring

Thoroughly cream shortening and sugar; add eggs and beat well.
Add applesauce, then sifted dry ingredients. Beat smooth and fold
in raisins. Grease and line pan with waxed paper. Bake. Serve
plain or frosted. This cake will remain moist several days in closely
covered container.

SPANISH BUN

7½x11-inch pan . . . Preheated oven—350° F. . . . Baking time—35
minutes

½ cup shortening   ¼ teaspoon salt
1 cup brown sugar   ½ teaspoon soda
1 whole egg   ½ teaspoon baking powder
1 egg yolk   ½ teaspoon cloves
1⅓ cups cake flour, sifted before   ½ teaspoon cinnamon
   measuring   ½ cup sour milk

Cream shortening and sugar. Add egg and egg yolk. Beat well.
Add dry ingredients, which have been sifted together, and sour
milk. Pour batter into greased and floured pan. Spread topping
(page 411) on cake and bake. Do not remove from pan after baking.

Topping

1 egg white
½ cup brown sugar

¼ cup nut meats, chopped

Beat egg white until it is stiff and holds a peak. Fold in brown sugar and spread on top of cake. Sprinkle with nut meats.

LEMON MERINGUE SQUARES

9x13-inch pan . . . Preheated oven—350° F. . . . Baking time—about 35 minutes

½ cup butter or margarine
½ cup powdered sugar
2 egg yolks
1 cup all-purpose flour, sifted
    before measuring

2 teaspoons lemon rind, grated
½ teaspoon salt

Topping

2 egg whites
½ cup sugar

1 tablespoon lemon juice
½ cup chopped nuts

Cream butter or margarine and sugar together. Add egg yolks and blend. Mix in flour, grated rind, and salt. Spread into an ungreased 9x13-inch pan and bake for 10 minutes at 350° F. Beat egg whites until stiff. Gradually add sugar and lemon juice. Fold in nuts. Spread over hot, partially baked batter and continue baking at 350° F. for 25 minutes. Cool, then cut into squares. Serve with or without a topping of ice cream. Serves 8.

CHEESECAKE

9-inch spring pan or tube pan . . . Preheated oven—325° F. . . . Baking time—60-70 minutes

3 cups zwieback crumbs
2 tablespoons sugar
2 tablespoons butter or
    margarine, melted
½ cup sugar
2 tablespoons flour

¼ teaspoon salt
5½ packages (3 ounces each)
    cream cheese
1 teaspoon vanilla
4 eggs, separated
1 cup light cream

Roll zwieback into fine crumbs. (Do this between two pieces of waxed paper, to save extra cleaning up.) Blend crumbs with sugar and melted butter or margarine. Press into bottom of pan. Blend ½ cup sugar with flour, salt, and cream cheese. Add vanilla. Add egg yolks, one at a time, mixing well after each yolk is added. Add cream; mix again. Fold in stiffly beaten egg whites. Pour mixture

on top of crumbs. Bake. Chill before removing from pan. Serves
8-10.

DELICATE SPICE CAKE (SWEDISH)

9-inch square cake pan . . . Preheated oven—350° F. . . . Baking
time—1 hour

3 tablespoons dry toasted bread
    crumbs
½ cup shortening
1½ cups brown sugar
2 eggs, separated
1½ cups all-purpose flour, sifted
    before measuring

2 teaspoons baking powder
2 teaspoons ground cardamom
    (or 1 teaspoon nutmeg and
    ½ teaspoon ginger)
2 teaspoons cinnamon
¾ cup light cream

Grease pan. Sprinkle with 3 tablespoons dry toasted bread crumbs.
Then cream shortening. Add sugar and cream until light and
fluffy. Beat in well-beaten egg yolks. Add sifted dry ingredients
and light cream. Mix well. Fold in stiffly beaten egg whites. Turn
into prepared pan. Bake and serve unfrosted from pan.

CRUMB CAKE

9-inch square pan or 8x12-inch pan . . . Preheated oven—375°F. . . .
Baking time—30 minutes

2 cups brown sugar
2 cups all-purpose flour, sifted
    before measuring
½ cup butter
1 egg, well beaten
1 cup sour milk

1 teaspoon soda
¼ teaspoon cinnamon
¼ teaspoon cloves
¼ teaspoon allspice
¼ teaspoon nutmeg

Mix brown sugar, flour, and butter together until crumbly, as for
pie crust. Divide crumbs in half. Add the well-beaten egg, milk,
soda, and spices to half the mixture. Pour batter into greased and
floured cake pan. Sprinkle remaining crumbs on top of batter
and bake. Serve from pan.

DATE CAKE WITH BROILED ICING

9x12-inch pan . . . Preheated oven—350° F. . . . Baking time—45
minutes

1 cup boiling water
¼ pound (1 cup) dates, chopped
1 teaspoon soda
1 cup granulated sugar
½ cup shortening

1 egg
1½ cups all-purpose flour, sifted
    before measuring
1 teaspoon salt
1 teaspoon vanilla

Pour boiling water over dates and soda. Let stand while mixing batter. Cream sugar and shortening. Add egg and beat again. Add flour and salt alternately with dates and soda mixture. Add vanilla. Pour into greased and floured pan and bake. Immediately after cake is baked, mix ingredients for icing and spread evenly over cake. Broil icing until lightly browned. Cool before serving. This is a very moist cake and will keep well for several days. Do not remove from pan. Makes 15 to 20 pieces.

Icing

4 tablespoons butter or margarine, melted	2 tablespoons milk
½ cup brown sugar	1 cup coconut or chopped nuts

Blend ingredients together and spread over top of baked cake.

CHOCOLATE ROLL

10x15-inch shallow pan . . . Preheated oven—400° F. . . . Baking time—15 minutes

6 tablespoons cake flour, sifted before measuring	4 egg yolks
½ teaspoon baking powder	1 teaspoon vanilla
¼ teaspoon salt	2 squares unsweetened chocolate, melted over hot water
4 egg whites	
¾ cup sugar	

Sift flour once, then measure and sift again with baking powder and salt. Beat egg whites until stiff and gradually beat in sugar. Fold in the egg yolks, which have been beaten until thick and lemon colored. Add vanilla. Fold in flour gradually, then melted chocolate, and mix all ingredients together. Pour into shallow pan which has been well greased and lined with greased waxed paper to within ½ inch of the edge. Bake. Remove from pan, cut off crisp edges of cake and turn out on cloth covered with powdered sugar. Remove paper. Spread half of mile-high icing on cake and roll as for jelly roll (page 316). Wrap in cloth and cool. When cool, cover with remaining icing.

TREAT: Chocolate roll recipe may be used to make a nice cool dessert. In place of mile-high icing, use ice cream for filling. Mint, vanilla, coffee, or strawberry ice cream makes delicious filling. Spread softened ice cream over the cake, roll as for jelly roll (page 316). Dust powdered sugar on outside of roll rather than covering with icing. Place in freeze chest until ready to serve.

FUDGE CAKE

2 8-inch square cake pans or 1 14x4-inch pan with 2-inch sides . . .
Preheated oven—350° F. . . . Baking time—30-35 minutes

2 squares chocolate, melted	1¼ cups white sugar
2 cups cake flour, sifted before measuring	2 eggs
½ teaspoon salt	1 teaspoon vanilla
1½ teaspoons cream of tartar	½ cup milk
½ cup shortening	¾ cup boiling water
	1 teaspoon soda

Melt chocolate over hot water. Sift flour four times with salt and cream of tartar. Cream shortening with sugar until light and fluffy. Add melted chocolate, then add eggs, one at a time, beating vigorously. Add vanilla. Add flour mixture alternately with milk, stirring until ingredients are well blended. Measure boiling water in cup, add soda, quickly add to cake mixture. Stir. This batter will be very thin. Pour in well-greased and floured cake pans. Bake. After cake has baked, remove immediately from pans. Cool on wire cake racks.

TRICK: You may use 3 egg yolks in place of the 2 eggs if preferred.

DEVIL'S FOOD CAKE

2 9-inch round cake pans . . . Preheated oven—350° F. . . . Baking time—40-45 minutes

2½ cups cake flour, sifted before measuring	4 eggs
¼ teaspoon salt	3 squares chocolate, melted and cooled
1 teaspoon soda	1 cup thick buttermilk
1 cup shortening	2 teaspoons vanilla
1½ cups sugar	

Sift flour three times with salt and soda. Cream shortening and sugar together until light and fluffy. Add eggs one at a time, beating well after each egg has been added. Add melted chocolate which has been cooled. Next add sifted dry ingredients alternately with the buttermilk, beginning and ending with the dry ingredients. Add vanilla last. Bake. After cake has baked, remove immediately from pan. Cool on wire cake racks.

TRICK: Sour cream may be used in place of buttermilk; in which case, decrease shortening to ⅔ cup.

WHITE FRUIT CAKE

3 bread pans . . . Preheated oven—250° F. . . . Baking time—3½-4 hours

1 pound candied pineapple, chopped	1 fresh coconut, grated, or 2 cans grated moist coconut
½ pound citron, chopped	6 cups all-purpose flour, sifted before measuring
½ pound candied lemon peel, chopped	1 pound butter or margarine
½ pound white raisins	2 cups sugar
½ pound almonds, chopped	9 eggs •
½ pound English walnuts or pecans, chopped	½ cup white corn sirup
1½ pounds candied cherries, chopped	½ cup sherry wine
½ pound candied orange peel, chopped	½ cup coconut milk, or ½ cup orange juice

Chop fruits and nuts and dredge well with 2 cups of the flour. Cream butter or margarine and sugar together until light and fluffy. Add eggs one at a time, beating well after each addition. Combine corn sirup, sherry wine, and coconut milk or orange juice and add alternately with remainder of flour to butter and sugar mixture. Fold in fruits and nuts last. Pour into well-greased and waxed-paper-lined bread pans and bake. Remove from pans immediately after baking and remove waxed paper. Cool on wire cake racks.

WHITE FRUIT CAKE (A CONFECTION)

2 small loaf pans or 1 small tube pan . . . Preheated oven—250° F. . . . Baking time—2-3 hours

2 cups all-purpose flour, sifted before measuring	1 cup nut meats, chopped
1 pound white raisins	2 teaspoons baking powder
1 pound mixed, cut-up candied fruit, ¼ of which consists of dates	¼ teaspoon salt
	½ cup butter or margarine
	1 cup white sugar
½ pound candied cherries, sliced	3 eggs
1 cup moist coconut	1 teaspoon orange extract
½ pound red and green candied pineapple, cut in small pieces	½ cup orange juice

Measure out ½ cup flour and mix with candied fruits and nuts. Sift remaining flour with baking powder and salt. Cream butter or margarine and sugar together until light and fluffy. Add lightly beaten eggs to shortening and sugar mixture and beat thoroughly. Add orange extract. Next add the dry ingredients alternately with orange juice to sugar and shortening mixture. Carefully fold in the candied fruit. Fill greased and waxed-paper-lined pans almost full with mixture. Bake. Remove from pans immediately after baking and remove waxed paper. Cool on wire cake racks.

Follow instructions for preparing pans given in dark fruit cake recipe (below). The baking time depends upon size of pan. Might keep out a few pieces of pineapple for decorating the top. When cake seems dry, wrap in cloth moistened with orange juice. Makes 5½ pounds.

DARK FRUIT CAKE

3-quart tube pan and 2 1½-pound bread pans . . . Preheated oven—
250° F. . . . Baking time—4 hours

1 pound currants	1 pound all-purpose flour, sifted before measuring
3 pounds seeded raisins	
½ pound candied orange peel, cut fine	1 pound butter or margarine
	1 pound brown sugar
½ pound candied lemon peel, cut fine	12 eggs, separated
	1 square chocolate, melted
1½ pounds citron, cut fine	2 teaspoons nutmeg
1 pound candied cherries	1 tablespoon cinnamon
1 pound candied pineapple, diced	1 tablespoon cloves
	1 teaspoon soda
1 pound shelled filberts, cut in halves	1 cup orange and lemon juice (half and half)
1 pound shelled almonds, cut lengthwise	

Grease pans thoroughly. Cut heavy waxed paper to fit bottom and sides of pans. Line pans with waxed paper, taking care that paper fits snugly into corners of pans. Lightly grease the waxed paper. This extra care in preparing the pans makes a much better finished product.

To prepare fruits and nuts, pick over, wash, and dry currants and raisins. Cut candied fruit into thin slices, excepting the cherries, which are cut in half. Blanch almonds and remove skin. Cut almonds and filberts into lengthwise strips. Mix all fruits and nuts (a large dishpan is excellent for mixing fruits) and half the flour. Mix together thoroughly until all particles of fruits and nuts are flour coated.

Cream butter or margarine, add sugar, and mix together until light and fluffy. (It is suggested that the electric mixer be used for blending all ingredients until ready to combine with fruit and nut mixture.) Add egg yolks one at a time, beating thoroughly. Then add melted chocolate.

Sift the remaining half of the flour with the spices and soda and add alternately with the fruit juice to the butter or margarine mixture. When thoroughly blended, add this mixture to the fruits and nuts. Beat egg whites until stiff and add to the well-blended cake mixture. Fill prepared pans ¾ full of batter. Bake. After baking, remove at once from pans and take off paper. May be baked in oblong bread pans, if desired. Makes about 14 pounds of fruit cake.

FRUIT CAKE IN CANDIED GRAPEFRUIT SHELLS

Holiday fruit cake baked in candied grapefruit shells is a delightfully original gift. It packs easily and travels well.

To Prepare the Shells

Select perfect grapefruits that are clean and free from blemishes. Wash and cut slice from top of each. Remove inside of fruit with teaspoon, being careful not to break shell. Cover shells with cold salted water (1 teaspoon salt to each quart water), bring to boil, and cook five minutes. Drain, cover again with fresh water and boil five minutes. Repeat process about three times until bitter flavor is gone from peel and peel is tender, but not tender enough to break apart. Invert shells and drain on a wire rack for at least an hour, preferably overnight.

Sirup for 10 to 12 Shells

8 cups water	2 cups corn sirup
8 cups sugar	1 tablespoon glycerin

There must be enough sirup to cover and float the fruit. Cook the shells in sirup until sirup gives a jelly test (about 250° F.). Let shells stand in sirup overnight, or longer. Reheat and cook 10 minutes. Cool in sirup until ready to use. Drain before filling with cake mixture. Use any fruit cake batter to fill shells. Fill shells about ¾ full.

To Cook the Cakes in Candied Shells

Steam about 1½ hours. This may be done on top of the range, in the oven or the roaster. (Place filled grapefruit shells on Lift-Out Rack in Inset Pan of Roaster-Oven. Pour 2 quarts of water in bottom of Inset Pan, set control at 300° F., and when steaming point is reached, steam cakes for 1½ hours.) After steaming has been completed, bake at 300° F. for ½ hour, or until center of cake is done when tested with a toothpick. Cool. Store in a covered container. If the confection seems dry, place a fresh orange in the container for a day or two. If properly stored, this confection will keep for a year. Serve by slicing through peel, either crosswise or lengthwise.

Cookies

There isn't a child, or an adult, either, for that matter, who can pass by a cooky jar filled with homemade cookies. There is no substitute for a filled cooky jar, and you will find that the little effort of making cookies is more than repaid by the pleasure they will give to your family and friends.

There are a few tricks to the business, however, that are worth learning before you start.

Flour to Use

Most recipes call for all-purpose flour. Be certain you sift it before measuring. Otherwise you'll end up with too much flour.

However, should the recipe call for cake flour, use it, because it's there for a reason—to make the cooky more tender and flaky.

Baking Pans

Be sure to use shiny aluminum or tin pans with very shallow sides. Cookies do not brown well when baked in pans with deep sides. Do not use a cooky pan that is so large it will block the heat circulation in the oven, and never use a blackened cooky sheet. Poor cookies will be nobody's fault but your own if your pan is too large or too black.

419

Tricks

When greasing the cooky sheets, do it sparingly. Here is a good place to save on your food budget, for you need only a thin film of grease over the baking sheet.

When removing cookies from baking sheets, it is wise to use a pancake turner or a small spatula, being careful not to break the brittle cookies. Place them on a wire cake cooler in a single layer and do not let them touch each other as they cool.

When a recipe calls for milk and flavoring, it is a smart trick to add the flavoring to the milk at the outset. That way you are sure not to forget the flavoring.

Rolled Cookies

If you are planning to roll cooky dough, refrigerate the dough at least 2 hours before rolling. Then divide the dough into halves or thirds and put the portion not being rolled back in the refrigerator.

Dust the rolling board lightly with flour, just enough to keep the rolled dough from sticking. Too much flour makes the cooky tough and tasteless. That's why it is best to refrigerate first, because then you can use the minimum of flour.

Drop Cookies

Always allow about 2 inches between cookies. They are going to spread when baked and will all run together unless space is left between.

Storing Cooky Dough

Cut both ends off a No. 2 can. Pack cooky dough in can. Cover each end with aluminum foil. Place in refrigerator. When ready to bake cookies, force dough out one end, slice, and bake. You get round cookies without any effort. Or, pack in empty butter or margarine carton. Or, you can shape them into 2-inch round rolls, wrap in waxed paper, and bake as needed. In other words, there is no reason why a cooky jar should go empty.

SUGAR COOKIES

10x14-inch cooky sheet . . . Preheated oven—375° F. . . . Baking time—10-12 minutes

2 cups all-purpose flour, sifted before measuring	⅔ cup shortening
	⅔ cup granulated sugar
2 teaspoons baking powder	2 eggs
½ teaspoon salt	1 teaspoon vanilla

Sift flour together with baking powder and salt. Cream shortening and sugar together until light and fluffy. Add unbeaten eggs, one at a time, beating thoroughly after each egg is added. Add vanilla and flour mixture. Beat vigorously until flour is completely blended. Put bowl of dough in refrigerator until it's quite cold, usually about 2 hours. Divide cooky dough in half. Roll each half out on lightly floured board. Roll until dough is about ⅛ inch thick. Then cut with 2- or 3-inch cooky cutter, sprinkle top with colored or plain sugar. Bake. After baking, remove cookies at once to cake cooler. Makes 2½ dozen.

TRICK: Tie a piece of cheesecloth or any plain muslin around the bottom of a water glass. Instead of rolling the dough, lift out small portions of it, about the size of an English walnut. Roll dough between palms of hand, until a little ball is formed. Do this quickly. Place on greased cooky sheet about 2 inches apart. Sixteen little dough balls will fill the cooky sheet.

Then press down on the ball of cooky dough with the cloth-covered water glass. You'll have nice round cookies without the bother of rolling the dough. It may be necessary to dust your hands lightly with flour before rolling dough into little balls.

ANISE COOKIES

10x14-inch cooky sheet . . . Preheated oven—325° F. . . . Baking
  time—10-12 minutes

1¾ cups all-purpose flour, sifted before measuring	1 tablespoon anise seed, or 1 teaspoon anise oil (you'll find the anise oil at a drugstore)
½ teaspoon baking powder	
3 eggs	
1 cup + 2 tablespoons granulated sugar	

Sift flour with baking powder. If you have an electric mixer you are in luck. Put eggs and sugar in mixer bowl and beat for 30 minutes on medium speed. (If you do not have an electric mixer, better skip this recipe.) To the eggs which have been beaten for ½ hour, add the flour and baking powder. Beat another 3 minutes. Add anise seed or oil. Blend quickly. Drop by teaspoons 2 inches apart onto greased and floured cooky sheet. Let set overnight. Bake. Remove from pans immediately after removing from oven. Makes 6 or 7 dozen.

SOUR-CREAM DROP COOKIES

10x14-inch cooky sheet . . . Preheated oven—375° F. . . . Baking
time—10-12 minutes

2 cups all-purpose flour, sifted before measuring	½ cup shortening
	1 cup brown sugar
1 teaspoon nutmeg	1 egg
½ teaspoon soda	½ cup rich, sour cream
2 teaspoons baking powder	½ cup nut meats, chopped
½ teaspoon salt	

Sift flour with nutmeg, soda, baking powder, and salt. Thoroughly
cream shortening and sugar; add egg and beat well. Add sifted
flour mixture alternately with sour cream to first mixture. Then
add nut meats. Mix well. Drop from teaspoon onto well-greased
cooky sheet. Bake for 10 minutes. Remove from pan to cake cooler
immediately after baking. Makes about 2½ dozen cookies.

JULIA'S SUGAR DROP COOKIES

10x14-inch cooky sheet . . . Preheated oven—375° F. . . . Baking
time—10-12 minutes

3¾ cups cake flour, sifted before measuring	1 cup shortening
	1½ cups granulated sugar
2 teaspoons baking powder	2 eggs
1 teaspoon soda	1 teaspoon vanilla
¼ teaspoon salt	1 cup sweet milk

Sift flour with baking powder, soda, and salt. Cream shortening
and sugar. Add eggs one at a time to shortening and sugar mixture,
beating well between each addition. Add vanilla to milk, then
add dry ingredients alternately with milk to creamed sugar mixture. Drop from teaspoon onto ungreased cooky sheet 2 inches
apart. Bake. Remove from pan to cake cooler immediately after
baking. Makes about 6 dozen cookies.

BOURBON BALLS

These do not require baking

3 cups vanilla wafers (about 1 pound), ground	3 tablespoons light corn sirup
	1½ tablespoons cocoa
1 cup pecans, ground	½ cup bourbon or rum
1 cup confectioners' sugar	

Mix all ingredients thoroughly and shape into balls the size of
an English walnut. Roll in confectioners' sugar. Serve with Christmas punch or eggnog. Makes 2½-3 dozen balls.

BUTTERSCOTCH NUT STICKS

8x8-inch square pan . . . Preheated oven—350° F. . . . Baking time
—20 minutes for bottom layer and 25 minutes for top layer

Bottom Layer

½ cup butter or margarine
½ cup brown sugar

1 cup all-purpose flour, sifted
before measuring

Cream butter or margarine. Add brown sugar and cream until
light and fluffy. Add flour and work into dough. Press firmly into
pan. Bake. Cool slightly before adding top layer.

Top Layer

2 eggs
1 cup brown sugar
1 teaspoon vanilla
2 tablespoons all-purpose flour

1 teaspoon baking powder
½ teaspoon salt
1½ cups corn flakes, crushed
1 cup nuts, chopped

Beat eggs until light and fluffy. Add brown sugar gradually and
beat until well blended. Add vanilla. Sift flour, baking powder,
and salt together and add to egg and sugar mixture. Stir in corn
flakes and nuts. Spread evenly over slightly cooled bottom layer.
Bake. Cool before cutting. If possible, leave in pan overnight.
Makes about 2 dozen sticks.

COCONUT COOKIES

10x14-inch cooky sheet . . . Preheated oven—375° F. . . . Baking
time—10-12 minutes

1 cup shortening
2 cups granulated sugar
2 eggs
1½ teaspoons vanilla
1 teaspoon lemon rind, grated
4 cups all-purpose flour, sifted
before measuring

1 teaspoon soda
2 teaspoons baking powder
½ teaspoon salt
⅔ cup thick sour cream
1 cup moist coconut

Cream shortening and sugar together. Add eggs and beat well.
Add vanilla and lemon rind. Sift flour with soda, baking powder,
and salt and add to creamed mixture, alternately with sour cream.
Stir in coconut. Chill overnight in refrigerator. Roll dough ⅛-inch
thick and cut with floured cooky cutter, or stamp dough with
glass covered with thin cloth (page 421). The latter method is
quicker than rolling. Bake. Remove from pan to cake cooler immediately after baking. Yields about 6 dozen cookies.

DATE REFRIGERATOR COOKIES

10x14-inch cooky sheet . . . Preheated oven—375° F. . . . Baking
time—10 minutes

1 cup shortening	3 cups all-purpose flour, sifted
2 cups brown sugar, pressed	before measuring
firmly in cup	1 teaspoon salt
2 eggs	1 teaspoon baking powder
1 cup dates, cut in pieces	½ teaspoon soda
1 teaspoon vanilla	

Cream shortening and sugar, add eggs, and beat thoroughly. Add
dates and vanilla. Sift flour with salt, baking powder, and soda
and add to creamed mixture. Shape into rolls, about 2 inches in
diameter. Wrap in waxed paper and let stand in refrigerator overnight, or until firm enough to slice. Cut ¼-inch slices and bake.
Remove from pan to cake cooler immediately after baking. Makes
about 5 dozen cookies.

HONEY CRISP COOKIES

10x14-inch cooky sheet . . . Preheated oven—350° F. . . . Baking
time—12 minutes

2¼ cups all-purpose flour, sifted	1 teaspoon soda
before measuring	¼ teaspoon salt
¼ teaspoon allspice	½ cup honey
¼ teaspoon cloves	½ cup shortening
¼ teaspoon cinnamon	

Sift flour with spices, soda, and salt. Boil honey and shortening
together one minute. Cool. Add sifted dry ingredients. Cool in
refrigerator. Roll to ⅛-inch thickness and cut with cooky cutter.
You can drop cooled dough from teaspoon onto cooky sheet if
you prefer. Saves time. Bake. Remove from pan to cake cooler
immediately after removing from oven. Makes about 3 dozen
cookies.

LEMON REFRIGERATOR COOKIES

10x14-inch cooky sheet . . . Preheated oven—400° F. . . . Baking
time—8-10 minutes

1 cup shortening	4 cups all-purpose flour, sifted
2 cups granulated sugar	before measuring
2 tablespoons lemon rind	2 teaspoons baking powder
2 tablespoons lemon juice	⅛ teaspoon salt
2 eggs	⅛ teaspoon nutmeg

Cream shortening, sugar, lemon rind, and lemon juice together until light and fluffy. Add eggs, one at a time, beating well after each addition. Sift flour with baking powder, salt, and nutmeg. Add to first mixture. Blend well. Chill dough in refrigerator, then shape into 3 rolls, each roll about 2 inches in diameter. Wrap in waxed paper. Chill. Or, the wrapped dough may be frozen. Bake as needed. Remove from pan to cake cooler immediately after baking. This makes a crisp cooky and yields about 5 dozen.

MINT SURPRISE COOKIES

10x14-inch cooky sheet . . . Preheated oven—375° F. . . . Baking time—12-15 minutes

3¼ cups all-purpose flour, sifted before measuring	½ cup firmly packed brown sugar
1 teaspoon soda	2 eggs
½ teaspoon salt	1 teaspoon vanilla
1 cup shortening	1 package (9 ounces) chocolate mint wafers
1 cup granulated sugar	

Sift flour, soda, and salt together. Cream shortening, granulated sugar, and brown sugar together until light and fluffy. Add eggs and vanilla. Beat thoroughly. Add dry ingredients and mix until well blended. Chill dough in refrigerator. Use approximately 1 tablespoon (level) dough for each cooky. Drop on greased cooky sheet, 2 inches apart. Press a mint wafer into center of each and fold dough around mint, so it is covered. Do not make cookies too large. If you wish, you may put a pecan or walnut half on top. Bake. Remove from pan to cake cooker immediately after baking. Makes about 5 dozen cookies.

NUT CRUNCHES

10x14-inch cooky sheet . . . Preheated oven—375° F. . . . Baking time—10 minutes

1½ cups all-purpose flour, sifted before measuring	¼ cup granulated sugar
½ teaspoon soda	1 egg
1 teaspoon salt	½ teaspoon vanilla
½ cup shortening	½ cup nut meats, chopped
½ cup brown sugar	½ cup raisins, chopped

Sift flour with soda and salt. Cream shortening, granulated sugar, and brown sugar together until light and fluffy. Add egg, beating well. Add vanilla, nuts, and raisins. Blend thoroughly. Add dry ingredients and beat until all ingredients are blended. Drop by teaspoons on ungreased baking sheet. Bake. Remove from pan to cake cooler immediately after removing from oven. Yields about 3 dozen cookies.

OLD-FASHIONED WASHBOARDS

10x14-inch cooky sheet . . . Preheated oven—350° F. . . . Baking time—8-10 minutes

4 cups all-purpose flour, sifted before measuring	2 cups brown sugar, firmly packed
1¼ teaspoons baking powder	2 eggs
1 teaspoon baking soda	1 teaspoon vanilla
¼ teaspoon salt	1 cup moist coconut
1 cup shortening	

Sift flour with baking powder, baking soda, and salt. Cream shortening and brown sugar until light and fluffy. Add eggs and beat well. Add vanilla and coconut. Add sifted dry ingredients to creamed shortening mixture. Chill in refrigerator about 2 hours. Roll dough about ¼ inch thick, and cut into shapes 1½x2½ inches. It might be helpful to make a cardboard pattern to cut around. Place on cooky sheet. Press lengthwise with tines of fork. If fork sticks to dough, dip fork in flour before pressing on cooky dough. Bake. Remove from pan to cake cooler immediately after baking. Yields about 4 dozen cookies.

HEAVENLY TARTS

10x14-inch cooky sheet . . . Preheated oven—350° F. . . . Baking time—10-12 minutes

1 cup butter or margarine	1 cup pecans or walnut meats, finely chopped
3 tablespoons confectioners' sugar	
2 cups cake flour, sifted before measuring	Extra confectioners' sugar

Cream butter or margarine and confectioners' sugar until light and fluffy—should have the appearance of whipped cream. Add sifted flour and nut meats. Place in refrigerator to chill for about 2 hours. Roll about ⅛ inch thick and cut into narrow, fingerlike strips. Bake on greased cooky sheet. These cookies should not get brown. Remove from pan to cake cooler immediately after baking. Yields about 2 dozen cookies.

SAND TARTS

10x14-inch cooky sheet . . . Preheated oven—400° F. . . . Baking
  time—8-10 minutes

1 cup shortening	2 eggs
1 cup butter or margarine	¼ teaspoon almond flavoring
2 cups granulated sugar	3 cups all-purpose flour, sifted
½ teaspoon salt	before measuring

Cream shortening, butter or margarine, sugar, and salt until light
and fluffy. Add well-beaten eggs and mix well. Stir in flavoring
and add sifted flour. Blend ingredients thoroughly. Roll in balls,
the size of a walnut, and place about one inch apart on a greased
cooky sheet. Bake. These will spread out and become thin, crisp
cookies when baked and will keep nicely in a covered crock for
at least two weeks. Remove from pan to cake cooler immediately
after baking. Makes about 5 dozen.

CHOCOLATE CLUSTERS

These do not require baking

5 cups puffed rice	½ teaspoon salt
½ cup small, unsalted peanuts	2 squares baking chocolate
¾ cup granulated sugar	1 tablespoon butter or margarine
¼ cup light corn sirup	1 teaspoon vanilla
½ cup water	

Heat puffed rice in a moderate oven (350° F.) for 10 minutes.
Pour into a large greased bowl and mix with peanuts. Combine
sugar, sirup, water, and salt in saucepan. Bring to a boil. Add
chocolate and continue cooking until a few drops tested in water
form soft balls. Add butter or margarine and vanilla. Stir until
butter or margarine has melted. Pour sirup gradually over the
puffed rice, mixing thoroughly. Grease hands and form small
patties or clusters. Makes about 3 dozen clusters.

REFRIGERATOR OR BUTTERSCOTCH COOKIES

10x14-inch cooky sheet . . . Preheated oven—400° F. . . . Baking
  time—10-12 minutes

3½ cups all-purpose flour, sifted	2 cups brown sugar, firmly
before measuring	packed in cup
1 teaspoon soda	3 eggs
1 teaspoon cream of tartar	1 teaspoon vanilla
1 teaspoon salt	1 cup nuts, cut in small pieces
1 cup shortening	

Sift flour with soda, cream of tartar, and salt. Place shortening and sugar in mixing bowl, cream until light and fluffy. Add whole eggs and vanilla, continue beating. Add flour mixture and mix until ingredients are blended. Add nuts and mix only until nuts are mixed through dough. Dough may be molded in empty butter cartons, chilled, and sliced for baking, or may be made into small oblong rolls, wrapped in waxed paper, placed in refrigerator, and sliced for baking as needed. Remove from pan to cake cooler immediately after baking. Makes about 5 dozen small cookies.

CHOCOLATE SQUARES

8x8-inch square pan . . . Preheated oven—350° F. . . . Baking time —30 minutes

2 squares bitter chocolate	3 eggs
½ cup shortening	1 cup sugar
¾ cup cake flour, sifted before measuring	1 teaspoon vanilla
	1 cup nut meats, chopped
1 teaspoon baking powder	

Melt chocolate and shortening together over hot water. Beat smooth. Sift flour with baking powder. Beat eggs until light, add sugar and vanilla and continue beating until thick. Add chocolate and shortening. Beat smooth. Add flour and baking powder. Mix thoroughly. Fold in nut meats. Pour into greased pan. Bake. Cut in squares while warm and remove from pan. Cool on wire cake rack. Makes 16-20 squares.

CHOCOLATE DREAMS

7x11-inch pan . . . Preheated oven—375° F. . . . Baking time—25 minutes

2 cups quick-cooking oatmeal, uncooked	1 package (6 ounces) chocolate chips
½ cup brown sugar	¼ cup dark corn sirup
¼ cup butter or margarine, melted	

Combine oatmeal and brown sugar. Add melted butter or margarine. Stir until well blended. Add chocolate chips and dark corn sirup. Stir until thoroughly blended. Pack mixture into greased oblong pan. Bake. Mixture will be bubbling when removed from oven. Let stand 10 minutes, no longer. Cut into small bars and remove from pan to finish cooling. Makes 16-20 bars.

WALNUT MACAROONS

10x14-inch cooky sheet . . . Preheated oven—325° F. . . . Baking time—20-25 minutes

½ cup butter or margarine
¼ cup granulated sugar
1 egg, separated
½ teaspoon vanilla
1 tablespoon lemon rind, grated
1 tablespoon lemon juice

1 cup cake flour, sifted before measuring
⅛ teaspoon salt
½ cup walnut meats, chopped
Candied cherries

Cream butter or margarine and sugar together until light and fluffy. Add egg yolk. Beat thoroughly. Add vanilla, grated lemon rind, and lemon juice. Beat again. Blend in the cake flour, sifted with salt. Chill dough 2 hours in refrigerator. Form into small balls, like a good-sized marble. Roll in egg white which has been beaten to a froth. Then roll in finely chopped nut meats. Top with half a candied cherry. Bake only until a very light brown. Remove from pan to cake cooler immediately after baking. Yields about 2½ dozen cookies.

LEBKUCHEN

10x14-inch cooky sheet . . . Preheated oven—400° F. . . . Baking time—12-15 minutes

1 cup brown sugar, firmly packed
¾ cup molasses
½ cup butter or margarine
2 eggs
¼ cup sour milk
4 cups all-purpose flour, sifted before measuring

1 teaspoon cinnamon, ground
¾ teaspoon cloves, ground
¾ teaspoon soda
¾ teaspoon salt
½ cup nut meats, broken
4 tablespoons candied fruit, finely cut

Heat the brown sugar and molasses until mixture is hot. Stir often to prevent sticking. Remove from heat, add butter or margarine, and allow mixture to cool. Add eggs and milk; stir vigorously until well blended. Sift flour with spices, soda, and salt. Add with nut meats and candied fruit to liquid mixture. Stir until ingredients are all blended. Cover. Let set in refrigerator or cool place for a day or so. Roll to ¼-inch thickness on lightly floured board. Cut with desired cutters. Bake. Remove from pan to cake cooler immediately after baking. Frost and decorate in any desired manner.

Wonderful cookies for Christmas time. Makes about 6½ dozen cookies.

CHOCOLATE NUGGETS

10x14-inch cooky sheet . . . Preheated oven—375° F. . . . Baking time—15 minutes

1½ cups all-purpose flour, sifted before measuring	2 eggs
2 teaspoons baking powder	¾ cup nut meats, coarsely cut
½ teaspoon salt	1 package (6 ounces) chocolate chips
⅔ cup shortening	
1 cup brown sugar, firmly packed	

Sift flour with baking powder and salt. Cream shortening and sugar together until light and fluffy. Add eggs; beat vigorously. Add flour mixture, nuts, and chocolate morsels. Mix well. Drop by teaspoonfuls on greased cooky sheet. Bake. Remove from pan to cake cooler immediately after baking. Makes about 5 dozen cookies.

GINGERSNAPS

10x14-inch cooky sheet . . . Preheated oven—375° F. . . . Baking time—15 minutes

1 cup granulated sugar	½ teaspoon salt
¾ cup shortening	1 teaspoon cinnamon
¼ cup molasses	½ teaspoon cloves
1 egg	¼ teaspoon nutmeg
2 cups all-purpose flour, sifted before measuring	1½ teaspoons ginger
1½ teaspoons soda	½ cup granulated sugar

Cream sugar and shortening together until light and fluffy. Add molasses and beaten egg. Beat thoroughly. Sift flour with soda, salt, and spices. Add to creamed mixture. Blend together carefully so that all ingredients are well mixed. Roll small portions of dough between palms of hands into small balls, about the size of small walnut. Roll balls in granulated sugar. Place 2 inches apart on greased cooky sheet. The cookies flatten out as they bake. When they are baked, remove at once from cooky sheet and cool on wire cake rack. Makes about 5 dozen cookies.

SOFT-SHELL COOKIES

10x14-inch cooky sheet . . . Preheated oven—375° F. . . . Baking
   time—10 minutes

1 cup shortening (part butter or margarine)	2 teaspoons baking powder
	1 cup sweet milk
1½ cups granulated sugar	1 teaspoon vanilla
2 eggs	½ pound pecan meats
3¾ cups cake flour, sifted before measuring	

Cream shortening and sugar until light and fluffy. Add eggs. Beat
well. Sift flour with baking powder and salt. Add alternately with
milk to creamed shortening mixture. Add vanilla. Blend ingredients carefully, but do not overbeat. Arrange pecans on ungreased
cooky sheet, 4 pecans in each group, in the shape of a cross. Drop
1 teaspoonful batter directly in the center of the 4 pecans, being
sure the batter covers the center tip of each pecan. Bake. Remove
from pan to cake cooler immediately after removing from oven.
Ice cooky portion with chocolate frosting (below) while cooky is
still warm. Yields about 3 dozen cookies.

Chocolate Frosting

3 tablespoons softened butter or margarine	3 tablespoons cocoa
	2 cups confectioners' sugar
1 tablespoon light cream	½ teaspoon vanilla
2 tablespoons strong hot coffee	½ teaspoon salt

Combine softened butter or margarine with cream and hot coffee.
Add cocoa and beat vigorously. Add confectioners' sugar and stir
until ingredients are well blended, then beat very hard. Add vanilla and salt.

WHIRLIGIG COOKIES

10x14-inch cooky sheet . . . Preheated oven—375° F. . . . Baking
   time—10-12 minutes

½ cup shortening	½ teaspoon soda
½ cup brown sugar	½ teaspoon salt
½ cup granulated sugar	1 package (6 ounces) chocolate chips
½ cup peanut butter	
1 egg, unbeaten	
1¼ cups all-purpose flour, sifted before measuring	

Cream shortening, brown sugar, granulated sugar, and peanut butter together thoroughly. Add egg; beat until light and fluffy. Sift flour with soda and salt. Add to egg mixture and blend well. Roll dough into oblong shape ¼ inch thick. Melt chocolate bits over hot boiling water. Cool slightly. Spread on rolled dough with spatula. Roll up like jelly roll and chill. Slice ¼ inch thick. Place on ungreased cooky sheet. Bake. Remove from pan to cake cooler immediately after baking. Yields about 3 dozen cookies.

PEANUT BUTTER COOKIES

10x14-inch cooky sheet . . . Preheated oven—375° F. . . . Baking
time—15-18 minutes

3 cups all-purpose flour, sifted before measuring	1 cup granulated sugar
	1 cup brown sugar
2 teaspoons soda	2 eggs, beaten
¼ teaspoon salt	1 cup peanut butter
1 cup shortening	1 teaspoon vanilla

Sift flour once with soda and salt. Cream shortening, granulated sugar, and brown sugar together. Add beaten eggs and mix until smooth. Add peanut butter, stir well, then add flour mixture. Mix to a stiff batter, then add vanilla. Form into tiny balls and press onto a greased cooky sheet. Press with back of fork to make a waffle design. Bake. Remove from pan to cake cooler immediately after baking. Makes 4 dozen small cookies.

FLORENCE'S MINCEMEAT COOKIES

10x14-inch cooky sheet . . . Preheated oven—375° F. . . . Baking
time—12-15 minutes

½ cup butter	3 cups all-purpose flour, sifted before measuring
½ cup shortening	
1 cup granulated sugar	1 teaspoon soda
½ cup brown sugar	1 jar (8 ounces) brandied
2 eggs	mincemeat, or mincemeat
1 teaspoon vanilla	soaked in brandy

Cream butter, shortening, and sugars. Add eggs and vanilla. Beat well. Sift flour and soda together. Add to creamed mixture. Chill dough for at least two hours. Form into small balls of dough (slightly larger than a walnut) and place on greased cooky sheet. Make a depression in dough with back of measuring spoon (1 teaspoon size) and fill with mincemeat. Be sure the mincemeat has been drained. Have cookies about 2 inches apart to allow for spreading. Bake. Remove from pan to cake cooler immediately after baking. Makes about 3 dozen cookies. DELICIOUS.

FAVORITE OATMEAL COOKIES

10x14-inch cooky sheet . . . Preheated oven—375° F. . . . Baking time—12-15 minutes

1 cup shortening	1 teaspoon soda
1 cup granulated sugar	4 tablespoons sour milk
2 eggs	2 cups all-purpose flour, sifted
1 teaspoon vanilla	before measuring
¼ teaspoon salt	2½ cups quick-cooking oatmeal,
1 cup raisins	uncooked

Cream shortening and sugar together until light and fluffy. Add eggs, one at a time, beating thoroughly. Add vanilla and salt. Pour boiling water over raisins and let stand a few minutes. Drain. Add to creamed shortening mixture. Dissolve soda in milk and add alternately with flour to creamed shortening mixture. Add oatmeal. Blend all ingredients thoroughly. Drop by teaspoonfuls on greased cooky sheet. Bake. Remove from pan to cake cooler immediately after baking. Makes 3½-4 dozen cookies.

OATMEAL COOKY MIX

3 cups all-purpose flour, sifted	2 teaspoons salt
before measuring	1 cup shortening
2½ cups sugar	3 cups quick-cooking oatmeal,
1 teaspoon soda	uncooked
1 teaspoon baking powder	

Sift flour, sugar, soda, baking powder, and salt together. Cut in shortening until the mixture resembles corn meal. Add uncooked oatmeal and mix well. Store in covered container at room temperature. This recipe makes 8 dozen cookies.

To Make 2 Dozen Cookies

10x14-inch cooky sheet . . . Preheated oven—375° F. . . . Baking time—12-15 minutes

1 egg	1 teaspoon vanilla
1 tablespoon milk	2 cups oatmeal cooky mix

Beat egg and add to milk and vanilla. Add to mix and beat until well blended. Drop by teaspoonfuls on a greased cooky sheet, about 2 inches apart. Bake. Remove from pan to cake cooler immediately after baking.

TREATS: For variation, add ½ cup of any of the following ingredients to above recipe for 2 dozen cookies:

½ cup chopped nuts   ½ cup seedless raisins
½ cup chopped coconut   ½ cup chocolate chips

OATMEAL CRISPIES

10x14-inch cooky sheet . . . Preheated oven—350° F. . . . Baking time—10-12 minutes

¾ cup all-purpose flour, sifted   ½ cup granulated sugar
   before measuring   1 egg
½ teaspoon salt   ½ teaspoon vanilla
½ teaspoon soda   1½ cups quick-cooking oatmeal,
½ cup shortening, softened but   uncooked
   not melted   ¼ cup nut meats, chopped
½ cup brown sugar, firmly
   packed

Sift flour with salt and soda. Add softened shortening, sugars, egg, and vanilla. Beat until smooth. Fold in oatmeal and nut meats. Shape dough in rolls, about 2 inches in diameter. Wrap in waxed paper and chill several hours in refrigerator. Slice ¼ inch thick and place on ungreased cooky sheet. Bake. Remove from pan to cake cooler immediately after baking. Makes about 3½ dozen cookies.

DATE SWIRLS

10x14-inch cooky sheet . . . Preheated oven—400° F. . . . Baking time—10 minutes

Dough

½ cup butter or margarine   2 cups all-purpose flour, sifted
½ cup brown sugar, firmly packed   before measuring
½ cup granulated sugar   ¼ teaspoon salt
1 egg   ½ teaspoon baking soda

Cream butter or margarine with sugars. Beat until light and fluffy. Add egg. Beat well. Sift flour with salt and baking soda and add to creamed sugar mixture. Beat until ingredients are well blended. Toss on lightly floured board. Knead until smooth. Roll out ¼ inch thick. Spread with date filling and roll like a jelly roll (page 316). Wrap in waxed paper. Place in refrigerator overnight to chill. Slice in ¼-inch slices. Bake on well-greased cooky sheet. Remove from pan to cake cooler immediately after baking. Makes about 3 dozen cookies.

Filling

½ pound pitted dates, cut in
    fourths
⅓ cup water

¼ cup sugar
¼ cup nut meats, chopped

Cook dates, water, and sugar together until thick, stirring constantly. Remove from heat. Add nuts. Cool before spreading on cooky dough.

APPLESAUCE BRAN COOKIES

10x14-inch cooky sheet . . . Preheated oven—375° F. . . . Baking
   time—12-15 minutes

½ cup shortening
1 cup sugar
1 egg
1¾ cups all-purpose flour, sifted
    before measuring
½ teaspoon salt
1 teaspoon cinnamon

½ teaspoon nutmeg
½ teaspoon cloves
1 teaspoon soda
1 cup sweetened applesauce
1 cup seedless raisins
1 cup All-Bran

Cream shortening and sugar together until light and fluffy. Add unbeaten egg and mix well. Sift flour with salt and spices. Add soda to applesauce and combine well. Add applesauce mixture and dry ingredients to the creamed mixture. Mix well. Add raisins and All-Bran last. Drop by teaspoonfuls on well-greased cooky sheet, about 2 inches apart. Bake. Remove from pan to cake cooler immediately after baking. Makes about 3 dozen.

CHINESE CHEWS

8x8-inch cake pan . . . Preheated oven—325° F. . . . Baking time—
   30-35 minutes

2 eggs
1 cup granulated sugar
¾ cup all-purpose flour, sifted
    before measuring
1 teaspoon baking powder

¼ teaspoon salt
1 cup pitted dates, cut in small
    pieces
1 cup pecans, broken

Beat eggs and sugar together until light in color and thick. Sift flour with baking powder and salt over dates and nuts. Fold fruit and nut mixture into beaten egg and sugar mixture. Spread in buttered cake pan. Bake. Cool in pan. Cut in 1x2-inch bars before removing from pan. Makes about 32 bars.

FRUIT BARS

8x8-inch cake pan . . . Preheated oven—350° F. . . . Baking time—
40 minutes

Dough

1 cup all-purpose flour, sifted before measuring	½ cup shortening
1 cup brown sugar, lightly packed	1½ cups quick-cooking oatmeal, uncooked
½ teaspoon salt	3 tablespoons milk

Mix flour, sugar, and salt. Cut in shortening until mixture resembles corn meal. Add uncooked oatmeal. Mix well. Add milk and blend thoroughly. Pack half of mixture into greased square pan. Spread fruit mixture (below) on top. Cover fruit with remaining flour mixture. Press down lightly. Bake. Cool on wire cake cooler. Cut in bars 1x2 inches. Makes 32 bars.

Filling

1 cup figs or dates, cut fine	1 tablespoon lemon juice
⅓ cup granulated sugar	1 tablespoon lemon rind, grated
½ cup water	

Cook fruit, sugar, and water until thick. Add lemon juice and lemon rind. Cool.

HOLIDAY FRUIT BARS

9½x5½x2¾-inch utility pan . . . Preheated oven—350° F. . . . Baking time—30 minutes

1½ cups all-purpose flour, sifted before measuring	1 cup raisins
1½ teaspoons baking powder	1 cup pitted dates, chopped
¾ teaspoon salt	½ cup maraschino cherries, chopped
3 eggs	½ cup candied pineapple, diced
1 cup sugar	1 tablespoon maraschino cherry juice
1 package semi-sweet chocolate morsels	Grated rind of orange
1 cup nut meats, chopped	

Sift flour with baking powder and salt. Beat eggs and add sugar. When well blended, add remaining ingredients to egg mixture. Add flour mixture last. Pour into pan. Bake. Cool. Cut in 1x2-inch bars. Makes 4 dozen.

MYSTERY BARS

8-inch square pan . . . Preheated oven—300° F. and 350° F. . . .
Baking time—20 minutes at 300° F., 25 minutes at 350° F.

½ cup butter or margarine	2 tablespoons all-purpose flour
1½ cups brown sugar	½ teaspoon baking powder
1 cup all-purpose flour, sifted before measuring	¼ teaspoon salt
	½ cup coconut, shredded
2 eggs	1 cup nut meats, chopped
1 teaspoon vanilla	

Cream butter or margarine with ½ cup of the brown sugar until
smooth. Add 1 cup sifted flour and mix to a crumbly mass. Pat
evenly into a well-greased pan and bake until pastry is delicately
brown. Remove from oven. Cool. Beat the 2 eggs until light and
lemon colored, add the 1 cup brown sugar and the vanilla, and
mix. Add the 2 tablespoons flour which has been sifted with baking
powder and salt. Add coconut and nut meats. Spread over the
baked and cooled pastry and bake at 350° F. for about 25 minutes.
Cool overnight. Cut in 1x4-inch lengths. Makes about 2 dozen.

CHOCOLATE HALFWAY COOKIES

2 8-inch square pans . . . Preheated oven—350° F. . . . Baking time—
30 minutes

½ cup shortening	¼ teaspoon salt
½ cup granulated sugar	1 teaspoon baking powder
½ cup brown sugar, firmly packed	¼ teaspoon baking soda
2 egg yolks, slightly beaten with 1 tablespoon water	1 package (6 ounces) semi-sweet chocolate morsels
1 teaspoon vanilla	
2 cups all-purpose flour, sifted before measuring	

Cream shortening and sugars. Add egg yolk, to which water has
been added, and vanilla. Blend well. Sift flour with salt, baking
powder, and baking soda. Thoroughly blend dry ingredients with
creamed shortening mixture. Put in greased square pans, sprinkle
the chocolate morsels on top, and press down slightly into the
dough. Next spread topping over the dough. Bake. Cool before
cutting. Yields about 3 dozen cookies.

Topping

2 egg whites	1½ cups brown sugar

Beat egg whites until stiff. Blend in the brown sugar and fold ingredients together until well blended.

KRINGLE MERINGUES

10x14-inch cooky sheet . . . Preheated oven—350° F. . . . Baking
time—15 minutes

⅛ teaspoon salt	½ teaspoon vanilla
1 egg white	1½ cups corn flakes
⅓ cup granulated sugar	

Add salt to egg white and beat until foamy. Add sugar, 2 tablespoonfuls at a time, beating after each addition until sugar is
blended. Then continue beating until mixture will stand in peaks.
Add vanilla. Fold in corn flakes. Drop from teaspoon onto greased
cooky sheet. Bake. Remove from pan to cake cooler immediately
after baking. Makes about 2 dozen cookies.

CEREAL MACAROONS

10x14-inch cooky sheet . . . Preheated oven—325° F. . . . Baking
time—15 minutes

1 can sweetened condensed milk	½ cup nut meats, chopped
5 tablespoons brown sugar	Maraschino or candied cherries
3 cups corn or wheat flakes	

Cook the milk and brown sugar over low heat until thickened. Stir
constantly. Remove from heat; stir in cereal flakes and nut meats.
Drop from teaspoon onto greased cooky sheet. Top with bits of
cherry. Bake. Remove from pan to cake cooler immediately after
baking. Makes 2½ dozen.

CORN FLAKE MACAROONS

10x14-inch cooky sheet . . . Preheated oven—350° F. . . . Baking
time—10 minutes

3 tablespoons butter or	¼ cup nut meats, chopped
margarine, melted	¼ cup moist coconut
¼ cup brown sugar	2½ cups corn flakes, slightly
¼ cup white sugar	crushed
1 egg	

Blend butter or margarine and sugars thoroughly; add egg. Beat
vigorously. Add nut meats, coconut, and corn flakes. Fold ingredients carefully, but thoroughly. Shape cookies, using a tablespoon
and pressing the filled spoon against the side of the bowl. Then
drop onto greased cooky sheet. Bake. Remove from pan to cake
cooler immediately after baking. Makes about 2 dozen.

DATE AND NUT MERINGUES

10x14-inch cooky sheet . . . Preheated oven—325° F. . . . Baking
time—20 minutes

4 egg whites	1 teaspoon vanilla
¼ teaspoon salt	1 cup dates, chopped
1½ cups granulated sugar	1 cup nut meats, chopped

Beat egg whites until frothy, add salt, then gradually add sugar,
beating continuously. Continue beating until egg whites will stand
in stiff peaks. Fold in vanilla, dates, and nut meats. Drop from teaspoon onto lightly greased cooky sheet. Bake. Remove from pan
to cake cooler immediately after baking. Makes about 2½ dozen.

COOKY-PRESS COOKIES

10x14-inch cooky sheet . . . Preheated oven—375° F. . . . Baking
time—8-10 minutes

1 cup butter or margarine	1 tablespoon lemon rind
1 package (3 ounces) cream cheese	2½ cups all-purpose flour, sifted before measuring
1 cup granulated sugar	1 teaspoon baking powder
1 egg, beaten	½ cup nut meats, finely chopped
1 tablespoon lemon juice	

Blend butter or margarine with cream cheese. Add sugar. Beat
until light and fluffy. Add egg, lemon juice, and rind; blend carefully. Sift flour and baking powder. Add to creamed mixture.
Place dough in refrigerator for about an hour to chill. Force 2-inch
ribbon strips through cooky press onto ungreased cooky sheet.
Bake. Remove from pan to cake cooler immediately after baking.
When cookies are cool, dip ends into frosting (below), then in
the chopped nuts. Makes about 4½ dozen cookies.

Frosting

1 cup confectioners' sugar	2 tablespoons lemon juice

Blend the confectioners' sugar with the lemon juice.

Candy

It would be neither right nor proper to write a cookbook that ignores the importance of candy. A sweet tooth can develop before the baby teeth are fully in and may endure through the age when teeth no longer ache. It is a wise homemaker who can anticipate the appetite of her family and provide them with home-made candy just at the time when they feel they want it most.

Tricks in Candy Making

Although a candy thermometer is a great help in candy making, the "cold-water" test is dependable if you do it carefully. This is the procedure to follow.

COLD-WATER TEST

Fill a glass custard or tea cup half full of very cold water. Drop a spoonful of the hot mixture into the glass. Shape with fingers. Be sure to use fresh cold water for each test and remember to take the saucepan of candy away from the heat while you make the test, particularly when candy is nearly done.

Perhaps the following chart will help you.

Stage	Thermometer	Cold-Water Test
Soft Ball	234° F.-238° F.	You should be able to shape the candy into a soft ball with your fingers which flattens when removed from water.
Firm	242° F.-250° F.	The candy should shape into a ball which offers some resistance to the fingers.
Hard Ball	260° F.-270° F.	You should be able to shape the candy mixture into a ball which is firm and chewy.
Hard Crack	270° F.-310° F.	When mixture is gathered together and hit against the side of the cup it breaks into small pieces.

When making fudge or any of the candies that cook to the soft-ball stage, never start beating until the bottom of the pan in which the candy was cooked is cool enough to hold your hand to it. In other words, don't give into impatience. The cooler the candy, the better the texture.

If you can find a marble slab, it is a wonderful surface on which to pour your candy. Since the marble slab is cool, the candy takes shape the minute it hits the slab.

ERMALEE'S FUDGE
234° F. or soft-ball stage

2 cups evaporated milk
1 cup white corn sirup
6 cups granulated sugar
6 squares unsweetened chocolate

½ cup butter or margarine
2 teaspoons vanilla
2 to 3 cups pecan meats, chopped

Combine milk, corn sirup, sugar, and chocolate. Bring to a quick boil, stirring constantly, then reduce heat to a medium setting. Wash crystals from sides of pan several times. Cook to 234° F., or soft-ball stage. Remove from heat, add butter or margarine, but do not stir. Let mixture cool until you can press your hand to the bottom of pan. Add vanilla, beat until mixture begins to hold shape. Add nuts and pour into greased pans. Makes approximately 4 pounds candy.

AUNT BEAL'S BROWN CANDY
242° F. or firm-ball stage

2 cups granulated sugar	½ cup butter or margarine
4 cups granulated sugar	¼ teaspoon soda
2 cups cream or evaporated milk	1 teaspoon vanilla
1 tablespoon white corn sirup	2 cups pecans, broken

Caramelize 2 cups granulated sugar over low heat (page 329). While doing this, place the 4 cups granulated sugar, cream or evaporated milk, and corn sirup into another sauce pan and bring to a boil. When sugar is caramelized, pour in a very thin stream into boiling mixture, stirring constantly. Cook over medium heat to 242° F. or firm-ball stage. Remove from heat, add butter and soda. Stir only until butter or margarine melts. Cool 20 minutes, add vanilla, and beat until gloss disappears. Add nuts and pour into greased pans. Makes about 4 pounds candy.

BROWN SUGAR FUDGE
234° F. or soft-ball stage

2 tablespoons butter or margarine	¼ teaspoon salt
	¾ cup light cream or top milk
2 cups brown sugar	¾ cup coconut, pecans, or walnuts

Melt butter or margarine in saucepan. Add sugar, salt, and cream and stir until sugar has dissolved. When mixture begins to boil, reduce heat to a medium setting and continue cooking to soft-ball stage. Remove from heat and do not stir until the outside of the pan is cool to the touch. Beat until creamy. Add coconut or nut meats. Press in greased pans. Makes approximately 1 pound.

FONDANT
238° F. or soft-ball stage

4 cups granulated sugar	¼ teaspoon cream of tartar
½ tablespoon white corn sirup	1 cup water

Dissolve sugar, sirup, and cream of tartar in water in a saucepan. Place over medium heat and bring to a boil. Cover saucepan at first so that the sugar crystals will wash down from sides of pan. Should sugar crystals form, tie a piece of damp cheesecloth around tines of a fork and wipe off sugar crystals. It is important no sugar crystals form on side of pan. Boil to 238° F. or soft-ball stage. Pour onto large platter which has been rinsed with cold water. DO NOT STIR WHILE POURING. Cool until barely warm. Scrape and turn mixture toward center with spatula until mixture is white and creamy. Knead with hands until smooth and velvety. Form into a loaf. Cover with a dampened tea towel and let stand for about 2 hours. Then slice or form into desired shape. Makes 2 pounds.

CREAM MINTS

Melt 1 cup fondant over hot water, flavor with 1 drop oil of peppermint, cloves, or wintergreen. (You buy these oils at the drugstore.) Color as desired. Drop from tip of teaspoon onto waxed paper or a marble slab. Dry thoroughly before removing.

STUFFED DATES

Remove pits from dates. Fill centers with small blobs of fondant. You may color the fondant, mix it with chopped nut meats, coconut, or chopped ginger.

DIVINITY FUDGE

238° F. or soft-ball stage and 270° F. or hard-ball stage

2 cups granulated sugar	4 egg whites
1 cup water	¾ cup nut meats, chopped
1¾ cups corn sirup	1 teaspoon vanilla
1 teaspoon salt	

Mix sugar, water, corn sirup, and salt together in a saucepan. Cook to soft-ball stage. Beat egg whites until they form a stiff peak. Just as soon as sirup reaches soft-ball stage, pour ⅛ of the hot sirup over the beaten egg whites, beating vigorously. Continue cooking the remaining sirup until it reaches the hard-ball stage. Continue beating the egg whites and sirup mixture, while the remainder of the sirup is cooking. Pour remaining sirup over egg white mixture. Beat until mixture will hold shape when dropped from a spoon. Add nuts and flavoring. Pour into boxes lined with waxed paper and slice as needed. This makes a wonderful candy to ship to youngsters away from home, because it keeps moist for a considerable length of time and can be cut as desired. Makes about 2 pounds.

UNCOOKED FUDGE

8x8-inch square pan

4 squares chocolate	1 tablespoon light cream
4 tablespoons butter or margarine	1 pound confectioners' sugar
1 egg, beaten	1 cup nut meats, chopped
1 teaspoon vanilla	

Melt chocolate and butter or margarine together over hot water or very low heat. Combine egg, vanilla, cream, and sugar. Then add to chocolate mixture. Stir in the nuts. Mix vigorously. Press into greased pan and chill several hours. Makes about 16 pieces.

HOSTESS CARAMELS

244° F. or firm-ball stage

- 2 cups granulated sugar
- ½ pound butter or margarine
- 1¾ cups corn sirup
- 1 can (14½ ounces) evaporated milk
- 1½ tablespoons vanilla
- 1 cup nut meats, chopped

Place all ingredients except vanilla and nut meats in saucepan and cook over high heat for about 5 minutes, stirring occasionally. If using a candy thermometer, cook over high heat until thermometer registers 210° F. Then reduce heat to a medium setting and continue cooking, stirring constantly until 244° F. or the firm-ball stage is reached. Remove from range and add vanilla and nut meats. Stir quickly and pour into greased pan. When thoroughly cold, turn out and cut into squares. Wrap each square in heavy waxed paper. If chocolate caramels are desired, add 3 squares unsweetened chocolate to mixture when first put on to cook.

VELVET MOLASSES CANDY

260° F. or hard-ball stage

- ½ cup sorghum molasses
- 1½ cups granulated sugar
- ½ cup water
- 1½ tablespoons vinegar
- ¼ teaspoon cream of tartar
- 4 tablespoons butter or margarine
- ⅛ teaspoon soda
- 1 teaspoon vanilla
- ½ teaspoon lemon extract

Cook molasses, sugar, water, and vinegar in heavy saucepan, stirring constantly. When boiling point is reached, add cream of tartar. Continue cooking until mixture forms a hard ball or has reached 260° F. Stir constantly. When nearly done, add butter or margarine and soda. Pour into greased pans to cool. When cool enough to handle, pull until porous and light colored, using tips of fingers and thumbs. While pulling, add vanilla and lemon extract, or any other desired flavoring. Cut into small pieces with sharp knife or scissors.

POPCORN BALLS

260° F. or hard-ball stage

1 tablespoon butter or margarine	½ teaspoon salt
1 cup granulated sugar	4 quarts popped corn
1 cup sorghum molasses	

Melt butter or margarine in saucepan, add sugar, molasses, and salt. Cook, stirring frequently, to hard-ball stage, or 260° F. Pour over corn. Stir corn thoroughly while pouring hot sirup over it. Butter hands and immediately shape mixture into balls. 1 cup hulled peanuts may be added, if desired. Makes 12-14 popcorn balls.

PEANUT BRITTLE

295° F. or hard-crack stage

1½ cups shelled peanuts	½ cup water
¼ teaspoon salt	2 tablespoons butter or
1 cup sugar	margarine
½ cup white corn sirup	½ teaspoon lemon extract

Sprinkle nuts with salt and warm in 300° F. oven. Put sugar, corn sirup, and water in saucepan, stir until mixture boils, and wash down sides of saucepan with dampened cloth. (See fondant recipe, page 443.) Cook to 295° F. or until mixture is very brittle when tried in cold water. Add butter, flavoring, and warmed nuts. Pour into a shallow, greased pan. As soon as the mixture can be handled, turn the mass over and pull and stretch it out as thin as possible. Break into irregular pieces. Makes about 1 pound.

ENGLISH TOFFEE

290° F. or hard-crack stage

1 pound granulated sugar	½ pound coating chocolate
1 pound butter or margarine	½ pound nut meats, finely ground
¼ teaspoon salt	

This candy is best made in a skillet. Put sugar in skillet first, then add butter or margarine, and salt. Cut butter or margarine into small pieces, coating well with sugar. Cook over high heat until butter or margarine has melted, then reduce heat to a medium setting. Cook mixture until it is a deep amber in color, stirring constantly. Be sure to work the mixture away from the sides of the skillet so it will not burn or become too dark in color. Cook to 290° F. or hard-crack stage. Pour into an ungreased shallow tray or marble slab. When cold, brush with melted chocolate and sprinkle finely ground nut meats over the chocolate, pressing the nuts down firmly into the chocolate. When chocolate is hardened on one side, turn candy over and repeat on other side. Break into irregular pieces. The candy will keep for several weeks if stored in a dry, cool spot. Makes about 2 pounds.

QUICK PARTY BARS

7x11-inch pan . . . Preheated oven—350° F. . . . Baking time—20 minutes

½ cup butter or margarine
½ cup brown sugar, firmly packed
1 teaspoon vanilla
1 egg, beaten
½ cup all-purpose flour, sifted before measuring

½ cup quick-cooking oatmeal, uncooked
1 cup semi-sweet chocolate morsels
½ cup chopped nut meats

Blend butter or margarine with sugar and vanilla. Beat vigorously. Add egg and continue beating until mixture is light and fluffy. Stir in flour and rolled oats. Spread in greased pan and bake. Remove from oven. Cool slightly. Melt chocolate morsels over hot water or low heat and spread over baked mixture. Sprinkle nuts over chocolate. Cut into bars while still warm. Makes about 16 pieces.

DOUGHBOY GLAZED ALMONDS

1 cup blanched almonds
½ cup granulated sugar

½ teaspoon cinnamon
Dash salt

Combine all ingredients in a heavy skillet and cook over very low heat until almonds are brown and sugar is thoroughly caramelized and brown. Do not burn the sugar. Stir continuously after sugar starts to melt. Pour onto well-buttered cooky sheet or pan and separate almonds. Cool.

UNCOOKED CANDY ROLL

1½ cups pitted dates
¼ pound shredded coconut
½ pound figs
½ cup nut meats, coarsely chopped

1 tablespoon orange juice
1 teaspoon grated orange rind

Grind dates, coconut, and figs through a food chopper. Add other ingredients and mix well. This mixture may be shaped into two rolls, 1½ inches in diameter, and rolled in chopped nuts. Place in refrigerator and slice when thoroughly chilled. The mixture may also be made into balls, and half a candied cherry or nut pressed on top. Or the balls may be rolled in granulated sugar. Good healthy candy for children.

Beverages

There is nothing so satisfying as a cold drink on a hot day—unless it be a hot drink on a cold day! Most beverages involve very little work, and perhaps it is for that reason that many people neglect to do the little extra things that can make an ordinary drink into a delicious and refreshing experience.

COFFEE

Some folks admit that they just *can't* make a good cup of coffee! But everyone *can* if they avoid the three common errors of coffee-making: inaccurate measurement of coffee or water; a coffeepot that has been imperfectly cleaned or insufficiently aired; or, finally, the use of the wrong grind of coffee for the type of coffeepot used.

These points are worth considering at greater length.

Accurate Measurements

It is impossible to have a well-flavored cup of coffee if the dump method is used for making the coffee. Use a regular measuring spoon for the coffee, and if the coffee maker doesn't have indicators showing the number of cups of water, use a standard measuring cup for the water. If you use the combination of a standard measuring spoon and measuring cup, use 2 level tablespoons coffee for each measuring cup of water.

If your coffeepot has lines indicating the number of cups in the pot, pay attention to those marks. For instance, if there is a mark indicating that you have six cups of water in the coffeepot, then put in 6 tablespoons coffee, plus one extra. In other words, always add 1 additional tablespoon coffee for the number of cups indicated on the coffeepot.

Of course you can vary this according to your own likes and dislikes. The average coffee cup holds about ⅔ cup of liquid, compared to standard measuring cup. Usually the indicators on coffeepots are for actual servings.

Keep the Coffeepot Clean

Many a poor cup of coffee can come from a stale coffeepot. After the meal is finished, never allow coffee to remain in the coffeepot, even though it may be one that automatically keeps it hot all day long. Coffeepots need to be washed and aired every day.

If the coffeepot is electric, never immerse it in water. Clean the inside with hot sudsy water, rinse with boiling water. Wash the top and any parts of the coffeepot used in making coffee. There are special brushes available for cleansing spouts, tubes, and narrow necks. NEVER, NEVER return all the parts to the coffeepot. But set the lid on slightly ajar so the pot will air during the day. Be sure all parts of any coffeepot are rinsed in boiling water, and aired during the day.

It may be necessary occasionally to fill the coffeepot with water, add a teaspoon of soda, and let the pot go through the regular cycle. Pour out this solution, scald with boiling water, and air.

If the inside of the coffeepot has become stained and corroded, it may be necessary to use a soft scouring pad. However, it is not desirable to do that too often, because it might also scour off the finish on the inside. It is far better to do a careful day-by-day cleaning job.

There are several new products on the market which remove coffee stain. When you use these, follow the directions on the outside of the package carefully.

If a coffeepot is seldom used, be sure it is not sealed tightly when put away. In other words, place the coffeepot in a spot free from dust, leave the lid off or slightly ajar, and all other parts outside of the pot, so they too can air.

The Correct Grind

Coffee comes in three grinds: (1) Regular, (2) Drip Grind, (3) Pulverized. For everyday use, and for most types of coffeepots, the Drip Grind gives the greatest satisfaction.

There is one vacuum-type coffee maker on the market with a glass rod for filtering the coffee. Probably the pulverized coffee is best for this type of coffee maker.

Those who are fond of a thick coffee, such as Cuban coffee, should use the pulverized grind. Sometimes this is also used when preparing afterdinner coffee.

Coffee Makers

You have your choice of four different types of coffee makers. The ordinary coffeepot, the percolator, the drip coffee maker, and the vacuum coffeepot. There is little need to go into detail about making coffee in these various coffee makers, for full directions for their use are always furnished when you purchase the pot, and there may be minor differences in the use of coffeepots of different manufacturers.

In general, however, choose whichever type of coffeepot you prefer, serene in the knowledge that any coffeepot will make "perfect" coffee if you remember to follow the three golden rules we have discussed.

TO MAKE COFFEE FOR 50

1 pound drip grind coffee   10 quarts water

Tie coffee loosely in a cheesecloth bag. If cheesecloth is very thin and open, use a double thickness. Fill the container with cold water, place bag of coffee in cold water, and when water reaches a full boil, remove coffee bag. Reduce heat so the coffee will stay piping hot, but will not boil.

TRICK: Your electric roaster is a wonderful convenience in making coffee for 50.

DEMITASSE

For truly delicious after-dinner coffee, which, as you know, is served in demitasse cups, use 3 level tablespoons coffee for each measuring cup of water. Each measuring cup of water will provide about 3 demitasse cups. Serve with sugar and cream if you wish.

INSTANT COFFEE

I have a very good friend who makes her instant coffee in an interesting way. She uses a saucepan with a tight-fitting lid. The cold water is measured by coffee cups, and she makes the exact amount of coffee she wants for that particular serving. To the cold water she adds the instant coffee, allowing 1 teaspoon instant coffee per cup of water. She brings this slowly to the boiling point and allows to boil about 30 seconds. It is a little more work, but the coffee is delicious and she doesn't have to bother with coffee grounds.

ICED COFFEE NO. 1

Use 4 level tablespoons drip grind coffee for each measuring cup of water. Make coffee in your coffee maker. Fill tall glasses with ice cubes. Pour hot coffee over ice. Serve with sugar and cream if you wish.

You still may be a little confused about this method. For instance, if you have a 10-cup coffee maker, use the required amount of coffee and just half the water. This is double strength, but pouring the hot coffee over the ice reduces the strength.

ICED COFFEE NO. 2

Make coffee the regular way. Cool. Pour over coffee ice cubes. For this method you must make two pots of coffee. Pour 1 pot coffee in the ice cube tray of your refrigerator and freeze. (You really are no better off than making the double strength to start with and freezing coffee ice cubes adds to the work; still, you may wish to experiment with this method.)

CAFÉ BRÛLOT

If you have a pretty silver bowl, or a chafing dish, and wish to dress up your party, you might try this delicious concoction. (If you have been in New Orleans, you have probably already been exposed to this treat.)

1 small stick cinnamon

6 whole cloves

1 medium sliver of lemon peel

1 medium sliver of orange peel

6-8 lumps sugar

6 ounces brandy, or 4 ounces brandy and 2 ounces rum

3 cups double strength coffee, very hot

Mix all ingredients excepting coffee in silver bowl or chafing dish. Heat and set afire with lighted match. Stir with silver ladle until sugar is dissolved, and liquor well blended through the ingredients. Slowly pour hot coffee over mixture. Serve in demitasse cups. Serves 6-8.

CAFÉ AU LAIT

This is a great favorite with many folks. The coffee must be very strong. Pour equal amounts of hot, strong coffee into coffee cup simultaneously with hot, scalded milk. Or you may put the scalded milk in the cup first, then the hot coffee.

TEA

A good cup of tea is worth any amount of trouble; and yet it may be made with very little trouble if you brew the tea properly.

Varieties of Tea

Black tea usually comes from India, Java, and Sumatra. The leaves go through a fermenting process before they are heated and dried.

Green tea comes from China and Japan.

Oolong tea comes from Formosa and is subjected to only a short fermenting process.

These are the basic teas, although many variations are created when different flowers and flavors are blended with the tea leaves as they are dried. Jasmine is one of the best-known teas of this sort.

How to Make Tea

Tea is best made in an earthen or china teapot. Before making the tea, heat the pot with boiling water. Otherwise, the tea will not be as hot as it should be when served.

Be sure to have the water boiling for your tea. Not simmering hot, but a full rolling boil.

Use ½ to 1 teaspoon tea per cup, according to your own likes. Allow tea to steep about 3 minutes after boiling water has been poured over the tea leaves. Do not boil tea.

If you use tea bags, pour boiling water into teapot, add bags of tea, allowing 1 bag of tea for each cup water in the pot. Allow to steep about 3 minutes, remove bags, and serve. If you want to make only one cup, place tea bag in teacup and pour boiling water over tea bag.

What to Serve with Tea

Some folks prefer their tea plain. Others like sugar, lemon slices, milk, cream, sugared ginger strips, or mint leaves, for added flavor.

ICED TEA

Make tea triple strength. Pour hot tea over ice cubes in tall glasses.

Or, use 3 level teaspoons of tea or 3 tea bags to each measuring cup of water. Pour cold water over tea. Place in pitcher and set in refrigerator for 10 to 12 hours. Many folks prefer this long, slow brewing in cold water, rather than ordinary brewing in boiling water.

MILK DRINKS

HOT COCOA

4 tablespoons cocoa	4 cups milk
4-6 tablespoons sugar	¼ teaspoon vanilla
1½ cups cold water	6 marshmallows (optional)
Few grains salt	

Combine cocoa, sugar, water, and salt. Cook over medium heat until mixture comes to boiling point, stirring frequently. Add the milk. Bring to boiling point but do not boil. Remove from heat, add vanilla. Add marshmallows just before serving. Serves 6.

TRICK: To keep cocoa from forming a thickened layer over the top, which will happen when it stands, give it a few brisk beatings with egg beater just after removing from heat.

READY-TO-SERVE COCOA

This type of cocoa comes in packages and has the cocoa, sweetening, and powdered milk already added. All you need to do is add boiling water, or scalded milk. Directions for making are given on the package.

QUICK HOT OR COLD COCOA

3 tablespoons chocolate sirup added to 2 cups scalded milk will make a quick cocoalike drink.

CHOCOLATE MILK SHAKE

1 pint ice cream	2 cups cold sweet milk
3 tablespoons chocolate sirup	

Scoop ice cream into tall glasses. Work with a spoon until softened. Then add chocolate sirup and milk. Stir vigorously. Serves 2 generously.

TRICK: Add 1 tablespoon malted milk to ice cream before mixing with the spoon.

EGGNOG

2 eggs	1 teaspoon vanilla
2 tablespoons sugar	2 cups whole milk
⅛ teaspoon salt	

An electric mixer is best for this. If one is not available, use a good rotary egg beater, because the goodness of the eggnog depends somewhat upon the fluffiness of the mixture. Break eggs into mixer bowl, add sugar and salt. Beat until the eggs are lemon colored and thick. Add vanilla and milk. Beat until well blended. Serves 2.

PUNCH

ORANGE BLOSSOM PUNCH

6 cups orange juice	½ cup maraschino cherry or
1 cup lemon juice	raspberry juice
4 cups water or gingerale	½ cup sugar

Combine ingredients and add ice cubes or large block of ice and citrus fruit garnishes. Makes 25-30 punch cup servings.

TREAT: Add 2 quarts lemon or orange sherbet to punch bowl just before serving. Looks beautiful, tastes wonderful.

TRICK: You may use frozen lemon or orange concentrate. Add the amount of water the concentrates call for, since the recipe above is for fresh orange and lemon juice.

COUNTRY CLUB PUNCH

3 cups sugar	12 lemons, juiced
3 quarts water	1 quart grape juice
1 cup strong tea	1 small can crushed pineapple
12 oranges, juiced	2 quarts gingerale

Boil sugar and water together for about 8 minutes. Add tea. Chill. Add orange, lemon, and grape juices. Add pineapple. Place in refrigerator to mellow about 2 hours. Before serving, add gingerale and ice cubes. If served in a punch bowl, add quarter slices of orange and lemon and one small bottle maraschino cherries, chopped fine. Makes 50-60 servings.

PARTY PUNCH BOWL

3 cups sugar
3 cups strong tea
6 lemons, juiced (save peel)

1 bottle Gold Label rum
Cubes of pineapple

Dissolve sugar in hot tea. Cool. Place in punch bowl. Add lemon juice; cut lemon peel in fine slivers and add. Place block of ice in punch bowl. Add rum. Stir well. Just before serving, add either fresh or canned pineapple, cut in small cubes. Serves 15-20.

MAY PUNCH

2 or 3 sprigs fresh mint
6 whole cloves
1 cup sugar
1 cup water
½ cup lemon juice

2 cups cubed pineapple
1 orange, unpeeled, sliced
2 large bottles Rhine wine or
sauterne
1 quart sparkling water

Crush mint leaves and whole cloves with sugar in punch bowl. Add water and lemon juice and stir until dissolved. Add pineapple cubes and orange slices. Just before serving, add large chunk of ice, then wine and sparkling water. Serves 12-15.

CHAMPAGNE PUNCH

3 cups sugar
2 cups lemon juice
1 fresh pineapple, cubed
1 cup sugar
1 block ice

1½ quarts sparkling water
1 quart chilled sauterne wine
1 quart strawberries, lightly
sugared
2 bottles champagne

Dissolve 3 cups sugar in lemon juice. Cube 1 fresh pineapple, dredge with 1 cup sugar and let stand for an hour or so. If fresh pineapple is not available, use sliced canned pineapple, cut in cubes, but do not dredge in sugar. Combine in a chilled punch bowl. Add block of ice, water, and sauterne. Just before serving, add 1 quart lightly sugared strawberries with hulls removed and 2 bottles champagne. Makes about 30 servings.

WHITE WINE SYLLABUB

1 quart coffee cream
1 cup fresh orange juice
  Grated rind of 2 oranges
  Grated rind of 1 lemon

3 cups sauterne
1 cup sugar
1 cup heavy cream

Combine coffee cream with orange juice, ½ of grated rind of orange, and all of lemon. Add wine and sugar. Beat until well mixed. Chill thoroughly. Serve from large glass bowl. Decorate with "islands" of whipped cream, sprinkled with rest of grated orange rind. Serves 8-10.

HOT SPICED WINE

1 cup sugar
3 cups boiling water
  Grated rind of ½ lemon
18 whole cloves

1 small stick cinnamon
2 bottles claret or Burgundy
  wine
  Grated nutmeg

Dissolve sugar in boiling water. Add lemon rind, cloves, and stick cinnamon. Boil together for 15 minutes. Strain. Place in chafing dish or in saucepan. Add wine. Cook over low heat, but do not boil. When piping hot, serve in punch cups or small earthenware cups. Sprinkle nutmeg over top. Serves 10-15.

PARTY PUNCH ORIENTAL

1 can (46 ounces) pineapple juice
1 can (No. 2) guava juice

1 quart gingerale
1 quart mint sherbet

Open cans of juice and freeze to just past mushy stage. Place sherbet in punch bowl. Pour juice and gingerale over sherbet. Makes about 30 servings.

MOCHA CREAM PUNCH

1 quart freshly made strong
  coffee
1 quart chocolate ice cream

½ pint heavy cream
¼ teaspoon almond flavoring
1 teaspoon grated nutmeg

Chill the coffee and pour into a punch bowl. Add half the ice cream and stir until partly melted. Add almond flavoring to cream and whip stiff. Spoon whipped cream and remaining ice cream into the mixture in punch bowl. This makes a beautiful topping over the punch. Sprinkle lightly with nutmeg. Serves 12-15.

Index

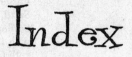

Index

The Betty Furness

P

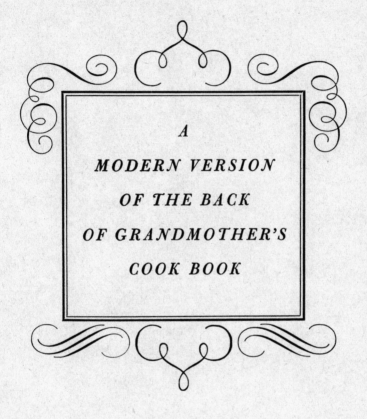

A

MODERN VERSION
OF THE BACK
OF GRANDMOTHER'S
COOK BOOK

A MODERN VERSION OF THE BACK
OF GRANDMOTHER'S COOK BOOK

If any of you are fortunate enough to have one of your grand-mother's old cook books, you probably have had a good many laughs over the information found in the back of the book. They always contained helpful hints on making washday easier. How-ever, in order to put these fine suggestions into use, Grand-mother had to have a fair-sized drugstore in her kitchen. For instance, to keep starch from sticking, she had to mix spermaceti and wax together, to clean silver she had to have hartshorn powder, to wash fragile, colored garments she first soaked them overnight in a turpentine solution. The stain chart alone must have been a worry, because among many other things it listed sulphurous acid, citric acid, copperas and beef gall. "Management of the stove" for washday included advice on laying the fire, filling the boiler, keeping the fire from going out, and so forth. Today we smile at such instructions and find it difficult to believe that not too many years ago homemakers everywhere were faced with such complex problems.

Do we homemakers appreciate the fact that today we live elec-trically? A flip of a switch and our work is done for us. Can you imagine laying a fire in a firebox to heat the wash water? Can you believe that not too many years ago Grandmother always got up before daybreak on washday? She had to, to have the washing finished by sundown.

Because electric living has made our work so much easier, we are apt to take it for granted. Our modern, automatic electric appliances have eliminated all the arduous work of homemaking, but we as homemakers still have a few responsibilities. For in-stance, when we prepare our three meals a day we fully realize the necessity of accuracy in measuring ingredients. With thermostat-ically controlled ovens in our electric ranges, food failures usually result because of hit-and-miss methods in measuring and mixing the ingredients.

The same is true of laundering clothes. Automatic washing machines and clothes dryers must be operated intelligently for best results. So, today, we also have recipes for washing, and it is with that thought in mind we have included some washday recipes with the other recipes in this book. For your convenience they are given in question-and-answer form.

QUESTION: **What types of automatic washers are on the market?**

ANSWER: There are two types of automatic washing machines on the market. The agitator type has the agitator wings or blades cast to a center shaft. The tumbler type has the agitators cast in the side of the tub. It is essential that washing recipes for each type be carefully followed.

QUESTION: **Can electric blankets be dry cleaned?**

ANSWER: No, they cannot be dry cleaned, because the dry cleaning fluid may injure the wiring system.

QUESTION: **Can electric blankets or electric sheets be washed in automatic washing machines?**

ANSWER: Yes, they can, and following are the directions for the two types of automatic washing machines:

Agitator-type automatic washing machine

Wash only one blanket at a time. Fill washer with tepid water, 100° F. Add 1 cup of synthetic detergent and agitate the machine until the detergent is dissolved. Stop washing machine and remove agitator. Place blanket in machine. Be sure blanket is submerged in water. Close cover and set control dial for 10 minutes' washing time. Allow machine to go through complete cycle. Remove blanket and dry. Replace agitator.

Tumbler-type automatic washing machine

Wash only one blanket at a time. Set Control Dial at Warm. Add ½ cup non-sudsing detergent. Start machine and as soon as it fills, stop it. Open door, put in blanket. Be sure blanket is submerged in water. Soak for 10 to 20 minutes depending upon soil.

After the soak period, start the washing machine and IMMEDIATELY ADVANCE THE CONTROL DIAL until water is drained out. Allow washer to fill again for the deep rinse. When tub is completely filled with the deep rinse water, IMMEDIATELY ADVANCE THE DIAL TO THE FINAL DRAIN PERIOD. Continue on through final spin cycle until washer shuts off.

QUESTION: **Can electric bedding be dried in an automatic clothes dryer?**

ANSWER: Recently manufactured automatic electric clothes dryers with Low Heat setting make it possible partially to dry electric bedding in the automatic clothes dryer. Otherwise, electric bedding should be line dried.

QUESTION: **What makes my white nylon garments turn yellow? (Grandmother never had this problem)**

ANSWER: White nylon garments should always be washed in your automatic washing machine in 140° F. water, and with an all-purpose synthetic detergent. When washed by hand in tepid water, the soil is not all removed, the garment is not properly rinsed, and the result is a yellowed garment. Some washing machine manufacturers recommend these garments be placed in a bag for washing; however, with the tumbler type washer this is not necessary.

QUESTION: **How can the yellow color be removed?**

ANSWER: It is impossible to restore the garment to its original whiteness. You can use a diluted solution of chlorine bleach, or a sodium perborate powdered bleach. However, once the garment is yellowed, there is little you can do.

QUESTION: **What can I do about the fine wrinkles which appear in my nylon curtains after they are washed?**

ANSWER: Unfortunately there is little that can be done. Nylon curtains must be made from a heat set nylon fabric if they are to look fresh and crisp after laundering. Unfortunately all weavers of nylon fabric do not heat set it, which is to nylon what Sanforizing is to cotton.

It gives the fabric stability and prevents shrinking. Buy curtains from a reputable store, and ask the clerk if material has been heat set.

QUESTION: **Why does my table linen appear limp after it is dried in the dryer?**

ANSWER: If you will remember back to the days when you hung your table linen on the clothes line, you carefully watched it, and always took it down when it was just right for ironing. You probably made a dozen trips to the back yard to make certain the linen did not become too dry.

The same is true with the dryer. Linen napkins and table cloths should be removed from the dryer when they are just the right dampness for ironing. Otherwise, the linen becomes limp and sprinkling does not restore the moisture lost in drying. Grandmother knew this; in fact, it is in the back of her old recipe book that linen must never be allowed to become thoroughly dry. Grandmother sometimes used a bit of starch to give the linen more body, but modern homemakers seldom do this.

QUESTION: **I have great difficulty with starch sticking to my iron. What do I do wrong?**

ANSWER: If you are using a cooked starch, it is possible you do not cook it long enough. Or, you may let it stand; thus a skin forms over the top which will cause spotty starching and sticking. You can buy a fine helper, which comes in bright-blue, wax-like cakes. One little square dissolved in a quart of hot, cooked starch really cuts down ironing time and prevents sticking. Remember Grandmother had to make her own additive by mixing spermaceti and wax together.

QUESTION: **Every so often I find tiny little holes and brown spots on my garments. They always seem to appear when I am ironing the garment. What causes this difficulty?**

ANSWER: It took the Bureau of Human Nutrition and Home Economics to solve that problem for us, and it cer-

tainly isn't one that ever bothered Grandmother. It's
zipper trouble. It seems that sometimes zippers are
made from two metals, copper and aluminum. During the time the dampened garment is rolled up for
ironing, electrolysis takes place and gives off enough
acid to damage the fabric. Then, when the hot iron
is applied, the damage shows up in brown spots or
holes. In addition to dampness, the fabric must
contain some substance that will conduct electricity,
such as minerals from hard water, salt in liquid
starch, or even some detergent not removed by rinsing. Yes, we have modern laundering problems, but
fortunately they are easily solved.

QUESTION: **How can I protect my garments from this damage?**

ANSWER: There are two easy ways. Take the garment from the
dryer or clothes line while still damp enough to iron.
If that is not possible, and if the garment must be
dampened for ironing, allow fabric around zipper to
dry and dampen the remainder of the garment.

QUESTION: **What causes rust stains on my clothes?**

ANSWER: There may be several causes. If you use liquid bluing, it could be responsible. Liquid bluing usually
has a Prussian-blue base, containing iron. Even with
thorough rinsing, alkali from soap or synthetic detergent may be left in the fabric. This alkali may combine with the iron in the bluing, and under the heat
of the iron or even in warm sunlight the alkali-iron
compound may oxidize, which in simple language
means rust spots.

   Or, the rust may be caused by corrosion of plumbing
in the home, or there may be iron in the original source
of water supply.

QUESTION: **How can iron rust stains be removed?**

ANSWER: Spread stained area over bowl of steaming hot water.
Apply oxalic acid solution with medicine dropper.
After a few minutes rinse thoroughly. Or apply a com-
mercially prepared rust remover, using manufacturer's
directions. These remedies may be used on white cot-

tons or linen, washable colored garments and nylon.
Note: Grandmother removed rust stains the same way.

QUESTION: **What causes white embossed-cotton garments and trimmings to turn yellow when they are washed?**

ANSWER: Embossing is done by applying a resin to the material; sometimes the resin used is not compatible with chlorine bleach and the fabric turns yellow. It's bleach that causes the change in color.

QUESTION: **Can anything be done to restore the garment to its original whiteness?**

ANSWER: Yes, indeed. Go to the drugstore or a photographic supply shop and buy a small amount of sodium sulphite. Dissolve 2 tablespoons of sodium sulphite in 1 quart water. Place garment in this solution, and the yellow disappears like magic. Rinse thoroughly.

QUESTION: **Can you give me a general recipe for a snowy white washing?**

ANSWER: That's easy. First of all an automatic washing machine. For all white and colorfast garments, and very soiled clothes, use hot water, at least 140° F., be sure the water is soft, and use a good, all-purpose detergent. Grandmother did just that. She boiled the clothes in a wash boiler, gently stirring and lifting them with a wooden stick. She always softened her water and used her good, homemade soap. The formula hasn't changed, only you have automatic laundry equipment and modern detergents to do it for you.

In Grandmother's cook book there was a formula for making liniment to rub on her aching back after washday. That is not included in this cook book, because you don't need it. You can live electrically; Grandmother couldn't.